Ain't No Makin' It

Praise for *Ain't No Makin' It*

"This book is simply one of the classic ethnographies of the growing number of men who live marginal lives in American society."

—Stanley Aronowitz
City University of New York

"That MacLeod had the patience and the courage to get inside the Hangers' world as completely as he did is impressive, and his lengthy quotes from them are gripping."

—Nicholas Lemann
The Washington Post

"A passionate and theoretically superb ethnographic study about the ideological and material constraints faced by working-class youths in a large northeastern city. One of the best critical ethnographies to appear in years. It gives new meaning to the notion and practice of critical ethnography in the way it links the language of critique with the discourse and promise of hope and possibility."

—Henry A. Giroux
Pennsylvania State University

"A sensitive and sophisticated ethnographer."

—Roger Waldinger, *The Annals of the American Academy of Political and Social Science*

"In his follow-up study of the youths of Clarendon Heights, Jay MacLeod charts the transformation of the American dream of opportunity into the nightmarish reality of inequality and marginality. He offers a much-needed, empirically grounded critique of the bankrupt ideologies of individual meritocracy and moral entrepreneurship."

—Loïc J. D. Wacquant
University of California–Berkeley

"The rich new material in Ain't No Makin' It *takes on an even greater urgency because it pitches even more directly the challenge of redeeming ourselves amidst the failures of democracy."*

—Peter McLaren
University of California–Los Angeles

Ain't No Makin' It

Aspirations and Attainment
in a Low-Income
Neighborhood

Jay MacLeod

WESTVIEW PRESS
Boulder • San Francisco • Oxford

All rights reserved. No part of this publication may be reproduced or transmitted in any form or by any means, electronic or mechanical, including photocopy, recording, or any information storage and retrieval system, without permission in writing from the publisher.

Copyright © 1987, 1995 by Westview Press, Inc.

Published in 1995 in the United States of America by Westview Press, Inc., 5500 Central Avenue, Boulder, Colorado 80301-2877, and in the United Kingdom by Westview Press, 12 Hid's Copse Road, Cumnor Hill, Oxford OX2 9JJ. Design and composition by Westview Press.

Library of Congress Cataloging-in-Publication Data
MacLeod, Jay.
    Ain't no makin' it : aspirations and attainment in a low-income neighborhood / Jay MacLeod.
        p.   cm.
    Part one largely unchanged republication of 1987 ed.
    Includes bibliographical references and index.
    ISBN 0-8133-1514-X (HC). — ISBN 0-8133-1515-8 (PB)
    1. Urban poor—United States—Case studies.   2. Socially handicapped youth—United States—Case studies.   3. Social mobility—United States—Case studies.   4. Equality—United States—Case studies.   I. Title.   II. Title: Ain't no making it.
HV4045.M33   1995
305.5'69'0973—dc20   95-2367
                                                                                                        CIP

Printed and bound in the United States of America

   The paper used in this publication meets the requirements of the American National Standard for Permanence of Paper for Printed Library Materials Z39.48-1984.

20 19

Contents

Part One   The Hallway Hangers and the Brothers as Teenagers

Part Two   Eight Years Later: Low Income, Low Outcome

IN THE SPRING OF 1981, as a college sophomore, I ventured into the Clarendon Heights public housing development for the first time. Two female students and I met with the Tenant Council about setting up a summer youth program. The Council—all women, mostly white, many clad in housecoats with their hair in curlers—questioned us closely about our motives, objectives, and funding. The meeting was disrupted when a mouse scurried under the table, and the conversation detoured into a discussion of the previous night's movie on HBO. Dwelling in candid detail on the sex scenes and laughing loudly, the women delighted in my discomfort. "Don't you worry, honey," one assured me, "we'll teach you a thing or two down here."

In fact, I did learn more hanging in the hallways of Clarendon Heights than studying in the hallowed halls of the university up the street. Working with youngsters in this poor neighborhood for several summers, I was struck by their forlorn hopes for the future and decided to write my undergraduate thesis on the occupational aspirations of two contrasting cliques of older teenagers in the project—the Hallway Hangers and the Brothers. I immersed myself in their peer cultures for a year and tried to understand the two groups from the inside. Exploring their aspirations brought me straight into a thicket of enduring social issues about the nature of poverty, opportunity, and achievement in the United States. I completed the research in February 1984 and submitted the thesis two months later. The study was published as a book in 1987. That first book, largely unchanged, constitutes Part One of this revised and updated edition.

The first edition of *Ain't No Makin' It* raised as many questions as it answered, the basic one being: What happened to these young men? The answer is of immense human and sociological interest. I kept in touch with the Brothers and Hallway Hangers while studying in England, and I spent a month in Clarendon Heights upon my return to America in September 1987. Having tracked down the young men, I outlined their progress between 1984 and 1987 in a short postscript that was tacked on to subsequent printings of the book. However, the postscript whetted rather than sated the curiosity of both reader and writer. So in the summer of 1991, after four years in Mississippi and before going back overseas, I returned to Clarendon Heights for a period of intensive fieldwork, hoping to discover how the men had fared in the eight years since the initial research.

If I had studied middle-class boys, I would have had to criss-cross the country to catch up with them as twenty-four-year-olds. But my own transatlantic travels contrasted sharply with the limited mobility of my subjects. The Clarendon Heights men, constrained geographically as well as socioeconomically, still lived nearby. Only those in prison resided far from the city. I managed to locate and interview every Brother and Hallway Hanger (the fieldwork is discussed in the Appendix). And I ended up with nearly eight hundred pages of interview transcripts and field notes, most of it as compelling as the original material gathered in 1983. Part One tells the story of the Brothers' and Hallway Hangers' teenage aspirations. Part Two relates the outcomes and explores the sociological implications of their young lives.

Jay MacLeod

Acknowledgments

THE MAKING OF THIS BOOK has spanned twelve years, and scores of people—too many to list—have helped along the way. I am especially grateful to Katherine McClelland, David Karen, Stephen Cornell, Dave Webb, Douglas Taylor, John Dickie, Jane Rosegrant, Dan Porterfield, David Finegold, Dean Birkenkamp, John Stern, Greg Johnson, Andrew Sum, Loïc Wacquant, and Paul Willis. My biggest debt is to Sally Asher, my wife. Apart from typing, transcribing, analyzing, organizing, editing, and proofreading, she's been generous with amnesties for domestic delinquency as I struggled to finish the second edition. To her and to the Brothers and the Hallway Hangers I dedicate this book.

J. M.

The Hallway Hangers and the Brothers as Teenagers

1

Social Immobility in the Land of Opportunity

A NY CHILD CAN GROW UP TO BE PRESIDENT." So says the achievement ideology, the reigning social perspective that sees American society as open and fair and full of opportunity. In this view, success is based on merit, and economic inequality is due to differences in ambition and ability. Individuals do not inherit their social status; they attain it on their own. Since education ensures equality of opportunity, the ladder of social mobility is there for all to climb. A favorite Hollywood theme, the rags-to-riches story resonates in the psyche of the American people. We never tire of hearing about Andrew Carnegie, for his experience validates much that we hold dear about America, the land of opportunity. Horatio Alger's accounts of the spectacular mobility achieved by men of humble origins through their own unremitting efforts occupy a treasured place in our national folklore. The American Dream is held out as a genuine prospect for anyone with the drive to achieve it.

"I ain't goin' to college. Who wants to go to college? I'd just end up getting' a shitty job anyway." So says Freddie Piniella,[1] an intelligent eleven-year-old boy from Clarendon Heights, a low-income housing development in a northeastern city. This statement, pronounced with certitude and feeling, completely contradicts our achievement ideology. Freddie is pessimistic about his prospects for social mobility and disputes schooling's capacity to "deliver the goods." Such a view offends our sensibilities and seems a rationalization. But Freddie has a point. What of Carnegie's grammar school classmates who labored in factories or pumped gas? For every Andrew Carnegie there are thousands of able and intelligent workers who were left behind to occupy positions in the class structure not much different from those held by their parents. What about the static, nearly permanent element in the working class, whose members consider the chances for mobility remote and thus despair of all hope? These people are shunned, hidden, forgotten—and for good reason—because just as the self-made individual is a testament to certain American ideals, so the very existence of an "underclass" in American society is a living contradiction to those ideals.

Utter hopelessness is the most striking aspect of Freddie's outlook. Erik H. Erikson writes that hope is the basic ingredient of all vitality;[2] stripped of hope, there is little left to lose. How is it that in contemporary America a boy of eleven can feel bereft of a future worth embracing? This is not what the United States is supposed to be. The United States is the nation of hopes and dreams and opportunity. As Ronald Reagan remarked in his 1985 State of the Union Address, citing the accomplishments of a young Vietnamese immigrant, "Anything is possible in America if we have the faith, the will, and the heart."[3] But to Freddie Piniella and many other Clarendon Heights young people who grow up in households where their parents and older siblings are undereducated, unemployed, or imprisoned, Reagan's words ring hollow. For them the American Dream, far from being a genuine prospect, is not even a dream. It is a hallucination.

I first met Freddie Piniella in the summer of 1981 when as a student at a nearby university I worked as a counselor in a youth enrichment program in Clarendon Heights. For ten weeks I lived a few blocks from the housing project and worked intensively with nine boys, aged eleven to thirteen. While engaging them in recreational and educational activities, I was surprised by the modesty of their aspirations. The world of middle-class work was entirely alien to them; they spoke about employment in construction, factories, the armed forces, or, predictably, professional athletics. In an ostensibly open society, they were a group of boys whose occupational aspirations did not even cut across class lines.

The depressed aspirations of Clarendon Heights youngsters are telling. There is a strong relationship between aspirations and occupational outcomes; if individuals do not even aspire to middle-class jobs, then they are unlikely to achieve them. In effect, such individuals disqualify themselves from attaining the American definition of success—the achievement of a prestigious, highly remunerative occupation—before embarking on the quest. Do leveled aspirations represent a quitter's cop-out? Or does this disqualifying mechanism suggest that people of working-class origin encounter significant obstacles to social mobility?

Several decades of quantitative sociological research have demonstrated that the social class into which one is born has a massive influence on where one will end up. Although mobility between classes does take place, the overall structure of class relations from one generation to the next remains largely unchanged. Quantitative mobility studies can establish the extent of this pattern of social reproduction, but they have difficulty demonstrating *how* the pattern comes into being or is sustained. This is an issue of immense complexity and difficulty, and an enduring one in the field of sociology, but it seems to me that we can learn a great deal about this pattern from youngsters like Freddie. Leveled aspirations are a powerful mechanism by which class inequality is reproduced from one generation to the next.

In many ways, the world of these youths is defined by the physical boundaries of the housing development. Like most old "projects" (as low-income public housing developments are known to their residents), Clarendon Heights is architecturally a world unto itself. Although smaller and less dilapidated than many urban housing developments, its plain brick buildings testify that cost efficiency was the overriding consideration in its construction. Walking through Clarendon Heights for the first time in spring 1981, I was struck by the contrast between the project and the sprawling lawns and elegant buildings of the college quadrangle I had left only a half hour earlier. It is little more than a mile from the university to Clarendon Heights, but the transformation that occurs in the course of this mile is startling. Large oak trees, green yards, and impressive family homes give way to ramshackle tenement buildings and closely packed, triple decker, wooden frame dwellings; the ice cream parlors and bookshops are replaced gradually by pawn shops and liquor stores; book-toting students and businesspeople with briefcases in hand are supplanted by tired, middle-aged women lugging bags of laundry and by clusters of elderly, immigrant men loitering on street corners. Even within this typical working-class neighborhood, however, Clarendon Heights is physically and socially set off by itself.

Bordered on two sides by residential neighborhoods and on the other two by a shoe factory, a junkyard, and a large plot of industrial wasteland, Clarendon Heights consists of six large, squat, three-story buildings and one high rise. The architecture is imposing and severe; only the five chimneys atop each building break the harsh symmetry of the structures. Three mornings a week the incinerators in each of the twenty-two entryways burn, spewing thick smoke and ash out of the chimneys. The smoke envelops the stained brick buildings, ash falling on the black macadam that serves as communal front yard, backyard, and courtyard for the project's two hundred families. (A subsequent landscaping effort did result in the planting of grass and trees, the erection of little wire fences to protect the greenery, and the appearance of flower boxes lodged under windows.) Before its renovation, a condemned high-rise building, its doors and windows boarded up, invested the entire project with an ambiance of decay and neglect.

Even at its worst, however, Clarendon Heights is not a bad place to live compared to many inner-city housing projects. This relatively small development, set in a working-class neighborhood, should not be confused with the massive, scarred projects of the nation's largest cities. Nevertheless, the social fabric of Clarendon Heights is marked by problems generally associated with low-income housing developments. Approximately 65 percent of Clarendon Heights' residents are white, 25 percent are black,[4] and 10 percent are other minorities. Few adult males live in Clarendon Heights; approximately 85 percent of the families are headed by single women. Although no precise figures are available, it is acknowledged by the City Housing Authority that significant numbers of tenants are second- and third-generation public housing residents. Social workers estimate that almost 70 percent of the families are on some additional form of public assistance.

Overcrowding, unemployment, alcoholism, drug abuse, crime, and racism plague the community.

Clarendon Heights is well known to the city's inhabitants. The site of two riots in the early and mid-1970s and most recently of a gunfight in which two policemen and their assailant were shot, the project is considered a no-go area by most of the public. Even residents of the surrounding Italian and Portuguese neighborhoods tend to shun Clarendon Heights. Social workers consider it a notoriously difficult place in which to work; state and county prison officials are familiar with the project as a source for a disproportionately high number of their inmates. Indeed, considering its relatively small size, Clarendon Heights has acquired quite a reputation.

This notoriety is not entirely deserved, but it is keenly felt by the project's tenants. Subject to the stigma associated with residence in public housing, they are particularly sensitive to the image Clarendon Heights conjures up in the minds of outsiders. When Clarendon Heights residents are asked for their address at a bank, store, or office, their reply often is met with a quick glance of curiosity, pity, superiority, suspicion, or fear. In the United States, residence in public housing is often an emblem of failure, shame, and humiliation.

To many outsiders, Freddie's depressed aspirations are either an indication of laziness or a realistic assessment of his natural assets and attributes (or both). A more sympathetic or penetrating observer would cite the insularity of the project and the limited horizons of its youth as reasons for Freddie's outlook. But to an insider, one who has come of age in Clarendon Heights or at least has access to the thoughts and feelings of those who have, the situation is not so simple. This book, very simply, attempts to understand the aspirations of older boys from Clarendon Heights. It introduces the reader not to modern-day Andrew Carnegies, but to Freddie Piniella's role models, teenage boys from the neighborhood whose stories are less often told and much less heard. These boys provide a poignant account of what the social structure looks like from the bottom. If we let them speak to us and strive to understand them on their own terms, the story that we hear is deeply disturbing. We shall come to see Freddie's outlook not as incomprehensible self-defeatism, but as a perceptive response to the plight in which he finds himself.

Although the general picture that emerges is dreary, its texture is richly varied. The male teenage world of Clarendon Heights is populated by two divergent peer groups. The first group, dubbed the Hallway Hangers because of the group's propensity for "hanging" in a particular hallway in the project, consists predominantly of white boys. Their characteristics and attitudes stand in marked contrast to the second group, which is composed almost exclusively of black youths who call themselves the Brothers. Surprisingly, the Brothers speak with relative optimism about their futures, while the Hallway Hangers are despondent about their prospects for social mobility. This dichotomy is illustrated graphically by the responses of Juan (a Brother) and Frankie (a Hallway Hanger) to my query about what their lives will be like in twenty years.

JUAN: I'll have a regular house, y'know, with a yard and everything. I'll have a steady job, a good job. I'll be living the good life, the easy life.

FRANKIE: I don't fucking know. Twenty years. I may be fucking dead. I live a day at a time. I'll probably be in the fucking pen.

Because aspirations mediate what an individual desires and what society can offer, the hopes of these boys are linked inextricably with their assessment of the opportunities available to them. The Hallway Hangers, for example, seem to view equality of opportunity in much the same light as did R. H. Tawney in 1938—that is, as "a heartless jest ... the impertinent courtesy of an invitation offered to unwelcome guests, in the certainty that circumstances will prevent them from accepting it."[5]

SLICK: Out here, there's not the opportunity to make money. That's how you get into stealin' and all that shit. ... All right, to get a job, first of all, this is a handicap, out here. If you say you're from the projects or anywhere in this area, that can hurt you. Right off the bat: reputation.

The Brothers, in contrast, consistently affirm the actuality of equality of opportunity.

DEREK: If you put your mind to it, if you want to make a future for yourself, there's no reason why you can't. It's a question of attitude.

The optimism of the Brothers and the pessimism of the Hallway Hangers stem, at least in part, from their different appraisals of the openness of American society. Slick's belief that "the younger kids have nothing to hope for" obviously influences his own aspirations. Conversely, some of the Brothers aspire to middle-class occupations partly because they do not see significant societal barriers to upward mobility.

To understand the occupational hopes of the Brothers and the Hallway Hangers—and the divergence between them—we must first gauge the forces against which lower-class individuals must struggle in their pursuit of economic and social advancement. Toward this end, the next chapter considers social reproduction theory, which is a tradition of sociological literature that strives to illuminate the specific mechanisms and processes that contribute to the intergenerational transmission of social inequality. Put simply, reproduction theory attempts to show how and why the United States can be depicted more accurately as the place where "the rich get richer and the poor stay poor" than as "the land of opportunity." Social reproduction theory identifies the barriers to social mobility, barriers that constrain without completely blocking lower- and working-class individuals' efforts to break into the upper reaches of the class structure.

Once we have familiarized ourselves with this academic viewpoint, we shall switch perspectives abruptly to the streets in order to consider how the Brothers and Hallway Hangers understand their social circumstances. How do they view their prospects for social upgrading, and how does this estimation affect their aspirations? What unseen social and economic forces daily influence these boys? How do they make sense of and act upon the complex and often contradictory messages emanating from their family, peer group, workplace, and school? In examining this terrain, we shall touch upon many theoretical issues: the role of education in the perpetuation of class inequality; the influence of ethnicity on the meanings individuals attach to their experiences; the causes and consequences of racism; the relationship between structural determinants (e.g., the local job market) and cultural practices (e.g., rejection of school); the degree of autonomy individuals exercise at the cultural level; the destabilizing roles of nonconformity and resistance in the process of social reproduction; the functions of ideology; and the subtlety of various modes of class domination. Our emphasis throughout, however, will be on the occupational aspirations of the Brothers and the Hallway Hangers, how these aspirations are formed, and their significance for the reproduction of social inequality.

Such an agenda can be addressed most thoroughly by a methodology of intensive participant observation. To do justice to the complexity and richness of the human side of the story requires a level of understanding and distinction that questionnaire surveys are incapable of providing. The field methods employed in this study are not unlike those of most sociological ethnographies in which the researcher attempts to understand a culture from the insider's point of view. But my methods are unique in some ways because of my previous involvement with the community. Having worked and lived in the neighborhood for three summers directing a youth program, I was already close friends with many Clarendon Heights residents prior to the beginning of my research. Without this entree into the community, as a college student from rural New Hampshire I would have faced massive problems gaining the trust and respect of my subjects. As it was, acceptance was slow, piecemeal, and fraught with complications. But with the hurdle of entree partially overcome, I was able to gather a large amount of sensitive data, most of it during a twelve-month period of participant observation in 1983 when I lived in the community.

This study concentrates not on Freddie Piniella and the other boys in my youth enrichment program, but on their high school–age role models whose aspirations are better developed. Only Mike, my oldest charge in the first summer of the youth program, later became a member of the Brothers and thus is included in the study. Nevertheless, my roles as community worker and researcher were never entirely distinct, and the dependence of the latter on the former is clearly illustrated by my first "interview," which was undertaken, strangely enough, not in Clarendon Heights but in my college dormitory.

One evening in late February 1983, Mike, with whom I had maintained a steady relationship since his graduation from the youth program a year and a half earlier, phoned my room. I had been down at the Heights that day and had stopped by his apartment, but Mike had not been home. His mother and grandmother had lamented to me about his poor performance in school, and I had offered to help in any way I could. On the telephone Mike gradually turned the conversation to school. He said he was doing fairly well, but he had failed English. I said I would help him prepare for tests, at which point he mentioned a report on Albert Einstein due in a few days. He had not had much luck researching the topic and hoped I could help. We arranged to meet the next day near the university. After reading an *Encyclopedia Britannica* article on Einstein and photocopying it, we got something to eat in the college dining hall and went up to my room. While I did some reading, Mike worked on his paper at my desk.

Before I knew what was happening my first unstructured interview was under way. Mike suddenly began talking about his future, about, in fact, his occupational and educational goals and expectations. The ensuing conversation lasted an hour and a half and touched on many subjects, but in that time Mike described the high school's curricula, spoke of his own experience in the Occupational Education Program, expressed his desire to work in the computer field, and graphically communicated the role of the achievement ideology in the school. His computer teacher, Mike mentioned, assured the class that a well-paid programming job could be secured easily upon graduation. When I asked Mike about all the unemployed teenagers in Clarendon Heights, his response betrayed his own internalization of the achievement ideology: "Well, you can't just be fooling around all the time. Those guys, they was always fucking off in class. You gotta want it. But if you work hard, really put your mind to it, you can do it."

Thus began my formal research, which was to involve me deeply with the community during the next year. The data focus on the fifteen teenage boys who constitute the Brothers and the Hallway Hangers. Much time was spent with these peer groups during all four seasons and at all hours of the day and night. The simultaneous study of both groups was a difficult undertaking because of the animosity that exists between them and the consequent aspersions that often were cast upon me by members of one group when I associated with the other. In the end, however, the effort was well worth the trouble, as the comparative material that I managed to gather is of great importance to the study.

Field notes, a record of informal discussions, and transcripts of taped, semistructured interviews with each boy (individually and, on occasion, in groups) make up the main body of the data. In the few instances where interviews were not taped, the dialogue is not verbatim. Rather, it is my best rendering of what was said, which was recorded as soon after the discussion as possible. To round out the research, discussions with some of the boys' parents and interviews with teachers, guidance counselors, and career counselors also were undertaken.

2

Social Reproduction in Theoretical Perspective

WHY IS THERE A STRONG TENDENCY for working-class children to end up in working-class jobs? It is this question, a perennial one in the field of sociology, that social reproduction theorists have addressed during the past twenty years. Drawing on the work of Max Weber, Emile Durkheim, and especially Karl Marx, reproduction theorists analyze how the class structure is reproduced from one generation to the next. They attempt to unravel how and why the poor are at a decided disadvantage in the scramble for good jobs. As reproduction theorists explore how the social relations of capitalist society are reproduced, they invariably are led to one site: the school. In the popular mind, school is the great equalizer: By providing a level playing field where the low and the mighty compete on an equal basis, schooling renders social inequality superfluous. Reproduction theorists, in contrast, show that schools actually reinforce social inequality while pretending to do the opposite. These theorists share a common interest in uncovering how status or class position is transmitted. But in doing so, they follow somewhat different approaches.

On one end of the spectrum are theorists who advocate deterministic models of reproduction; on the other end are those who put forth models that allow for the relative autonomy of individuals in their own cultural settings. Deterministic theories take as their starting point the structural requirements of the capitalist economic system and attempt to demonstrate how individuals are obliged to fulfill predefined roles that ensure the perpetuation of a class society. Culturally attuned models begin with the experiences of individuals, and only after understanding people on their own terms do these models attempt to connect those experiences with the demands of capitalist social relations. In this review of reproduction theory, I shall begin with Samuel Bowles and Herbert Gintis, who represent the economic determinist end of the spectrum, progress through the works of Pierre Bourdieu, Basil Bernstein, and Shirley Brice Heath, and finally consider Paul Willis and Henry Giroux on the other end of the continuum.

Samuel Bowles and Herbert Gintis:
Schooled by Social Class

As Marxists, Bowles and Gintis begin their analysis with the forces and relations of production. Marx writes in *Capital,* "The capitalist process of production … produces not only commodities, not only surplus-value, but it also produces and reproduces the capitalist relation itself; on the one hand the capitalist, on the other the wage-labourer."[1] Building on Marx's basic point, Bowles and Gintis show how the American educational system is subordinated to and reflective of the production process and structure of class relations in the United States. Thus, they suggest that "the major aspects of the structure of schooling can be understood in terms of the systemic needs for producing reserve armies of skilled labor, legitimating the technocratic-meritocratic perspective, reinforcing the fragmentation of groups of workers into stratified status groups, and accustoming youth to the social relationships of dominance and subordinancy in the economic system."[2] In short, argue Bowles and Gintis, schools train the wealthy to take up places at the top of the economy while conditioning the poor to accept their lowly status in the class structure.

Bowles and Gintis emphasize their "correspondence principle," which highlights the similarity between the social relations of production and personal interaction in the schools. "Specifically, the relationships of authority and control between administrators and teachers, teachers and students, students and students, and students and their work replicate the division of labor which dominates the work place."[3] Bowles and Gintis argue that strong structural similarities can be seen in (1) the organization of power and authority in the school and in the workplace; (2) the student's lack of control of curriculum and the worker's lack of control of the content of his or her job; (3) the role of grades and other rewards in the school and the role of wages in the workplace as extrinsic motivational systems; and (4) competition among students and the specialization of academic subjects and competition among workers and the fragmented nature of jobs.[4] In short, the social relations of the school reflect those of the capitalist mode of production; through its institutional relationships, the system of education in the United States "tailors the self-concepts, aspirations, and social class identifications of individuals to the requirements of the social division of labor."[5]

Insofar as these conditions apply to all students, however, their influence cannot explain the reproduction of class relations. An effective explanation must indicate the ways in which the educational system treats students differently depending on their social origins. In taking up this task, Bowles and Gintis elaborate the factors that contribute to class-based differences in socialization. They begin by demonstrating that there are major structural differences among schools. Schools serving working-class neighborhoods are more regimented and emphasize rules and behavioral control. In contrast, suburban schools offer more open classrooms that "favor greater student participation, less direct supervision, more student electives, and, in general, a value system stressing internalized standards of control."[6]

These variations reflect the different expectations of teachers, administrators, and parents for children of different class backgrounds. Working-class parents, for example, know from their own job experiences that submission to authority is an important value for success in the workplace; they will insist that the schools inculcate this value. Middle-class parents, reflecting their position in the social division of labor, will expect more open schools for their children.[7] Even within the same school, argue Bowles and Gintis, educational tracks, which cater to different classes of students, emphasize different values.

According to Bowles and Gintis, schooling functions at a material level to ensure the successful accumulation of capital by providing employers with trained workers. But the American educational system also functions at an ideological level to promote the attitudes and values required by a capitalist economy. Children of workers attend schools and are placed into educational tracks, both of which emphasize conformity and docility and prepare them for low-status jobs. By contrast, the sons and daughters of the elite are invited to study at their own pace under loose supervision, to make independent decisions, and to internalize social norms—all of which prepares them to boss rather than to be bossed. In short, Bowles and Gintis argue that schools socialize students to occupy roughly the same position in the class structure as that of their parents.

Pierre Bourdieu: Cultural Capital and Habitus

Pierre Bourdieu, a prominent French sociologist, is more indebted to Weber and Durkheim than to Marx, yet Bourdieu also is influenced by the French structuralist movement, which seeks to delve beneath the surface of observed cultural forms to find the "deep" principles and logic according to which empirical reality functions. Drawing on these perspectives, Bourdieu forges an original theory in which class structure plays a more nuanced role, but one that does not preclude deterministic elements.

Bourdieu's most important contribution to reproduction theory is the concept of cultural capital, which he defines as the general cultural background, knowledge, disposition, and skills that are passed from one generation to the next. Cultural capital is the centerpiece of Bourdieu's theory of cultural reproduction. Children of upper-class origin, according to Bourdieu, inherit substantially different cultural capital than do working-class children. By embodying class interests and ideologies, schools reward the cultural capital of the dominant classes and systematically devalue that of the lower classes. Upper-class students, by virtue of a certain linguistic and cultural competence acquired through family upbringing, are provided with the means of appropriation for success in school. Children who read books, visit museums, attend concerts, and go to the theater and cinema (or simply grow up in families where these practices are prevalent) acquire a familiarity with the dominant culture that the educational system implicitly requires of its students for academic attainment. As Giroux contends, "Students whose families have a tenuous connection to forms of cultural capital highly valued by the dominant society are at a decided disadvantage."[8] Hence, schools serve as the trading post where socially valued cultural capital is parlayed into superior academic performance. Academic performance is then turned back into economic capital by the acquisition of superior jobs. Schools reproduce social inequality, but by dealing in the currency of academic credentials, the educational system legitimates the entire process.

There are four main points in Bourdieu's theory. First, distinctive cultural capital is transmitted by each social class. Second, the school systematically valorizes upper-class cultural capital and depreciates the cultural capital of the lower classes. Third, differential academic achievement is retranslated back into economic wealth—the job market remunerates the superior academic credentials earned mainly by the upper classes. Finally, the school legitimates this process "by making social hierarchies and the reproduction of those hierarchies appear to be based upon the hierarchy of 'gifts,' merits, or skills established and ratified by its sanctions, or, in a word, by converting social hierarchies into academic hierarchies."[9]

Bourdieu's model is not quite that simple, however. He recognizes, for instance, that the conversion of economic capital into cultural capital is not a precise one and thus that "the structure of distribution of cultural capital is not exactly the same as the structure of economic capital."[10] Moreover, in the upper reaches of the class structure, despite the decline of the family firm, economic capital is still passed on directly to the next generation, and the importance of educational attainment and cultural capital is correspondingly lower. Bourdieu also argues that "children's academic performance is more strongly related to parents' educational history than to parents' occupational status"[11] and contends that class-based differences in cultural capital tend to have a decreasing importance as one ascends the educational ladder. For Bourdieu, "social class background is mediated through a complex set of factors that interact in different ways at different levels of schooling."[12] Giroux captures the essence of Bourdieu's argument when he observes that "rather than being directly linked to the power of an economic elite, schools are seen as part of a larger social universe of symbolic institutions that, rather than impose docility and oppression, reproduce existing power relations subtly via the production and distribution of a dominant culture that tacitly confirms what it means to be educated."[13]

In addition to cultural capital, Bourdieu employs the concept of habitus, which he defines as "a system of lasting, transposable dispositions which, integrating past experiences, functions at every moment as a matrix of perceptions, appreciations, and actions."[14] The habitus "could be considered as a subjective but not individual system of internalized structures, schemes of perception, conception, and action common to all members of the same group or class."[15] Put simply, the habitus is composed of the attitudes, beliefs, and experiences of those inhabiting one's social world. This conglomeration of deeply internalized values defines an individual's attitudes toward, for example, schooling. The structure of schooling, with its high regard for the cultural capital of the upper classes, promotes a belief among working-class students that they are unlikely to achieve academic success. Thus, there is a correlation between objective probabilities and subjective aspirations, between institutional structures and cultural practices.[16]

Aspirations reflect an individual's view of his or her own chances for getting ahead and are an internalization of objective probabilities. But aspirations are not the product of a rational analysis; rather, they are acquired in the habitus of the individual. A lower-class child growing up in an environment where success is rare is much less likely to develop strong ambitions than is a middle-class boy or girl growing up in a social world peopled by those who have "made it" and where the connection between effort and reward is taken for granted. "The habitus is the universalizing mediation which causes an individual agent's practices, without either explicit reason or signifying intent, to be none the less 'sensible' and 'reasonable.'"[17]

The habitus engenders attitudes and conduct that enable objective social structures to succeed in reproducing themselves. The educational and job opportunity structures are such that individuals of lower-class origin have a very reduced chance of securing professional or managerial jobs. This fact filters down to the lower-class boy (for a girl the outlook is even bleaker) situated in his habitus from the experiences and attitudes of those close to him. Responding to the objective structures, the boy loses interest in school and resigns himself to a low-level job, thereby reinforcing the structure of class inequality. Essentially, Bourdieu posits a circular relationship between structures and practices, in which "objective structures tend to produce structured subjective dispositions that produce structured actions which, in turn, tend to reproduce objective structure."[18]

In Bourdieu's scheme, habitus functions as a regulator between individuals and their external world, between human agency and social structure. As Loïc Wacquant argues, habitus "effects, from within, the reactivation of the meanings and relations objectified 'without' as institutions."[19] It is the mediating link between individuals and their social world. As a conceptual bridge between subjective, inner consciousness and the objective, external constraints of the material world, habitus disposes individuals to think and act in certain ways.[20] Thus, Freddie Peniella announces in the streets of Clarendon Heights, "I ain't goin' to college," while an eleven-year-old counterpart across the city may enter his father's study to confirm a preference for Harvard over Yale.

Through the concepts of cultural capital and habitus, Bourdieu seeks to explain how social inequality is perpetuated and why this process of social reproduction is so readily accepted by exploiter and exploited alike. "Every established order," he notes, "tends to produce the naturalization of its own arbitrariness."[21] At the same time, the mechanisms of cultural and social reproduction remain hidden, because the social practices that safeguard the political and economic interests of the dominant classes go unrecognized as anything other than the only natural, rational, or possible ones. And schooling is crucial to the reproduction and legitimation of social inequality.

> Surely, among all the solutions put forth throughout history to the problem of the transmission of power and privileges, there does not exist one that is better concealed, and therefore better adapted to societies which tend to reuse the most patent forms of the hereditary transmission of power and privileges, than that solution which the educational system provides by contributing to the reproduction of the structure of class relations and by concealing, under an apparently neutral attitude, the fact that it fulfills this function.[22]

Thus success or failure in school is determined largely by social class. But cloaked in the language of meritocracy, academic performance is apprehended as the result of individual ability by both high and low achievers. Such is the magic of school-mediated exclusion: It implants in those it marginalizes a set of cognitive and evaluative categories that lead them to see themselves as the causal agents of a process that is actually institutionally determined. Bourdieu shows how schooling entrenches social inequality by reproducing class privilege and simultaneously sanctifying the resultant inequality.

Basil Bernstein and Shirley Brice Heath: Linguistic Cultural Capital

Whereas Bourdieu paints an elegant theory with broad brush strokes, Basil Bernstein, an innovative British sociologist, zeroes in on one important link in the process of social reproduction—language patterns. Through his theory of language codification and its relationship to social class on the one hand and schooling on the other, Bernstein links micro- and macro-sociological issues. Influenced by Durkheim and the French structuralist movement, Bernstein, in some respects, goes well beyond Bourdieu in terms of methodological rigor by analyzing both structures and practices and actually demonstrating their relationship. Nevertheless, for all its distinctiveness, Bernstein's work is understood most easily in the context of Bourdieu's theory of cultural capital.

Bourdieu argues that schools require cultural resources with which only specific students are endowed; Bernstein looks specifically at the educational ramifications of divergent linguistic patterns among children of different social strata. Bernstein begins by tracing the implications of social class for language use. In a highly complex argument, he contends that class membership generates distinctive forms of speech patterns through family socialization. Working-class children are oriented to "restricted" linguistic codes, while middle-class children use "elaborated" codes. By *linguistic codes* Bernstein does not mean the surface manifestations of language such as vocabulary or dialect, but rather the underlying regulative principles that govern the selection and combination of different syntactic and lexical constructions.[23]

Linguistic codes, which ultimately are rooted in the social division of labor, derive from the social relations and roles within families. While rejecting an outright correlation between social class and linguistic code, Bernstein claims that working-class children generally grow up in homes where common circumstances, knowledge, and values give rise to speech patterns in which meanings remain implicit and dependent on their context (a restricted code). Middle-class families, in contrast, use elaborated codes to express the unique perspective and experience of the speaker; meanings are less tied to a local relationship and local social structure and consequently are made linguistically explicit.[24] In their introductory essay to *Power and Ideology in Education,* Karabel and Halsey explain how distinct class-specific forms of communication are engendered.

> Participation in working-class family and community life, in which social relations are based upon shared identifications, expectations, and assumptions, tends to generate a "restricted code," for the speaker who is sure that the listener can take his intentions for granted has little incentive to elaborate his meanings and make them explicit and specific. Middle-class culture, in contrast, tends to place the "I" over the "we," and the resultant uncertainty that meanings will be intelligible to the listener forces the speaker to select among syntactic alternatives and to differentiate his vocabulary. The result is the development of an "elaborated code" oriented to the communication of highly individuated meanings.[25]

Because "one of the effects of the class system is to limit access to elaborated codes"[26] and because schools operate in accordance with the symbolic order of elaborated codes, working-class children are at a significant disadvantage. "Our schools are not made for these children; why should the children respond? To ask the child to switch to an elaborated code which presupposes different role relationships and systems of meaning ... may create for the child a bewildering and potentially damaging experience."[27] By conceptualizing the social structure as a system of class inequality, tracing this structure's implications for language, and demonstrating the ways in which schools value the elaborated codes and other linguistic devices characteristic of the upper classes, Bernstein puts forth a theory that focuses on a powerful mechanism of social reproduction.

Shirley Brice Heath's research into language patterns at home and in the classroom also highlights the importance of linguistic cultural capital. Whereas Bernstein elucidates the relationship among schooling, social class, and language in Britain, Heath looks at race as well in her sensitive ethnography of schooling in America's Piedmont Carolinas. Heath examines the way language is used in Trackton (a working-class African American community) and nearby Roadville (a working-class white neighborhood). She uncovers important linguistic differences between the two neighborhoods, but the real contrast is between the language patterns of these two rural communities and the way the middle-class townspeople talk. The townspeople, including teachers, use discrete interrogative questions when they talk to their children at home. Through the everyday speech patterns prevalent in their households, these middle-class children are taught to label and name objects, to identify the features of the objects, and to talk about referents out of context: precisely the skills demanded of students in school. The children of Trackton learn different skills. They are less often questioned by their parents, who tend to use imperatives or statements. And in any case, questions that are asked at home usually require comparative or analogical answers rather than specific information. The result is that the black working-class children are not socialized to cope with the language patterns used in school and quickly fall into a pattern of academic failure. The white working-class children from Roadville fare better in that they develop many of the cognitive and linguistic patterns required in elementary school. But they fail to develop "the integrative types of skills necessary for sustained academic success."[28] Like their Trackton counterparts, only later, many Roadville students fall behind, drift through school in a fog of failure, or drop out altogether.

Heath's basic point is the same as Bernstein's: The mismatch between the language used at home and the language demanded by the school is a serious stumbling block for working-class and nonwhite pupils. Like many of the mechanisms of social reproduction, linguistic socialization is an invisible impediment that goes unacknowledged. Disadvantaged students blame themselves for failure, whereas wealthier pupils take their cultural capital for granted and accept full credit for their success. By stripping schools of their innocence, social reproduction theorists show that formal education actually functions "to certify lower status youngsters as socially inferior at an early age and to initiate the process that keeps many of them economically and socially inferior in adulthood."[29]

Paul Willis: The Lads and the Ear'oles

Like Heath, Paul Willis, author of *Learning to Labor,* begins with the lived culture of his subjects. In this impressive ethnographic study of a group of disaffected, white, working-class males in a British secondary school, Willis undertook extensive participant observation in order to grasp this "counter-school culture's" distinctive pattern of cultural practices. Willis found that the complex and contradictory nature of the "sources of meaning" on which these boys draw and the determinants of their behavior "warns against a too reductive or crude materialist notion of the cultural level."[30]

This is not to say, however, that Willis denies the importance of structural influence. On the contrary, writing in the Marxist tradition, Willis believes that these boys' class background, geographical location, local opportunity structure (job market), and educational attainment influence their job choice. But he reminds deterministic Marxists that these structural forces act through and are mediated by the cultural milieu. If we are to understand social reproduction, we must understand

> *how* and *why* young people take the restricted and often meaningless available jobs in ways which seem sensible to them in their familiar world as it is actually lived. For a proper treatment of these questions we must go to the cultural milieu ... and accept a certain autonomy of the processes at this level which defeats any simple notion of mechanistic causation and gives the social agents involved some meaningful scope for viewing, inhabiting, and constructing their own world in a way which is recognizably human and not theoretically reductive.[31]

By viewing social reproduction as it actually is lived out, we can understand the mechanisms of the process.

In his study of a working-class school, Willis finds a major division between the students. The great bulk of the students are the "ear'oles" who conform to the roles defined for students, aspire to middle-class occupations, and comply with the rules and norms of the school. The counterschool culture of the "lads," in contrast, rejects the school's achievement ideology; these nonconformist boys subvert teacher and administrator authority, disrupt classes, mock the ear'oles (to whom they feel superior), and generally exploit any opportunity to "have a laff," usually at the expense of school officials. In short, the lads use whatever means possible to display their open opposition to the school.

Willis directs almost all his attention to understanding the lads. Their rejection of school, according to Willis, is partly the result of some profound insights, or "penetrations," into the economic condition of their social class under capitalism. The lads believe that their chances for significant upward mobility are so remote that sacrificing "a laff" for good behavior in school is pointless. The lads repudiate schooling because they realize that most available work is essentially meaningless and that although individuals are capable of "making it," conformism for their group or class promises no rewards.[32] As Michael Apple puts it, "Their rejection of so much of the content and form of day to day educational life bears on the almost unconscious realization that, as a class, schooling will not enable them to go much further than they already are."[33] According to Willis, this type of insight into the nature of capitalism has the potential to catalyze class solidarity and collective action.

The promise of these cultural penetrations, however, is dimmed by certain "limitations" in the lads' cultural outlook. The lads equate manual labor with masculinity, a trait highly valued by their working-class culture; mental labor is associated with the social inferiority of femininity.[34] This reversal of the usual valuation of mental versus manual labor prevents the lads from seeing their placement in dead-end, low-paying jobs as a form of class domination. Instead, they positively choose to join their brothers and fathers on the shop floor, a choice made happily and apparently free from coercion. Val Burris, in a review of *Learning to Labor,* brings this point into sharp focus.

> What begins as a potential insight into the conditions of labor and the identity of the working class is transformed, under the influence of patriarchal ideology, into a surprising and uncritical affirmation of manual labor. It is this identification of manual labor with male privilege which, more than anything else, ensures the lads' acceptance of their subordinate economic fate and the successful reproduction of the class structure.[35]

The lads' nonconformist cultural innovations, which ultimately contribute to the reproduction of the class structure, are often complex and contradictory. An understanding of these mechanisms of social reproduction requires an ethnographic approach based on a theory that postulates the relative autonomy of the cultural sphere. Although a Marxist, Willis eschews theories based on economic determinism or a correspondence principle as explanations for the perpetuation of class inequality. Rather, he gives explanatory power to the cultural level and the social innovations of the individuals involved. In this way, we can see how structural forces are mediated by the cultural sphere through which they must pass.

Willis insists that the cultural attitudes and practices of working-class groups are not necessarily reflective of, or even traceable to, structural determinations or dominant ideologies. Although the mode of production wields a powerful influence on the attitudes and actions of individuals, people do not simply respond to the socioeconomic pressures bearing down on them with passivity and indifference. The cultural level is marked by contestation, resistance, and compromise. Culture itself implies "the active, collective use and explorations of received symbolic, ideological, and cultural resources to explain, make sense of and positively respond to 'inherited' structural and material conditions."[36] Subordinate groups can produce alternative cultural forms containing meanings endemic to the working class. Termed "cultural production" by Willis, this process is by nature active and transformative. Still, these behavioral and attitudinal innovations, as the lads illustrate, are often ultimately reproductive. As Liz Gordon remarks in her review of Willis's work, it may seem contradictory to refer to cultural production as both transformative and reproductive, but "Willis wishes to move away from an oversimplistic either/or model. He points out that there is no clear separation between agency and structure; these cannot be understood in isolation from one another."[37]

Henry Giroux: Student Resistance to School

Bridging the division between structure and agency maintained by theories of social reproduction has been one of the ongoing theoretical concerns of Henry A. Giroux, who contends that separation of human agency and structural analysis either suppresses the significance of individual autonomy or ignores the structural determinants that lie outside the immediate experience of human actors.[38] Giroux insists on the need to admit "wider structural and ideological determinations while recognizing that human beings never represent simply a reflex of such constraints."[39] Structuralist theories, which stress that history is made "behind the backs" of the members of society, overlook the significance and relative autonomy of the cultural level and the human experiences of domination and resistance. "In the structuralist perspective human agents are registered simply as the effects of structural determinants that appear to work with the certainty of biological processes. In this grimly mechanistic approach, human subjects simply act as role-bearers."[40] Culturalist theories, on the other hand, pay too little attention to how structurally embedded material and economic forces weigh down and shape human experience. "Culturalism begins at the right place but does not go far enough theoretically—it does not dig into subjectivity in order to find its objective elements."[41]

Giroux argues for a rigorous treatment of ideology, consciousness, and culture in order to move reproduction theory past the theoretical impasse imposed by the structure-agency dualism. He proposes a dialectical treatment of subjectivity and structure in which structure and human agency are seen to affect each other and thinks it crucial "to understand more thoroughly the complex ways in which people mediate and respond to the interface between their own lived experiences and structures of domination and constraint."[42]

In exploring these issues, Giroux develops a theory of resistance. He takes as his starting point the ethnographic studies of Willis, Hebdige, and Corrigan, which analyze how socioeconomic structures work through culture to shape the lives of students.[43] Giroux follows their lead in examining student nonconformity and opposition for their sociopolitical significance. Giroux considers resistance a response to the educational system, a response rooted in "moral and political indignation,"[44] not psychological dysfunction. Student countercultures and their attendant social attitudes and practices, according to Giroux, need to be analyzed carefully for "radical significance"; not all forms of oppositional behavior stem from a critique, implicit or explicit, of school-constructed ideologies and relations of domination. The violation of a school rule is not in itself an act of resistance unless committed by a youth who, for example, sees through the schools' achievement ideology and is acting on that basis. The logic of resistance runs counter to the social relations of schooling and calls for struggle against, rather than submission to, domination.[45] By insisting that oppositional behavior be scrutinized and that resistance be mined for its broader significance, Giroux sets the program for future studies in social reproduction.

Student resistance represents a fertile area for academic study because it offers the possibility of transcending the structure-agency dualism. Resistance theory examines the ongoing, active experiences of individuals while simultaneously perceiving in oppositional attitudes and practices a response to structures of constraint and domination. Taking Willis's concept of cultural production seriously, Giroux suggests that working-class subordination is not a simple reaction to the logic of capitalist rationality. Rather, oppositional cultural patterns draw on elements of working-class culture in a creative and potentially transformative fashion. Thus, the mechanisms of class domination are neither static nor final.

As Giroux is well aware, a thorough understanding of student resistance is difficult to come by. Oppositional behavior is not self-explanatory. It must be linked with the subjects' own explanations of their behavior and contextualized within the nexus of peer, family, and work relations out of which resistance emerges.[46] Unfortunately, Giroux himself undertakes no such investigation, and most studies of social reproduction concentrate on the role of schooling in the perpetuation of class inequality, thus giving only token consideration to the other vehicles of socialization.

Social Reproduction in Clarendon Heights

This book intends to delve beneath the surface of teenage behavior to recover the interests, concerns, and logic that render it comprehensible. In *Learning to Labor*, Willis gives us a complete and sophisticated analysis of how the lads experience the process of social reproduction. But what of the ear'oles? Both groups are working class. What causes the lads to respond to the school and to the occupational structure in a completely different way than do the ear'oles? Are the ear'oles, as Burris suggests, prepared for their economic fate by passive submission to structural and ideological forces? Or do the ear'oles actively respond to structural pressures bearing down on them and develop their own novel cultural practices and meanings? If economic determinants have the overriding importance that theorists such as Bowles and Gintis suggest, how can two groups from the same social location embody two distinctly different cultural orientations? Will the educational and occupational outcomes be much the same for the lads and ear'oles, or will they differ? In the process of social reproduction, what is the relationship between structural forces and cultural innovation? How much autonomy do individuals have at the cultural level?

Although the British and American contexts are obviously different, such questions are crucial to our understanding of how social inequality is reproduced in the United States. The chapters that follow examine in an intensive fashion two very different groups from the same social location and in the process illuminate some of the mechanisms, both structural and cultural, that contribute to social reproduction. In particular, occupational aspirations, as a mediating link between socioeconomic structures (what society offers) and individuals at the cultural level (what one wants), play a crucial role in the reproduction of class inequality. At the interface between structural determinants and human agency, aspirations offer the sociologist a conceptual bridge over the theoretical rift of the structure-agency dualism. Bourdieu and Willis both emphasize the importance of aspirations in their theoretical writings. For Bourdieu, the relationship between aspirations and opportunity is at the root of "the educational mortality of the working classes."[47] We have seen that a disparity in aspirations is the major difference between the lads and the ear'oles. Indeed, of all the factors contributing to social reproduction (e.g., tracking, social relations of schooling, class-based differences in linguistic codes), the regulation of aspirations is perhaps the most important.

Now that we have familiarized ourselves with some of the major aspects of social reproduction literature, we are in a position to examine in depth the male teenage world of Clarendon Heights. The experiences of the Brothers and the Hallway Hangers, if properly elucidated, bear on the issues of social reproduction more directly than any sociological theory ever could. Thus, it is to the boys of Clarendon Heights that we now turn.

Notes

1. Karl Marx, *Capital* (Harmondsworth: Penguin, 1976), p. 724.

2. Samuel Bowles and Herbert Gintis, *Schooling in Capitalist America* (New York: Basic Books, 1976), p. 56.

3. Ibid., p. 12.

4. Ibid.

5. Ibid., p. 129.

6. Ibid., p. 132.

7. Ibid., pp. 132–133.

8. Henry A. Giroux, *Theory & Resistance in Education* (London: Heinemann Educational Books, 1983), p. 88.

9. Pierre Bourdieu, "Cultural Reproduction and Social Reproduction," in Jerome Karabel and A. H. Halsey, eds., *Power and Ideology in Education* (New York: Oxford University Press, 1977), p. 496.

10. Ibid., p. 507.

11. David Swartz, "Pierre Bourdieu: The Cultural Transmission of Social Inequality," *Harvard Educational Review* 47 (November 1977):548.

12. Ibid.

13. Giroux, *Theory & Resistance*, p. 87.

14. Pierre Bourdieu, *Outline of a Theory of Practice* (Cambridge: Cambridge University Press, 1977), pp. 82–83.

15. Ibid., p. 86.

16. Pierre Bourdieu and Jean-Claude Passeron, *Reproduction in Education, Society and Culture* (London: Sage, 1977), p. 156.

17. Bourdieu, *Outline of a Theory of Practice*, p. 79.

18. Swartz, "Pierre Bourdieu," p. 548.

19. Loïc J. D. Wacquant, "Sociology as Socioanalysis: Tales of *Homo Academicus*," *Sociological Forum* 5 (1990):684.

20. Richard Jenkins, *Pierre Bourdieu* (London: Routledge, 1992), pp. 74–84.

21. Bourdieu, *Outline of a Theory of Practice*, p. 164.

22. Bourdieu and Passeron, *Reproduction in Education*, p. 178; translation adapted by Loïc Wacquant and cited in "On the Tracks of Symbolic Power," *Theory, Culture, and Society* 10 (August 1993):2.

23. Paul Atkinson, *Language, Structure and Reproduction* (London: Methuen, 1985), pp. 66, 68, 74.

24. Basil Bernstein, "Social Class, Language, and Socialization," in Karabel and Halsey, *Power and Ideology*, p. 477.

25. Karabel and Halsey, *Power and Ideology*, p. 63.

26. Ibid., p. 478.

27. Ibid., p. 483.

28. Shirley Brice Heath, *Ways with Words* (Cambridge: Cambridge University Press, 1983), p. 343.

29. Carol Camp Yeakey and Clifford T. Bennett, "Race, Schooling, and Class in American Society," *Journal of Negro Education* 59 (Winter 1990):5.

30. Paul E. Willis, *Learning to Labor* (Aldershot: Gower, 1977), p. 171.

31. Ibid., p. 172.

32. Ibid., pp. 126–129.

33. Michael W. Apple, *Education and Power* (Boston: Routledge and Kegan Paul, 1982), p. 99.

34. Willis, *Learning to Labor*, p. 148.

35. Val Burris, rev. of *Learning to Labor*, by Paul Willis, *Harvard Educational Review* 50 (November 1980):525.

36. Paul Willis, "Cultural Production and Theories of Reproduction," in *Race, Class and Education*, ed. Len Barton and Stephen Walker (London: Croom Helm, 1983), p. 112.

37. Liz Gordon, "Paul Willis—Education, Cultural Production and Social Reproduction," *British Journal of Sociology of Education* 5 (1984):113.

38. Giroux, *Theory & Resistance*, p. 119.

39. Ibid., p. 38.

40. Ibid., p. 136.

41. Ibid., p. 135.

42. Ibid., p. 108.

43. Ibid., pp. 98–99.

44. Henry A. Giroux, "Theories of Reproduction and Resistance in the New Sociology of Education: A Critical Analysis," *Harvard Educational Review* 53 (August 1983):289.

45. Ibid., p. 290.

46. Ibid., p. 291.

47. Bourdieu and Passeron, *Reproduction in Education*, p. 156.

3

Teenagers in Clarendon Heights:
The Hallway Hangers
and the Brothers

O N ANY GIVEN DAY, except during the coldest winter months, the evening hours in Clarendon Heights are filled with activity. At one end of the housing development, elderly women sit on wooden benches and chat. In the center of the project, children play street hockey, kickball, stickball, or football, depending on the season. At the other end, teenage boys congregate in the stairwell and on the landing of one of the entries—doorway #13.

The Hallway Hangers: "You Gotta Be Bad"

This doorway and the area immediately outside it are the focus of activity for the Hallway Hangers, one of the two main peer groups of high-school-age boys living in Clarendon Heights. Composed of a core of eight youths, but including up to ten additional people who are loosely attached to the group, the Hallway Hangers are tough, streetwise, individuals who form a distinctive subculture. Except for Boo-Boo, who is black, and Chris, who is of mixed racial parentage, the Hallway Hangers are white boys of Italian or Irish descent. The eight members considered here range in age from sixteen to nineteen. Five have dropped out of school, two graduated last year,[1] and one continues to attend high school. They all smoke cigarettes, drink regularly, and use drugs. All but two have been arrested. Stereotyped as "hoodlums," "punks," or "burnouts" by outsiders, the Hallway Hangers are actually a varied group, and much can be learned from considering each member.

Frankie, the acknowledged leader of the Hallway Hangers, is of only medium height and weight, but his fighting ability is unsurpassed among teenagers in

Clarendon Heights. Missing two front teeth from one of his few unsuccessful encounters, Frankie maintains a cool, calculating demeanor that only occasionally
gives way to his fiery temper. He commands the respect of the other boys because
he is a natural leader and because he comes from a family that is held in high esteem by the city's underworld. His brothers have been involved in organized
crime and have spent time in prison; four of them were incarcerated at the time I
conducted my research. Although Frankie is the ringleader of the Hallway Hangers, he has never been arrested—no small feat considering the scope of the group's
criminal activity.

Whereas Frankie combines physical toughness and mental acuity, Slick, although no weakling, clearly possesses an abundance of the latter attribute. Very
articulate and perceptive, Slick scored high on standardized tests and fared well in
school when he applied himself (he dropped out last year). Slick gets along well
on the street, where his quick wit and sharp tongue are major assets. Although his
status falls short of Frankie's, Slick is accorded much respect by the other boys of
Clarendon Heights.

As Slick is known for the strength of his intellect, Shorty is known for his physical toughness. When a teacher at the local high school remarked, "What makes
someone tough has nothing to do with size or even muscle—it's the fear factor. If
someone's fearless, crazy, he'll do anything," he doubtless had Shorty in mind. As
his nickname implies, Shorty is small, but well built. His temper is explosive, and
under the influence of alcohol or drugs, he has been known to accost strangers,
beat up friends, or pull a knife on anyone who challenges him. On one occasion,
he repeatedly stabbed himself in the head in a fit of masochistic machismo. Although Frankie and Slick also consider themselves alcoholics, Shorty's drinking
problem is more severe. The county court ordered him to a detoxification center—an arrangement Shorty has slyly managed to avoid.

Like the other three boys, Chris is a self-professed alcoholic who also admits to
being dependent on marijuana. Chris's father (who does not live at home) is
black, and his mother is white, which gives Chris an ethnic heritage that makes
his acceptance by the rest of the Hallway Hangers difficult. A tall, very slender
youth, Chris is loud and talkative but without the self-confidence and poise of
Slick or Frankie. He is often the object of the other boys' abuse, both verbal and
physical, but nevertheless has some stature in the group largely because of his loyalty and sense of humor.

Boo-Boo, the other black member of the Hallway Hangers, is a tall, quiet, dark-
skinned youth. His serious nature makes him a less frequent target of abuse,
which begins as playful racial barbs but often degenerates into downright racial
animosity. Like Chris, Boo-Boo is a follower. A sincere and earnest boy, his general demeanor is at odds with the violence and bluster that characterize the group
as a whole. Nevertheless, Boo-Boo has been known to fight—and quite effectively—when seriously antagonized and generally is held in moderate esteem by
the rest of the boys.

Like Boo-Boo, Stoney is a bit of a loner. The only Hallway Hanger to hold stable employment, Stoney works full time in a pizza shop. His regular income, which he recently used to buy a car, earns him a measure of deference from the other boys, but Stoney lacks the cockiness and bravado necessary for high stature within the group. Skinny and averse to street fights, Stoney perpetually but ineffectively strives to rid himself of the label "pussy." Stoney does share with the other boys an enthusiasm for beer and drugs; he has been arrested for possession of mescaline and is psychologically dependent on marijuana. He has a steady girlfriend (another anomaly for the Hallway Hangers, who generally reject serious relationships in favor of more casual romantic encounters) with whom he spends much of his time, but Stoney still values the friendship of the Hallway Hangers and remains an integral member of the group.

Steve, Slick's younger brother, is the stereotypical project youth. Constantly on the lookout for a free ride, Steve is insolent and loud but lacks his brother's sophistication. He is courageous, full of energy, and fights well, but Steve is not particularly popular with the other boys, who tolerate him as Slick's brother and as a person who can be counted on for support and loyalty in the most trying situations. Steve is the only Hallway Hanger still in school; he expects to graduate in two years (1986).

In contrast to Steve, Jinks is a sensitive, shy boy who shares with Stoney and Chris a psychological dependence on marijuana. Although he is considered immature and is taunted as a "mama's boy" by some of the Hallway Hangers, Jinks seems to have inner reserves of confidence and self-esteem that protect his ego from such assaults. Lighthearted and understanding of others, Jinks is the only white member of the Hallway Hangers who is not overtly racist. Although he takes a good deal of abuse from the others, especially Frankie and Shorty, Jinks's acceptance as a bona fide member of the group is beyond question.

These boys come together in the late afternoon or early evening after dinner and "hang" in doorway #13 until late at night. They come to "see what's up," to "find out what's goin' down," to "shoot the shit," and, generally, to just pass the time. Smelling of urine, lined with graffiti, and littered with trash and broken glass, this hallway is the setting for much playful banter, some not so playful "capping" (exchange of insults), and an occasional fight. The odors of cigarette smoke, beer, and marijuana are nearly always present. During the weekend, there may be a case or two of beer, a nearly constant circulation of joints, and some cocaine, mescaline, or "angel dust" (PCP). Late at night, one occasionally stumbles upon a lone figure shooting up heroin.

In an inversion of the dominant culture's vocabulary and value scheme, the subculture of the Hallway Hangers is a world in which to be "bad" is literally to be good. A common characteristic of lower-class[2] teenage peer cultures, this emphasis on being bad is inextricably bound up with the premium put on masculinity, physical toughness, and street wisdom in lower-class culture. Slick, in articulating the prominence of this value for the Hallway Hangers, states in definite terms what being bad often involves.

(in an individual talk)

SLICK: You hafta make a name for yourself, to be bad, tough, whatever. You hafta be, y'know, be with the "in" crowd. Know what I mean? You hafta—it's just all part of growing up around here—you hafta do certain things. Some of the things you hafta do is, y'know, once in awhile you hafta, if you haven't gotten into a fight, if you have a fight up the high school, you're considered bad. Y'know what I mean? If you beat someone up up there, especially if he's black, around this way ... if you're to be bad, you hafta be arrested. You hafta at least know what bein' in a cell is like.

(In a group discussion)

JM: So how is it that to be what's good down here, to be respected ...

SLICK: You gotta be bad.

FRANKIE: Yeah, if you're a straight A student, you get razzed.

SLICK: Then you're a fucking weirdo, and you shouldn't be living here in the first place.

SHORTY: No, you got people down here who don't drink and don't smoke.

SLICK: Who? Name one.

SHORTY: Crane. Bruce Crane.

FRANKIE: Yeah, but like he's sayin', whadda we think of Bruce Crane?

SHORTY: Fucking shithead (*all laugh*).

Thus, good grades in school can lead to ostracism, whereas time spent in prison earns respect. To be bad is the main criterion for status in this subculture; its primacy cannot be overemphasized, and its importance is implied continually by the boys.

Frankie carries the notion of being bad to the extreme, despite its offensiveness to conventional American values. In June 1983, John Grace, a bartender in a pub across the city, shot two police officers and was himself wounded in a gunfight in Clarendon Heights. All three survived, and at the time of this interview, Grace was awaiting trial in a county jail where two of Frankie's brothers were also serving time. "Fucking Grace, he's my man. He's taken care of. My brother says he'll have a fucking joint when he see him in his cell. He's in lock-up, but they take care of him. He's a big fucking dude. He's respected up there, man. He's the baddest. He shot a fucking cop. He's golden, he's there. That's the best you can fucking do."

Although such a drastic view is seldom voiced or acted upon by the Hallway Hangers, success for members of the peer group does involve physical and emotional toughness. In addition, a quick wit is essential, for much time is spent capping on one another.

(*in the hallway late one afternoon*)

SHORTY: (*drunk*) Hey Steve, what are you doing tonight?

STEVE: Nuttin'. Why?

SHORTY: You wanna suck my dick?

STEVE: You're the only gay motherfucker around here.

SHORTY: Yeah? Ask your girlfriend if I'm gay.

STEVE: Yeah, well, you ask your mother if I'm gay.

This type of sportive banter is common, a diversion to interrupt the boredom inherent in hanging in hallways for a good portion of the day.

JINKS: Everyone gets ragged on out there. It's just when you're high, y'know, you're drunk—you start ragging on people. Helps the time go by.

Sometimes, of course, real venom lies behind the words. In that case, size and strength are the crucial elements for success in an altercation. For behind all the posturing lies the reality of the pecking order, which is determined primarily by physical toughness. Fighting ability is the deciding factor for status demarcation within the group; those lacking in physical stature must compensate for it with aggressiveness and tenacity or learn to live with a lot of abuse, both verbal and physical.

For the Hallway Hangers, being bad entails the consumption of alcohol and the use of drugs on a regular basis. The boys are intoxicated for a good portion of almost every weekend and drink heavily during the week. During the summer, the level of drinking reaches staggering proportions, often involving the consumption of two or more "beer balls" (the equivalent of two and half cases of beer pressurized into a plastic ball about two feet in diameter) a day for a group of eight or ten boys. Although none of the Hallway Hangers is drunk constantly, Frankie, Shorty, Slick, and Chris all consider themselves alcoholics.

FRANKIE: See, the way we are right now, technically we are alcoholics. Y'know, I can go days without drinking alcohol. It ain't like I need it, but right now I want it, y'know; it helps me get through. Y'know, get through problems, whatever; it helps me get through. Take away all the fucking problems down here, and there would be no problems with alcohol.

Shorty is honest about the debilitating effects of his dependence on alcohol.

(*in a group discussion*)

SHORTY: I think when you're an alcoholic like me, man, you ain't gonna be able to hold no fucking job. You say things you fucking forget.

FRANKIE: Yeah, yeah. I hear ya.

SHORTY: I mean, I don't remember trying to stab my own brother in the back; my other brother caught me. That's when I knew I was dead-up an alcoholic. Then I stabbed myself and three other people.

JM: How'd you get to be an alcoholic in the first place?

SHORTY: Being with these motherfuckers (*all laugh*). These got me going. Frankie always used to drink before me. I only used to drink about a beer a night, and I used to get buzzed every night. It's like this now: six pack—Monday through Friday. Friday, it's a case, and when summer comes, it's ...

ALL: Beer balls!

Most of these boys began drinking beer regularly at the age of thirteen or fourteen; their preferences now include whiskey and Peppermint Schnapps.

The Hallway Hangers also began smoking marijuana when they were twelve or thirteen years old, a tendency that has led many to use an assortment of heavier drugs as well. Most of them describe stages in their adolescence during which they used PCP, mescaline, valium, or THC (the chief intoxicant in marijuana). Only Chris admits to having used heroin; Frankie's experience is more typical of these boys.

(*in a group interview*)

FRANKIE: My drug was, my freshman and sophomore year, I was into THC, right? And you get a tolerance and shit, and you start doing three and four hits.

SLICK: Frankie was a junkie.

FRANKIE: Well, yeah, I didn't boot it [shoot it up], but I was addicted to it, definitely.

Having moderated what they now see as their youthful enthusiasm for different drugs, the Hallway Hangers generally limit themselves to marijuana and cocaine. All the Hallway Hangers smoke a great deal of marijuana; Chris, Jinks, and Stoney acknowledge their dependence on the drug. Marijuana joints circulate in doorway #13 almost as often as cans of beer, and all admit they get high before and during school.

(*in an individual interview, before he dropped out of school*)

JM: Chris, you get high a lot in school?

CHRIS: Oh, yeah. I'm high every time I go to school. I gotta be. Sometimes I even drink before I go—I'll have a few beers. It's too much if you don't. I'm a fucking alcoholic. I do a lot of cocaine. I'll do up cocaine whenever I can get it. Fucking expensive though.

Despite their own widespread use of marijuana and occasional consumption of cocaine, the Hallway Hangers have no respect for junkies or "dustheads," those who are addicted to heroin or angel dust.

(*in an interview with Shorty and Slick*)

SHORTY: Little Tony and them, fuckin' ten, twelve years old, smoking pot, taking drugs. And that ain't good, at that age, cuz me and him don't do drugs, maybe coke, y'know? Coke and pot. But a lot of other dudes out here, they'll be taking; they'll be shooting up and everything. We don't even bother with them.

Obviously, underage drinking and drug use are illegal, and the Hallway Hangers have made their share of trips to the police station and the courthouse. Stoney has three convictions, twice for possession of narcotics and once for passing stolen property. Boo-Boo has been arrested for "hot boxes" (stolen cars). Chris has assault with a deadly weapon in addition to some less serious convictions on his record. Shorty has been to court for larceny, assault with a deadly weapon, and other less substantial crimes. One of the older teenagers on the fringes of the Hallway Hangers was convicted of rape and sentenced to eighteen months in the maximum security state prison after his sophomore year in high school.

These, of course, represent only the crimes at which the Hallway Hangers have been caught. Their criminal activity is actually much more widespread. Those trusted by the Hallway Hangers are occasionally approached with offers for good deals on bicycles, stereo equipment, or musical instruments, all of which have been stolen. Chris makes serious money dealing drugs. Other Hallway Hangers make small amounts of cash selling drugs to friends and acquaintances.

JINKS: We all know how to make a fast buck on the street. Buy the pot, roll up joints, sell 'em for two bucks a joint. Pay thirty for a bag; get twenty-five bones out of a bag—there's fifty bucks for thirty bucks.

Jimmy Sullivan, an experienced and perceptive teacher of the adjustment class in which Frankie, Shorty, and Steve are, or were at one time, enrolled, gives a good description of the Hallway Hangers' criminal careers.

JS: One thing about these kids: Crime pays, and they know it. ... It's so easy to go over to the hallowed halls across the street there [a large university] and pick up a bike. I know three or four stores in the city that will pay thirty to forty dollars for a good bike, no questions asked. They'll turn it over for a hundred fifty or two hundred bucks. What do these kids need money for? What do they care about? Beer, sneakers, joints. They're not going to work when they can make easy money through virtually riskless criminal enterprises. Only suckers are gonna work for that. As long as their expectations stay low and they only need a hundred bucks a week—as Steve said, "All I want is my beer money"—they're all set. Up to when they're seventeen years old there's no risk. But when they turn about eighteen, the peer group doesn't accept that anymore. If they could go on stealing bikes for the rest of their lives, I think they would. But when you're seventeen or eighteen and someone says, "Hey man, where'd you get the cash?" it's unacceptable to say, "Oh, stealing bikes, man." You've got to be into cars, dealing drugs, or holding people up. That's when the risk and fear start coming into it. For many of them, the easiest route is to get a job. Of course, some of them don't, and they end up in jail.

Although this dynamic certainly plays a role in the Hallway Hangers' rationale, the legal system's distinction between a juvenile and an adult is more important in their determination of whether or not crime pays.

(*in a group interview*)

JM: Most of you are seventeen or over now?

SLICK: Only Chris is sixteen.

JM: Doesn't that make a big difference in terms of what you're doing to get money?

SHORTY: Hey, I'm doin' good. I don't deal no more, Jay. I got a good job coming at the weapons lab; most likely I'm gonna get my brother one there.

FRANKIE: Yeah, you slow down. Seventeen—you're an adult.

SLICK: Yeah, at seventeen you start slowing down.

SHORTY: You gotta start thinking.

(*in a separate interview*)

FRANKIE: Now that I think about it, I should've did more crime when I was a juvenile cuz when you're a juvenile you get arrested a good eight or nine times before they put you away. So I could've did a lot more crime, but I don't really mind. It was all right. But yeah, that's what most people do is once they go to seventeen, they smarten up and say that's big-time prison. And I've had many good examples of what not to do. I know jail ain't no place for nobody, even though some of my brothers make a living out of it.

Like many urban slums, the teenage underworld of Clarendon Heights is characterized by predatory theft, and some of the Hallway Hangers specialize in "cuffing" drugs, stolen merchandise, and money off those who themselves are involved in illegal activity. Shorty and Frankie have sold hundreds of fake joints, robbed other drug pushers, and forced younger or less tough boys to give them a share of their illegal income. The consensus among the Hallway Hangers is that this type of thievery is morally more defensible than conventional theft. More importantly, there is less risk of detection, for the authorities are unlikely to become involved.

(*in a group discussion*)

SLICK: You chump off thieves, and then you're like a hero. At least you got him back, y'know? You steal off a fucking thief who makes his life off stealing off other people, then its like you're fucking …

FRANKIE: You rip off illegal people, y'know? You rip off dealers.

SHORTY: That's why if you deal, you gotta be able to kill.

FRANKIE: Yeah, sometimes it could mean your life if you get caught. But you can't get put in jail.

For those raised with a strong sense of law and order, these attitudes are difficult to fathom. The Hallway Hangers, for their part, however, cannot understand the contempt and disdain the upper classes display for their lifestyle and launch a counterattack of their own.

(*in a group interview*)

SLICK: All right, you get people making fucking over fifty thousand dollars, and they fucking ask us why do we hang there? What the fuck, man?

CHRIS: What else are we gonna do?

JINKS: They can go fuck themselves.

CHRIS: They want us to deal the drugs so they can buy them.

SLICK: See, they don't know what the deal is. See, they're just doing what we're doing, except they're doing it in a more respectable way. They're ripping off each other up there. That's all they're doing. They're all ripping each other off up there. But they're doing it in a fucking legal way.

FRANKIE: Yeah, check this out.

SHORTY: We ain't doin' it behind anybody's back.

FRANKIE: All them fucking businessmen, man. All them stockbrokers and shit in New York. All them motherfuckers are out to rip people off. There's more fucking scamming going on up there. They're like legally ripping everyone off.

SLICK: We're just doing it illegally.

This is an insightful, if incomplete, critique of the social order, but not one about which the Hallway Hangers get particularly upset. Rather, they accept it as a simple fact of life with an acquiescent attitude that is typical of their outlook.

An important characteristic of the subculture of the Hallway Hangers is group solidarity. Membership in the Hallway Hangers involves a serious commitment to the group: a willingness to put out for others and to look out for the rest of the group's well-being as well as one's own. This loyalty is the glue that holds the group together, and honoring it is essential. The requirements and limits of this commitment to the group are seldom expressed, but are such that Slick would not leave Shorty "hanging with the cops," even though to stay with Shorty resulted in his own arrest.

SHORTY: See, that's how Slick was that day we were ripping off the sneakers [from a nearby factory]. He figured that if he left me that would be rude, y'know? If he just let me get busted by myself and he knew I had a lot of shit on my head, that's what I call a brother. He could've. I could've pushed him right through that fence, and he coulda been *gone*. But no, he waited for me, and we both got arrested. I was stuck. My belly couldn't get through the fucking hole in the fence.

This cohesion between members of the Hallway Hangers is a striking characteristic of their subculture and one to which they constantly draw attention. Not only are they proud of their adoption of communitarian values, but they also see their "brotherhood" as inconsistent with conventional middle- and upper-class attitudes.

(*in a group discussion*)

SLICK: What it is, it's a brotherhood down here. We're all fucking brothers. There's a lot of backstabbing going on down here, down in the streets. But we're always there for each other. No shit. There's not a guy in here that wouldn't put out for one of the rest of us. If he needs something and I got it, I'll give it to him. Period. That's the way it works. It's a brotherhood. We're not like them up there—the rich little boys from the suburbs or wherever. There's a line there. On this side of the line we don't fuck with each other; we're tight.

FRANKIE: We'd chump them off [rob] on the other side, though.

SLICK: Fucking right. If he's got four hundred bucks in his pocket, there's more where that came from. Fuck him. But they also chump each other off; only they do it legally. How do you think they got rich—by fucking people over. We don't do that to each other. We're too fucking tight. We're a group. We don't think like them; we think for all of us.

FRANKIE: That's the fucking truth. If you don't have your fucking buddies, where are you? You're fucking no one. Nuttin'.

SLICK: If I had the choice, and this isn't just me but probably everyone in here, if I had the choice between being a good person and making it, I'd be a good person. That's just the way I am. If I had my bar exam tomorrow and these guys needed me, I'd go with them. That's just the way it is down here.

SHORTY: Yeah, you wanna be here with your family, with your friends; they're good people. You're comfortable with them. You don't feel right with these other people. I dunno. ... You wanna be like them, y'know? You see they're rich; you wanna be rich. You can't be the poor one out of the crowd. You got all the crowd, and places like that—the suburbs—they're all rich. Y'know, a lot of places, they say quiet places; around here, you'll just be able to hang together, and nobody has that much money.

SLICK: But I'll tell you right now, you cannot find better friends because everybody's in the same boat. You'll find a few assholes, rats, whatever, but mostly when you have all of us, we all know everybody's poor. You're not better than me; I'm not better than him, y'know? Like, say if I have a hundred dollars or he has a hundred dollars, y'know, it's not just his or mine—it's *our* money. It goes between us, y'know what I mean? Like up there, it's not as tight. People aren't tight up there. I just came back from Fort Lauderdale, and I seen it up there. Real rich people, it's not like this at all.

These comments bear ample testimony to the solidarity that characterizes the subculture of the Hallway Hangers. This solidarity is not an ideal to which they only pay lip service; shared money, shared drugs, and shared risks in criminal activity are all facts of life in doorway #13.

At the same time that these boys affirm the lifestyle and values of people in their neighborhood, they assert with peculiar constancy their deeply felt desire to move with their families out of Clarendon Heights. Many of them want to make enough money to get their families out of the projects forever.

(all in separate discussions, unsolicited by me)

SLICK: Most of the kids down here, most of 'em wanna make money so they can help their families and help themselves to get out of this place. ... My main concern is to get my family out of the projects.

CHRIS: I just wanna get my mother out of the projects, that's all.

SHORTY: All's I'm doing, I'm gonna get enough money, save enough money to get my mother the fuck out of here.

These statements are evidence of the stigma the Hallway Hangers, as public housing tenants, feel as a matter of course. Their pride in their lifestyle is pierced by the dominant culture's negative judgments. One implication of the culture's achievement ideology is that those of low socioeconomic stature are personally deficient. This negative evaluation and the inability of the Hallway Hangers to shield themselves completely from it combine to produce the deep ambivalence the boys feel toward themselves and their community.

Daily life for the Hallway Hangers is marked by unrelieved boredom and monotony. The boys are generally out of work, out of school, and out of money. In search of employment or a "fast buck on the street," high or drunk a good deal of the time, many are preoccupied with staying out of prison—a struggle some already have lost—and with surviving from one day to the next.

(in a discussion with Shorty and Slick)

SLICK: All through the teenage years around here, you hafta learn to survive, before you learn to do anything else.

SHORTY: Nobody learns anything from school around here. All it is is how to survive and have money in your pocket.

SLICK: You hafta learn how to survive first.

SHORTY: This is the little ghetto.

SLICK: Y'know, you hafta learn how to survive; if you can't survive, especially around here, that's why you see so many people who are just down and out. It's tough. That's what it is. It's tough.

Growing up in Clarendon Heights is indeed tough, and the frustrations of project life find release through the racist attitudes held by the boys. Racism among members of the Hallway Hangers runs very deep. Frankie and Shorty are violent in their prejudice against black people, while Slick, Steve, and Stoney are racist in a less strident manner. Only Jinks has a measure of empathy and respect for blacks.

According to the Hallway Hangers, their antipathy toward blacks stems from an incident in the early 1970s. At that time, a full-scale riot erupted in Clarendon Heights between the project's mostly white residents and black youths from the predominantly black Emerson Towers housing project a half mile away. The conflict lasted several days and involved the National Guard and riot police. Frankie describes how this event crystallized his own racist attitudes.

JM: So why is it, why is there like this tension between the whites and the blacks?

FRANKIE: Well, when I grew up here, when I was fucking second, third grade, there was racial riots right in front of my window every night. My brothers, I have seven brothers, were all out there, y'know, stabbin' niggers, beating niggers up. I was brought up thinking fucking niggers suck. Went over to Hoover School, no fuckin' black people there at all. Y'know, third grade, we had one black kid. His name was Sonny. Y'know, everyone fucked him up. So it was this through the racial riots. I was brought up to hate niggers.

Although the riots contributed to the racism of the Hallway Hangers, surprisingly enough, they also account for the acceptance of Boo-Boo and Chris into the group.

(*in an interview with Jinks and Chris*)

JM: Now Chris, you're an interesting case cuz, except when Boo-Boo's around, you're the only black guy out there. How'd that come about?

CHRIS: It goes back to the days of the riots.

JINKS: Back in the days of the riots, when the whites used to fight the blacks at the Heights ...

CHRIS: Nobody fucked with my family.

JINKS: Chris's family was always like neutral. They'd help out anybody. And besides, as he's grown older, I've related to him more because my brother married a black lady. And I got nieces and nephews that are like him: mulatto. I've just related to him more. I see things from his point of view more. Cuz I know how he feels when people start capping on him: "Hey Breed."

JM: So that's how it came about with you?

CHRIS: Yeah. When the riots were going on, right, they'd be out there: the niggers against the whites; I'd be sleeping over his house and shit, y'know? His brothers would be fucking hating niggers, man; like his brother John, they'd be killing them.

Boo-Boo also gives a similar reason for his membership in the Hallway Hangers.

JM: What happened with your family during the riots?

BOO-BOO: My father knew both. He used to have all the kids in the house and shit.

JM: What happened with Chris's family?

BOO-BOO: People they knew wouldn't do nothing. If someone was hurting real bad and needed a towel or something, they'd get it. They knew both. Y'know, Chris's mother is real nice—she'd help both the whites and blacks.

Other factors have contributed to Chris's and Boo-Boo's affiliation with the Hallway Hangers. Boo-Boo's family was one of the first black households to be moved by the city's Housing Authority into the Heights. When he was growing up, he naturally made friends with white youngsters. His younger brother Derek went to a private grammar school; most other black youths who now live in Clarendon Heights had yet to move in. Boo-Boo's expressed reason for being a Hallway Hanger is simple: "I grew up with them, since I was real small."

The situation was much the same for Chris; in addition, his acceptance into the Hallway Hangers has been facilitated because he is half white.

(*in a group interview*)

FRANKIE: It ain't like he's living with his black daddy; he's living with his white mommy.

SHORTY: His white brothers.

(*in a separate discussion*)

JINKS: My brothers always liked his family though …

CHRIS: Cuz my brothers were white, y'know.

JINKS: His brothers were mulatto, but they looked like a white person. … It just looked like he had a nice tan all year round. And he was one of my brother's best friends. Y'know, it's just families hanging around.

Although both Chris and Boo-Boo are full members of the Hallway Hangers, their position often seems tenuous because of their race. Both take a lot of ribbing for their skin color. Chris routinely is referred to as nigs, nigger, breed, half-breed, or oreo; Boo-Boo gets less direct abuse but is the butt of racist jokes and occasional taunts. Both tend to deal with it in the same way: They "play it off," make a joke of it, or ignore it.

(*in an individual discussion*)

JM: So you naturally hung with Frankie and them. Are there any problems with you being black?

BOO-BOO: No. They say things but they're just fooling around. I take it as a joke. They're just fooling around. It doesn't bother me at all. If they hit me or something, that's a different story.

Chris occasionally will play along with the other Hallway Hangers by agreeing with their racist statements and denigrating other blacks.

One balmy night in late autumn, I walked into doorway #13 at about eleven o'clock to find Frankie, Chris, and two older guys on the fringes of the Hallway Hangers, Joe and Freddy, smoking a joint and drinking beer. I struck up a conversation with Frankie, but I was interrupted by Joe, a twenty-three-year-old man whose six-foot frame boasts a lot more brawn than mine. "Hey Jay," he said in a mocking, belligerent tone, glancing sharply up at me from his two empty six packs of Miller, "You're a fucking nigger. You're a nigger. You play basketball with the niggers. You talk like a nigger. You're a fucking nigger." This reference to a basketball game a few days earlier in which I played with the Brothers demanded a response that would not provoke a fight but would allow me to maintain some poise and dignity in front of the others. (I had learned long since that to confront the Hallway Hangers' racism was a fruitless exercise and not particularly conducive to entry into the group.) In the end, although I escaped with my pride and body intact, Chris was not so lucky. The exchange that followed highlights his deep ambivalence toward his ethnic identity.

JOE: Did you hear me? I said you're a nigger, a motherfucking nigger.

JM: What, you'd rather play four on six? It's not my fault we won; maybe it's yours.

JOE: You're a nigger, a fucking nigger. You act like a nigger.

JM: You must be really rat-assed drunk or that must be really good herb, cuz it isn't that fucking dark in here. My skin looks white to me.

FRANKIE: (*in an attempt to steer the conversation away from confrontation*) No, really though Jay, you don't have to have black skin to be a nigger.

CHRIS: Yeah, look at me. My skin is black, right? But I ain't a nigger. I ain't. It's not cool. The Brothers, I don't like them. I ain't like them. I ain't a nigger.

FRANKIE: Chris, you're a fucking nigger.

CHRIS: No, I ain't, Frankie. You know that.

Chris will go so far as to shout racial epithets at fellow blacks and to show enthusiasm for fighting with the Hallway Hangers against other black youths.

Much of this attitude, however, is expedient posturing that enables Chris to maintain his sometimes tenuous status in the group. His real feelings are quite different.

CHRIS: I've lived here for fourteen years. I've always hung with these guys. I dunno, maybe it's cuz I never knew many black people back then. These guys are all right though. They fuck with me some, but not like with some kids. I mean, after fourteen fucking years you get used to them calling you nigger every ten minutes. It doesn't do no good to get upset. I just let it slide. Fuck it. I've gotten used to it. I'm glad you're not prejudiced though. The only time they get real bad is when they've been drinking; then I gotta watch myself. I know how these guys think. That's something too—understanding how they think. I've been here fourteen fucking years, and I know how these motherfuckers think. Like, I can tell when they're gonna fuck with me. When they're trashed, they'll be looking at me a certain way and shit. Then another one will do it. I get the fuck out of there because I know they're gonna fuck with me. Yeah, when they're drunk, they'll get like that. Fucking assholes. But when they haven't been pounding the beers, they're the most dynamite people around. Really.

The rest of the Hallway Hangers are quick to deny any animosity toward Chris.

(*in a group interview*)

JM: Chris, it can't be easy coming from down here and being half black and half white.

SHORTY: The blacks bother him cuz he hangs with whites—us.

JM: Yeah, and you fuck with him cuz he's black.

FRANKIE: No, see, cuz we just razz him because he's black.

SHORTY: We done that all his life and he knows it.

CHRIS: It don't bother me.

Nevertheless, outright hostility toward Chris does come to the surface at times, especially when people are under the influence of alcohol or drugs. It seems that whenever Chris threatens the status of others in the group with his street hockey ability, his knack for making a fast buck selling drugs, or his success with girls, racial antagonism comes to the fore. One particular incident is illustrative of this dynamic. Frankie and I were talking in the doorway when we noticed two white girls giving Chris a few lines of cocaine on the landing above us. As they came down the stairs on their way out, Frankie demanded in a very abrasive tone, "What are you getting that fuckin' *nigger* high for? You don't fucking do that." As the door slammed behind them, Frankie muttered, "They want to suck his black cock, that's why. Fuckin' cunts."

Although the Hallway Hangers attribute their racist attitudes to the riots that occurred in Clarendon Heights during their childhoods, such an explanation cannot account for the racial antagonism that gave rise to the riots in the first place. Racism in Clarendon Heights is a complex phenomenon that does not lend itself to easy interpretation or explanation. Nevertheless, in the attitudes and comments of the Hallway Hangers, it is possible to discern evidence in support of the proposition that racism in lower-class communities stems from competition for scarce economic resources.[3] Shorty, for example, bitterly attributes his brother's unemployment to affirmative action policies: "He got laid off because they hired all Puerto Ricans, blacks, and Portegis (Portuguese). It's cuz of the fuckin' spics and niggers." In a separate discussion of the harshness of unemployment, Smitty, an older youth on the fringes of the Hallway Hangers, put forth a similar view.

SMITTY: All the fuckin' niggers are getting the jobs. Two of them motherfuckers got hired yesterday [at a construction site]; I didn't get shit. They probably don't even know how to hold a fuckin' shovel either.

FRANKIE: Fuckin' right. That's why we're hanging here now with empty pockets.

The perceived economic threat blacks pose to the Hallway Hangers contributes to their racism. The racial prejudice of the Hallway Hangers, a subject of academic interest in its own right, also has important ramifications for social reproduction. In Chapter 11 we see how it now only harms blacks but is ultimately self-destructive as well.

Although the Hallway Hangers can be hostile to Boo-Boo and Chris, their real racial venom is directed against the Brothers, the black peer group at Clarendon Heights. Interestingly, when considering each member of the Brothers individually, the Hallway Hangers admit respect and esteem for a number of them. Considered as a group, however, there is little feeling aside from bitter racial enmity. As with Chris, the enmity is at its sharpest when the Brothers are perceived as threatening in some way. The following interview segment, quoted at length, captures the essence of the Hallway Hangers' attitude toward the Brothers.

JM: What do you think of Super and the rest of them?

SLICK: Fuck 'em, they're niggers.

FRANKIE: Fuck 'em, they're niggers, that's right.

SHORTY: They're niggers, man.

FRANKIE: Pretty soon, pretty soon, we're gonna be beefing [fighting] them motherfuckers, and they're not gonna like it.

SLICK: Once they're ready to take a beating, that's when …

FRANKIE: No, no. I'll tell you. They're ready; they're ready. Summertime. Summertime, we'll be fighting.

SLICK: Yeah, this summer we'll be fighting them.

FRANKIE: Definitely, we'll be fighting them.

SHORTY: Even though we did before, and they were the same age as us, but if we beat them up bad, they'd fucking, y'know …

SLICK: They'd call the cops and shit.

SHORTY: (*sarcastically*) Or their big tough fathers would come out. You see what we'll do to their fathers. We'll fight their fathers worse than we'll fight them.

JM: (*with my disgust undisguised*) So why are you so into that?

SHORTY: No, we ain't into it. We don't like their attitude.

FRANKIE: They don't like us, man. What're you crazy? They're niggers.

SHORTY: They move in here. We don't bother them. Once they start with us …

FRANKIE: Hey, they're coming on our fucking land. Fuck them motherfuckers. They don't like us, man, and I sure as hell don't like them.

SHORTY: I've lived here all my fucking life, and no new nigger is gonna move in and fucking start [a fight] with me.

FRANKIE: And I'll tell ya, I'll stick any of them; I'll beat any of them. Fuck them fucking niggers.

SHORTY: Jay, listen to this. They move in here, right?

JM: But how do they move in here, huh?

SHORTY: They just move in here, y'know?

JM: But wait. Into the projects? It's not like you pick which one you wanna move into.

SHORTY: Bullshit!

JM: I think they said, "There's too many white people in here and people been complaining." So they started moving black people in here.

FRANKIE: (*still yelling*) Yeah, that's what happened last time. They moved too many fucking niggers in, and then in '71 and '72 we had the fucking riots.

SHORTY: The last time they did that was ten years ago. Watch!

JM: All's I'm sayin' is that it's not their fault that they moved in. It's the Housing Authority that sends 'em in.

SHORTY: Will you fucking listen, Jay?

JM: Yeah, but I mean, if you were black, would you wanna live here? I fucking wouldn't.

FRANKIE: (*very angrily*) They come in here with a fucking *attitude,* man. They ain't gettin' no [inaudible] attitude. Fucking niggers are getting *hurt* this summer. I'm telling you, man.

SHORTY: Jay, *listen.* When they first moved in here, they were really cool and everything. We didn't bother them. But once more and more black families moved in, they said, "Wow, we can overrun these people. We can overpower them." That's what their attitude was.

SLICK: Slowly but surely, man, they're trying to fucking fuck us over. It's gonna be '71 and '72 all over again.

SHORTY: They come in here walking with their buddies now with sticks and shit and look at us and laugh. Y'know what we could do to them so bad? It's just that a lot of us don't fucking wanna …

SLICK: No one can really afford to get arrested anymore, or we'll go away. No one wants to go away. No one wants to go to fucking jail.

FRANKIE: Yeah, but I'll tell you. Them niggers, man. It's just about time. This summer.

The resentment the Hallway Hangers feel toward blacks and the destructive consequences that flow from this hatred could not be more plainly exposed. By pointing to the economic and social factors that feed this racism, I do not mean to absolve the Hallway Hangers of responsibility for their racist attitudes and beliefs, much less for the violence to which these give rise. Racism is a sickness that rots American society, but those who see it simply as a matter of individual pathology overlook the social conditions that contribute to its outbreak and spread. We can blame the Hallway Hangers, but we also must blame the economic and social conditions of lower-class life under competitive capitalism.

The Brothers: Conspicuous by Their Conventionality

In contrast to the Hallway Hangers, the Brothers accommodate themselves to accepted standards of behavior and strive to fulfill socially approved roles. It is the white peer group from Clarendon Heights that is at odds with mainstream American culture. Nonconformity fascinates the sociologist, and if in this book undue attention is given to the distinctive cultural novelty of the Hallway Hangers, it should be borne in mind that the Brothers also pose an interesting and in many ways exceptional case. However, because my primary interest is the role that aspirations play in social reproduction, and because the Hallway Hangers undergo the process of social reproduction in a unique fashion, my emphasis in both the presentation of ethnographic material and in its analysis inevitably falls on the Hallway Hangers.

The most obvious difference between the two peer groups is in racial composition: The Brothers have only one white member. When one considers that this peer group emerges from the same social setting as do the Hallway Hangers, other striking differences become apparent. Composed of a nucleus of seven teenagers and expanding to twelve at times, this peer group is not a distinctive subculture with its own set of values defined in opposition to the dominant culture. The Brothers attend high school on a regular basis. None of them smokes cigarettes, drinks regularly, or uses drugs. None has been arrested.

Craig is a quiet, tall, dark-skinned youth with a reserved manner and easy smile, except on the basketball court. A graceful athlete, he is on the varsity basketball team at the high school. He moved to the projects six years ago and was one of a few black children to attend the neighborhood grammar school. His family is tightly knit; he lives with his parents, four brothers and sisters, and two stepsiblings. Self-assured and agreeable, Craig maintains a leadership role in the peer group, although such status demarcations are much less clearly defined among the Brothers than among the Hallway Hangers.

In contrast to Craig, Super is a fiery, loud, yet often introspective lad who, despite his medium size, never backs down from a fight. Hesitant in speech and uncomfortable with written material, Super struggles in the classroom. He is, however, a natural athlete. His speed, quickness, and agility lend themselves to football and basketball but his carefree attitude toward sport and his flare for flashy moves do not sit well with high school coaches and have prevented success in these areas at the varsity level. Super's home life is turbulent; his temper, apparently, is matched by his father's, and the confrontations between father and son have prompted Super to leave home for safer environs for a week or two on at least three occasions.

Originally from the Dominican Republic, Juan is the only Brother to have finished school, but he currently is unemployed. He is slight of build, a sincere and sensitive youth. Juan speaks in somewhat broken English, was not particularly successful in school, and is not a good athlete. His loyalty, kind manner, and sense of fair play, however, are attributes that have earned him respect. Such remarks as these are typical of him: "Yup," he said, as he left one evening to meet his girlfriend, "there's the three things everyone needs—a job, a car, and a girl. And the girl's the most important. Because otherwise you'd be lonely. You need someone to talk to and somebody to love." In a neighborhood notorious for its toughness, such a comment is remarkable for its honesty and tenderness.

Mokey is a quick-tempered boy whose impatience with others often borders on insolence. Stocky and of medium height, Mokey commits himself with vigor and enthusiasm to whatever he is pursuing but has difficulty sustaining this drive for an extended period of time. One week he is enthused about his prospects on the school football team, but two weeks later he has quit the squad and exhibits a newfound zeal for track and field. Full of energy and constantly on the move, Mokey chafes against the tight rein his mother keeps on him but generally accedes to her wishes. When necessary, his father, who does not live with the family, is called in to straighten out any problems.

James, a junior at the high school, is very small for his age. He manages to compensate for his diminutive size, however, with a quick and caustic tongue. He is not as well integrated into the group as the other boys, perhaps because of a long, involved relationship with a girl that recently ended. A year ago, James was a fixture in one of the city's video arcades during school hours; now he attends school every day as well as on Thursday evenings to make up for failed subjects. This turnabout resulted from a serious talk with his father, whose presence in the household is sporadic. James's wit, sense of humor, and toughness have earned him the esteem of the Brothers.

Derek is Boo-Boo's half brother. The two boys have different friends, interests, and attitudes and are not particularly close, but they do maintain an amiable cordiality outside their home, which is a considerable achievement in view of the animosity between the Brothers and Hallway Hangers. (I take up the siblings' substantially divergent outlooks and membership in different peer groups in Chapter 8.) Their paths parted when, as a third grader, Derek's scholastic achievements enabled him to secure a government scholarship to a prestigious private school. Derek attended Barnes Academy through the eighth grade with great success; his grades were good, and he had many friends. Nevertheless, he decided to attend the city high school, where he has continued his academic achievement. Although lacking in athletic prowess, Derek is admired by the other boys for his scholastic success and personal motivation.

Mike is the sole white member of the Brothers. He lives with his mother and grandmother and rules the household. His large frame and strength have made him a valuable asset to the high school's football, wrestling, and track and field squads. His athletic ability and an aversion to drugs and alcohol inculcated by his mother as well as a strong and lasting friendship with Super all account for Mike's allegiance to the Brothers. He is subject to some abuse from his white peers on this account but seems to take their ribbing in stride.

The Brothers, in contrast to the Hallway Hangers, are not a distinctive subculture with its own set of shared values. The Brothers accept the dominant culture's definitions of success and judge themselves by these criteria. A night in the city jail would permanently tarnish a Brother's reputation rather than build it up. In the eyes of the Brothers, John Grace, the bartender who was involved in the shootout in Clarendon Heights, only would be worthy of disdain, and perhaps pity, rather than the respect Frankie accords him. While the Hallway Hangers have little concern for the judgments of the dominant culture, the Brothers become uncomfortable and embarrassed when recounting disciplinary problems they have had at home or in school. Such a "confession" for a member of the Hallway Hangers, on the other hand, might be accompanied by laughter and a sense of triumph.

Just as the Brothers accept the values of the dominant culture, their behavior generally conforms to societal expectations. Whereas the Hallway Hangers are conspicuous in their consumption of cigarettes and beer, the Brothers reject both. Although many of the Brothers drink beer in moderation every once in a while at a party or on a similar occasion, their consumption of alcohol is very limited. Likewise, although most of the Brothers have tried marijuana, they rarely smoke it, and they never use other drugs.

The Brothers are uncomfortable with simply "hanging"; they cannot tolerate such inactivity. They often can be found playing basketball in the park or the gym. If a pick-up game of basketball cannot be mustered in the immediate neighborhood, they often will walk a half mile to the Salvation Army gym or another housing project. Energetic and spirited, the Brothers dislike the idleness of the Hallway Hangers.

DEREK: I would never hang with them. I'm not interested in drinking, getting high, or making trouble. That's about all they do. ... I don't like to just sit around.

Although the Brothers do not adopt those practices that symbolize rejection of authority or basic societal values, their peer group does have its own distinctive attributes. The Brothers carry themselves in ways familiar to most urban black Americans, although somewhat scaled down. Their style of dress, mode of speech, and form of greeting clearly set them apart from other residents of Clarendon Heights. However, the caps, neck chains, and open shirts so prevalent among teenagers in the predominantly black sections of the city are lacking among the Brothers, whose residency in a white neighborhood has important implications for much more than their dress.

Athletics is one activity into which the Brothers channel their energies. Many excel in organized youth, church, and school basketball leagues as well as in regular pick-up games. Mike, Super, and Mokey also play on the school football team. Only Juan and Derek are not good athletes, and even they maintain an interest in sports, often rounding out the teams for a pick-up game of basketball.

Girls also claim much of the Brothers' time. A frequent topic of conversation, their interest in girls seems much more widespread than is the case for the Hallway Hangers. While the Hangers tend to go out with girls on a casual basis (typically for a weekend), the Brothers often have steady girlfriends, with whom they are constantly speaking on the phone, to whose house they are forever headed, and about whom they always are boasting. Whereas the Hallway Hangers focus on their beer and drugs, the Brothers have their basketball and girlfriends.

Since Juan bought an old worn-out Vega for two hundred dollars and fixed it up complete with paint job and functioning engine, cruising the streets also has become a favorite pastime for the Brothers. It gives them access to the "Port" and the "Coast," the black sections of the city. Considering the tense racial atmosphere of the Clarendon Heights community, it is no wonder that the Brothers do not spend as much time in the vicinity of the Heights as the Hallway Hangers do and instead prefer the black neighborhoods.

In addition to being the objects of many of the Hallway Hangers' racist slurs and insults, the Brothers suffer from even more substantive racial abuse. Super tells how the windows in his family's car have been broken year after year and how one morning last spring he awoke to find "KKK" drawn in spray paint on the side of the car. Juan recounts with anger accompanied by matter-of-fact acceptance how his mother was taunted by some members of the Hallway Hangers, which led his father into a confrontation with them. His father was lucky to escape unharmed from the ensuing argument. Juan has a measure of understanding for the Hallway Hangers: "When they call me a nigger, I usually don't let it bother me none. They drunk or high, y'know. They don't know what they're doing." In his freshman year of high school, however, Juan was beaten up by Shorty for no apparent reason; he still bears the scar on his lip from the fight, and the memory of it burns in his mind, fueling the resentment he feels toward the Hallway Hangers.

Although the Brothers are not submissive in the face of racial animosity from the Hallway Hangers, they are outnumbered and outmatched, and they usually find it expedient to walk away before a confrontation explodes into a street fight. They are accustomed to the violent racial prejudice of the Hallway Hangers. In fact, Craig, instead of being upset that a simple basketball game threatened to erupt into a racial brawl, merely commented, "That was good of Shorty to come over and tell us we better leave before his friends start all sorts of trouble." Although the Brothers are hesitant to answer openly the insults of the Hallway Hangers, they do vent their contempt for the Hallway Hangers in private discussions.

(all in separate interviews)

JUAN: I don't like their attitude, their gig, what they do. ... They'll be there, hanging in front of the Heights, fighting and arguing and stuff like that. ... It wasn't until I moved here that I heard the word "nigger." I had heard about people in the projects; I knew they'd be a pain in the ass sometimes. ... I swear, if I ever see one of them touching my mother or doing something to my car, I don't care, I'll kill them. Cuz I don't like none of them. I'm afraid I'm gonna hurt one of them real bad. Every time I hear them call me nigger, I just don't say anything, but I can't take the pressure of people getting on my case every time, y'know?

CRAIG: I don't know why they just hang out there being crazy and getting drunk and bothering people. Maybe cuz they need attention or something. They got nuttin' better to do so they might as well cause trouble so people will think they're bad and stuff. They're just lazy. They wanna take the easy way out—that is, hang around outside all day.

JAMES: They're not gonna get anywhere except for standing at that same corner going (*imitating someone who is very benumbed*), "Hey man, got some pot, man? Hey Frank, let's get high."

DEREK: We just have different attitudes. We like to stay away from the projects as much as possible, or they'll give us trouble. That's about all they do: make trouble.

SUPER: They smoke reefer; they drink. They ain't friendly like people, y'know what I'm sayin'? They go around the street laughing at people, ragging them out, y'know what I mean? They just disrespect people.

MIKE: They're just a bunch of fuck-ups.

Such perceptions are often voiced by the Brothers. The situation between the two peer groups, however, is not one of constant strife. Rather, there is a constant underlying tension that surfaces occasionally—often during basketball games or when the Hallway Hangers have been drinking excessively—but that threatens to erupt into considerable violence.

Aside from racial factors, the character of the two peer groups differs markedly in other ways. The Brothers have no pecking order based on fighting ability. Although Craig is generally respected most, there is no hierarchy in the group, hidden or otherwise; the Brothers do not playfully abuse each other, physically or verbally. Loose and shifting cliques develop among the members and sometimes encompass outsiders. Friendships wax and wane according to the season and the extracurricular activities and responsibilities of the boys. During the winter, for example, Craig is so tied up with the basketball team that he effectively drops out of the group, and his best friend, Super, becomes closer to Derek and Mokey. During the school day, the Brothers often see little of each other and, once out, invariably break up into smaller friendship groups, coming all together only once in awhile. In short, the Brothers are no more than a peer group, whereas the Hallway Hangers are a much more cohesive unit with its own subculture.

The Hallway Hangers, who reject the values of the dominant culture and subscribe to their own distinctive cultural norms, have a sense of solidarity that is noticeably absent from the Brothers' peer group. Internal cohesion and the adoption of communitarian values, in which the Hallway Hangers take pride, are missing among the Brothers. Although all the Brothers would support each other in a fight, the ties that bind them are not as strong and are not as strongly affirmed as those that bind the Hallway Hangers.

The Brothers do not compare themselves to members of the upper classes, nor do they feel as keenly the stigma or shame associated with life in public housing. (An explanation of these differences is undertaken in Chapter 7.)

Daily life for the Brothers is far less circumscribed than it is for the Hallway Hangers. Active, enthusiastic, and still in school, the Brothers are not preoccupied with mere survival on the street. Their world extends into the classroom and onto the basketball court, and it extends into the home a great deal more than does the world of the Hallway Hangers, as we shall see in the next chapter.

Notes

1. All temporal citations in Part One have as their reference point February 1984, when the first draft of the book was written. Thus, "presently" and "currently" refer to the winter of 1984 and "last year" means June 1983. The present tense is used throughout the book, and no developments after February 1984 are included in Part One.

2. *Lower-class,* as the term applies to public housing residents, is not used in this book as an analytical construct but as a descriptive term that captures their position at the lower end of the socioeconomic spectrum. Similarly, the term *upper classes* is used to refer to all those whose position is higher on the socioeconomic scale; *middle class* refers more specifically to salaried white-collar workers, including professional and managerial personnel.

3. See, especially, David T. Wellman, *Portraits of White Racism* (Cambridge: Cambridge University Press, 1977); and Donald Neal, "A Theory of the Origin of Ethnic Stratification," *Social Problems* 16 (Fall 1968):157–172.

4

....

The Influence
of the Family

AS THE FOCAL SOCIALIZING AGENCY, especially in the early years of a child's life, the family plays a crucial role in the process of social reproduction. In this chapter, we consider the particular circumstances of each boy's family and how the family influences his expectations for the future. In describing the families of these boys, we must be attentive to a number of factors, such as the presence of a father in the household, the occupational histories of parents and older siblings, and the length of the family's tenancy in public housing.

All families living in Clarendon Heights are lower class. For a family of four to qualify for federal housing projects, its annual income must not exceed $14,000; for state housing developments the limit is approximately $1,500 lower. These are, of course, the upper boundaries; the annual income of most families living in Clarendon Heights is well below the limit.

The Hallway Hangers' Households

Chris lives with his white mother and two younger sisters. Their father, who is black, moved out of the house a few years ago. "I kicked my father out," boasts Chris in a group interview. Chris also has two half brothers and one half sister who live on their own. His brothers work in unskilled, manual labor jobs; his sister is a part-time secretary. Chris seems to have free run of the household. His mother, a kind, friendly woman who has never married, has been pleading with Chris for two years to attend school regularly, but to no avail. Although she does not work regularly, for much of the year she babysits in her home for one and sometimes two young children from working-class families. In exchange for her labors (nine hours per day), she receives a small wage. Chris's family has lived in Clarendon Heights for sixteen years, prior to which his mother lived with her other children in private housing.

Boo-Boo also has lived in Clarendon Heights for his entire life. He and his older brother have a different father than his younger brother Derek (a member of the Brothers) and his younger sister. Both fathers live out of state and very seldom venture to Clarendon Heights. Their mother, a high school dropout, has stable employment assembling computer and electronic parts in a nearby suburb. Boo-Boo's father, who graduated from high school, has been in the merchant marine "for a long, long time." Boo-Boo's older brother has a drug dependency problem. He dropped out of high school a few years ago, recently has joined the army reserves and is struggling to acquire a General Equivalency Diploma (G.E.D.) so that he can join the army.

Stoney's mother's occupational history is a modest success story. She attended St. Mary's Catholic High School in the city but had to drop out during her freshman year to find work after her mother died. She subsequently earned a G.E.D. as well as a secretarial degree and has worked her way up to a supervisory position as secretary of a department in a state welfare office. Stoney's father's experience has been altogether different. Confined to the county house of correction a year and a half ago for passing a bad check, he broke out with only a month remaining on his sentence. With no place to go and unable to see his family, however, he subsequently turned himself in. After serving the remainder of his sentence plus some additional months for the escape, he has now found short-term work cleaning carpets. But like so many others from Clarendon Heights with a criminal record, Stoney's father probably will have a difficult time securing stable employment and is likely to end up back behind bars. Stoney's family moved to the Clarendon Heights neighborhood only three years ago; before that time they lived in Emerson Towers housing project, where Stoney's mother grew up. In contrast to the rest of the Hallway Hangers, Stoney's mother has a strong influence on him. A strict disciplinarian, she sets a nightly curfew for him, which he respects with diligence.

Frankie's family lived in the Heights for thirty years, and although his mother recently moved to another project in the city, Frankie spends nearly all of his time in the Clarendon Heights community. His mother and father both grew up in separate working-class neighborhoods in the city. Frankie's father attended City Tech for a few years before quitting school. He died when Frankie was seven years old. Frankie is the only Hallway Hanger whose mother graduated from high school; she currently works full-time at a camera factory. His sister also graduated from high school, but none of his seven brothers has earned a diploma. As mentioned earlier, all of Frankie's brothers have served time in prison; four of them presently are scattered around the state in various institutions. When out of prison, they find work in construction, landscaping, or painting. One of his brothers tends bar at the local pub, where recently he was shot trying to break up a fight. Most of Frankie's brothers work irregularly; at any given time, one or two may be unemployed.

Slick and Steve are the only members of the Hallway Hangers whose family has moved recently to public housing. Although their mother grew up only a few blocks from the Heights, the family lived in a neighboring city until they moved to Clarendon Heights about six years ago. Their father has never lived with the family, his background is hazy, and Steve's feelings about him are ambivalent. "I haven't seen that bastard for a long time. ... I think he got put away when he was a kid." Neither parent graduated from high school. "My mom quit in the ninth or tenth grade. She quit cuz she had to put money in the house. And, y'know, she was on her own by the time she was eighteen," declares Slick. Currently out of work due to ill health, their mother, an aggressive and strong-willed woman, usually is employed as a nurse's aide. Slick and Steve have a brother and sister, both younger.

Jinks, like Frankie, is part of a large family that has lived in Clarendon Heights for close to thirty years. Both of his parents grew up in the city and are currently employed full-time. His father has worked for the city maintenance department for nearly thirty years, while his mother has been employed at a hotel as a chambermaid for six or seven years. Neither parent graduated from high school, nor did five of his six older siblings, including his only sister. The one high school graduate is in the navy; of the other three brothers, one paints houses, one works in a factory assembling clothes racks, and one is unemployed, having himself completed a stint in the navy. Jinks's fifth brother died of natural causes at the age of sixteen. His sister recently obtained her own apartment in Clarendon Heights; she has a small daughter to look after and consequently does not work. Given that the largest apartment in Clarendon Heights contains only three bedrooms, Jinks's family must have been very cramped before his sister and her daughter moved out. Even now, six people live in the unit.

Shorty's family is even larger. He has ten older brothers and sisters, three of whom have graduated from high school.

SHORTY: I got seven brothers. We lived here for thirteen years. ... I mean, we been through the riots and everything. My brother Joe had to quit school when he was sixteen years old, just because my father was an alcoholic. He had to go out and get a job. My [other] brother, he was a bikey; he had to sell pot. But Joe was out gettin' a job at sixteen to support all the kids. ... He [went back to school and was subsequently employed as] a cop for two months; he got laid off. He was working at the weapons lab as a security guard. You ask him. He's our father. That's what he really is—he's our father. My father got put away for nine months. He didn't live with us for six years. Every fucking penny that my brother got he threw right into the family, right into the house. Cuz my mother can't work. She almost died three times; she has a brain tumor.

Aside from this account, information on Shorty's family is very sketchy, as he will very seldom speak about his home life. In a separate interview, however, Shorty did mention that with the exception of Joe, all the boys in his family have at one time or another been in the military service, as was his father.

Despite the difficulty inherent in generalizing about such diverse family histories, it is clear that the Hallway Hangers share certain family characteristics that may affect their aspirations. Foremost among these are the duration of these families' tenancy in public housing. With the exception of Slick and Steve, all the Hallway Hangers and their families have lived in the projects for many years: Shorty for thirteen years, Chris for sixteen, Boo-Boo's family for at least eighteen, Jinks's family for twenty-seven years, and Frankie's and Stoney's families for thirty years. Like most of the project residents, the educational attainment of these boys' parents and older brothers and sisters is very low; of their parents, only Boo-Boo's father and Frankie's mother graduated from high school. The sporadic employment record of family members is another common characteristic. For those who are able to find employment at all, it is typically menial, low paying, and unstable. Other less widespread commonalities between the families of these boys include the fathers' absence from the household, the large size of the families, and the numerous encounters of family members with the law.

The Brothers' Families

Super's family has lived in public housing for eighteen years. The family moved to Clarendon Heights only five years ago but prior to that lived in a large housing project in a nearby city. Super's mother and father came to the north from South Carolina and Tennessee respectively in the early 1960s. Neither graduated from high school. Super's mother does not work; his father is a general laborer in construction but currently is unemployed, a typical predicament for low-level employees in the seasonal construction business. Super has two younger sisters and an older sister who attends a Catholic high school. Super has left home repeatedly, citing his parents' strict and inflexible disciplinary code as the reason. Although many parents in Clarendon Heights use force when disciplining their children, Super is the only boy who admits to being abused physically by his father.

Details about Mokey's home life are scarce. Mokey is not sure whether or not his parents graduated from high school. Apparently a heavy drinker, Mokey's father is a custodian in an office building in the commercial and financial district of the city. Although his father moved out of the house at least four years ago, Mokey frequently meets him at work to help with the evening cleanup, especially during the summer. His mother works part-time at a nearby day care center. He has a brother who is two years younger than he is and a five-year-old sister who has just entered kindergarten. His family lived in a very small public housing development before moving into Clarendon Heights.

James has lived in the Clarendon Heights community for his entire life. His mother, who is originally from Georgia, quit school when she was in the eighth grade. She is unemployed temporarily because she injured her shoulder about six months ago, but she usually works as a nurse's aide for the elderly. James's father graduated from high school and currently works in a factory that manufactures zippers and buttons. When asked if his father lives in the household, James shakes his head no, but adds, "He didn't really move out. He comes and he goes." James's two younger sisters are excellent students, but his thirteen-year-old brother has a much more lackadaisical attitude toward his education. As noted previously, James's approach to school recently has undergone a dramatic change from ambivalence to commitment.

Craig's family came to this country from Haiti about eleven years ago and has lived in the Clarendon Heights neighborhood for six years. Although the educational system is somewhat different in Haiti, both his parents attained the rough equivalent of a high school diploma. His mother works part-time as a "homemaker"; she prepares meals, cleans, and performs other domestic chores for an elderly couple. Craig's father works as a janitor for an engineering company. Craig took pains to explain to me that his father has worked his way up to a supervisory role in the maintenance department.

CRAIG: I think he's a supervisor.

JM: So what exactly does he do?

CRAIG: Before he used to do it himself—cleaning—but now he makes sure others do it.

Craig lives with his parents and six brothers and sisters. "Actually, I got four brothers and sisters, right? But since my father was messin' around, I got six brothers and sisters." The half siblings as well as his four full brothers and sisters all live in the household. His two older sisters have been very successful academically; there seems to be a supportive atmosphere for academic achievement in his home. His brother is in his second year at a technical college. One of the older sisters, who was a straight-A student in high school, is studying medicine at a local college.

Juan's family is also from the West Indies, in this case the Dominican Republic. His mother and father were divorced there, at which time Juan's mother came to the United States. Juan and his younger sister came to join her ten years ago; their three brothers preferred to remain in their home country. At some point, his mother remarried, and the family of four moved into Clarendon Heights in 1978. Juan's stepfather is presently unemployed.

JUAN: He can't find a job.

JM: What's his trade?

JUAN: He used to work in a hotel, like in management—a boss. He decided to quit, and then he went to another hotel. Then the same thing happened: He decided to quit. Don't know why.

Juan's mother does not work either. Both his stepfather and mother graduated from high school in the Dominican Republic. He sorely misses his older brothers and hopes to return to his homeland in the near future.

Mike lives with his unmarried mother and grandmother. His father, an Italian immigrant, was a very successful professional wrestler, but Mike knows of him only from television. Mike has lived in public housing since he was two years old, first in Emerson Towers and, since 1977, in Clarendon Heights. His grandmother retired from her work in a local factory a few years ago. His mother, a high school dropout, has held a series of jobs. Most recently, she worked at Woolworth's and subsequently on the night shift at a large hotel. She found that job physically draining and currently is employed as a homemaker who takes care of elderly people. Neither woman has much success disciplining Mike; periodically, however, his uncle is brought in to help with the task, which Mike loathes. A navy veteran, Mike's uncle is the stereotypical tough, no-nonsense, blue-collar worker. His uncle recounts stories of painful encounters with his own father when his self-discipline slipped perceptibly and threatens Mike with the same type of punishment.

UNCLE: When my father said something, he meant it. When he said to be in at eleven o'clock, he meant eleven o'clock. I can remember being out with the boys one night and running all the way home—got in at 11:05. My old man was sitting there waiting for me. He looked at me, looked at the clock, and that was it. He knocked the shit out of me.

MIKE: (*grimacing*) That's crazy. Jay, tell him that's crazy.

UNCLE: It worked. And it'll work on you too. Damn right it will.

Indeed, the approach does have the desired effect, for now his mother exercises more control of Mike by threatening to summon his uncle.

In general terms, the Brothers' families are typical of lower-class households and are much like the families of the Hallway Hangers. Family structure is not of the conventional nuclear type; most are "broken homes." Educational achievement is low, and employment, for those who have a job, is typically in nondescript, uninteresting, unskilled work. There are, however, some differences between the families of the Brothers and of the Hallway Hangers in these areas.

Whereas among the Hallway Hangers only Jinks's father lives regularly in the household, three of the Brothers have a male authority figure living with them. Nearly half the parents of the Brothers have graduated from high school; of the Hallway Hangers, only Boo-Boo and Frankie have a parent who has obtained a high school diploma. With the exception of Derek, all the Brothers are either the oldest male sibling or have older brothers and sisters whose educational achievement is significant; for the Hallway Hangers, on the other hand, it is more typical to find that an older sibling has been sent away to prison. In addition, all the Brothers' fathers work except Juan's, whereas among the Hallway Hangers, only Jinks's father works regularly. Moreover, the Hallway Hangers' families have lived in public housing for at least twenty years, and some are second-generation tenants (Stoney's, Jinks's, and Frankie's). The Brothers' families have lived in public housing for five to thirteen years (the exceptions are James, whose family has been in public housing for sixteen years, and Derek, who is Boo-Boo's brother). An even more pointed contrast arises when we consider how long the families of each peer group have lived in the Clarendon Heights neighborhood. Of the Hallway Hangers, only Steve's and Slick's family has moved to the area within the last twelve years. The opposite is true of the Brothers. Only James's family (and, of course, Derek's) has lived in Clarendon Heights for more than six years. In analyzing the feelings of hopelessness, immobility, and stagnation that plague the Hallway Hangers, this contrast will prove important.

The subjective side of these structural elements also shapes the boys' aspirations. Although rejection of parental authority is a common attribute of adolescent subcultures, the Hallway Hangers seem to respect the views of their parents, even though their parents do not play a large role in their lives. What we see in most cases is an unspoken but mutually accepted limitation of the parental role. At sixteen, seventeen, and eighteen years of age, these boys have gained a maturity from years of hard living on the street that is incommensurate with their chronological age. It appears that both they and their parents respect the notion that parental authority is incompatible with this maturity.

The boys' comments point to the limited role their parents play in their lives. In describing his mother's influence, Frankie says, "She wants me to do what I want to do." But, although she has little direct control of her son and does not exercise much authority, Frankie respects her wishes. He knew, for example, how badly she wanted one of her sons to graduate from high school. For reasons that will become clear in the next two chapters, Frankie wanted to leave school. "The only reason I got my diploma wasn't for me; it was for my mother. My mother wanted a diploma." The limited influence Slick's mother had concerning the same issue is apparent from the following exchange.

(in a discussion with Slick and Shorty)

JM: So did she [his mother] pressure you at all to stay in school when you decided to quit?

SLICK: No. She wanted me to stay in high school, but at the time, things were tough, y'know?

SHORTY: She knows his attitude is all right.

SLICK: She knows what I want, and she's not gonna stop me from getting it my way.

This type of interaction is typical of the relationship between parent and son among the Hallway Hangers.

The respect these parents have for the autonomy of their sons extends to the way in which they influence their sons' occupational aspirations. When asked about the effect their parents have on their ambitions, the Hallway Hangers are unanimous in their declaration that such a determination is left up to them alone. Indeed, even Stoney's mother, the most authoritarian of the parents, does not feel it is her place to sway Stoney's aspirations. She thinks it inappropriate to foster high aspirations in her children, fearing that unrealistically high goals only will result in disappointment, frustration, and feelings of failure and inadequacy. "It's not like he's growing up in the suburbs somewhere. Sure, he could probably make it if everything went right for him, but lemme tell you, the chances aren't great. He's got his goals, and they're probably good, realistic ones. I personally think he should've stayed in school. I think he fucked up by dropping out. But he didn't think it was worth it, and what the hell, maybe it isn't."

Other parents also are hesitant to encourage hefty ambitions in their children; as the Hallway Hangers tell it, there is little stimulus from home to raise their aspirations.

JM: What kind of work does your mother [do your parents] want you to do for a living?

(*all in separate interviews*)

BOO-BOO: Anything. She doesn't really care, as long as I'm working.

FRANKIE: She don't fucking care. I mean, I'm sure she cares, but she don't push nothing on me.

SLICK: She wants me to make a buck so I can move for myself.

STEVE: Anything, man. Somethin'. I dunno. Just a fuckin' job.

JINKS: They don't talk about it. They hardly ever talk about it. Just as long as I'm not out of work. My mother hates when I'm unemployed.

If such an attitude is widespread among parents in Clarendon Heights, then the conventional sociological wisdom requires revision. The premise that lower-class parents project their frustrated ambitions onto their children in an attempt to reach their goals vicariously is a widely accepted notion among social psychologists and one to which Robert Merton alludes in his essay "Social Structure and Anomie." Citing work he and some colleagues undertook on the social organization of public housing developments, Merton reports that a substantial portion of both black and white parents on lower occupational levels want their children to have professional careers.[1] Before we challenge the sociological perspective on intergenerational mobility, however, we should consider the attitude of the Brothers' parents toward this issue.

In contrast to the Hallway Hangers, the Brothers' parents exercise a good deal of authority over them. All the Brothers have a relatively early curfew, which they conscientiously obey. They are expected to perform up to a certain standard at school, both in terms of academic achievement and discipline. Furthermore, they are expected to respect prohibitions against smoking cigarettes, drinking alcohol, and using drugs. Failure to meet expected standards of behavior invariably results in punishment. In these instances, the youth is confined to his family's apartment for specified times during the day. Sometimes one of the Brothers will be restricted to his room after school, occasionally for periods as lengthy as one month. By their obedience and consent to these restrictions the Brothers acknowledge the control their parents exercise. Comparable manifestations of parental authority are altogether absent among the Hallway Hangers. In fact, Craig explicitly made this point in comparing the differences in attitude and behavior between the Brothers and the Hallway Hangers. "I guess our parents are a lot tighter than their parents. Y'know at least they tell us what to do and stuff. From the very beginning, ever since we were born, y'know, they'd always be telling us, 'Do this; do that.' Always disciplining us. As far as their parents go, I can't really say their parents are bad, but their parents aren't helping any."

Parental influence on the Brothers' aspirations accords with Merton's findings. James, for instance, feels that his parents project their own frustrated educational and occupational ambitions onto him.

JAMES: My father had to quit school when he had to go to work. But he went back to school. He was one of the top people in his class; he could've went to college. But he didn't have the money to go to college. He had to go to work. So now he wants us all to go to college.

(later in the same interview)

JM: What do your mother and father want you to do for a living?

JAMES: They wanted me to be a lawyer when I was a little kid. They wanted me to grow up and be a lawyer.

James also attributes his dramatic turnaround in school performance to his father's influence.

JM: So how'd you get back on track then? Why've you started working hard now? This year.

JAMES: I decided I need to have good marks, so ...

JM: Did anyone help you decide that or just ...

JAMES: *Yeah.* My father.

JM: Yeah?

JAMES: He didn't hit me or anything; he just talked to me. Told me I wouldn't be able to go and do what I want to when school's over. Wouldn't be able to get no good job.

Other members of the Brothers indicate that similar processes are at work in their families.

SUPER: One thing I know they want me to do, they're always sayin' is finish school. They want me to go to college.

JM: They want you to finish high school and college?

SUPER: Uh-huh. ... They want me to get a good job; I know that. And not no job with hard labor, y'know, standin' on my foot; they want me sittin' down, y'know, a good job, in an office.

Derek, Juan, and Craig also mention that their parents have high hopes for them. Craig's parents were the key figures in his decision to try becoming an architect. Juan's father wants him to get a job where "you can keep yourself clean." Derek's family nurtured hopes their son would enter a professional career. "They wanted me to be a lawyer. Ever since I went to Barnes Academy."

In addition to the Brothers' accounts, we have further evidence from the parents themselves. Mokey's mother, for instance, feels that her expectations heavily influence Mokey and undoubtedly will play a large part in whatever he decides to do. She insists that he pursue a career "which gives a successful future," such as management or ownership of a small business. She also believes that Mokey should "plan to be a success and reach the highest goal possible. The sky's the limit. That's what my mother told me, and that's what I tell my children. The sky is the limit."

Thus, the Brothers present a significant contrast to the Hallway Hangers with respect to their parents' influence in their lives. The Brothers' parents wield a substantial degree of authority, both in the present and in shaping their children's educational and occupational aspirations. These parents may be projecting their own unfulfilled occupational ambitions onto their children by nurturing in them high hopes for the future.

Some of the Brothers also have older siblings who serve as role models. Craig, Super, and James all have older brothers and sisters who have achieved at least moderate success in school. These three boys see that the path to academic achievement can be followed. Juan, Mokey, and Mike have no older siblings; they see a path that is as yet untried. In contrast, the Hallway Hangers, with the exception of Stoney and Slick, have older siblings who have failed in school; thus, the Hallway Hangers see a tortuous path that is difficult to negotiate. The Brothers all may not have older brothers and sisters who are high academic achievers, but, with the exception of Derek, at least they are not confronted exclusively with examples of academic failure, as most of the Hallway Hangers are. This difference between the two peer groups also has a significant impact on the boys' hopes for the future, which are the subject of the next chapter.

Notes

1. Robert K. Merton, *Social Theory and Social Structure* (New York: Free Press, 1968), p. 213.

5

···

The World of Work:
Aspirations of the
Hangers and Brothers

 IVEN THAT WORK DETERMINES ONE'S SOCIAL CLASS, the perpetuation of
class inequality requires that boys like the Hallway Hangers and the Brothers go
on to jobs that are comparable in status to the occupations of their parents. Thus,
the attitudes of these boys toward the world of work are critical to our understanding of social reproduction. In this chapter, their previous employment records, their general impressions of work, their aspirations and expectations, and
their perceptions of the job opportunity structure are considered.

Before describing the boys' orientation toward work, I would like to make an
analytical distinction between aspirations and expectations. Both involve assessments of one's desires, abilities, and the character of the opportunity structure. In
articulating one's aspirations, an individual weighs his or her preferences more
heavily; expectations are tempered by perceived capabilities and available opportunities. Aspirations are one's preferences relatively unsullied by anticipated constraints; expectations take these constraints squarely into account.[1]

The Hallway Hangers: Keeping a Lid on Hope

Conventional, middle-class orientations toward employment are inadequate to
describe the Hallway Hangers' approach to work. The notion of a career, a set of
jobs that are connected to one another in a logical progression, has little relevance
to these boys. They are hesitant when asked about their aspirations and expectations. This hesitancy is not the result of indecision; rather it stems from the fact
that these boys see little choice involved in getting a job. No matter how hard I
pressed him, for instance, Jinks refused to articulate his aspirations: "I think

61

you're kiddin' yourself to have any. We're just gonna take whatever we can get."
Jinks is a perceptive boy, and his answer seems to be an accurate depiction of the
situation. Beggars cannot be choosers, and these boys have nothing other than
unskilled labor to offer on a credential-based job market.

It is difficult to gauge the aspirations of most of the Hallway Hangers. Perhaps
at a younger age they had dreams for their futures. At ages sixteen, seventeen, and
eighteen, however, their own job experiences as well as those of family members
have contributed to a deeply entrenched cynicism about their futures. What is
perceived as the cold, hard reality of the job market weighs very heavily on the
Hallway Hangers; they believe their preferences will have almost no bearing on
the work they actually will do. Their expectations are not merely tempered by
perceptions of the opportunity structure; even their aspirations are crushed by
their estimation of the job market. These generalizations may seem bold and
rather extreme, but they do not lack ethnographic support.

The pessimism and uncertainty with which the Hallway Hangers view their futures emerge clearly when the boys are asked to speculate on what their lives will
be like in twenty years.

(*all in separate interviews*)

STONEY: Hard to say. I could be dead tomorrow. Around here, you gotta take life
day by day.

BOO-BOO: I dunno. I don't want to think about it. I'll think about it when it
comes.

FRANKIE: I don't fucking know. Twenty years. I may be fucking dead. I live a day
at a time. I'll probably be in the fucking pen.

SHORTY: Twenty years? I'm gonna be in jail.

These responses are striking not only for the insecurity and despondency they reveal, but also because they do not include any mention of work. It is not that work
is unimportant—for people as strapped for money as the Hallway Hangers are,
work is crucial. Rather, these boys are indifferent to the issue of future employment. Work is a given; they all hope to hold jobs of one kind or another in order
to support themselves and their families. But the Hallway Hangers, like the lads in
Willis's study, believe the character of work, at least all work in which they are
likely to be involved, is essentially the same: boring, undifferentiated, and unre-
warding. Thinking about their future jobs is a useless activity for the Hallway
Hangers. What is there to think about?

For Steve and Jinks, although they do see themselves employed in twenty years,
work is still of tangential importance.

JM: If you had to guess, what do you think you'll be doing twenty years from now?

(*in separate interviews*)

STEVE: I don't fucking know. Working probably. Have my own pad, my own house. Bitches, kids. Fucking fridge full of brewskies. Fine wife, likes to get laid (*laughs*).

JINKS: Twenty years from now? Probably kicked back in my own apartment doing the same shit I'm doing now—getting high. I'll have a job, if I'm not in the service, if war don't break out, if I'm not dead. I just take one day at a time.

As Jinks suggests, work is contingent on realities over which the Hallway Hangers have no control. Thus, far from being a priority in its own right, work makes possible more pleasurable activities. For the Hallway Hangers, as for many Americans, work is important not as an end in itself but as a means to an end—money.

In probing the occupational aspirations and expectations of the Hallway Hangers, I was able to elicit from them some specific hopes. Although Shorty never mentions his expectations, the rest of the Hallway Hangers have responded to my prodding with some definite answers. The range of answers as well as how they change over time are as significant as the particular hopes each boy expresses.

Boo-Boo's orientation toward work is typical of the Hallway Hangers. He has held a number of jobs in the past, most of them in the summer. During his freshman year in high school Boo-Boo worked as a security guard at school for $2.50 an hour in order to make restitution for a stolen car he damaged. Boo-Boo also has worked on small-scale construction projects through a summer youth employment program called Just-A-Start, at a pipe manufacturing site, and as a clerk in a gift shop. Boo-Boo wants to be an automobile mechanic. Upon graduating from high school, he studied auto mechanics at a technical school on a scholarship. The only black student in his class, Boo-Boo was expelled early in his first term after racial antagonism erupted into a fight. Boo-Boo was not altogether disappointed, for he already was unhappy with what he considered the program's overly theoretical orientation. (Howard London found this kind of impatience with academic study typical of working-class students in the community college he studied.[2]) Boo-Boo wanted hands-on training, but "all's they were doing was telling me about how it's made, stuff like that." Boo-Boo currently is unemployed, but he recently had a chance for a job as a cook's helper. Although he was not hired, the event is significant nevertheless because prior to the job interview, Boo-Boo claimed that his ambition now was to work in a restaurant. Here we have an example of the primacy of the opportunity structure in determining the aspirations of the Hallway Hangers. One job opening in another field was so significant that the opening prompted Boo-Boo to redefine totally his aspirations.

In contrast to the rest of the Hallway Hangers who are already on the job market, Steve wants to stay in school for the two years required to get his diploma. Yet he has a similar attitude toward his future work as do the other youths. He quit his summer job with the Just-A-Start program and has no concrete occupational aspirations. As for expectations, he believes he might enlist in the air force after graduation but adds, "I dunno. I might just go up and see my uncle, do some fuckin' construction or something."

Many of these boys expect to enter military service. Jinks and Frankie mention it as an option; Stoney has tried to enlist, but without success. Although Jinks refuses to think in terms of aspirations, he will say what he expects to do after he finishes school.

JM: What are you gonna do when you get out?

JINKS: Go into the service, like everybody else. The navy.

JM: What about after that?

JINKS: After that, just get a job, live around here.

JM: Do you have any idea what job you wanna get?

JINKS: No. No particular job. Whatever I can get.

Jinks subsequently quit school. He had been working twenty hours a week making clothesracks in a factory with his brother. He left school with the understanding that he would be employed full-time, and he was mildly content with his situation: "I got a job. It ain't a good job, but other things will come along." Two weeks later, he was laid off. For the past three months he has been unemployed, hanging full-time in doorway #13.

Shorty has worked construction in the past and has held odd jobs such as shoveling snow. Shorty, an alcoholic, has trouble holding down a steady job, as he freely admits. He was enrolled in school until recently. Ordered by the court to a detoxification center, Shorty apparently managed to convince the judge that he had attended enough Alcoholics Anonymous meetings in the meantime to satisfy the court. He has not returned to school since, nor has he landed a job. Given that Shorty is often on the run from the police, he is too preoccupied with pressing everyday problems to give serious thought to his long-term future. It is not surprising that my ill-timed query about his occupational aspirations met with only an impatient glare.

Stoney is one of the few Hallway Hangers with a definite ambition. In fact, he aspires to a middle-class occupation—to own his own pizza shop. Although Stoney's goal is exceptionally high for a Hallway Hanger, ownership of one's own business, according to Ely Chinoy, is a common ambition for at least part of the blue-collar workforce.[3] Still, Stoney himself considers his aspiration unusually ambitious and is automatically defensive about his chances for success.

JM: What's your ambition?

STONEY: To *own* a store. One of these days I will. Watch. People might laugh at me now, but one of these days I will. It might be in fifty or sixty years. No, after a few years—if I'm about thirty years old, I can get a loan to get a store easy. Really. Get me some financial credit, buy me a little shop, work my way up.

Averse to both heavy manual work and "sitting behind a desk—I'd hate that," Stoney went straight to a local pizza establishment when he was put on a special work-study arrangement at school. He worked twenty-five hours per week, attending school in a special class from three to six in the afternoon. Stoney finally "got real sick and tired of school" and started working full-time, only to be fired soon thereafter. "I was working part-time anyway and I could work more if I wanted, so I told him [the boss] to put it up to thirty [hours per week] and I cut down my school more. Then I went up to forty. That's when I quit school. Then I got fired (*laughs*)."

Stoney can afford to laugh. In contrast to Jinks, he has a marketable skill—making pizza—and immediately found another job in a small pizza shop in a different part of town. He soon left that "gig," returning to his original job. Shortly thereafter, he was fired once again for "being mouthy." The very next day, he was hired by a third pizza shop. Stoney has worked there for the past seven months, earning $5.00 per hour under the table. He likes his boss, the small size of the operation, and the relatively good wage.

A year ago, however, when Stoney was employed by the larger establishment, was working for a boss he did not like, and was making only slightly more than minimum wage, he tried to join the navy. "I wanted to get into the navy and travel for awhile. For two years, see the world, travel. I just found out real quick that they weren't gonna take me cuz of my drug record." Stoney was arrested last year for possession of mescaline. Although he could still have joined the army, he was not interested: "I don't want no bullshit army." According to Stoney, it is just as well that he was not accepted into the navy. "I like what I'm doing now, so I'll probably be here for awhile."

Like most of the Hallway Hangers, Slick already has held quite a few jobs. Between the ages of nine and thirteen Slick worked under the table in a supermarket that his uncle managed. He also has worked construction and as a clerk in a shoe store as well as odd jobs such as snow shoveling and minor landscaping. Slick quit school his junior year and began bagging groceries in another supermarket. "I just decided I had to put any kind of money away; whatever was available I would do, right? When I went down there (*pointing to doorway #13*), a lot of people would say, 'Well, fuck it; it's just bagging,' y'know? But you ain't gonna get no $20,000 a year job right off the streets anyway. You have to start somewhere, doin' somethin'."

Just the same, Slick could not take bagging groceries for long. He quit that job last June and enlisted in the army the next day. Slick really wanted to join the marines, but without a high school diploma, one must score exceptionally high on the standardized tests the marines administer to potential recruits. Slick missed by one point.

Once he was reconciled to entering the army, Slick was disappointed to find that without a high school diploma, he did not qualify for many of the benefits. Not one to accept a setback so easily, Slick did something about it. "I started talkin' about the bonuses and shit [with the recruiter], cuz I seen them on the paper up there, and I asked him. He said 'Well, you have to have your high school diploma.' So right across the street was the Adult Education Center." He enrolled in some classes at considerable cost but managed to have a bona fide diploma by midwinter. Although originally scheduled to report for service in October, Slick postponed his entry until late December when he expected to have his diploma.

By December, however, Slick had what he considered a better job lined up as a security guard at a local defense contracting firm the Hallway Hangers call "the weapons lab." Although he would not be able to start that job until mid-January, Slick somehow managed to cancel his enlistment. Shortly thereafter, however, his contact at the weapons lab was fired, and with him went Slick's prospective job. He currently is unemployed and, like Jinks, spends much of his time hanging at the Heights.

Despite these setbacks, Slick dreams of becoming a lawyer. Apparently, I was the first person to whom he voiced this hope. In a subsequent group interview in which five of the Hallway Hangers were discussing their plans for the future, an embarrassed Slick mentioned his aspiration in front of the group. The manner of this disclosure, which amounted to a confession, and the response of the group are instructive.

SLICK: (*sheepishly*) I'm gonna be a lawyer.

(*This response elicits surprise and whistles from the group.*)

CHRIS: My boy ain't talkin' no petty cash.

SHORTY: My boy wants to be a lawyer. He ain't even graduated from high school. Got himself a shit-ass diploma. Signed up for the army.

FRANKIE: I know. My boy bought his diploma and shit.

Slick himself is the first person to admit that he is not likely to achieve this goal, although his pride prevents him from expressing his reservations to the group.

Slick, like Jinks and the rest of the Hallway Hangers, realizes that there is usually little room for choice in occupational decisions. "Well, *if I had the choice,* if I couldn't be a lawyer, I'd like to either do landscaping or construction (*my emphasis*)." Although his expectations are far different from his aspirations, Slick is the only Hallway Hanger who aspires to a professional career.

Like so many of the Hallway Hangers, Frankie's aspirations and expectations are in a constant state of flux. What follows are Frankie's comments on his occupational expectations on four separate occasions spanning a one-year period.

(2/22/83)

FRANKIE: I'm getting out [of school] this spring.

JM: What are you gonna do then? I mean for work.

FRANKIE: I don't fucking know. Probably work construction. That'll be good. I'll make like seventy-five bucks a day. Under the table. Sixty or seventy-five bucks a day. I could do that for the rest of my life. I get paid cash, every day. My brother sets it up for me.

(4/15/83)

JM: Have any idea what you'll be doing for work when you graduate, Frankie?

FRANKIE: I don't fucking know. If I can't get anything else, I'll just join the fucking service.

On May 13, 1983, the day he graduated, Frankie was feeling very strongly the sense of uncertainty surrounding his prospects for future employment.

FRANKIE: (*unsolicited*) I gotta get a job, any fucking job.

JM: What about the construction?

FRANKIE: Yeah, I can work with my brother, but that's under the table. Besides, he's in Bradford [state prison] now.

During the summer, when he was unemployed, Frankie was on the verge of joining the army. Finally, he landed a temporary job as a garbage collector for the city. He was laid off in November and since that time has been out of work.

In an in-depth interview in December, Frankie articulated a new occupational aspiration, which he presently nurtures. "My kind of job is like, y'know, I did a lot of construction. That's the kind of job like I want. What I want to do is save up some money and go to tractor trailer school and take heavy equipment. I don't wanna drive no eighteen wheeler, but I want to do heavy equipment like payloading. Hopefully, some day I can do it. I got to get up the cash first."

An aspiration to blue-collar work, such as this, is not easy to achieve. Coming up with the cash, Frankie realizes, is no easy task. In addition, even if he were able to get his heavy equipment license, there would be no guarantee that he will land the job he envisions. Frankie is aware of the problems; the scenario he foresees contains many "ifs." "If I do get my license, and say if I get a job with a construction company, I'll tell 'em I got my license, but I'm starting off as a laborer anyway. Gettin' in fuckin' holes, y'know. Then if higher jobs come up in it, I'd have a better chance than anyone, instead of them sending someone to school. Y'know, 'This kid already got his license, give him a couple of days to get back in the swing of things.'" Considering these contingencies, it is no wonder Frankie has yet to act on these hopes.

Whereas Frankie is lucid about his aspiration and how to achieve it, Chris is in doubt about his future. He never has held a steady job for any significant period of time and presently makes his money dealing drugs (mostly marijuana and cocaine) in the Clarendon Heights neighborhood. He works quite hard, actively seeking out customers and making himself available through the afternoon and evening hours. Because he is currently the sole major outlet of drugs for the teenagers of Clarendon Heights, Chris makes a good deal of money (about $150 per week). Although dealing pays well, the risks are high. He admits that the police seem to be watching him closely, and if he is convicted of another offense, he may well be sent away. The threat of violence from other kids trying to make a fast buck is an additional and sometimes greater risk, one brought home to Chris when he mentioned his occupational aspirations in a group interview.

CHRIS: I wanna sell cocaine, no lie. I wanna deal cocaine, be rich.

SLICK: (*somewhat dubiously*) That's what he wants to do.

CHRIS: I'm just tellin' you the truth, man. That's what I'm s'posed to do, right man?

SLICK: He's gonna get fuckin' blown away (*laughter*).

FRANKIE: I'll cuff off him a thousand dollars.

Like Frankie, who also used to make his money illegally (and still does to a lesser degree), Chris may weigh the risks and alter his aspirations, or he may take his chances and try to make a future out of selling drugs.

One cannot help but be struck by the modesty of the Hallway Hangers' hopes for the future. Only Slick aspires to a professional career; Stoney is the only other individual who aspires to a middle-class job. Refusing the risk of hope, the remainder adjust their occupational goals to the only jobs that they perceive to be available—unskilled manual work. Many expect to enter military service, not because they find it particularly appealing but because of the paucity of other opportunities. The concept of an aspiration is essentially alien to the Hallway Hangers. Most simply expect to take whatever they can get.

The Hallway Hangers are quite honest about their occupational expectations and aspirations, but it is not comforting to look closely at one's future when bleakness is its main characteristic. When free of the psychological complications inherent in considering one's own future, the Hallway Hangers predict even more inauspicious outcomes for the peer group in general.

JM: What sorts of jobs do you think the rest of the guys will have?

(*all in separate interviews*)

STONEY: Shitty jobs. Picking up trash, cleaning the streets. They won't get no good jobs.

SLICK: Most of the kids around here, they're not gonna be more than janitors or, y'know, goin' by every day tryin' to get a buck. That's it. ... I'd say the success rate of this place is, of these people ... about twenty percent, maybe fifteen.

STEVE: I dunno. Probably hanging around here. I dunno. Shit jobs.

JINKS: I think most of them, when and if a war comes, they're all gone. In the service. Everyone's going. But for jobs—odds and ends jobs. Here and there. No good high-class jobs. I think they'll all end up working for the city, roofers, shit like that.

In Frankie's answer to the same question, we get a real feel for the deep sense of pessimism that dominates the Hallway Hangers' outlook on their future. Listening to him talk, one can detect a poignant fear for his own destiny.

FRANKIE: Well, some of them are gonna do okay, but, I dunno, some of them are just gonna fuck up. They'll just be doing odd jobs for the rest of their lives, y'know. Still be drinking, y'know; they'll drink themselves to death, what's some of 'em'll do. That's what I hope I don't do. Yeah, some of them are gonna drink themselves to death, but some of them, y'know, they're gonna smarten up. Get married, have some kids, have a decent job. Enough to live off anyways, to support a wife and kids. But some of them, they're gonna fuck up; they'll be just a junkie, a tramp. They'll be sitting out on the lawn for the rest of their life with their fucking bottle. Going to work every morning, getting laid off. Fucking, y'know, they're just gonna fuck up. That's what I hope I don't do. I'm trying not to anyways.

The definitions of aspirations and expectations given at the beginning of this chapter suggest that an assessment of the opportunity structure and of one's capabilities impinge on one's preferences for the future. However, the portrait of the Hallway Hangers painted in these pages makes clear that "impinge" is not a strong enough word. But are the leveled aspirations and pessimistic expectations of the Hallway Hangers a result of strong negative assessments of their capabilities or of the opportunity structure?

This is not an easy question to answer. Doubtless, both factors come into play, but in the case of the Hallway Hangers, evaluation of the opportunity structure has the dominant role. Although in a discussion of why they do not succeed in school the Hallway Hangers point to personal inadequacy ("We're all just fucking burnouts"; "We never did good anyways"), they look to outside forces as well. In general, they are confident of their own abilities.

(in a group interview)

JM: If you've got five kids up the high school with all A's, now are you gonna be able to say that any of them are smarter than any of you?

SLICK: (*immediately*) No.

JM: So how'd that happen?

SLICK: Because they're smarter in some areas just like we're smarter in some areas. You put them out here, right? And you put us up where they're living— they won't be able to survive out here.

SHORTY: But we'd be able to survive up there.

FRANKIE: See, what it is—they're smarter more academically because they're taught by teachers that teach academics.

JM: Not even streetwise, just academically, do you think you could be up where they are?

FRANKIE: Yeah.

CHRIS: Yeah.

SHORTY: Yeah.

JM: When it comes down to it, you're just as smart?

FRANKIE: Yeah.

SLICK: (*matter-of-factly*) We could be smarter.

FRANKIE: Definitely.

CHRIS: On the street, like.

FRANKIE: We're smart, we're smart, but we're just smart [inaudible]. It's fucking, y'know, we're just out to make money, man. I know if I ever went to fucking high school and college in a business course …

SLICK: And concentrated on studying …

FRANKIE: I know I could make it. I am a businessman.

JM: So all of you are sure that if you put out in school …

FRANKIE: Yeah! If I went into business, I would, yeah. If I had the fucking money to start out with like some of these fucking rich kids, I'd be a millionaire. Fucking right I would be.

Although these comments were influenced by the dynamics of the group interview, they jibe with the general sense of self-confidence the Hallway Hangers radiate and indicate that they do not have low perceptions of their own abilities.

If their assessments of their own abilities do not account for the low aspirations of the Hallway Hangers, we are left, by way of explanation, with their perceptions of the job opportunity structure. The dominant view in the United States is that American society is an open one that values and differentially rewards individuals on the basis of their merits. The Hallway Hangers question this view, for it runs against the grain of their neighbors' experiences, their families' experiences, and their own encounters with the labor market.

The Clarendon Heights community, as a public housing development, is by definition made up of individuals who do not hold even modestly remunerative jobs. A large majority are on additional forms of public assistance; many are unemployed. Like most old housing projects, Clarendon Heights tends to be a cloistered, insular neighborhood, isolated from the surrounding community. Although younger residents certainly have external points of reference, their horizons are nevertheless very narrow. Their immediate world is composed almost entirely of people who have not "made it." To look around at a great variety of people—some lazy, some alcoholic, some foolish, but many energetic, dedicated, clever, and resourceful—and to realize all of them have been unsuccessful on the job market is powerful testimony against what is billed as an open society.

The second and much more intimate contact these boys have with the job market is through their families, whose occupational histories only can be viewed as sad and disillusioning by the Hallway Hangers. These are not people who are slothful or slow-witted; rather, they are generally industrious, intelligent, and very willing to work. With members of their families holding low-paying, unstable jobs or unable to find work at all, the Hallway Hangers are unlikely to view the job opportunity structure as an open one.

The third level of experience on which the Hallway Hangers draw is their own. These boys are not newcomers to the job market. As we have seen, all have held a variety of jobs. All except Steve are now on the job market year round, but only Stoney has a steady job. With the exceptions of Chris, who presently is satisfied with his success peddling drugs, and Steve, who is still in school, the Hallway Hangers are actively in search of decent work. Although they always seem to be following up on some promising lead, they are all unemployed. Furthermore, some who were counting on prospective employment have had their hopes dashed when it fell through. The work they have been able to secure typically has been in menial, dead-end jobs paying minimum wage.

Thus, their personal experience on the job market and the experiences of their family members and their neighbors have taught the Hallway Hangers that the job market does not necessarily reward talent or effort. Neither they nor their parents, older siblings, and friends have shared in the "spoils" of economic success. In short, the Hallway Hangers are under no illusions about the openness of the job opportunity structure. They are conscious, albeit vaguely, of a number of class-based obstacles to economic and social advancement. Slick, the most perceptive and articulate of the Hallway Hangers, points out particular barriers they must face.

SLICK: Out here, there's not the opportunity to make money. That's how you get into stealin' and all that shit.

(*in a separate interview*)

SLICK: That's why I went into the army—cuz there's no jobs out here right now for people that, y'know, live out here. You have to know somebody, right?

In discussing the problems of getting a job, both Slick and Shorty are vocal.

SLICK: All right, to get a job, first of all, this is a handicap, out here. If you say you're from the projects or anywhere in this area, that can hurt you. Right off the bat: reputation.

SHORTY: Is this dude gonna rip me off, is he ...

SLICK: Is he gonna stab me?

SHORTY: Will he rip me off? Is he gonna set up the place to do a score or somethin'? I tried to get a couple of my buddies jobs at a place where I was working construction, but the guy says, "I don't want 'em if they're from there. I know you; you ain't a thief or nothing."

Frankie also points out the reservations prospective employers have about hiring people who live in Clarendon Heights. "A rich kid would have a better chance of getting a job than me, yeah. Me, from where I live, y'know, a high crime area, I was prob'ly crime-breaking myself, which they think your nice honest rich kid from a very respected family would never do."

Frankie also feels that he is discriminated against because of the reputation that attaches to him because of his brothers' illegal exploits. "Especially me, like I've had a few opportunities for a job, y'know. I didn't get it cuz of my name, because of my brothers, y'know. So I was deprived right there, bang. Y'know they said, 'No, no, no, we ain't havin' no Dougherty work for us.'" In a separate discussion, Frankie again makes this point. Arguing that he would have almost no chance to be hired as a fireman, despite ostensibly meritocratic hiring procedures, even if he scored very highly on the test, Frankie concludes, "Just cuz fuckin' where I'm from and what my name is."

The Hallway Hangers' belief that the opportunity structure is not open also emerges when we consider their responses to the question of whether they have the same chance as a middle- or upper-class boy to get a good job. The Hallway Hangers generally respond in the negative. When pushed to explain why, Jinks and Steve made these responses, which are typical.

(*in separate interviews*)

JINKS: Their parents got pull and shit.

STEVE: Their fucking parents know people.

Considering the boys' employment experiences and those of their families, it is not surprising that the Hallway Hangers' view of the job market does not conform to the dominant belief in the openness of the opportunity structure. They see a job market where rewards are based not on meritocratic criteria, but on "who you know." If "connections" are the keys to success, the Hallway Hangers sense that they are in trouble.

Aside from their assessment of the job opportunity structure, the Hallway Hangers are aware of other forces weighing on their futures. A general feeling of despondency pervades the group. As Slick puts it, "The younger kids have nothing to hope for." The Hallway Hangers often draw attention to specific incidents that support their general and vague feelings of hopelessness and of the futility of nurturing aspirations or high expectations. Tales of police brutality, of uncaring probation officers and callous judges, and of the "pull and hook-ups of the rich kids" all have a common theme, which Chris summarizes, "We don't get a fair shake and shit." Although they sometimes internalize the blame for their plight (Boo-Boo: "I just screwed up"; Chris: "I guess I just don't have what it takes";

Frankie: "We've just fucked up"), the Hallway Hangers also see, albeit in a vague and imprecise manner, a number of hurdles in their path to success with which others from higher social strata do not have to contend.

Insofar as contemporary conditions under capitalism can be conceptualized as a race by the many for relatively few positions of wealth and prestige, the low aspirations of the Hallway Hangers, more than anything else, seem to be a decision, conscious or unconscious, to withdraw from the running. The competition, they reason, is not a fair one when some people have an unobstructed lane. As Frankie maintains, the Hallway Hangers face numerous barriers: "It's a steeplechase, man. It's a motherfucking steeplechase." The Hallway Hangers respond in a way that suggests only a "sucker" would compete seriously under such conditions.

Chris's perspective seems a poignant, accurate description of the situation in which the Hallway Hangers find themselves.

CHRIS: I gotta get a job, any fucking job. Just a job. Make some decent money. If I could make a hundred bucks a week, I'd work. I just wanna get my mother out of the projects, that's all. But I'm fucking up in school. It ain't easy, Jay. I hang out there [in doorway #13] 'til about one o'clock every night. I never want to go to school. I'd much rather hang out and get high again. It's not that I'm dumb. You gimme thirty bucks today, and I'll give you one hundred tomorrow. I dunno. It's like I'm in a hole I can't get out of. I guess I could get out, but it's hard as hell. It's fucked up.

The Brothers: Ready at the Starting Line

Just as the pessimism and uncertainty with which the Hallway Hangers view their futures emerge when we consider what they perceive their lives will be like in twenty years, so do the Brothers' long-term visions serve as a valuable backdrop to our discussion of their aspirations. The ethos of the Brothers' peer group is a positive one; they are not resigned to a bleak future but are hoping for a bright one. Nowhere does this optimism surface more clearly than in the Brothers' responses to the question of what they will be doing in twenty years. Note the centrality of work in their views of the future.

(*all in separate interviews*)

SUPER: I'll have a house, a nice car, no one bothering me. Won't have to take no hard time from no one. Yeah, I'll have a good job, too.

JUAN: I'll have a regular house, y'know, with a yard and everything. I'll have a steady job, a good job. I'll be living the good life, the easy life.

MIKE: I might have a wife, some kids. I might be holding down a regular business job like an old guy. I hope I'll be able to do a lot of skiing and stuff like that when I'm old.

CRAIG: I'll probably be having a good job on my hands, I think. Working in an office as an architect, y'know, with my own drawing board, doing my own stuff, or at least close to there.

James takes a comic look into his future without being prompted to do so. "The ones who work hard in school, eventually it's gonna pay off for them and everything, and they're gonna have a good job and a family and all that. Not me though! I'm gonna have *myself.* I'm gonna have some money. And a different girl every day. And a different car. And be like this (*poses with one arm around an imaginary girl and the other on a steering wheel*)."

The Brothers do not hesitate to name their occupational goals. Although some of the Brothers are unsure of their occupational aspirations, none seems to feel that nurturing an aspiration is a futile exercise. The Brothers have not resigned themselves to taking whatever they can get. Rather, they articulate specific occupational aspirations (although these often are subject to change and revision).

Like all of the Brothers, Super has not had extensive experience on the job market; he only has worked at summer jobs. For the past three summers, he has worked for the city doing maintenance work in parks and school buildings through a CETA-sponsored summer youth employment program. During the last year, Super's occupational aspirations have fluctuated widely. His initial desire to become a doctor was met with laughter from his friends. Deterred by their mocking and by a realization of the schooling required to be a doctor, Super immediately decided that he would rather go into business: "Maybe I can own my own shop and shit." This aspiration, however, also was ridiculed. "Yeah, right," commented Mokey, "Super'll be pimping the girls, that kinda business." In private, however, Super still clings to the hope of becoming a doctor, although he cites work in the computer field as a more realistic hope. "Really, I don't know what I should do now. I'm kinda confused. First I said I wanna go into computers, right? Take up that or a doctor." The vagueness of Super's aspirations is important; once again, we get a glimpse of how little is known about the world of middle-class work, even for somebody who clearly aspires to it. Of one thing Super is certain: "I just know I wanna get a good job."

Although Super does not distinguish between what constitutes a good job and what does not, he does allude to criteria by which the quality of a job can be judged. First, a good job must not demand that one "work on your feet," a distinction, apparently, between white- and blue-collar work. Second, a good job implies at least some authority in one's workplace, a point Super makes clearly, if in a disjointed manner. "Bosses—if you don't come on time, they yell at you and stuff like that. They want you to do work and not sit down and relax and stuff like that, y'know. I want to try and be a boss, y'know, tell people what to do. See, I don't always want people telling me what to do, y'know—the low rank. I wanna try to be with people in the high rank." Although Super does not know what occupation he would like to enter, he is certain that he wants a job that is relatively high up in a vaguely defined occupational hierarchy.

Mokey has not given as much thought to his occupational aspirations as have most of the Brothers. His contact with the job market has been minimal. His only job has been part-time janitorial work with his father. Mokey plans to attend college and does not envision working full-time until after graduation, several years from now.

JM: So what do you think you wanna do when you get out of school?

MOKEY: I have no idea really.

JM: Don't think about it that much?

MOKEY: Not really. Before, I wanted to be a motorcyclist, like motocross. That was it.

JM: Didn't you tell me mechanic?

MOKEY: And mechanic. That was when I wanted to be a motor mechanic. For motorcycles. I wanted to be a motocross, that's what I wanted to be.

JM: How'd you decide on that?

MOKEY: I seen a motorcycle race before and I've ridden a couple of minibikes before, and I just decided.

Usually, the aspirations of the Brothers reflect more thought than those Mokey articulates. Although his mother reports that he is interested in "general management, of his own or someone else's business," Mokey's aspirations are sketchy and contradictory.

In contrast to Mokey, James's aspirations are defined clearly. Since his eighth grade class visited the high school and James viewed the computer terminals, he has aspired to design video games. This is a goal to which James is strongly committed. His plans are well developed; he has even considered his prospective employers: Atari, Intelevision, or Colecovision. His enthusiasm for his foreseen occupation is unmatched by the other boys. "I like jobs that are fun and make money too. Like making computer games; it would be fun. ... I want computers. I love computers. I fell in love with computers, so I know I want to do computers."

James is confident that he will achieve his occupational goal, despite the difficulty he has had finding any kind of summer employment. Last summer, after a two-month job search, James did maintenance work for the city recreation department. Paid and hired through the CETA job program, he spent the summer clearing parks and buildings.

The only boy whose plans are more definitively developed is Derek. Derek has never worked in his life; his summers have been spent traveling with a wealthy friend from Barnes Academy. Since he was a young boy, however, Derek has dreamed of joining the military. He wants to learn electronics and become a helicopter pilot, an aspiration Derek took a big step toward fulfilling by enlisting in the navy this past summer. He is on delayed entry until he receives his diploma this June; then he will report to basic training in July and will serve for six years.

Considering that the decision to enter the service is usually a last resort for most Heights teenagers, it is noteworthy that Derek aspires to a career in the navy, particularly given his success in high school and at Barnes Academy. Of all the Brothers and Hallway Hangers, he seems to have the best educational credentials and the best chance to move on to high-status employment. But Derek does explain his choice.

DEREK: At first, they [his parents] wanted me to be a lawyer. Ever since I went to Barnes. But there's no way I could do that. I need a job that has action. I need to be active. I couldn't sit behind a desk all week to make a living; that wouldn't be right.

JM: What do you mean, it wouldn't be right?

DEREK: I just couldn't do it. I like all the activities the navy has. And, y'know, sometimes I like to take orders. Carry them out. I don't want to just sit around.

This devaluation of white-collar work as inactive and boring, according to Paul Willis, is the main cultural innovation of the nonconformist lads that deters them from entering, or even trying to enter, white-collar work. This distaste for office work, which is bound up inextricably with the working-class culture's ideal of masculinity, serves to level the aspirations of the lads, thereby spurring them to work on the shop floor. A close examination of the Hallway Hangers and Brothers, however, reveals no such definitive cultural process at work, although we can detect traces of such an attitude among the Hallway Hangers (and with Derek). However, Super and his parents denigrate work that would require that he stand on his feet, a view shared by Juan.

Juan, whose previous employment record consists of a number of summertime jobs, aspires to be a cook. Like Super, he hopes to avoid manual work (a hope his father shares). "I like clean job, y'know, where you can keep yourself clean. That's what my father said. 'You should get a job where you can keep yourself clean.' I found out that the one that was better off for me was cooking. I like mechanic, but, no man, too rough for me."

Despite this aversion to auto mechanics, which Juan expressed last summer, he currently is seeking employment in precisely that area. The only Brother to have graduated from high school and thus currently on the job market, Juan has been unable to find work in food preparation. Although he retains his aspiration to be a cook because "it's fun; I like it," the unpleasant experience of unemployment for eight months has forced Juan to lower his expectations.

Craig, who like most of the Brothers has "never held a real job, just, y'know, summer jobs," hopes to be an architect. Craig has been a good artist since his earliest years and his father suggested that he consider architecture as a career. Craig has nurtured this aspiration since sixth grade and sees himself working for an architecture firm in the future. He adds, however, that if he is frustrated in his attempt to find employment in this field, he would like to be a computer operator or programmer.

This tendency to express contingency plans in case of failure is articulated fully by Mike. During the course of a year, Mike has revealed a hierarchy of aspirations and expectations. Mike's dream is to be a professional athlete: a wrestler, like his father, or a football player. He realizes this would come about only "if I get a big break." The occupational aspiration about which he talks the most is in the computer field, apparently a common aspiration for these boys because of the emphasis put upon the subject in high school. One step below that on his hierarchy of occupational preferences is more traditional blue-collar work, particularly as an electrician. Finally, he says, "If I don't make it in like, anything, if I flunk out or something, I'll probably join the service or something."

Like most of the Brothers, Mike is very concerned about the quality of his future employment. "Mostly," he comments, "I just wanna get ahead in life, get a good job." Specifically, he wants to avoid the dull, monotonous type of work he experienced last summer as a stock boy in a large hardware warehouse. "It's for fucking morons," he exclaims. Mike also has held a summer job in which he learned some carpentry skills doing weatherization work for the City Action to Save Heat project, another CETA program. He hated taking orders from a strict supervisor who, Mike recalls, "just sat on his fat ass all day anyway. Then again," he added upon reflection, "I wouldn't mind doing that."

Despite the Brothers' absorption with athletics and the status of professional sports in American culture, the Brothers have few illusions about the extent to which sports are a ticket to success. While their younger siblings speak incessantly about "making it in the pros," the Brothers no longer aspire seriously to a career in professional athletics. Only Mike and Craig see sports as a means to get a college education.

Although not all the Brothers aspire to professional or managerial work, all do have hopes for the future. The notion of a career makes sense when applied to their visions of future employment. They are committed to acting on their hopes, and although they realize that there is no guarantee that their dreams will come to fruition, they are not resigned to failure. In short, the Brothers are optimistic about their future employment, while the Hallway Hangers are deeply pessimistic about their prospective occupational roles.

In contrasting the Brothers and the Hallway Hangers, however, we must resist the temptation to define the two groups only in relation to one another. Certainly in comparison to the Hallway Hangers, the Brothers have high aspirations. To assert that the Brothers aspire to middle-class jobs while the Hallway Hangers do not, however, would be overly simplistic. In a society in which the achievement of a prestigious occupation is considered a valid goal for everyone, it is significant that a few of the Brothers have only modest goals.

The Brothers display none of the cockiness about their own capabilities that the Hallway Hangers exhibit. Instead, they attribute lack of success on the job market exclusively to personal inadequacy. This is particularly true when the Brothers speculate about the future jobs the Hallway Hangers and their own friends will have. According to the Brothers, the Hallway Hangers (in Super's words) "ain't gonna get nowhere," not because of the harshness of the job market, but because they are personally lacking. The rest of the Brothers share this view.

JM: Some of those guys who hang with Frankie, they're actually pretty smart. They just don't channel that intelligence into school, it seems to me.

CRAIG: I call that stupid, man. That's what they are.

JM: I dunno.

CRAIG: Lazy.

(*in a separate interview*)

SUPER: They think they're so tough they don't have to do work. That don't make sense, really. You ain't gonna get nowhere; all's you gonna do is be back in the projects like your mother. Depend on your mother to give you money every week. You ain't gonna get a good job. As you get older, you'll think about that, y'know. It'll come to your mind. "Wow, I can't believe, I should've just went to school and got my education."

(*in a separate interview*)

MOKEY: They all got attitude problems. They just don't got their shit together. Like Steve. They have to improve themselves.

In the eyes of the Brothers, the Hallway Hangers have attitude problems, are incapable of considering their long-term future, and are lazy or stupid.

Because this evidence is tainted (no love is lost between the two peer groups), it is significant that the Brothers apply the same criteria in judging each other's chances to gain meaningful employment. James thinks Mokey is headed for a dead-end job because he is immature and undisciplined. He also blames Juan for currently being out of work. "Juan's outa school, and Juan does *not* have a job (*said with contempt*). Now that's some kind of a senior. When I'm a senior, I'm gonna have a job already. I can see if you're gonna go to college right when you get out of school, but Juan's not doin' nothin'. He's just stayin' home." Juan, in turn, thinks that Mokey and Super will have difficulty finding valuable work because of their attitudes. He predicts that Derek and Craig will be successful for the same reason.

These viewpoints are consistent with the dominant ideology in America; barriers to success are seen as personal rather than social. By attributing failure to personal inadequacy, the Brothers exonerate the opportunity structure. Indeed, it is amazing how often they affirm the openness of American society.

(*all in separate interviews*)

DEREK: If you put your mind to it, if you want to make a future for yourself, there's no reason why you can't. It's a question of attitude.

SUPER: It's easy to do anything, as long as you set your mind to it, if you wanna do it. If you don't want to do it … you ain't gonna make it. I gotta get that through my mind: I wanna do it. I wanna be somethin'. I don't wanna be livin' in the projects the rest of my life.

MOKEY: It's not like if they're rich they get picked [for a job]; it's just mattered by the knowledge of their mind.

CRAIG: If you work hard, it'll pay off in the end.

MIKE: If you work hard, really put your mind to it, you can do it. You can make it.

This view of the opportunity structure as an essentially open one that rewards intelligence, effort, and ingenuity is shared by all the Brothers. Asked whether their chances of securing a remunerative job are as good as those of an upper-class boy from a wealthy district of the city, they all responded affirmatively. Not a single member of the Hallway Hangers, in contrast, affirms the openness of American society.

This affirmation of equality of opportunity is all the more astounding coming from a group of black, lower-class teenagers. Only Juan mentioned racial prejudice as a barrier to success, and this was a result of personal experience. Juan's mother was forced out of her job as a clerk in a neighborhood grocery store when some of the customers complained about the color of her skin. "Most of the time it depends on the boss, whether or not he has something against black. If they judge by the attitude, by the way they act, then that's it; there'll be an equal chance, but it's not usually that way."

Whereas the Hallway Hangers conclude that the opportunity structure is not open, the Brothers reach an entirely different, and contradictory, conclusion. Considering that both groups share neighbors and that the families of the boys have similar occupational histories, this discrepancy is all the more problematic. Indeed, we have uncovered quite a paradox. The peer group whose members must overcome racial as well as class barriers to success views the occupational opportunity structure as essentially open, whereas the white peer group views it as much more closed. The Brothers, whose objective life chances are probably lower than those of the Hallway Hangers, nevertheless hold positive attitudes toward the future, while the Hallway Hangers harbor feelings of hopelessness. To unravel this paradox is a challenge, one that we shall face in Chapter 7.

If the Hallway Hangers view their predicament as a race in which they, as members of the lower class, must jump a number of hurdles, while the rest of the pack can simply sprint, the Brothers see it as an even dash. The Hallway Hangers believe a strong finish, given their handicap, is out of the question and drop out of the race before it begins. They cannot understand why the Brothers compete seriously. Apparently, explains Slick, the Brothers do not see the hurdles. "It's a question of you wanna see it, and you don't wanna see it. They might not wanna see all the obstacles. In the long run, it'll hurt them. You hafta hear what's going on, or it's gonna hurt you later on."

The Brothers, for their part, are lined up at the start, unsure of their ability, but ready to run what they see as a fair race. They do not understand why the Hallway Hangers fail to take the competition seriously. It is, after all, the only game in town.

DEREK: I don't know. I really don't. I guess they just don't realize what they have to do. It just doesn't get through to them. I dunno. I don't think anyone has really told them straight out what it takes to make it, to be a winner.

Before we analyze how the same race can be viewed in two fundamentally different ways, we must investigate how the two peer groups prepare themselves for the competition. School is the training ground, the place where this preparation takes place. As we might expect, the boys who plan to run the race competitively approach their training in a fundamentally different way than do those who already have conceded defeat.

Notes

1. Archibald O. Haller undertook extensive conceptual and empirical work on aspirations and introduced this distinction between aspirations and expectations. The study that led to subsequent empirical work by Haller and others is Archibald O. Haller and Irwin Millers's *The Occupational Aspirations Scale* (Cambridge, Mass.: Schenkman, 1972). For a

6

School: Preparing for the Competition

$\mathcal{S}$ CHOOL IS AN INSTITUTION in which the Hallway Hangers and the Brothers are forced into daily contact. Many of the attitudes we already have uncovered are played out in school, and made manifest in the boys' conduct. Before we can consider this intriguing cultural and institutional mix, however, we must familiarize ourselves with the school itself.

Almost all the teenagers from Clarendon Heights who attend school go to Lincoln High School (LHS). LHS, a comprehensive school of more than 2,800 students and 300 faculty, is organized into four regular academic houses (A,B,C,D), four alternative programs (Enterprise Co-op, Pilot School, Achievement School, Fundamental School), and a separate Occupational Education Program that offers both academic and vocational courses. Two additional programs—the Building Trades and Services Program (BTS) and the Adjustment Class—also come under our purview.

Lincoln High School students from all four grades in the main academic program are sorted randomly into the four main houses of the school, as are staff members from all the academic areas. These 400–500 students and approximately 50 teachers are each assigned to one area of the building—their house. Freshmen, and sophomores take most of their subjects within their house, while juniors and seniors often cross over to other houses as their elective program expands. The house system is designed to create a smaller setting that promotes better communication and accountability; it also is intended to build strong relationships between students' families and the administrators and counselors who work with the students all four years. In House D, in addition to the more than 300 students in the conventional curriculum, the Bilingual Program teaches the standard course work to about 200 students in their native languages: Portuguese, French-Haitian, Spanish, and Chinese.

According to the course catalogue, the Occupational Education Program provides new options to secondary school students: a high school diploma as well as

marketable skills in an occupation of one's choice. Karen Wallace, a career counselor at the school, describes the Oc. Ed. Program as "a spinoff from the old technical school. It's for kids who like to work with their hands." Students enrolled in
Oc. Ed. carry an academic program that meets LHS graduation requirements, but
they also carry a full vocational program that according to the course catalogue
"insures access to a career at a skilled level."

As freshmen, students in Occupational Education spend two periods each day
in the exploratory program, in which they sample each of the twelve shops: auto
body, auto mechanics, carpentry, computers, culinary arts, drafting, electrical,
electronics, machine, metals, printing, and welding. According to Bruce Davis,
guidance counselor for the Occupational Education Program, at the end of the
year each freshman lists three shops in which he or she prefers to major. In con-
sultation with the shop teachers, the guidance counselors decide, on the basis of
the interest, aptitude, and behavior each student has demonstrated, each student's
shop major. Most of the students, claims Davis, end up with their first choice.
During their sophomore year, students spend three periods per day in their shop.
"During the third and fourth years," explains Davis, "they spend three periods in
shop plus three periods per week in what we call a theory class where they learn
about the occupation itself." The Occupational Education Program enrolls approximately 300 students.

Enterprise Co-op is an alternative, career-oriented program that includes stu-
dent-run businesses for dropouts and potential dropouts. The curricula of the
standard English, math, and social studies courses also include academic work relating directly to the students' experiences in the businesses. A wood shop and extensive food services are operated in an atmosphere that simulates the real business world. Students receive shares in the co-op based on their productivity, and
their dividend checks reflect the increase or decrease in profits for a particular pay
period. "It is anticipated that, after one year of participation in Enterprise Co-
op," states the course catalogue, "a student will be prepared either to re-enter the
mainstream high school program, or to secure entry-level employment in a career
of his/her choosing."

The Pilot School, founded in 1969, is an alternative high school program that
accommodates approximately 200 students. According to Wallace, the Pilot
School came into being when a group of parents decided that the curriculum and
atmosphere of the high school were too regimented. "The teachers act as counselors to the students; there are weekend trips and lots of outdoor activities. You
have a much closer teacher/pupil relationship. The onus of responsibility is on the
student to take charge for his work." Candidates for admission are selected at random after steps have been taken to ensure that the student body approaches a representative cross section of the school population with respect to geographical
area, race and/or ethnic background, sex, academic interest, and parental occupation. The course catalogue bills the Pilot School as an attempt to create a commu-

nity of students, parents, and educators accountable to each other for the goals of the program and the successful operation of the school.

The Fundamental School, which originated when a group of parents decided that the high school was not regimented enough, employs an educational philosophy at the other end of the spectrum. The school (with 400–500 students) "emphasizes basic academic requirements with few frills." The catalogue describes this alternative program as one that "stresses academic excellence and student accountability and enlists parental involvement and support in reinforcing the discipline code." For Stephen, a ninth grader who at his parents' insistence has chosen to go into the Fundamental School as did his brother Mokey, the Fundamental School is simply a lot stricter than the regular program: "I mean, you can't cut class in Fundamentals. If you do, bang, you'll get caught."

"The Achievement School," according to Wallace, "is for kids who haven't quite made it out of elementary school, but who are old enough to be in high school." With a maximum student population of forty, the Achievement School is designed to provide intensive compensatory education in the basic academic subjects for students with special needs (e.g., underachievers, perceptually handicapped). Wallace explains that kids "do cross over and are mainstreamed, but they have their own graduation."

Like Enterprise Co-op, the Building Trades and Services Program enrolls "high risk" students: dropouts and potential dropouts with truancy and disciplinary problems. Students from grades nine through twelve attend classes in math, science, English, history, and social studies in a small, self-contained environment from 8:00 until 11:30 A.M. A lunch break follows; then from 12:00 until 2:30 P.M. the students learn carpentry skills and occasionally travel to work at small-scale construction sites around the city. Teachers seldom mention the program, and when they do, it is typically in a negative vein: "There's Building Trades with very easy academics. I don't know what the hell you learn to do there, be a janitor or something."

Like all public high schools in the state, LHS has provisions for those students who are considered emotionally disturbed. These students are required to meet regularly with an adjustment counselor. Depending on a psychiatrist's perception of the severity of the problem, a student meets with his or her adjustment counselor weekly, daily, or for two periods each day. Adjustment counselors have more flexibility than do guidance counselors, which enables them to spend a lot more time and energy on each of their assigned students. According to Wallace, "[The adjustment counselor will] go to court with them, make sure they see their probation officer, and that type of thing. The student is required to spend a block of time with his adjustment counselor each week." Those with severe problems are enrolled full-time in the Adjustment Class, the last step before residential schooling or institutionalization.

Whereas secondary school adjustment programs, according to state statutes, serve emotionally disturbed students, the teachers describe the youngsters assigned to the programs in a different manner. Wallace portrays them simply as "kids whose academics are very poor or who are in trouble" and "who are really into drugs, have bad home lives, or things like that." Lincoln students sense the ambiguity about whom the Adjustment Class serves. "That's more or less for the slow kids, but they say the crazy kids," relates Jinks. "Y'know, you gotta act stupid in school, go off, crazy, shit like that." The students in the Adjustment Class realize they are classified as emotionally disturbed, but if the seriousness with which they take their mandatory appointments with the school psychiatrist is any indication, they are none too concerned about the designation.

FRANKIE: I would toy with him more than he'd try to fuck with me. Y'know, like once I caught him with a tape recorder in his drawer. I would've been cool if he told me it was on. But he didn't tell me, and like I knew it was on, so I waited five minutes. He was asking me "What bothers you?" I said, "You wanna know what bothers me? I'm pretty pissed that you fuckin' put that tape recorder on." I slammed open his drawer and shut the fucker off. I said, "That's what's pissing me off and I don't feel pissed off no more," and I sat back down. And like one time, y'know, I seen *Caine Mutiny,* and I went and I got some marbles. Y'know, Humphrey Bogart, he was a paranoiac, and he went in there always playing with marbles. So I went in there and played with marbles. The guy asked me why I was doing it. I says, "Cuz I know you're getting paid eighty-five bucks for this one hour, and I'm gonna make you work for it for once."

Jimmy Sullivan, the teacher of the Adjustment Class for fourteen years, describes his students variously as those "who've been in fights and are general pains in the ass," as "kids who have had emotional problems in the past and have shown an inability to be mainstreamed," as "those who couldn't hack the other programs," and "kids who are tough, from very, very rough backgrounds." Sometimes, he simply refers to those in his class as "crazy."

That the Adjustment Class is unique is beyond doubt. Walking into the room after school, one beholds a large, sand-filled punching bag suspended from the ceiling, weights and barbells sprinkled on the floor, magazines such as *High Times, Sports Illustrated,* and *Soldier of Fortune* left on the easy chairs and couches that line the room and a small punching bag in one corner. Both Jimmy and his assistant have black belts in karate; the twelve kids in the class are encouraged to work out with the weights and to learn martial arts. Posters of Bruce Lee adorn the walls to provide further inspiration.

The program is very flexible. Students must arrive at school by 9:30 in the morning and leave by 12:30. Upon arrival, the boys (there are no girls in the class) pick up their folders, which contain their daily assignments in math, reading, vocabulary, history, and a lesson from a job opportunities book. Most of the reading is on a fifth grade level; the daily math assignment includes basic addition, subtraction, multiplication, and division as well as work in decimals and fractions. In an interview, Jimmy expressed his teaching philosophy and gave an indication of the atmosphere that predominates in the class.

js: The kids are judged on their ability to get the work done. They've got the folder; that's it. It doesn't matter if they have this problem or that problem; everybody's got a fucking problem. Regardless of the problems, you've got to get your work done. I'd say the work can usually be done in two hours. Y'know, they come in here, some take a nap on the couch, some get a cup of coffee over at the store. There's a lot of freedom, but they have to get the work done. If you come in three days but only did the work two days, that's a forty percent. ... They'll get twenty-five credits each semester for being in here; you need one hundred and eighty to graduate. They can get ten extra credits for my version of work-study. I didn't give any work-study credits this year. I mean, you have to hold a job for more than a fucking week.

With its unique approach, the Adjustment Class deserves a separate in-depth study of its own. Although we shall temporarily reserve judgment on the effectiveness of the class, considering the positive attitudes of the enrolled students toward the class and the respect they accord Jimmy, the class is, by the school's standards, unusually successful. In contrast to the other programs, the boys attend regularly and control themselves while in class.

LHS formally practices tracking (as do 80 percent of the country's public high schools); classes in almost all programs are organized so students of similar learning achievement or capability are put together. According to their performance in each subject area in grammar school, pupils are placed into tracks, which also are called ability groupings and streams. Almost all the subject areas are divided into general, intermediate, and advanced level courses. Of the basic academic subjects, only the Social Studies Department, reflecting a commitment to heterogeneous classroom populations, offers a significant number of nonleveled courses. Even outside the core academic areas, most courses in business education, home economics, art, photography, dramatic arts, music, and physical education are leveled according to ability or achievement. Classes in the Fundamental School as well as academic classes in the Occupational Education Program also are leveled. Only classes within the Pilot School are all heterogeneous and untracked. But at Lincoln High School there are actually two levels of tracking—among programs (with Oc. Ed., Enterprise Co-op, BTS, and the Adjustment Class at the bottom) and within them. The practice of tracking on both levels has widespread implications for students' academic achievement, self-esteem, and postsecondary school educational and occupational plans, implications that are considered later in this chapter.

Although racial tension at LHS never has been as severe as at schools in a city such as Boston, Massachusetts, an incident in 1980 nevertheless focused attention on the severity of the problem at Lincoln. In a fight between black and white students on school grounds, a white boy was stabbed fatally. The ensuing review of the schools' policies revealed a significant shortage of black teachers. When the school system moved to rectify the problem by bringing in more black staff, a backlash from a number of white students accompanied the changes. Wallace, who is black, reports that white students, especially those from the Clarendon Heights neighborhood, "resented the fact that the black students now had somewhere to go, someone to relate to. And they did come—in droves. The white kids thought they were getting special attention." Indeed, the Hallway Hangers continue to believe that black students are favored at the high school.

The Brothers: Conformity and Compliance

Super, like all other pupils, had to decide in the middle of eighth grade what high school program he wanted to enroll in. As part of this process, the high school sends a guidance counselor down to each eighth grade grammar school class to explain the various programs and curricula at the high school. Booklets detailing the programs and their constituent courses are distributed to students; tours of the high school by all eighth grade classes are arranged; and parents are invited to the high school for an information night, during which high school counselors present each program and answer questions. Finally, a high school guidance counselor meets individually with every eighth grader to discuss what the LHS course catalogue calls his or her "high school choice, occupation or career plans, sports, interests and hobbies, and personal concerns." Considering the importance of the student's program choice and the implications it may have for his or her future, the provisions the high school makes to ensure an informed, carefully weighed decision are understandable. For thirteen and fourteen year olds, however, the choice of programs is not always based exclusively on logic or long-term considerations. Super's expressed rationale for entering the Occupational Education Program is typical: "Really, I picked Oc. Ed. because my friends picked it. That's why, y'know."

In contrast to the rest of the Brothers, Super changed his program after he entered LHS. Super was involved in several fights stemming from racial tension in the predominantly white Occupational Educational Program and was suspended from school (another anomaly among the Brothers) three months into his first term. Subsequently, he enrolled in House C, part of the regular academic program.

Super is now well integrated into the school. He respects his teachers and truly wishes to be successful academically. Super accepts the disciplinary code of the school. He occasionally cuts classes but openly chastises himself for this weakness in self-resolve. Similarly, although he later expresses regret, Super often ignores his homework for the pursuit of more pleasurable activities—playing basketball and flirting with girls. Super's scholastic performance is mediocre; his grade average (on the standard scale whereby sixty is the lowest passing mark) during the one-and-a-half year period he has been enrolled in the high school hovers just below a seventy.

A natural athlete, Super has been involved in sports at LHS, which is further evidence of his successful integration into the school. This past fall he played on the junior varsity football team; last year he made the freshman basketball team but quit when he found the daily practices too time consuming. Super's earnest involvement in both academic and athletic pursuits, with only fair success in each, typifies the Brothers' approach to school.

Mokey undergoes the rigors of schooling in a similar way. Enrolled in the Fundamental School at his mother's insistence, he is generally obedient and hard working. Despite his positive attitude, Mokey's grades have not been good. He failed a course last year, thereby prompting him, again at his mother's urging, to apply to the Upward Bound Program, into which he was accepted. Upward Bound, a year-round, federally sponsored program for underachieving high school students, stresses development of academic skills and motivation for students who traditionally are not considered college bound. Mokey attended an overnight summer school at a nearby college campus and presently spends three hours every Thursday afternoon in the program. Although he now names four colleges he would like to attend, Mokey actually has fared less well in school since his participation in the program, having failed two classes in the fall semester of his junior year. Despite his unsatisfactory performance, Mokey's attitude toward school is positive. His conduct and effort seem to be at a high level, and, like Super, he enjoys playing on the junior varsity football team.

James's attitude toward school has fluctuated dramatically during the past three years. After a dismal sophomore year, during which he cut nearly all his academic classes and only attended his computer shop for three periods daily, James has made a real turnaround. He now attends every class assiduously and is making up last year's failed classes after school on Thursdays. Whereas last year James spent school hours playing video games in a local sub shop, this year he recently was elected president of the science club despite having failed his science course in the fall semester.

Of all the boys from Clarendon Heights, Derek's educational history is the most unusual. After finishing third grade at the neighborhood grammar school, Derek was selected to attend Barnes Academy, a prestigious prep school located on the outskirts of the city. At Barnes, Derek enjoyed great success. He earned A's and B's and immediately gained the respect of students and staff. Nevertheless, instead of attending grades nine through twelve at Barnes, Derek chose to attend Lincoln High School. Tired of the heavy workload, sick of the pressure to achieve in order to requalify for his scholarships, and bored with his subjects, he transferred to House D in Lincoln.

DEREK: I like to work, but not too much. That's why I quit Barnes after eighth grade. I just lost interest. It got to be too much—all the bills and everything.

JM: You were on a scholarship though. Didn't it pay for everything?

DEREK: Yeah, as long as I kept my grades up, then the government would pay for it.

Derek's scholastic achievement at the high school has been quite high; he has been on the honor roll several times and maintains a strong B average.

Although his grades are not as high as Derek's, Craig works very hard in school. Self-disciplined and conscientious, Craig spends a good deal of time each evening on his homework, often passing up pick-up basketball games in favor of studying. Presently a senior, Craig picked the Fundamental School in eighth grade in part because it was at the time housed in a separate building located in the northern reaches of the city. By entering the Fundamental School, Craig hoped to avoid the racial tension in the main high school, a hope that went unrealized when the Fundamental School was moved into the Lincoln building just prior to his freshman year.

JM: You're in the Fundamental School, right?

CRAIG: Fundamental, yeah.

JM: Now, why'd you choose that one, way back in eighth grade?

CRAIG: Cuz I heard their reputation was something.

JM: What's their reputation?

CRAIG: Their reputation was that they have very good teachers and stuff. My sister and her friends said it was a very good school.

JM: Do they have technical drawing in Oc. Ed.?

CRAIG: In Oc. Ed.—oh, they have a lot of that stuff.

JM: How come you didn't decide to go into there?

CRAIG: I didn't know Oc. Ed. was like that. … I didn't want to go into it cuz I thought, I thought, really, I thought most of the kids in there are stupid.

JM: Do you think that now?

CRAIG: No, they're smarter than I am.

JM: In technical drawing?

CRAIG: Yeah, they went through a better program. See, if I was in Oc. Ed. I'd have like three periods each day.

JM: All this wasn't clear to you back in the eighth grade?

CRAIG: Well, to be truthful, the main reason I picked Fundamental was cuz the main high school was real tense. Y'know, there was fights up there—a white kid got stabbed to death, and when I was in the eighth grade it was still pretty bad. See, the Fundamental School used to be way up by, uh …

JM: Columbia Street?

CRAIG: Yeah, I thought by going up there I'd miss all the hassles. But then they moved the year I was graduating [from eighth grade]. They just moved into Lincoln.

Craig, during the course of his three and a half years at the school, has maintained a seventy-five average.

Juan, a 1983 graduate of the high school, studied culinary arts in the Occupational Education Program. Describing his performance in school as "pretty good," Juan never failed a subject and once received a ninety-four in a class for his efforts. In his honest, sincere, and straightforward manner, Juan describes his behavior in school. "I wasn't any angel in the class; most of the time I was okay. I was in between, because sometimes I came in a bad mood in some classes. But usually I wouldn't bother nobody, because I wasn't ready to go through no hassle. … Most teachers knew me as a nice kid. I don't know if I was a nice kid (*smiles widely*), but they know me as a nice kid." Although many of his black friends, like Super, eventually dropped out of the Occupational Education Program, Juan stuck with it.

Mike is generally obedient and disciplined, although he periodically cuts classes and occasionally sneaks down into the school basement with his girlfriend. Nevertheless, he respects the rules of the school; like many of the Brothers, he becomes embarrassed and almost apologetic when recounting episodes of misbehavior. Mike's academic performance is mediocre. Last year he failed English, which prompted his enrollment in a six-week summer school course. His grades have not improved much this year; his first semester's marks were a B, two C's, and two D's. Although his performance in the classroom has been dismal, Mike has excelled on the athletic fields. As a sophomore, he has made the varsity football, wrestling, and track teams.

In general, the Brothers are integrated fully into the school. Although many of them turn in only fair academic performances, they honor and respect the standards, conventions, and judgments of the school. They show no evidence of disrespect for teachers or other school officials, and their disciplinary records are for the most part clean. Their course of study is stable; once they choose a particular program, most of them stay with it until graduation. Their participation in extra-curricular activities, especially athletics, gives them a chance to excel in an activity that is sometimes prized as highly as academics. In short, the Brothers are typical high school students.

The Hallway Hangers: Teacher's Nightmare

For the most part, Frankie exemplifies the Hallway Hangers' attitudes toward school; he is unusual only in that he graduated. Placed in a special program limited to fifty students his freshman year (which has since been discontinued), Frankie was expelled from the high school for repeated fights, especially with black students, and for striking a teacher in the face. He was prevented from gaining entry into any alternative program and thus was barred from the school altogether. He then attended the King School, a certified, tuition-free, private, alternative high school for low-income youths that employs a politically radical educational philosophy and curriculum. Dissatisfied with the teachers, whom Frankie variously terms "fuckin' liberals," "flakes," and "burnouts from the sixties," he left the King School after one year. When Frankie threatened to take Lincoln High School to court for refusing to readmit him, he gained entry into the Enterprise Co-op Program. Although he did well at first, he was struggling to stay in the program after the first month because of a drug problem that severely impaired his performance. Frankie was ingesting three and four "hits" of THC each day and was "gettin' real fuckin' high, veggin' out, not doin' my work." After a month, he was kicked out of Enterprise Co-op.

At that point, there was only one program in which Frankie could be enrolled—the Adjustment Class. A sympathetic guidance counselor who had gained Frankie's trust arranged for his admittance into Jimmy Sullivan's class. For the first time in his life, Frankie really admired and respected his teacher; he stayed in Jimmy's class for three years, graduating in 1983. The respect Jimmy elicits from his students is based on his toughness, his streetwise reputation, and the perception that his financial success (he has significant real estate holdings) is independent of his position as a teacher. In an interview before he graduated, Frankie comments on Jimmy's Adjustment Class.

FRANKIE: I didn't give a shit at the school. I used to tell teachers to their face to fuck themselves. That's why I like this class I'm in. Jimmy, he'll say, "You wanna fuck with me, then fight me." He's a fucking black belt in karate. ... Jimmy makes more fucking money than anyone else in that school. He's a real estate broker.

(*in a separate interview*)

FRANKIE: I went there, y'know. It was cool, cuz like you went in there, fuckin' you talk to Jimmy, and you know Jimmy's real cool. I never had a teacher that says, "Fuck this and fuck that" and "I'll kick your ass if you fuck up." The teachers in the King School, they were flakes; they swore and shit, but you just told them to shut the fuck up, and they shut up. They were scared. Jimmy, he ain't scared of no one.

Faced with the simple choice of doing his daily two hours of academic work and getting credit or of not doing it and failing, he attended school conscientiously.

FRANKIE: Jimmy, he says to me, "Look, come in and do your work if you want to; if you don't, screw! Get the fuck out of here." ... I listened to him, y'know, sat there until was fuckin' got through my head. I fuckin' realized, hey man, I gotta get my diploma, keep my moms happy. I started doing my work and, y'know, you fuck around and shit but Jimmy was cool. He let you fuck around—if you do your work you can do whatever you want to. I used to work out, used to do a lot of boxing and shit. ... I was there for awhile, three years. It was pretty cool.

Frankie was the first Hallway Hanger to enter Jimmy's class. In fact, when Frankie was first accepted into the class, he was the only student not to have been sent there by the court system. Most of the students had come directly from prison; some were shuttled daily from the county jail where they were incarcerated. Now, however, the average age of the students has fallen from nineteen to seventeen, and most are referred to the class after having problems in other high school programs.

Steve, for example, made a similar trek through the different programs, finally landing in the Adjustment Class. He picked Occupational Education in the eighth grade "cuz all my friends were there and I thought it'd be all right." Steve lasted only a month in that program before he was switched to regular academics, House C, because of discipline problems and excessive truancy. He lasted only two weeks in House C before he was assigned to Enterprise Co-op. "I didn't go. And I told them to go to hell, and I left. I didn't show up for school for a *long* time. Then they transferred me over to Co-op. And then so I went there. It was all right, but I really didn't like it either. Then I just said the hell with that and missed the whole rest of the year. Didn't get no credits either." When he returned to school the next year, Steve kicked in a window in a hallway, exclaiming that he wanted to be put in Jimmy's class. The Hallway Hangers acknowledge that Steve's antic amounted to a deliberate attempt to get into the Adjustment Class, and Steve himself admits, "Yeah, I wanted to cuz they had me on the list and shit, so I said fuck it, I'm in."

The effort paid off; Steve was admitted to Jimmy's class almost immediately, has attended for one year, and plans to stay in it until he graduates in two years. Like Frankie, he respects Jimmy and finds the class superior to the other programs.

STEVE: Jimmy's class has been real good for me, man.

JM: Yeah? What's it like in there?

STEVE: Oh, it's bad. It's way better than the other school. Come in at 9:30, get out at 11:30. The guy is just like us; he swears and shit, tells all the other teachers to go fuck themselves; he don't care. Got weights, punching bag; we get out early.

Aside from the streetwise teacher and the unique atmosphere of the classroom, students in the Adjustment Class like the light academic workload. As Jimmy himself admits, "This is the easiest way to graduate." Whatever the reason, it is because of Jimmy's class that Frankie managed to graduate and Steve has stayed in school.

For Shorty, however, Jimmy's class was not enough. Shorty was admitted to the Adjustment Class because he was a chronic truant and had a habit of threatening teachers. Shorty accounts for his downward spiral into Jimmy's class this way.

SHORTY: You start school as a freshman and you start cutting one class, right, and when that teacher starts giving you a hard time—this is how it started with me: I wasn't good in history and spelling and shit—and he wouldn't ever have got me a tutor or nothing. So then I said, "Fuck it." He wasn't passing me so then I stopped going to his class. Then he would spread the word around to the other teachers, and they would give me a hard time, and I'd stop going to their classes. Finally, I ended up in Jimmy's class.

Although he successfully completed one year of the Adjustment Class, Shorty, hearing that there was a warrant out for his arrest, became convinced that he would be sent to a detoxification center or prison and dropped out of school altogether this past November (1983). Although he managed to avoid incarceration, Shorty never went back to school, figuring he could not bring up his average enough to get credit for the fall semester.

Slick has a somewhat different educational history. He lived in a neighboring city until sixth grade and scored well enough on a test to gain admission to Latin Academy, a public school for gifted students. He attended Latin Academy for one year, enjoyed the challenging academic work, and was disappointed with the local grammar school when his family subsequently moved to Clarendon Heights.

SLICK: When I was at Latin, it was fucking real hard, right? Then I moved here cuz my grandfather died and my mother wanted to be closer to my grand-mother so we could help her out. So we moved over here, and it would've cost three thousand dollars for me to go there (*to Latin Academy, where nonresidents of the city in which it is located pay tuition*), and we ain't got that kinda money, so I couldn't go. I went here [the local grammar school] during my seventh and eighth grade and then up the high school. It was a big letdown from Latin. It was much slower, and I knew everything they were teaching me. So I just didn't go to the school.

Given the apparently high level of his academic training at Latin Academy, it is curious that Slick chose to enter the Occupational Education Program upon en-tering the high school. In answer to my query, he revealed his logic. "Because I was already working with my brain. I wanted to try to learn something with my hands, know what I mean? If I just kept on doing fucking academics, it wasn't gonna fucking help me anyways. It was stuff I already knew." In a separate inter-view, Slick intimated that he thought at the time that he needed to learn a trade to maximize his chances of getting a job.

Once at the high school, however, Slick was dissatisfied with Oc. Ed. and switched to regular academics before his sophomore year. During his second year, bored with his classes, he started to cut more frequently. Like many of his friends, Slick voices dissatisfaction with what he perceives as favoritism toward black stu-dents at the high school. Indeed, this is the expressed reason that Slick quit school in the middle of his junior year.

SLICK: The regular academics I didn't like because there was certain favoritism. By my junior year, I quit school. Went to work.

JM: What do you mean? What was the favoritism?

SLICK: You see, because of what happened a few years ago, they have to lean to-wards the minorities more. Because of, you know what happened, some kid got stabbed up there. So if there's like a fight between a white kid and a black kid, the white kid's always wrong. So I didn't like that; so I just quit school.

Jinks also began in the Occupational Education Program "because I wanted to learn a career for when I got out of school." As a field of specialization, he chose computers, but left the program in favor of regular academics because he "couldn't deal with sitting at a desk all day typing. It was too fucking boring." Pre-viously a strong B student (according to the other boys), Jinks started cutting most of his classes and spending his time at Pop's, a store about five blocks from the school. The Hallway Hangers and a number of other students frequent the back room of Pop's during school hours, playing cards, smoking marijuana, and drinking beer. This past fall, at the beginning of his senior year, Jinks dropped out of school. He already was working twenty hours per week and expected to be hired full-time. "I like working better than I like going to school. I just prefer working. Going to work, getting paid. I need the money. The holidays are coming; gotta buy them gifts. I got a part-time job now. When I quit school, it'll be a full-time job, my boss said." Shortly after Jinks quit school, he was laid off.

Aside from Frankie, Boo-Boo is the only other Hallway Hanger who has graduated from high school. He entered the Oc. Ed. Program "cuz everybody else was" and attended school diligently for two months before starting to cut most of his classes in favor of "smoking a few bones" at Pop's. Eventually, Boo-Boo stopped going to school at all for four months and did not receive so much as a phone call from the school authorities. Then Boo-Boo was arrested for auto theft in the middle of his freshman year (he was fifteen). After he was placed on probation as a result of his conviction in juvenile court, Boo-Boo's school performance was monitored by his probation officer. He was switched into the Building Trades and Services Program and began to attend school regularly. "I was only fifteen, and when you're on probation, you have to go to school. They kept giving me a hard time, and I didn't want to hear it, so I kept going." Boo-Boo stayed in BTS for four years and graduated in 1983.

Like many of the Hallway Hangers, Chris enrolled in Oc. Ed. his freshman year because he believed that knowing a trade would make it easier to get a job. During his freshman year, Chris was switched into BTS because "I was fucking up in Oc. Ed. I threw a chair at a teacher. I couldn't take the shit they were dishing out." Claiming that the academic work in BTS is far too simple ("We were just doing multiplication tables and shit—what a fucking joke"), Chris skipped all but his first two classes, hanging at Pop's the rest of the day. Unfamiliar even with the names of his afternoon teachers, Chris acknowledges that when he did attend school, he was impaired by drugs or alcohol. "Oh yeah, I'm high every time I go to school. I gotta be. Sometimes I even drink before I go; I'll have a few beers. It's too much if you don't." This past fall, Chris quit school altogether. Although he still frequents Pop's to sell drugs and occasionally ventures onto school grounds for the same purpose, Chris is no longer subject to the school's authority, an arrangement he prefers.

Stoney chose to enter the regular academic program in the high school but attended classes for only two weeks before he started cutting regularly. "I never went. I'd go to a couple classes, and then I'd cut a class here, cut a class there, cut another class—before you know it, you got fifty cuts, detentions, and then I stopped going to school." According to Stoney, he was suspended a couple of times, and school administrators wanted to expel him, but because he was too young, they put him in a special after-school program. Working part-time and attending school from three to six in the afternoon, Stoney was satisfied with the situation until the middle of his junior year. Given the opportunity to work more hours and tired of the school routine from which he felt he was learning little

("We rarely did work in there. They thought I was stupid or something; they had us do stupid stuff"), he quit school completely and started working full-time.

As a group, the Hallway Hangers experience school in a way much different than the Brothers do. Whereas the Brothers are fully integrated into the school, the Hallway Hangers' attitudes toward the educational system can be summed up by Stoney's words: "Fuck school. I hate fucking school." Most of the Hallway Hangers have dropped out. While officially enrolled, most spent little time in school anyway, preferring the fun, companionship, and drugs at Pop's. When in class, they generally were disruptive and undisciplined. None of the Hallway Hangers participated in any extracurricular activities. By their own accounts, they were high or drunk much of the time they spent in school. No one picked a school program and stayed in it; they all switched or were switched into different classes, some spiraling down through the array of alternative programs at amazing speed, landing in the last stop on the line. Some stayed there; most have dropped out altogether.

What factors explain the wide discrepancy between the educational pattern of the Brothers and the Hallway Hangers? The school cites the personal problems with which the Hallway Hangers are burdened. They are slow, unmotivated, undisciplined, or emotionally disturbed. More sympathetic teachers, like Jimmy Sullivan, attribute this type of fundamental difference between students to the ability of some to "talk about themselves in the long range, to project themselves into the future." However, a deeper level of analysis is necessary to explain the Hallway Hangers' and the Brothers' different experiences in school.

The Underlying Logic of Student Behavior

As with many urban high schools, Lincoln High School is preoccupied with maintaining discipline. The team of security guards policing the hallways is ample evidence of this fact. Aside from specific sanctions (suspensions, detentions, parent notifications), teachers attempt to secure discipline by reinforcing the achievement ideology: "Behave yourself, work hard, earn good grades, get a good job, and make a lot of money." This line of reasoning rests on two assumptions: what I shall term the efficacy of schooling—the notion that academic performance is the crucial link to economic success—and the existence of equality of opportunity. Although used primarily to ensure proper behavior by highlighting its eventual rewards, the ideology has more than a disciplinary function.

Before we move on to consider the implications of this line of reasoning, we must address the question of how commonly it is used in the school. This task is not difficult, for both students and teachers draw attention to its prominence. Karen Wallace, the career counselor, in an unsolicited remark, mentioned that this argument is constantly reinforced by teachers: "We tell them that if they try hard enough, work hard enough, and get good grades, then anything is possible." On another occasion, Mike, excited about the prospects of securing a lucrative computer job, recounted the computer teacher's remark about a friend who makes two thousand dollars a week working with computers. The teacher assured his students that comparable jobs are available in the computer industry "for those who don't fool around and really learn the trade." In another unsolicited remark, Chris drew attention to this tendency of teachers to forge a secure link between success in school and success on the job market: "They tell you they'll get you a job when you're done. They say that to you right at the beginning. They say it to you all the time." The difference between Mike and Chris, and more generally, as we shall see, between the Brothers and the Hallway Hangers, is that Mike believes this line of reasoning, whereas Chris reacts to it with: "That's *bullshit.* They don't fucking give you shit."

Swallowing the Achievement Ideology

In the previous chapter, I noted the Brothers' widespread belief in the reality of equality of opportunity. Like most Americans, they view this society as an open one. Crucial to this widely held notion is a belief in the efficacy of schooling. As the achievement ideology propagated in school implies, education is viewed as the remedy for the problem of social inequality; schooling makes the race for prestigious jobs and wealth an even one. The Brothers have a good deal of faith in the worth of schooling.

The Brothers' belief in the equality of opportunity and the efficacy of schooling emerges very strongly from their responses to particular interview questions. When asked whether they feel they have an equal chance to do as well in school as would a wealthy boy from an affluent part of the city, the nearly unanimous response is "yes," as it is when they are asked if they have an equal chance to get as good a job as the same hypothetical wealthy boy would. With respect to their views on the efficacy of schooling, the Brothers' responses to the question of why they work hard in school are illustrative.

(*all in separate interviews*)

DEREK: I know I want a good job when I get out. I know that I have to work hard in school. I mean, I want a good future. I don't wanna be doing nothing for the rest of my life.

CRAIG: Because I know by working hard it'll all pay off in the end. I'll be getting a good job.

MIKE: Get ahead in life; get a good job.

When asked whether their academic achievement will influence the type of job they will be able to secure, the Brothers all agree that it will.

This viewpoint explains the Brothers' commitment to their school work and the relatively high level of effort that characterizes their academic participation. But whereas their acceptance of the achievement ideology accounts for the ease with which the Brothers are integrated into the school, their mediocre academic performance requires further explanation.

One cannot attribute the Brothers' lack of scholastic success to lack of effort; as we have seen, they try hard in school. Moreover, the Brothers generally are intelligent and able. Although their scores on I.Q. tests, which purport to measure intelligence, are not available, three years of acquaintance with the boys leaves me assured that, on average, they are not substantially less "gifted" or "clever" than my university classmates. What, then, accounts for the academic mediocrity of the Brothers?

In attempting to answer this question, we find ourselves in the company of many eminent sociologists who have tackled the problem of the "educability" of the lower classes. The consistent tendency of working-class children to perform less well in school than their middle-class counterparts is demonstrated by a wealth of empirical evidence,[1] but the actual processes and mechanisms by which this comes about remain almost completely obscured.

Many conventional sociologists look to the working-class family to explain differential academic performance by social class, an approach that has yielded little in the way of concrete results. As Olive Banks admits in *The Sociology of Education*:

> The consistent tendency of working-class or manual workers' children to perform less well in school, and to leave school sooner than the children of non-manual workers, calls for explanation, and it has seemed reasonable to look for that explanation in the working-class family.
>
> It would, however, be far from the truth to conclude that the attention paid by sociologists in recent years to this problem has taken us very far towards a solution. We have many studies into the relationship between social-class background and educational achievement, and many different aspects of that background have been suggested as causal factors in the link between home and school, but up to now we have very little knowledge of the precise way in which these different factors interrelate to depress intellectual performance.[2]

In addition to the inability of this approach to account for the problem of differential academic achievement, this emphasis on the family, in its extreme form, has produced some very dubious conclusions and destructive results. Propagated in the United States since the 1960s in an attempt to explain the low educational attainment of black and lower-class white children, the concept of cultural deprivation attributes their problems solely to the cultural deficiencies of their families. The view that the problem resides almost exclusively with the children and their families, and that some sort of cultural injection is needed to compensate for what they are missing, is not only intellectually bankrupt but also has contributed to the widespread popular notion that the plight of poor whites and minorities is entirely their own fault.

To understand the problems lower-class children face in the American educational system demands that attention be paid not just to their families but also to the school. Theories that give primacy to the family inhibit critical scrutiny of the nation's schools. The problem is not that lower-class children are inferior in some way; the problem is that *by the definitions and standards of the school,* they consistently are evaluated as deficient. The assumption of some mainstream sociologists that the problem must lie with the contestants, rather than with the judge, is simply unfounded.

Conventional sociologists as well as Marxist theorists have been singularly unable to put forth a convincing explanation of lower-class "educability." As Karabel and Halsey point out, the only explanation Bowles can muster is the vague assertion that the "rules of the game" favor the upper classes. Although this sentiment undoubtedly is true, he offers us no explanation of how the rules are biased and reproduced. Clearly, what is needed is a comprehensive analysis of how the educational system's curricula, pedagogy, and evaluative criteria[3] favor the interests of the upper classes.

Although such a formidable task has yet to be undertaken, the guiding theoretical concept for the endeavor has been provided by Bourdieu—the notion of cultural capital. To recapitulate: Bourdieu's theory maintains that the cultural capital of the lower classes—their manners, norms, dress, style of interaction, and linguistic facility—is devalued by the school, while the cultural capital of the upper classes is rewarded. As Halsey, Heath, and Ridge put it, "The ones who can receive what the school has to give are the ones who are already endowed with the requisite cultural attributes—with the appropriate cultural capital."[4] Although Bourdieu is primarily a theorist, Paul Dimaggio has substantiated Bourdieu's concept by analyzing data sets with measures for cultural attitudes, information, and activities for more than 2,900 eleventh grade boys and girls. He found that the impact of cultural capital on high school grades is "very significant," which confirms "rather dramatically the utility of the perspective advanced here [by Bourdieu]."[5]

Although neither Bernstein nor Nell Keddie self-consciously situates his or her empirical work within Bourdieu's theoretical framework, both provide analyses of actual classroom processes that enforce class-linked differences in educational achievement. These analyses fit nicely into Bourdieu's theoretical perspective. As we saw in Chapter 2, Bernstein actually demonstrates how class-based differences in speech patterns affect academic achievement and place working-class students like Frankie and Craig at a disadvantage with respect to their middle-class counterparts. Keddie's study also demonstrates how observed classroom phenomena—the different expectations teachers hold for students of different social origins, the determination of what counts as knowledge, teacher-student interaction, the tracking of courses—serve to handicap the performance of the lower classes.[6] As Karabel and Halsey remind us, because dominant social groups determine what is valued in the educational system, it should not surprise us that subordinate social groups are judged deficient by the criteria set by the powerful.[7]

These complex mechanisms of social reproduction are embedded deeply in the American educational system; they are well hidden, and thus the Brothers are unaware of the processes that work to hinder their performance. The Brothers believe in equality of opportunity and reject the idea that they have less of a chance to succeed in school than do middle- or upper-class students. Instead, the Brothers attribute their mediocre academic performance to personal inadequacy—laziness, stupidity, or lack of self-discipline.

(*all in separate interviews*)

SUPER: I would try—if I had more study skills, I bet you I'd be trying my hardest. I bet I'd be getting good grades. ... I dunno; I just can't seem to do it.

MOKEY: I try my best to do as good as anyone else. But there's some real smart people up there, plus I can't seem to get myself to work, especially during football. It's hard.

MIKE: I did horrible [my freshman year in high school]. I used to do good. I got all A's in grammar school. Now I'm doing shitty. I guess I started out smart and got stupider.

If one accepts the equality of opportunity line of reasoning, those who are not "making it" have only themselves to blame.

Clearly, the self-esteem of the Brothers suffers as a result of their inferior academic performance. A careful review of the literature on the effects of academic achievement and particularly track placement on students' sense of self, undertaken by Maureen Scully in a 1982 unpublished essay, reveals that although we can expect academic self-esteem to vary according to scholastic performance, students' general self-esteem is often more resilient. Because some high school students do not value academic achievement very highly and instead emphasize nonacademic activities and values, their general sense of self-esteem is sheltered from the negative onslaughts of academic failure.[8] The Brothers, however, care a great deal about their academic performance, and thus their general self-esteem is sensitive to academic failure.

In summary, the Brothers believe that American society is an open one; equality of opportunity is perceived as a reality. Moreover, schooling is regarded by the

Brothers as the means to economic success; consequently, they care about school, accept its norms and standards, and conform to its rules. As black lower-class students, however, the Brothers are lacking in the cultural capital rewarded by the school system—hence their poor academic achievement and placement into low tracks. The Brothers blame themselves for the mediocrity of their scholastic performance. The implications of this dynamic are important to an understanding of the overall process of social reproduction (which will be taken up in the next chapter).

Spurning the Achievement Ideology

The school experiences of the Hallway Hangers suggest that they are a group of disaffected, rebellious, undisciplined boys who have been labeled "emotionally disturbed," "learning impaired," and "slow." Beneath their uncooperative conduct and resistance, however, lies a logic that makes sense to these boys and informs their attitudes toward school.

The Hallway Hangers do not "buy" the achievement ideology because they foresee substantial barriers to their economic success, barriers this ideology fails to mention. It is important to note that the Hallway Hangers could reject the notion that equality of opportunity exists but accept the reasoning that school can still help them. Just because one does not have the same chance to succeed in school or on the job market as a middle- or upper-class student does not mean necessarily that achievement in school will be of no use in securing a job. Indeed, the connection between schooling and occupational achievement is so deeply ingrained in the minds of most Americans that it is difficult to imagine people completely rejecting it.

The Hallway Hangers, however, challenge the conventional wisdom that educational achievement translates into economic success. In their view of the opportunity structure, educational attainment is of little importance. Convinced that they are headed into jobs for which they do not need an education, the Hallway Hangers see little value in schooling. Jinks perfectly summarizes this view: "Even if you get a high school diploma, that don't mean shit. A lot of people say, 'Oh, you need it for that job.' You get a high school diploma, and they're still gonna give you a shitty job. So it's just a waste of time to get it."

Because this point of view runs counter to a deeply rooted, collective belief, it offends our sensibilities. In fact, however, it is a rational outlook based on experience. Jinks looks at his four older brothers, one of whom graduated from high school, and observes that the one with the diploma is no better off than the rest of them. The brother who struggled through the four years of high school is in the navy, as was another who did not graduate.

Stoney feels the same way. He insists that school performance has no effect on what kind of job one will get. He argues instead that "fucking experience, man, it comes in handy," particularly in the case of his current job in a pizza shop.

STONEY: So the very next day, I went looking for another job. Went into this place, told him my experience, made a few pies. That was it; he hired me on the spot. No application or nothing.

JM: No high school diploma.

STONEY: That's right. He didn't want one.

JM: For your goals, how would it help you to have a diploma?

STONEY: (*immediately*) It won't, cuz I don't need no diploma to open a store. Like I said, if you know how to do something, you do it. If you don't, you don't.

JM: Do you think it would help you at all if you got fired tomorrow, and you went up to another pizza shop somewhere? Do you think it would help you if you could show them a diploma?

STONEY: No, it wouldn't help me. They wanna see what you got, what you can do. If you can do the job. I used to always get hired on the spot. They'd look at me and be real surprised a young kid can make pizza this good.

Relevant job experience is much more important than educational attainment for landing a job in food preparation, at least in Stoney's experience. The same logic holds true for a prospective construction worker or auto mechanic.

Shorty draws on the experiences of his brothers, much like Jinks, to reach a similar conclusion regarding the efficacy of schooling. Two of Shorty's brothers have graduated from high school; one of these apparently graduated from college as well. Nevertheless, neither has been able to secure desired employment. The college graduate is working security at a local research firm. Despite relatively high educational achievement, "they don't seem to be getting anywhere," comments Shorty.

Frankie need only look at his own experience to assert that schooling is generally incapable of doing much for the Hallway Hangers. In interviews, he constantly reiterates this theme.

JM: Okay, so why is it that some kids, even coming from down here, will go to school, and they'll work real hard, go to all their classes, and do all the work? Why do some kids take that route?

FRANKIE: Well none of my friends take that route. But I dunno. I never took that route. But I guess, I dunno, they're dopes. I dunno, I guess, y'know, they fuckin' think if they go through high school and go through college, they think they're gonna get a job that's gonna pay fifty grand a year. Y'know, a white-collar job. I don't think that's true.

JM: Do you think how you do in school is gonna affect what kinda job you get?

FRANKIE: I got my diploma, and you don't even need that. Y'know, my diploma ain't doing me no good. It's sitting in my bottom drawer. Y'know, it ain't gonna help me. I got my diploma, and you don't even need that. ... All those Portegi [Portuguese] kids, they never went the fuck to school. Now they fuckin' got good jobs, cars—y'know, they fucking made it. They went out and fuckin' worked machinery and mechanics. So a high school diploma really isn't fucking shit.

(*in a separate interview*)

FRANKIE: They dropped out of school, and they got better fucking jobs than we do. I got my fuckin' diploma, and I ain't got jack shit. So it wasn't worth it for me to get my high school diploma. If I dropped out when I was sixteen—that was two years ago—I prob'ly would've already been through a job training program, and I'd already have a fucking job, saving me fucking money.

(*following an assertion by me that schooling is of some use on the labor market*)

FRANKIE: (*angrily*) But, but (*stuttering because he is upset*), still, I *did*, I did, I *did* the fucking, I did my school program, I went to school, I fuckin', I got my diploma, I went what you're s'posed to do. 'Cept you're s'posed to further your education—college and many more thousands of fucking dollars. Look how many fucking college graduates ain't got jobs. You know how fucking hard it is. They got educations. What the fuck they doin' with it? They ain't doin' shit. So fucking school ain't paying off for no one.

This last assertion—that school does not pay off for anybody—is not one to which all the Hallway Hangers would give their support. Even Frankie, in a less tense moment, would agree that some kids do "make it" and that success in school is a crucial ingredient for economic and social advancement. Nevertheless, although exaggerated in this case, Frankie's comment is indicative of the general attitude of the Hallway Hangers.

The Hallway Hangers do not maintain that schooling is incapable of doing anything for anyone because they all know Billy. Billy used to hang with the Hallway Hangers, getting high every day before, during, and after school, drinking excessively, and stealing cars. During his freshman year and the early part of his sophomore year, however, Billy underwent a number of personal crises out of which he emerged a much different person. Part of a large family, Billy had a father who was an alcoholic and has a mother who is mentally ill. In the span of a year and a half, Billy's mother was deemed unfit by the Department of Social Services to have custody of her children, so Billy moved in with his father, who died shortly thereafter. At about the same time, Billy's best friend was murdered brutally in an abandoned building a few blocks from Clarendon Heights. Billy, who currently lives in a three bedroom apartment in Clarendon Heights with his aunt and uncle, three cousins, and a baby nephew, is a senior at Lincoln High School. Goalie of the varsity hockey team and recipient of a special college scholarship for "individuals of extraordinary ability and need," Billy has switched from Oc. Ed. to the Fundamental School in preparation for college.

The view among the Hallway Hangers is that Billy is "making it." He is living testimony to the fact that schooling can work, that it can pay off. So the Hallway Hangers are not of the view that success in school is irrelevant but rather that the odds of "making it" are simply too slim to bet on. In what can be likened to a cost-benefit analysis, the Hallway Hangers, much like Willis's lads, conclude that the possibility of upward social mobility is not worth the price of obedience, conformity, and investment of substantial amounts of time, energy, and work in school.

For the Hallway Hangers, perhaps the biggest cost of going to school every day is the deferred income from full-time work. As Giroux reminds us, the economic issue often plays the crucial role in a working-class student's decision whether to attend school full-time, part-time, or not at all.[9] The issue of potential work earnings entered into all the boys' decisions to drop out of school. Chris and Jinks comment on the tension between school and employment directly.

(*in a joint interview*)

CHRIS: Jay, lemme tell you how I feel about school. I wanna go to school; I'd like to go til like 11:30 and then at about twelve o'clock work until about five. Y'know, so I could go to school plus make some money.

JINKS: You won't like that brother, cuz that's what I do. That's what I do. He'll start going to work, getting a little money in his pocket, and he'll always want more.

(*later in the same interview*)

CHRIS: So Jay, people should fucking give us a break, y'know? (*laughing*) Pay us to go to school, y'know?

JM: How would that work?

CHRIS: Give us forty bucks a week to go to school 'til twelve o'clock. At twelve we go to work and make about fifty bucks.

JM: What would be in it for them?

CHRIS: They'd get a lot of people to go (*laughing*). They'd get a helluva lot more than they got now, I'm tellin' ya.

CHRIS: On Friday, I'd say, "Oh *yeah!* Got my job."

JINKS: Got my ounce all paid for.

This last comment is revealing. The world that the Hallway Hangers inhabit, with its preponderance of drugs and alcohol, demands financial resources. The pressure to come up with money is keenly felt by all these boys, a pressure to which Slick alludes often.

SLICK: (*motioning to doorway #13*) Hey, everyone out there has a goal. Their goal is one thing and that's money. You hafta have money, to make it. ... That's what depresses them. That's what puts them into the pressure situation. They hafta make money; they know they hafta do it. The name of the game is money. You hafta get it. If you don't get it, there's no way you're gonna be able to do anything. You hafta make it.

Locked into the present by the pressing need for money, the Hallway Hangers, in contrast to middle-class teenagers, do not have the resources to bide their time while long-range educational or occupational plans come to fruition. Moreover, believing they have missed out on the indulgences of American consumerism, they are starved for immediate financial success.

(*in a group interview*)

SLICK: Y'know what it is, Jay? All of us down here, we just don't wanna make a buck; we wanna make a fast buck. We want it *now*. Right fucking now. And you know why? Not cuz we're stupid and can't wait for anything, but because we've never had it.

SHORTY: Fuckin' right. We're all poor as shit.

SLICK: No one in this room has thirty bucks in his pocket. Fuckin' right we want it. We've never had it.

The desire of these boys to go for the fast buck, to focus only on the present, becomes understandable in light of the uncertainty of the future and their bona fide belief that they may be in prison or dead.

In considering the experiences of the Brothers in school, we have seen that the effects of schooling on their self-esteem are significant. The Hallway Hangers also feel a measure of personal inadequacy with respect to their dismal educational attainment, but for them schooling is merely tangential to the overall experience of being a lower-class teenager in an urban setting. Hence, little of their self-esteem is tied up in school; academic performance has less effect on their sense of self. It is possible, however, that this apparent indifference toward school is itself in part a defense mechanism that protects the boys from assaults on their self-respect. Evidence for this type of failure-avoidance strategy has been documented in a number of quantitative studies of students' self-esteem.[10] For the Hallway Hangers, the prospects of failure in school and the accompanying feelings of inadequacy are further reasons not to invest themselves in education; the potential threat to self-esteem is another item on the cost side of the equation.

The cost of deferred work earnings, the price of obedience and conformity to rules and authority that run counter to the peer group's ethos, the risk of failure, and the investment of time and energy all make up the costs of school involvement for the Hallway Hangers. On the benefit side are improved prospects for social mobility resulting from educational achievement. For the Hallway Hangers, who see through the achievement ideology and have little faith in the efficacy of schooling, the improved prospects for social mobility are not worth the price that schooling exacts. Although their approach to school assuredly is not based on a rational cost-benefit analysis, these considerations do underlie their orientation toward education.

This logic dictates that the Hallway Hangers drop out of school or at least minimize their involvement with it. That most of the Hallway Hangers pursue this latter course is evident from their paths into the less demanding programs at Lincoln High School, such as BTS, the Adjustment Class, Enterprise Co-op, and the after-school program. With teachers for whom they have more respect, fewer rules, and lighter academic workloads, entry into these alternative programs sometimes minimizes the costs to the point where schooling becomes worthwhile. Both high school graduates (Boo-Boo and Frankie) and the one boy currently enrolled in school (Steve) are or were in such alternative programs. Even for the boys in these programs, however, schooling often is not worth the price that must be paid, and thus most have dropped out. For Frankie to stay in school, for instance, the added benefit of "keeping my moms happy" was necessary to swing the balance in favor of schooling.

Whereas at first glance the rebellious behavior, low academic achievement, and high dropout rate of the Hallway Hangers seem to stem from lack of self-discipline, dullness of wit, laziness, or an inability to project themselves into the future, the actual causes of their rejection of school are quite different. Their unwillingness to partake of the educational system stems from an assessment of the costs and benefits of playing the game. Their view is not that schooling is incapable of propelling them up the ladder of social mobility, but that the chances are too slim to warrant the attempt. The Hallway Hangers' alienation from school rests not so much on a perceived lack of the means to succeed in school as of the means to convert that success into success on the labor market. Convinced that they are headed into dead-end jobs regardless of their educational attainment, the Hallway Hangers dismiss school as irrelevant.

Given this logic, the oppositional behavior of the Hallway Hangers is a form of resistance to an institution that cannot deliver on its promise of upward social mobility for all students. Furthermore, Lincoln High School, like almost all American schools, is essentially a middle-class institution. Its curriculum, grading system, and disciplinary code all reward middle-class traits, values, and skills. In coping with the difficulties of growing up poor in America, the Hallway Hangers have developed a set of survival skills of which they are very proud. These skills, however, are accorded little or no recognition in the school setting; instead, students must relinquish their street identities and move beyond their neighborhood ties. The Hallway Hangers resent the fact that the school, because of its middle-class orientation, ignores the skills they have picked up on the street. Thus, they do anything they can to express themselves in an institution that denies and violates their cultural identities.

The maturity and independence the boys have gained from years of hard living in Clarendon Heights clash with the authoritarian structure of the school. Teachers, as the agents of repression, are especially difficult for the Hallway Hangers to tolerate.

(*all in separate interviews*)

CHRIS: I hate the fucking teachers. I don't like someone always telling me what the fuck to do. Especially the way they do it. They make you feel like shit. I couldn't take their shit.

SLICK: It's with the maturity here—you wanna do what you want to do, and you don't want anyone to tell you what to do.

JINKS: You gotta get high to go to class. You gotta, to listen to the teachers talk their shit. Tell you, "Do this, do that, and do that" and a lot of people just say, "Fuck you. You do it yourself. I ain't doing shit for you."

Although teacher condescension and the institution's demand for unquestioning obedience to authority are sore points, the Hallway Hangers' resentment is not focused on teachers as a generic category as much as it is directed at middle-class teachers in particular. The Hallway Hangers constantly refer to the perceived social class disjuncture between themselves and the schools' teaching staff. Jimmy Sullivan, who comes from the same class as these students and still displays many characteristics of that class culture, is respected because "he doesn't take no shit from anybody," including students. The middle-class teachers at the King School, in contrast, are held in contempt by Frankie because "they swore and shit, but you just told them to shut the fuck up and they shut up." The Hallway Hangers are willing to accept the authority of Sullivan and Harry Jones, a former resident of public housing. The same authority in the hands of other teachers, however, draws nothing but scorn from the boys.

(*in a group interview*)

JM: What about the teachers? You all seem to like Sullivan and Jones. What's the difference between them and the rest of 'em?

CHRIS: The other ones are all pussies.

SHORTY: Cuz they don't know how to deal with us kids.

FRANKIE: And the reason Harry Jones is cool is cuz Harry was brought up in the city his whole life; he used to live in Emerson Towers and his brothers and shit—they ain't all fucking angels, y'know. That's why he's cool. ... And, y'know, there's a couple of other teachers that are fuckin' from around here and know what the fuck is happening. Y'know, but other teachers, they live in the suburbs and shit. They're coming into a city to work. They don't know what the fuck city kids are.

(in a discussion with Shorty and Slick)

SLICK: Certain teachers you can talk to up there. But most of the teachers that are up there, a lot of them are too rich, y'know what I mean? They have money, and they don't give a fuck about nobody. They don't know how it's like to hafta come to school late. "Why'd you come to school late?" "I had to make sure my brother was in school. I had to make sure certain things—I had to make sure that there was breakfast."

SHORTY: Responsibilities. See, that's what I mean. Now, the teachers will not understand. He ain't got no father, right? The father ain't living there, just like me. He's the oldest kid now. And he has big responsibilities at home because his brothers are growing up and his sister—he's got to keep an eye on 'em. Now you gotta do all that, and you got teachers giving you a hard fucking time?

SLICK: It's tough.

SHORTY: You got teachers like Harry Jones. They know; they understand where you come from, that you're trying to support your family.

SLICK: Like Harry Jones, when I got into his class, he talked to me, y'know? He'd understand what I'm doing.

SHORTY: He grew up around here all his life.

(in a group interview)

FRANKIE: Y'know, I'll admit I fucked up, y'know? Hey man, I got fucking problems, y'know? And the teacher just don't want to deal with it. Well, fuck them.

(in a discussion with Jinks and Chris)

JM: Do any of the teachers know the people?

JINKS: A few. Like Harry Jones, Jimmy Sullivan. All the rest are all bitchy. They don't understand us; they don't try to understand us.

Similar effects of social class differences between teachers and students have been found in other studies. In his analysis of the culture of a community college, Howard London found that subtle class antagonism between students and teachers was at the root of problems in conduct, absenteeism, and negative attitudes on the part of both toward the school.[11] The expressed antipathy of the Hallway Hangers toward middle-class teachers should not surprise us, for they are the most obvious symbols of the middle-class orientation of the school.

The school demands respect for its staff. But for the Hallway Hangers to show respect or even deference for individuals who by their standards do not deserve it is a real struggle. Thus, in trying to understand the approach the Hallway Hangers take toward school, we also must be cognizant of the costs involved in meeting the school's requirement of respect for teachers (loss of self-respect, condemnation from peers, forfeiture of feelings of ascendancy over other students).

The Brothers do not have problems with respecting teachers, for in many ways the teachers symbolize what the boys hope to become. Many of the Brothers aspire to middle-class jobs and, in any case, harbor no ill will toward middle-class values and norms. Indeed, the Brothers, consciously or unconsciously, emulate the middle-class traits of the teachers and endeavor to embody middle-class values. This phenomenon, termed "anticipatory socialization" by Robert Merton,[12] is an important source of dissimilarity between the Brothers and the Hallway Hangers.

In marked contrast to the Hallway Hangers, the Brothers feel that they are headed up the ladder of social mobility and believe that schooling is going to get them there. That two peer groups of the same social class, indeed from the very same neighborhood, hold such radically different attitudes toward school presents a challenging puzzle to the sociologist. In the next chapter, I attempt to meet this challenge directly.

Notes

1. See, for example, studies by the following: David Dillon, "Does the School Have a Right to Its Own Language?" *The English Journal* 69 (April 1980):1460–1474; Warren G. Findley and Mirian M. Bryan, "Ability Grouping: A Review of the Literature," Part 3 (Washington, D.C.: Office of Education, 1970); Melvin L. Kohn, *Class and Conformity: A Study in Values* (Chicago: University of Chicago Press, 1977); Charles Miller, John A. McLaughlin, John Madden, and Norman M. Chansky, "Socioeconomic Class and Teacher Bias," *Psychological Reports* 23 (1968):806–810; Ray C. Rist, "Student Social Class and Teacher Expectations: The Self-Fulfilling Prophecy in Ghetto Education," *Harvard Educational Review* 40 (August 1970):411–451; Morris Rosenberg and Roberta G. Simmons, *Black and White Self-Esteem: The Urban School Child* (Washington, D.C.: American Sociological

Association, 1971); and Charles B. Schultz and Roger H. Sherman, "Social Class, Development, and Differences in Reinforcer Effectiveness," *Review of Educational Research* 46 (1976):25–59.

2. Olive Banks, *The Sociology of Education* (London: B. T. Batsfield, 1976), pp. 68, 69.

3. These are the three major areas Bernstein has identified as crucial to our understanding of the socially determined value placed on various types of knowledge. See *Class, Codes and Control*, vol. 3 (London: Routledge and Kegan Paul, 1975), p. 85.

4. A. H. Halsey, A. F. Heath, and J. M. Ridge, *Origins and Destinations* (Oxford: Clarendon Press, 1980), p. 7.

5. Paul Dimaggio, "Cultural Capital and Social Success," *American Sociological Review* 47 (April 1982):189–201.

6. Nell Keddie, "Classroom Knowledge," in *Knowledge and Control*, ed. Michael F. D. Young (London: Collier, 1972), pp. 133–160.

7. Jerome Karabel and A. H. Halsey, eds., *Power and Ideology in Education* (New York: Oxford University Press, 1977), p. 67.

8. Maureen Anne Scully, "Coping with Meritocracy" (Thesis, Harvard College, 1982), pp. 85–101.

9. Henry A. Giroux, *Theory and Resistance in Education* (London: Heinemann Educational Books, 1983), p. 95.

10. See the following: Viktor Gecas, "Contexts of Socialization," in *Social Psychology: Sociological Perspectives*, eds. Morris Rosenberg and Ralph H. Turner (New York: Basic Books, 1981); Rosenberg and Simmons, *Black and White Self-Esteem;* Morris Rosenberg, *Conceiving the Self* (New York: Basic Books, 1979); Morris Rosenberg, "The Self-Concept: Social Product and Social Force," in *Social Psychology: Sociological Perspectives;* Richard J. Shavelson, Judith J. Hubner, and George C. Stanton, "Self-Concept: Validation of Construct Interpretations," *Review of Educational Research* 46 (Summer 1976):407–411; Arthur L. Stinchcombe, *Rebellion in a High School* (Chicago: Quadrangle Books, 1964).

11. Howard B. London, *The Culture of a Community College* (New York: Praeger, 1978).

12. Robert K. Merton and Alice S. Rossi, "Contributions to the Theory of Reference Group Behavior" in *Social Theory and Social Structure* (New York: Free Press, 1968), pp. 319–322.

7

Leveled Aspirations: Social Reproduction Takes Its Toll

WITH THE ETHNOGRAPHIC DESCRIPTION from the preceding chapters at our disposal, we now can attempt to analyze the forces that influence the aspirations of these two groups of boys from Clarendon Heights. That many boys in both groups do not even aspire to middle-class jobs is a powerful indication of how class inequality is reproduced in American society. These youths' prospects for socioeconomic advancement are doomed before they even get started; most of the boys do not even get a foothold on the ladder of social mobility. In this chapter, the task before us is to illuminate in as much detail and depth as possible the process of social reproduction as it is lived by the Hallway Hangers and the Brothers.

The regulation of aspirations is perhaps the most significant of all the mechanisms contributing to social reproduction; however, aspirations themselves are largely a function of structural mechanisms that should be considered when possible. Mention already has been made of the effects of tracking and the school's valuation of the cultural capital of the upper classes, both of which influence aspirations but also have independent effects on reproducing class structure. An additional and essential component of social reproduction is the process by which individuals in a stratified social order come to accept their own position and the inequalities of the social order as legitimate.

Whereas force and coercion often have ensured the cohesion of societies and the maintenance of oppressive relationships, ideology is more important in fulfilling this function in contemporary America. In particular, the achievement ideology is a powerful force in the legitimation of inequality and, ultimately, in social reproduction. In short, this ideology maintains that individual merit and achievement are the fair and equitable sources of inequality of American society. If merit is the basis for the distribution of rewards, then members of the lower classes attribute their subordinate position in the social order to personal deficiencies. In this way, inequality is legitimated.[1]

In their theoretical formulations, both Weber and Marx touch on the role of ideology in the maintenance of social cohesion. In Weber's terms, ideology is the "myth" by which the powerful ensure belief in the validity of their domination. "Every highly privileged group develops the myth of its natural superiority. Under conditions of stable distribution of power ... that myth is accepted by the negatively privileged strata."[2] Although Marx considered economics the major determinant in the perpetuation of class relations, he discusses the function of ideology in preserving exploitative relations in capitalist societies. Ideology, which is proffered to the subordinate classes as an accurate depiction of the social order, is actually a "false consciousness," an apparently true but essentially illusory set of views that disguises and distorts the true workings of the capitalist system. The ruling class, in order to justify its dominance, "is compelled ... to represent its interest as the common interest of all the members of society. ... It has to give its ideas the form of universality, and represent them as the only rational, universally valid ones."[3] Thus, by obscuring the truth of conflictual relations and exploitation, ideology serves to make capitalist societies appear legitimate.[4]

In contemporary America, the educational system, by sorting students according to ostensibly meritocratic criteria, plays a crucial role in the legitimation of inequality. Because the school deals in the currency of academic credentials, its role in the reproduction of inequality is obscured. Students believe that they succeed or fail in school on the basis of merit. By internalizing the blame for failure, students lose their self-esteem and then accept their eventual placement in low-status jobs as the natural outcome of their own shortcomings. If individuals are convinced that they are responsible for their low position in society, then criticism of the social order by the subordinate classes is deflected. The process of social reproduction goes on, unscrutinized and unchallenged.

If this legitimation function is working, then members of the lower classes will suffer from low self-esteem, which originally was developed in the school and then carried into later life to reconcile them to their position. In gauging the degree to which lower-class individuals accept the social order and their position in it as legitimate, we must determine whether they attribute their inferior social position to personal inadequacy or to external forces as well.

The Hallway Hangers: Internalizing Probabilities, Rescuing Self-Esteem

According to Bourdieu, the aspirations of the Hallway Hangers should reflect their objective probabilities for upward mobility. Immersed as they are in their social universe at the bottom of the class structure, their subjective hopes should be as modest as their objective chances are slim. Indeed, this is the case. The Hallway Hangers view their prospects for substantial upward mobility as very remote, which accounts for their low occupational aspirations. Drawing on the experiences of their families, and on their own encounters with the job market, the boys' appraisals of the possibility for social upgrading often preclude the formation of any aspirations at all. Moreover, the available evidence indicates that the boys' parents do not intercede significantly in their children's aspiration formation. In general, the parents of the Hallway Hangers have little influence in their sons' lives. Like most parents, they want the best for their children, but if Stoney's mother is any indication, they also are hesitant to encourage excessively high aspirations in their sons for fear of setting them up for disappointment.

Although the families of the Hallway Hangers have a pervasive influence on their aspirations, so have their own work experiences. All the Hallway Hangers have held summertime employment since they have been of working age. Apart from Steve, they are searching for full-time work. In their struggles to find meaningful, stable employment all have been thwarted. Invariably, once they think they finally have found a decent job, the opportunity falls through. This type of firsthand experience on the job market further deflates any illusions they might have had about the openness of the opportunity structure. When a boy searches in vain for work that pays seventy-five cents more than minimum wage, his estimation of the prospects for significant upward mobility is bound to be low.

In addition to family and work, school has an important, if less direct, influence on aspirations. Because the school devalues the cultural capital of the Hallway Hangers, their chances for academic success are diminished substantially. Although the Hallway Hangers do not see the intricacies of this process taking place, half have remarked that students from "higher" social backgrounds have a better chance to do well in school. The Hallway Hangers have seen their older siblings fail in school; they see their friends fail as well. Even their Clarendon Heights peers who try to succeed in school meet with only modest success; for verification of this the Hallway Hangers need only look to the Brothers. Thus, the Hallway Hangers question their own capacity to perform well in school, a view that informs their assessment of the chances for social mobility.

Of more importance is the Hallway Hangers' belief that performance in school is of only tangential importance in securing a job. They challenge the widely held notion that success in school translates into success on the job market. But if they feel that schooling will not boost them up the ladder of social mobility, what will? In essence, the Hallway Hangers see a ladder with no rungs on it, or at least none they can reach. They believe that the educational system cannot deliver on its promise of upward social mobility for those who perform well in school. Thus, in part, their leveled aspirations reflect their feeling that schooling is incapable of doing much for them.

In concentrating on this point, however, it is easy to miss some of the intraschool processes that affect the aspirations of the Hallway Hangers. The school is distinctive not for what it does but for what it fails to do.

Lincoln School officials are aware of the process of social reproduction (although they would not conceptualize it in these terms). Bruce Davis, a young, enthusiastic, and dedicated guidance counselor in the Occupational Education Program acknowledges social reproduction as a simple fact of life.

BD: These kids [those enrolled in the Oc. Ed. Program] go directly into hard jobs. They're generally from homes where people are laborers. I mean, kids who go to college are from families whose parents went to college. That's how it works, it seems to me. That's where these kids are coming from; they're geared to manual labor jobs, like their brothers, sisters, fathers, uncles, whatever—mothers, like the jobs they have.

Rather than attempting to use the resources of the school to mitigate this process, school officials seem content to let it unfold unhindered. The Oc. Ed. Program, for example, is designed to prepare its students for the rigors of manual work.

BD: We constantly stress to the kids that they have to be responsible, reliable, and dependable, that they can't be a screw-off. Really, we're just trying to make the kids accountable for themselves. Y'know, most of these kids won't go to college. When they leave here, they can't sleep 'til eleven and then get up and go to three classes. They've really got to be disciplined. They're going to be right out there working. In Oc. Ed., that's really what we're all about. We're trying to simulate a work experience, make class just like a job. It's not just their competency that matters; to be a good worker, your willingness to cooperate, your attitude, is so important.

Bowles and Gintis's argument that working-class students are socialized for working-class jobs and that the social relations of school mirror those of the workplace hardly could be better substantiated.

My point here is not that the school, consciously or unconsciously, levels the aspirations of some students but that it accepts and exacerbates already existing differences in aspirations. By requiring the Hallway Hangers, as eighth graders, to choose their educational program, the school solidifies what is often a vaguely felt and ill-defined preference for manual work or a desire simply to be with one's friends into a definite commitment to a future in manual work. The decision is essentially their own, and it makes a good deal of sense considering that experience in a trade ostensibly will be of some advantage on a difficult job market. Slick's decision to enter the Oc. Ed. Program, despite his high level of achievement in grammar school, typifies the quandary of these boys. Very few middle-class students with decent grades would select a vocational program, but Slick felt the need to do so in order to improve his chances of getting work after graduation.

Although the boys chose their various programs, there are grounds for skepticism about the degree to which this was a completely uncoerced choice. James

Rosenbaum, in his 1976 study of a working-class high school, found that guidance counselors and teachers applied subtle and not-so-subtle techniques to channel students into particular tracks and keep them there, sometimes against the students' wishes. But the school officials did this in such a manner that both the youngsters and their parents believed it was a free choice.[5]

Lincoln High School boasts a more liberal educational philosophy than that of Rosenbaum's school, so we hardly can extrapolate his findings to Lincoln High. Nevertheless, in response to a question concerning the process by which students choose their program, Wallace responded, "Oh, that's done for them in grammar school." Sensing that I had picked up on the "for them," she hastily went on to say that it is a process that initially involves a conference between the eighth grade counselor and the student as well as parents. "According to however they performed in grammar school, the counselor will come up with a suggested schedule and send it home for approval. Of course, the parent can disagree and pick other courses."

Resolution of the extent to which this is a decision of self-selection requires detailed ethnographic data on the transition from grammar school to Lincoln High, without which we must stop short of Rosenbaum's conclusion that the school exacerbates and actually creates inequality by its discriminatory tracking procedures. There is no doubt, however, that the school, by requiring that such choices be made at a young age, reinforces existing differences in aspirations.

In trying to understand the impact of family, work, and schooling on the aspirations of the Hallway Hangers, Bourdieu's theory that the habitus engenders aspirations that reflect objective probabilities seems accurate. According to Bourdieu and Passeron:

> The structure of the objective chances of social upgrading according to class of origin and, more precisely, the structure of the chances of upgrading through education, conditions agents' dispositions towards education and towards upgrading through education—dispositions which in turn play a determining role in defining the likelihood of entering education, adhering to its norms and succeeding in it, hence the likelihood of social upgrading.[6]

But the concept of the internalization of objective probabilities, because it limits the scope for human agency and creativity, has little explanatory value when we consider the influence of the peer group on the Hallway Hangers. This is a serious deficiency because according to our ethnographic sketch the peer group, especially for the Hallway Hangers, is of primary importance in these boys' lives.

In a country in which success is largely measured by income and occupational status, the Hallway Hangers have a problem. Unemployed, living in public housing, at the very bottom of the socioeconomic spectrum, they are regarded as failures, both by others and, at least to some extent, by themselves, a phenomenon Sennett and Cobb document for working-class people in general in *The Hidden Injuries of Class*.[7] The Hallway Hangers have been enrolled in programs that are designed for "fuck-ups" (as Mike of the Brothers put it), have been placed in the lowest educational tracks, and have received failing grades; all these constitute part of the emotional attack the boys suffer in school. The Hallway Hangers may have little of their self-esteem tied up in school, but, as Scully argues, they cannot help but feel "a judgment of academic inferiority cast upon them, be it by teachers, classmates, or their seemingly objective computerized report card."[8] The subculture of the Hallway Hangers must be understood as an attempt by its members to insulate themselves from these negative judgments and to provide a context in which some semblance of self-respect and dignity can be maintained.

To characterize the subculture of the Hallway Hangers as a defense mechanism against these onslaughts to their self-esteem, however, would be incomplete. Scully argues that most student countercultures have both defensive and independent features;[9] studies by Sennett and Cobb, Stinchcombe, and Willis verify this duality. The Hallway Hangers, like Willis's lads, have their own distinct set of values. These values are indigenous to the working class; they do not arise simply in opposition to the school. The Hallway Hangers' valuation of physical toughness, emotional resiliency, quick-wittedness, masculinity, loyalty, and group solidarity point to a subculture with its own norms, which are passed on from the older to the younger boys. Frankie describes how the subculture of the Hallway Hangers is learned and passed on.

(in a group interview)

FRANKIE: We were all brought up, all we seen is our older brothers and that gettin' into trouble and goin' to jail and all that shit. Y'know, seeing people— brothers and friends and shit—dying right in front of your face. You seen all the drugs, Jay. Well, this place used to be a thousand times worse than it is now. We grew up, it was all our older brothers doing this. We seen many fucking drugs, all the drinking. They fucking go; that group's gone. The next group came. It's our brothers that are a little older, y'know, twenty-something years old. They started doing crime. And when you're young, you look up to people. You have a person, everybody has a person they look up to. And he's doing this, he's drinking, he's doing that, he's doing drugs, he's ripping off people. Y'know, he's making good fucking money, and it looks like he's doing good, y'know? So bang. Now it's our turn. We're here. What we gonna do when all we seen is fuckin' drugs, alcohol, fighting, this and that, no one going to school?

By providing a realm in which to be bad and tough are the main criteria for respect, the peer group of the Hallway Hangers reverses conventional cultural norms. Like almost all subcultures, however, the Hallway Hangers cannot escape the dominant culture's definitions of success. No matter how strong and insular the group, contact with the dominant culture, especially through school and work, is inevitable. Listening to the Hallway Hangers describe their descent through the school's programs, one detects a sense of shame, despite all their bravado. For Frankie to report that he finally found work, but as a temporary employee with the city's sanitation department as a garbage collector, clearly involved quite a swallowing of pride.

This inability on the part of a subculture to shelter itself completely from the dominant culture's values and norms has been documented widely: Willis's lads are pained by teachers' insults; the children Sennett and Cobb describe as having developed their own "badges of dignity" still have much of their sense of self-worth tied up in academic performance and teacher approval; and, the inside world of black streetcorner men who congregate at Tally's Corner in Elliot Liebow's study "is no more impervious to the values, sentiments and beliefs of the larger society than it is to the blue welfare checks or to the agents of the larger society, such as the policeman, the police informer, the case worker, and the landlord."[10]

Despite the fact that the Hallway Hangers' subculture affords its members only partial protection from the negative judgments of the dominant culture, it does provide a setting wherein a person can salvage some self-respect. The Hallway Hangers, who have developed alternative criteria for success, understand their situation in a way that defends their status; they manage to see themselves differently from the way the rest of society sees them. This is not entirely a self-protective psychological inversion; their ways of understanding their situation also are real. The Hallway Hangers are not living a fantasy. The world of the street exists— it is the unfortunate underside of the American economic system, the inevitable shadow accompanying a society that is not as open as it advertises. Moreover, the Hallway Hangers *are* physically hard, emotionally durable, and boldly enterprising. Those of us who are supposed to be succeeding by conventional standards need only venture into their world for the briefest moment to feel as though our badges of success are about as substantive and "real" in that environment as the emperor's new clothes.

The subculture of the Hallway Hangers is at odds with the dominant culture. The path to conventional success leads in one direction; the path to a redefined success lies in another. A boy cannot tread both paths simultaneously; orthodox success demands achievement in school, a feat that only can be accomplished by respecting the authority of teachers, which is inconsistent with the Hallway Hangers' alternative value scheme. All the current members of the Hallway Hangers have chosen, more or less definitively, to tread the path to a redefined success. (It should be remembered, however, that this choice is not an altogether free one; the Hallway Hangers see the path to conventional success as blocked by numerous obstacles.) Nevertheless, some do choose the path to conventional achievement; Billy, who expects to attend college next year, is being studied carefully by the Hallway Hangers as a testament to what they may have passed up.

The decision to break away from the group and pursue conventional success is not just a matter of individual calculation, however. More complicated forces are at work, forces that strain the individualistic orientation of American society. The solidarity of the Hallway Hangers is very strong. We have seen, for example, that the sense of cohesion and bonds of loyalty are such that Slick would not leave Shorty at the scene of a crime, preferring to be arrested himself. These communitarian values act to restrain individual Hallway Hangers from breaking away from the group and trying to "make it" conventionally. Slick, for example, scores very well on standardized tests, attended Latin Academy for a year, and is very articulate. Despite class-based barriers to success, he had a relatively good chance of "making it." But Slick also demonstrates the strongest sense of loyalty to the group. In a group interview, for example, he commented, as the rest of the group nodded their heads in agreement, that "money is secondary to friendship; I think friendship is more important than money." Jinks realizes that this loyalty can constrain individuals from striving for upward social mobility.

(*in an individual interview*)

JM: Do you have anything else to add about kids' attitudes down here?

JINKS: I'd say everyone more or less has the same attitudes towards school: fuck it. Except the bookworms—people who just don't hang around outside and drink, get high, who sit at home—they're the ones who get the education.

JM: And they just decided for themselves?

JINKS: Yup.

JM: So why don't more people decide that way?

JINKS: Y'know what it is Jay? We all don't break away because we're too tight. Our friends are important to us. Fuck it. If we can't make it together, fuck it. Fuck it all.

One of the forces operating to keep the Hallway Hangers from striking out on their own is the realization that there is little chance of their making it as a group and to leave the others behind is to violate the code of loyalty. Recall how Slick contrasts the Hallway Hangers and the "rich little boys from the suburbs." "How do you think they got rich? By fucking people over. We don't do that to each other. We're too fucking tight. We're a group. We don't think like them. We think for all of us." This group loyalty rests on some very strong communitarian values and vaguely parallels an affirmation of class solidarity over individual interests, a point to which I shall return.

With respect to the influence of the peer group on social reproduction, there are some complicated processes at work that Bourdieu's theory fails to capture. Conceptually "flat," the model Bourdieu develops with Passeron struggles to account for the resistance and nonconformity characteristic of the Hallway Hangers' subculture. To some extent, membership in the subculture of the Hallway Hangers tends to level one's aspirations. Although influenced by the definitions of the dominant culture, the value scheme of the peer group devalues conventional success; the norm among the Hallway Hangers is low aspirations. This ethos, passed down from older to younger boys, is a powerful force on the individual. In addition to the general climate of the peer group, there is a tendency among the Hallway Hangers to resist raised aspirations because to act on them would involve breaking one's ties and leaving the group, a transgression of the code of loyalty.

It is possible to examine the workings of the process of legitimation as it applies to the Hallway Hangers. We have seen that their self-esteem is relatively resilient to poor academic performance, for little of each boy's sense of self is invested in the school. In addition, the peer group subculture affords the Hallway Hangers additional protection for their self-esteem and alternative ways of generating self-esteem through the value system of the group. Although failure in school is psychologically debilitating for the Hallway Hangers in some ways, their self-esteem is partially buttressed from the assaults of the educational system.

If legitimation were functioning smoothly, the Hallway Hangers, in addition to low self-esteem, would internalize their failure and point only to personal inadequacy as the cause of their plight. But such is not the case; the Hallway Hangers realize that internal and external factors contribute to their low social position. Although they do blame themselves to some degree for their failure, they also recognize external barriers to success.

When the Hallway Hangers talk, one almost can feel the struggle being waged in their minds between the tenets of the achievement ideology and the lessons distilled from their own experiences. This tension produces a deep-seated ambivalence. At times the boys are prone to take full responsibility for their dismal social status, but on other occasions they blame external obstacles to their social advancement. Boo-Boo reproaches himself at the beginning of an interview ("I just screwed up") but later maintains that boys from a middle-class neighborhood have an advantage when it comes to achieving social and economic prosperity. Other boys hold a similarly dichotomous outlook.

CHRIS: I guess I just don't have what it takes.

(*in a separate interview*)

CHRIS: We don't get a fair shake and shit.

FRANKIE: We're all just fucking burnouts. ... We never did good anyways. ... We've just fucked up.

(*in the same interview*)

FRANKIE: If I had the fucking money to start out with like some of these fucking rich kids, I'd be a millionaire. Fucking right, I would be.

SHORTY: I'd go in there, and I'd try my hardest to do the work, right? I'd get a lot of problems wrong cuz I never had the brains much really, right? That's what's keepin' me back.

(*in a different interview*)

SHORTY: Hey, you can't get no education around here unless if you're fucking rich, y'know? You can't get no education. … And you can't get a job once they find out where you come from. "You come from Clarendon Heights? Oh shit. It's them kids again."

The Hallway Hangers see through parts of the achievement ideology, but at some level they accept the aspersions it casts on lower-class individuals, including themselves. However, although the Hallway Hangers do not escape emotional injury, neither does the social order emerge unscathed. In the eyes of the Hallway Hangers the opportunity structure is not open, a view that prevents them from accepting their position and the inequalities of the social order as completely legitimate.

Although the legitimation of inequality could be working more efficiently with respect to the Hallway Hangers, the whole process is not ready to collapse. Like the lads in Willis's study, these boys' insights into the true workings of the system are only partial, and often vague and ill-defined at that. Moreover, although they are cognizant of external barriers to success, the Hallway Hangers raise no fundamental challenge to the fairness or efficacy of the system as a whole. For the most part, in the absence of any systematic critique of capitalism, the Hallway Hangers simply are plagued by a sense of unfairness and the uneasy conviction that the rules of the contest are biased against them. Thus, there is a discrepancy between their strongly felt conviction that they are getting "the short end of the stick," and their inability to understand fully how this is so.

They conveniently fill this gap with racism. The Hallway Hangers seem to believe that if they are stuck with the short end of the stick, it must be because the "niggers" have the long end. Their feelings of impotence, frustration, and anger are subsumed in their hatred of blacks and in their conviction that their own plight somehow has been exacerbated, if not caused, by the alleged economic and social advancement of black Americans. Recall how Shorty attributed his brother's unemployment to the "Spics and niggers." Frankie and Smitty account for their predicament with one reason.

SMITTY: All the fuckin' niggers are getting the jobs.

FRANKIE: Fuckin' right. That's why we're hanging here now with empty pockets.

Affirmative action affords the Hallway Hangers a handy explanation for their own demise. Slick, despite his perceptiveness, succumbs to the same misunderstanding. Although his decision to quit school was undoubtedly the result of many factors, Slick insists that he dropped out of school solely because of supposed favoritism toward black students at Lincoln High. In a different interview, Slick begins by accusing the school of class-based prejudice but muddles the issue by suddenly bringing blacks into the discussion: "They favor all them fucking rich kids at that school. All the rich people. They fucking baby 'em. They baby all the fucking niggers up there."

This confusion between class bias and alleged reverse racial discrimination is symptomatic of the Hallway Hangers' outlook. By directing their resentment at affirmative action and those who benefit from it, the Hallway Hangers can spare themselves blame, but then the social order also is spared any serious scrutiny. In Willis's terms, racism is a serious "limitation" on the cultural outlook of the Hallway Hangers. Just as the lads' reversal of the usual valuation of mental versus manual labor prevents them from seeing their placement into dead-end, low-paying jobs as a form of class domination, so does the Hallway Hangers' racism obscure reality.

Thus, the Hallway Hangers harbor contradictory and ambivalent beliefs about the legitimacy of their social position. Their identification of class-based barriers to success and their impression that the deck is unfairly stacked against them, insights that could catalyze the development of a radical political consciousness, are derailed by their racism. On the one hand, the Hallway Hangers puncture the individualistic orientation of American society by their adoption of communitarian values to the point where a realization that the entire group cannot "make it" prevents individuals from striving for conventional success—a point of view that runs in the same direction as a class logic. But on the other hand, the Hallway Hangers support some politically conservative values and leaders. The prevalence of this type of dual, contradictory consciousness, embodying both progressive, counterhegemonic insights and reactionary, distorting beliefs, is discussed at length by Antonio Gramsci.[11] More recently, Michael Mann has argued convincingly that ambivalence about social beliefs leads to "pragmatic acceptance" of the social order rather than complete acceptance of it as legitimate.[12]

It is instructive to compare in detail this analysis of the Hallway Hangers with Willis's depiction of how social reproduction takes place for the lads in his study. The Hallway Hangers, as residents of public housing, are from a lower social stratum than the lads, who are from stable working-class families. Moreover, the British working class, with its long history, organized trade unions, and progressive political party, has developed an identity, pride, and class consciousness that are lacking in the United States. Despite these differences, substantial similarities in the way each peer group experiences the process of social reproduction warrant a comparison.

Willis argues that the lads' rejection of the achievement ideology and of the values and norms of the educational system is based on some key insights into the situation of their class under capitalism. However, the crucial element in the process of social reproduction—placement into manual labor jobs—is experienced by the lads as an act of independence and self-election, not a form of oppression. Because of the value placed on machismo in the wider working-class culture, which the lads appropriate for their own, they choose to enter the bottom of the occupational structure. At the root of social reproduction for the lads is the cultural inversion by which manual labor, equated with the social superiority of masculinity, is valued over white-collar work, which is associated with the inferior status of femininity.

Whereas the lads reject school because it has no bearing on the manual labor jobs they intend to pursue, the Hallway Hangers reject school for different reasons. For the lads, the seeds of leveled aspirations, and hence social reproduction, lie in their cultural affirmation of manual labor. Like the lads, the Hallway Hangers place a heavy premium on masculinity; their emphasis on being cool, tough, streetwise—in a word, bad—indicates the prevalence of machismo in their cultural outlook. Nevertheless, this emphasis on masculinity seldom is linked with distaste for white-collar work. The subculture of the Hallway Hangers contains no systematic bias toward manual work; their depressed aspirations result from a look into the future that sees stagnation at the bottom of the occupational structure as almost inevitable. The Hallway Hangers' outlook is more pessimistic than that held by the lads; there is no room on the job market for independence, election, or even choice. Thus, the Hallway Hangers reconcile themselves to taking whatever job they can get. Given this resignation, their belief that education can do little for them, and their assessment of the costs of educational success, the Hallway Hangers reject the institution of school. Although they do not experience unemployment or entry into low-level jobs as acts of triumph but rather as depressing facts of lower-class life, neither do the Hallway Hangers incriminate the social order as entirely unjust. In both cases the structure of class relations is reproduced, largely through the regulation of aspirations, but the processes through which it happens for the lads and the Hallway Hangers vary. The lads' sexism keeps them from decrying class domination; the racism of the Hallway Hangers serves the same purpose.

It is difficult to conceptualize the process of social reproduction when it is depicted in general terms. To facilitate our understanding of how the aspirations of the Hallway Hangers are leveled, I now describe the mechanisms associated with social reproduction as they affect Jinks. By looking at his experiences, the processes we have been discussing can be rendered concrete.

According to one of his friends, Jinks was an A student in his freshman year. At first, he worked hard and conformed to the rules of the school, but during his sophomore year, he started to weigh the costs and benefits of attendance and hard work. Every morning, he would socialize with the rest of the boys at Pop's for about fifteen minutes, maybe smoke a joint, and then head to class. "Hey, man, what the fuck? Sit down and smoke another bone. Whaddya wanna go to school for? You like them teachers better than us?" After leaving the group to comments like this, in class his mind would wander back to his friends sitting in Pop's, getting high, relaxing. He would think about his brother who dropped out of school at the age of sixteen and had a union job at the shipyards. He would think about another brother who had graduated the year before and joined the navy, and about his oldest brother, who was dead. He would think about the older boys at the Heights, some graduates of high school, some dropouts—all unemployed or in lousy jobs. Gradually, Jinks's attitude toward school started to change.

JINKS: I started hanging around, getting high, just not bother going to school … started hanging down Pop's. Cutting, getting high.

JM: What were the reasons behind that? Why'd you start going down to Pop's?

JINKS: Friends, friends. … I'd go to my classes and meet them at lunch, but when I was with 'em, I'd say, "The hell with it. I ain't even going." Besides, I didn't really care to try in school. … You ain't got a chance of getting a good job, even with a high school diploma. You gotta go on to college, get your Masters and shit like that to get a good paying job that you can live comfortably on. So if you're not planning on going to college, I think it's a waste of time.

By his junior year, Jinks attended school only sporadically, and when he did go to class, he was often drunk or high, a necessity if he was to "listen to the teachers talk their shit."

Faced with the need for income to pay for, among other things, his weekly ounce of marijuana, Jinks began to deal drugs on a small scale, stopping only after a close call with the police. After four months of searching and waiting, Jinks landed a job and began working in the afternoons, attending school for a few hours each day. Convinced that school was doing him little good and faced with the opportunity to work full-time, Jinks quit school, only to be laid off shortly thereafter. Although his parents wanted him to finish school, Jinks downplays their influence on him: "They want me to graduate from high school, but I ain't gonna. They'll be mad at me for a week or two, but that's life."

Now that he is out of school, out of work, and out of money, Jinks does not have much to which he can look forward. Nevertheless, he is not as "down and out" as we might think. He has plenty of time for his friends and accepts his predicament placidly, with neither thorough disrespect for the system nor for himself. The situation is, after all, not much different than he had expected.

The Brothers: Internalizing Failure, Shorn of Self-Esteem

If the mechanisms by which the Hallway Hangers and lads end up in dead-end jobs are somewhat different, the process of social reproduction as it operates with respect to the Brothers presents an even sharper contrast. Applied to the Brothers,

Bourdieu's concept of the internalization of objective probabilities does not ring true. Undoubtedly, the Brothers do internalize their chances of "making it," and this calculation certainly moderates their aspirations. Yet, their view of the probabilities for social advancement is informed not only by the objective opportunity structure but also by their parents' hopes for their future and the achievement ideology of the school. In this sense, there is no such thing as the internalization of objective probabilities, for all perceptions of the opportunity structure necessarily are subjective and influenced by a host of intervening factors. The actual habitus of the Brothers is much more complex than Bourdieu and Passeron would have us believe. A theory stressing a correspondence between aspirations and opportunity cannot explain the excessive ambitions of the Brothers because it underestimates the achievement ideology's capacity to mystify structural constraints and encourage high aspirations. The Hallway Hangers reject the achievement ideology, but the situation for the Brothers is quite different.

Like the Hallway Hangers, the Brothers come from families in which their parents either hold jobs that are at the bottom of the occupational structure or are unable to find work at all. An important difference, however, is that, with the exception of Derek, all the Brothers are either the oldest male sibling in the family or have older brothers and sisters who attend college. Thus, the Brothers are not faced with a picture of nearly uniform failure in school. In addition, the parents of the Brothers actually encourage high aspirations in their children, as a tool to motivate them to achieve in school and perhaps as a projection of thwarted ambitions. Thus, from their families, the Brothers take away a contradictory outlook. On the one hand, they see that hard work on the part of their parents has not gotten them very far, an implicit indictment of the openness of the opportunity structure, but on the other hand, they are encouraged by these same people to have high hopes for the future.

For the Brothers, work is an exclusively summertime affair; only Juan is on the job market full-time. Thus, their experience on the labor market is very limited, and that experience has been sheltered from the rigors and uncertainties of finding work. Most of these boys have been enrolled almost exclusively in federal summer youth employment programs and only have had to fill out an application form to be placed in a summer job. Whereas the more extensive contact of the Hallway Hangers with the world of work tends to level their aspirations, a comparable process has not taken place for the Brothers—at least not yet.

The Brothers' peer group does not tend to level their hopes for the future. Because the Brothers do not comprise a distinctive subculture but rather accept the norms and values of the dominant culture and strive to embody them, their peer group does not provide them with a redefinition of success. The Brothers are achievement oriented, prize accomplishments in school and obedience to the law, and measure success as does the rest of society. The ethos of their group encourages high aspirations and reinforces behavior that contributes to the realization of their goals.

The Brothers unconditionally accept the school's achievement ideology, a step that requires a belief in equality of opportunity and the efficacy of schooling. But at the same time that their aspirations tend to rise because of their faith in these precepts, the Brothers are being prepared psychologically for jobs at the bottom of the occupational structure. In low educational tracks and the recipients of poor grades, the Brothers struggle in school. They blame themselves for their mediocre academic performances because they are unaware of the discriminatory influences of tracking, the school's partiality toward the cultural capital of the upper classes, the self-fulfilling consequences of teachers' expectations, and other forms of class-based educational selection. Conditioned by the achievement ideology to think that good jobs require high academic attainment, the Brothers may temper their high aspirations, believing not that the institution of school and the job market have failed them, but that they have failed themselves.

For most of the Brothers, this "cooling-out" process, documented by Burton Clark in his study of a community college,[13] will not be completed until they actually graduate from high school and are face to face with the job market. Armed with a high school diploma and a good disciplinary record, the Brothers will have a better chance to land suitable jobs than the Hallway Hangers do, but the Brothers' opportunities still will be quite limited. Juan, the only Brother to have graduated, already has begun to "cool out."

Juan, who left high school with a diploma and a skill (he spent 1,500 hours in school learning culinary arts), has lowered his aspirations significantly after six months of unemployment. Although he previously expressed distaste for a job in auto mechanics because of its association with dirty manual work, Juan now hopes to find work in precisely that area. We can expect many of the Brothers to undergo a similar reorientation after graduation.

From the description of the Brothers' experiences in school it seems clear that the legitimation of inequality is working smoothly for them. In general, the Brothers, without the protection of a peer group with a distinctive subculture, suffer from low self-esteem as a result of their academic performances. In addition, they do not acknowledge the existence of external barriers to their success in school and instead blame themselves for their mediocre performance. We can expect that the same will be true for what may turn out to be their low occupational status.

Whereas the Hallway Hangers are analogous to Willis's lads, the Brothers are closer to the ear'oles. Although our picture is complicated by the variable of ethnicity, the Brothers' experiences illuminate the process of social reproduction as it is undergone by conformist lower-class youth, a subject into which Willis does not delve. Reflecting their acceptance of the achievement ideology and the concomitant notion that all those who are capable can get ahead on their own merits, the Brothers have developed significant ambitions. Relative to the depressed aspirations of the Hallway Hangers, the middle-class aspirations of the Brothers attest to their belief that they are involved in a fair competition. If they fail to get ahead, they will probably attribute their social and economic fate to their own incapabilities, to their own lack of merit.

But we cannot be sure. Will the Brothers and the ear'oles become disillusioned with themselves when they are "cooled out," or will their disillusion encompass the social order as well? This issue demands a longitudinal study spanning a number of years, without which no definite pronouncements are possible. I suspect that although some cynicism about the openness of American society will result, the achievement ideology has been internalized so deeply by the Brothers that their subsequent "careers" will be interpreted in its light. Moreover, if one of the Brothers should be lucky enough to "make it," those that do not will be all the more likely to blame themselves. Far from contradicting the social reproduction perspective, the limited social mobility that does take place in liberal democracies plays a crucial role in the legitimation of inequality. ("If Billy can make it, why can't I? The problem must reside in me.") This "controlled mobility" encourages working-class self-reproach and goes a long way toward explaining why in the United States working-class students with Super's outlook far outnumber those with Jinks's perspective and why in Britain there are more ear'oles than lads.

When Super switched from the Occupational Education Program to House C in the regular academic program, he was placed in the lowest educational tracks for nearly all his subjects because of his low academic performance in grammar school and the fact that switching into the classes in the middle of the semester would have been difficult for him academically. Now in his sophomore year, Super still is enrolled in the "basic" tracks and maintains a high D average.

Super aspires to professional or middle-class work, which reflects his parents' insistence that Super aim for a white-collar job, the premium his peer group places on conventional success, his minimal contact with the job market, and the achievement ideology of the school. Within the course of a year he variously expressed hopes of becoming a doctor, a businessman, or a computer specialist. Reconciling these aspirations with his academic performance is a difficult exercise for Super. At the same time that he affirms the achievement ideology ("It's easy to do anything as long as you set your mind to it") and his own effort ("I swear, I'll be tryin' real hard in school"), Super admits that his performance is lacking ("I just can't seem to do it"). The only explanation left for him is that his own abilities are not up to par, a conclusion that Super accepts, despite its implications for his sense of self-worth. Every lower-class student who internalizes the achievement ideology but struggles in school finds himself or herself in this dilemma. Moreover, the way is clear for lower-class students again to attribute their failure to personal inadequacies when they find themselves in a low-status job. The feeling is a harsh one, but the American school system and the structure of class relations demand that it be borne by many. That Super and the other Brothers feel it strongly is evidence that the legitimation function of the school and the larger process of social reproduction are at work.

If schooling is the training ground at which students are prepared to participate in the race for the jobs of wealth and prestige, the Brothers are being cheated.
Told over and over again that the race is a fair one and led to believe that they are
given as much attention during the training as anyone, the Brothers step to the
starting line for what they see as an equitable race. When the starter's gun goes off
and they stumble over the first few hurdles while others streak ahead, they will in
all likelihood blame only themselves and struggle to keep going.

The Hallway Hangers see that the race is unfair. They reject official declarations
of equity and drop out of the training sessions, convinced that their results will be
unsatisfactory no matter how hard they train. They expect to do poorly, and even
those who might stand a chance stay back with their friends when the race starts.
Instead of banding together, however, and demanding that a fair race be held, the
Hallway Hangers never really question the race's rules and simply accept their
plight.

This leaves us with an important question: How can the same race be viewed so
differently? Why is it that the entrants who have racial as well as class-based hurdles to overcome are the ones who see no hurdles at all?

The Sources of Variation

Although the distinctive processes of social reproduction that have been detailed
previously make internal sense, what accounts for the variance between them?
What factors contribute to the fundamental incongruity between the two peer
groups in the first place? Why is the influence of the family so different for the two
peer groups? Why are their experiences in school so dissimilar?

To answer these questions, we must move to a deeper level of analysis that is
centered on the role of the achievement ideology. The Hallway Hangers reject this
ideology; the Brothers accept it. It is at this point that their paths diverge and the
groups experience the process of social reproduction in different ways.

The achievement ideology runs counter to the grain of all these boys' experiences. Neither the residents of their neighborhood nor the members of their families have "made it." In a housing project plagued by unemployment and crime,
we might expect both groups of boys to question the existence of equality of opportunity, yet only the Hallway Hangers do so. Of course, they have their own experiences on the job market to which they can point, but this explanation is only
of limited value because in most instances they have dismissed the ideology even
before experiencing the job market firsthand. The question remains: Why do the
Hallway Hangers dismiss the achievement ideology while the Brothers accept it?

The Hallway Hangers reject the achievement ideology because most of them
are white. Whereas poor blacks have racial discrimination to which they can point
as a cause of their family's poverty, for the Hallway Hangers to accept the achieve-

ment ideology is to admit that their parents are lazy or stupid or both. Thus, the achievement ideology not only runs counter to the experiences of the Hallway Hangers, but is also a more serious assault on their self-esteem. Acceptance of the ideology on the part of the Brothers does not necessarily involve such harsh implications, for they can point to racial prejudice to explain their parents' defeats. The severe emotional toll that belief in the achievement ideology exacts on poor whites relative to poor blacks explains why the Hallway Hangers dismiss the ideology while the Brothers validate it.[14]

The Brothers believe the achievement ideology to be an accurate depiction of the opportunity structure as it exists in the United States today because they perceive the racial situation to be substantially different for them than it was for their parents. Whereas their parents were barred from lunch counters and disqualified from the competition before it began, the Brothers see themselves in entirely different circumstances. Mokey's mother, for example, in commenting on Mokey's chances of "making it," says, "I feel Mokey has a equal chance to [be successful], regardless of money or color. That's a chance I never had." We saw in Chapter 5 that of all the Brothers only Juan believes that young blacks face any racial barriers to success. Indeed, it is amazing how often the Brothers affirm the openness of the opportunity structure. Presumably encouraged by perceived gains made in the last two decades, the Brothers seem to believe that equality of opportunity exists today as it did not in their parents' time. This view allows them to accept the achievement ideology without simultaneously indicting their parents. Because the Brothers fully expect to "make it" themselves, embracing the achievement ideology involves little assault on their self-esteem.

This belief that the situation for blacks has improved in the United States also explains why the parents of the Brothers encourage high aspirations in their children while the Hallway Hangers' parents do not. Believing the situation that contributed to their own condition to have changed, the Brothers' parents are convinced that their children have a better chance of "making it" and see no danger in encouraging lofty aspirations. The Hallway Hangers' parents, in contrast, believe that the deck is stacked against their children as it was against them and are wary of supporting unrealistically high aspirations.

Quantitative studies on the generation of ambition have produced equivocal results about whether blacks have higher aspirations than whites from the same socioeconomic background. In general, more recent studies indicate higher aspiration levels for blacks, while those utilizing data from the 1960s and early 1970s find that whites maintain higher aspirations than blacks. The only issue on which there is a consensus amongst quantitative practitioners is that the aspiration levels of blacks seem to have risen during the past ten to fifteen years,[15] a finding consistent with the attitudes of the Brothers and their families.

A number of factors can account for the increased aspirations of blacks. Because black youths perceive a change in the opportunity structure their parents faced (a change that may or may not have occurred to the degree perceived), they may feel that affirmative action has reduced the occupational handicap of color and that discrimination in employment has abated. Or it may be that the incontrovertible gains of the civil rights movement (e.g., affirmation of basic political and civil rights for blacks, an end to legal Jim Crow segregation, the emergence of black leaders on the national stage) have imbued many blacks with a general sense of progress and improvement that has affected their occupational aspirations. Or political mobilization itself may have created feelings of efficacy and resistance to being "cooled out" that have led to the higher aspirations. To the extent that the civil rights movement was about aspirations and dreams and a refusal to be reduced to hopelessness, blacks may feel that diminutive aspirations are somehow a form of surrender and a betrayal of past gains.

The divergence between how the Brothers and Hallway Hangers react to the achievement ideology is not entirely racial. As I noted in Chapter 4, many of the Hallway Hangers and their families have lived in low-income housing projects for a long period of time, and some have been on public assistance for as many as three generations. This extended duration of tenancy in public housing cannot help but contribute to a feeling of hopelessness and stagnation on the part of the Hallway Hangers. With family histories dominated by failure, the Hallway Hangers' cynicism about the openness of the opportunity structure and their rejection of the achievement ideology are understandable.

The Brothers' situation is quite different. Their families have lived in public housing, on average, for less than half the time the Hallway Hangers' families have. The Brothers' families also have resided in the Clarendon Heights neighborhood for a substantially shorter period of time. Many of the families see their move to the neighborhood as a step up in social status; some families came from worse projects in the area, others from tenement flats in the black ghetto. Moreover, some of the Brothers' parents (Super's, James's, Mokey's) have moved up from the south, bringing with them a sense of optimism and hope about making a fresh start, feelings that have not yet turned into bitterness. For those families that have come to the United States from the West Indies in the last twelve years (Craig's, Juan's), this buoyancy is even stronger. Like the optimism felt by turn-of-the-century immigrants despite their wretched living conditions and the massive barriers to success that they faced, the Brothers' outlook encompasses a sense of improved life chances. Although at the bottom of the social ladder, the Brothers feel that they are part of a collective upward social trajectory, a belief that is conducive to acceptance of the achievement ideology.

Another factor that bears on the Hallway Hangers' rejection of the achievement ideology and the Brothers' acceptance of it is the way in which these peer groups define themselves in relation to one another. The character of the Brothers' peer group is in some measure a reaction to distinctive attributes of the Hallway Hangers. Thus, we can understand, in part, the Brothers' aversion to drugs and alcohol and their general orientation toward achievement as a response to the Hallway Hangers' excessive drinking, use of drugs, and general rejection of the standards and values of the dominant culture. As Super remarks pointing at a group of the Hallway Hangers loitering in doorway #13, "As long as I don't end up like *that*." Having moved into a predominantly white neighborhood that is generally un-friendly toward blacks and having been taunted and abused by a group of disaf-fected, mostly white boys, the Brothers' reaction has been to disassociate them-selves completely from the Hallway Hangers and to pursue a distinctly different path—one that leads to success as it is conventionally defined.

For these and other reasons, the Brothers are not representative of poor black teenagers generally. One might discover black peer groups with a similar ethos in other lower-class, predominantly white communities, but if one ventures into any black ghetto, one finds an abundance of black youths hanging in doorways who are pessimistic about the future and cynical about the openness of American soci-ety. These youths have formed subcultures with values similar to those of the Hallway Hangers and present a marked contrast to the Brothers in outlook and behavior. The sources of these differences are explored in Chapter 8.

To view the general orientation of the Brothers' peer group as a mere reaction to that of the Hallway Hangers would be a vast oversimplification that fails to ac-count for both the complexity of their reaction to the situation in which they find themselves and their powers of social discernment. We have seen that the Hallway Hangers see through the achievement ideology, not so much because of greater insight into the workings of the system but because of the assault this ideology makes on their self-esteem. The Brothers' acceptance of the ideology and their own individualistic orientations toward achievement are not entirely uncritical. The Brothers are not ideological dupes. They make their own partial "penetra-tions"[16] into their economic condition, and these insights inform their actions.

The Brothers' decision to "go for it," to work hard in school in pursuit of a de-cent job, makes a good deal of sense in view of the Hallway Hangers' decision to opt out of the competition. With the number of "good" jobs fixed, one's objective chances increase as individuals remove themselves from contention. Thus, the bi-polarity between the Hallway Hangers and the Brothers should not surprise us. In deciding whether to purchase a raffle ticket, the wily individual takes note of how many others are buying them, conscious that the less sold, the more sense it makes to purchase one. Lower-class individuals generally do not have a good chance of "making it," but as one social group eschews the contest, others see it in their interest to vie seriously. Where we have a group like the Hallway Hangers, it is only natural that we have a group with the outlook of the Brothers. Willis notes a similar logic in *Learning to Labor:* "The ear'oles' conformism ... takes on a more rational appearance when judged against the self-disqualification of the lads."[17]

The Brothers' orientation toward individual achievement is even more under-standable when we consider affirmative action measures. Although a far cry from what is needed to ameliorate racial injustice in the United States, affirmative ac-tion for minorities does increase the Brothers' objective chances of securing stable employment. There is, of course, no analogous measure offered to the lower classes as a whole to mitigate class injustice in the United States, so the anger of the white working class about affirmative action should not surprise us. The perception among whites in Clarendon Heights is that blacks now have an advantage on the job market. There may even be a measure of support for this view among blacks. Chris, for example, believes that although the white boys will face unemployment, his fate could be different: "Watch when I go for a job for the city or something: I'll get it. They'll say, 'Minority—you got the job.'" The Brothers' decision to "buy into" the system also seems to be based on the understanding that, all other things being equal, affirmative action can give them an advantage over their white lower-class peers on the labor market. The sharpening of racial division in the lower classes about affirmative action policies, alluded to throughout this study, also has important political ramifications that are taken up in the final chapter.

There are, then, a number of factors that contribute to the dissimilarity between the Brothers and the Hallway Hangers. The Brothers, who have moved to the northeastern United States within the last generation and recently have moved into public housing, see themselves on a social upswing. This ambiance of ascension is intensified by their impression that racial injustice has been curtailed in the last two decades, thereby making the opportunity structure they face more pliant than the one their parents encountered. The Hallway Hangers have no such grounds for optimism, having been left behind when much of the white working class moved to the suburbs. Whereas Clarendon Heights seems a step up for the Brothers' families, the Hallway Hangers believe they cannot slide much lower. Hailing from families who have resided in the projects for many years, some in Clarendon Heights for three generations, the Hallway Hangers feel that little has changed and consequently are despondent about their own futures. We also might point to variances in the families of the two groups as a source of their divergent outlooks. The Brothers' family members, especially their older siblings, have achieved a slightly higher status in terms of educational and occupational achievement than have the Hallway Hangers' family members.

Although all these factors contribute to the optimism of the Brothers and the pessimism of the Hallway Hangers, they do not in themselves account for the wide disparity between the two groups, nor do they explain the distinctive subculture of the Hallway Hangers. This oppositional culture partially shelters the Hallway Hangers from the abnegations of the dominant society, the negative judgments they sustain as poor members of an ostensibly open society. The Brothers are pained by these appraisals, too, of course, but the achievement ideology represents a more potent assault on the Hallway Hangers because as white youths they can point to no extenuating circumstances to account for their poverty. The subculture of the Hallway Hangers is in part a response to the stigma they feel as poor, white Americans. Finally, the differences between the two groups seem to be amplified by their tendencies to define themselves in relation (i.e., in opposition) to one another.

Where are these two paths likely to lead? In all probability, the Brothers will be better off than the Hallway Hangers. With a high school diploma, a positive attitude, and a disciplined readiness for the rigors of the workplace, the Brothers should be capable of landing steady jobs. An individual or two may work his way into a professional or managerial occupation, and a few might slide into a state of chronic unemployment, but the odds are that most of the Brothers will end up members of the stable working class, generally employed in jobs that are toward the bottom of the occupational ladder but that afford some security.

The Hallway Hangers probably will end up quite differently. Dependent on alcohol or drugs or both, disaffected and rebellious, and without qualifications in a credential-based job market, the Hallway Hangers generally will end up as Slick predicts: "They're not gonna be more than janitors or, y'know, goin' by every day tryin' to get a buck." An alcoholic himself, who becomes more despondent every day that he remains unemployed, Slick may well meet the same fate, despite his exceptional intelligence and articulate nature.

Of course, the Hallway Hangers do not deny that upward social mobility is possible. Their rejection of school was based not on the premise that they could not succeed but on the premise that the prospects for limited social mobility did not warrant the attempt, given the costs involved in the try. This is a calculation they all now have come to question. Having experienced life on the streets without a job, the Hallway Hangers generally indicate that if they had it to do over again, they would apply themselves in school.

JM: Would you do anything different if you could do it over again?

(*all in separate interviews*)

BOO-BOO: Yeah, lots. Wouldn't screw up in school as bad as I did, wouldn't get high with my friends as much.

CHRIS: I dunno, man, wouldn't fuck up in school. I guess I shoulda learned to live with their shit. It's just the way I am. Like, if I decide, if I say I'm not going to do something, I don't give a fuck what they do to me. I'm not going to do it. That's just the way I am. I guess that's what's gonna fuck me over in the long run.

FRANKIE: Yeah, definitely. I wouldn't have fucked up as much. I coulda been a—I fucked it up for myself, maybe. Maybe I woulda tried going to school more. But still, I don't think I woulda come out much better. So, y'know, just fuckin' bein' less rude to people, truthfully.

STEVE: Yeah, I'd make sure I got more credits my freshman year. I only got five fucking credits, man. That's rough to fuckin' jump back on and shit. It's a bitch.

JINKS: I'd probably get more interested in school, but it's too late now.

Almost any price would be worth paying to avoid the pain and misery of hope-lessness at such a young age.

Notes

1. Maureen Anne Scully, "Coping with Meritocracy" (Thesis, Harvard College, 1982), p. 6.

2. Max Weber, *Economy and Society* (Berkeley: University of California Press, 1970), p. 953.

3. Karl Marx and Friedrich Engels, *The German Ideology* (New York: International Publishers, 1947), pp. 65–66.

4. Scully, "Coping with Meritocracy," p. 3.

5. James Rosenbaum, *Making Inequality* (New York: Wylie and Sons, 1976).

6. Pierre Bourdieu and Jean-Claude Passeron, *Reproduction in Education, Society, and Culture* (London: Sage, 1977), p. 156.

7. Richard Sennett and Jonathan Cobb, *The Hidden Injuries of Class* (New York: Vintage Books, 1972).

8. Scully, "Coping with Meritocracy," p. 83.

9. Ibid., p. 85.

10. Elliot Liebow, *Talley's Corner* (Boston: Little, Brown, 1967), p. 209.

11. Antonio Gramsci, *Selections from Prison Notebooks* (London: Lawrence and Wishart, 1971).

12. Michael Mann, "The Social Cohesion of Liberal Democracy," *American Sociological Review* 35 (June 1970):423–439.

13. Burton Clark, "The 'Cooling Out' Function in Higher Education," *American Journal of Sociology* 65 (1960):576–596.

14. I am not arguing that blacks living in poverty are psychologically better off than their white counterparts. Given the internalized effects of racism on blacks, such is clearly not the case. It is only in considering the effect of the achievement ideology alone that I am making a comparative statement about the emotional suffering of poor blacks and poor whites.

15. Kenneth I. Spenner and David L. Featherman, "Achievement Ambitions," *Annual Review of Sociology* 4 (1978):388.

16. The term, of course, is borrowed from Willis, who first directed my attention to the penetrations of the Brothers after reading a draft of the book.

17. Willis, *Learning to Labor* (Aldershot: Gower, 1977), p. 148.

8

Reproduction Theory Reconsidered

T HE THEORETICAL LITERATURE comprising reproduction theory was discussed in Chapter 2. Conceptualizing reproduction theory as a spectrum, with one end dominated by economically determinist theories and the other by theories asserting the autonomy of the cultural level, we reviewed the work of Bowles and Gintis on the determinist end of the spectrum, progressed through the theories of Bourdieu, Bernstein and Heath, and Willis and Giroux at the other end of the spectrum. Having examined in detail the specific mechanisms of the process of social reproduction as they occur in one low-income neighborhood, we are now in a position to assess the cogency of the theories outlined in the first chapter and to develop a revised theoretical perspective.

Building on Bourdieu

This book's basic finding—that two substantially different paths are followed within the general framework of social reproduction—is a major challenge to economically determinist theories. Two groups of boys from the same social stratum who live in the same housing project and attend the same school nevertheless experience the process of social reproduction in fundamentally different ways. This simple fact alone calls into question many of the theoretical formulations of Bowles and Gintis. If social class is the overriding determinant in social reproduction, what accounts for the variance in the process between the Brothers and Hallway Hangers? Bowles and Gintis, in considering a single school, maintain that social reproduction takes place primarily through educational tracking. Differential socialization through educational tracking prepares working-class students for working-class jobs and middle-class students for middle-class jobs. But the Hallway Hangers and the Brothers, who are from the same social class background and exposed to the curricular structure of the school in the same manner, un-

135

dergo the process of social reproduction in substantially different ways. The theory of Bowles and Gintis cannot explain this difference.

Bowles and Gintis do give an excellent account of the hidden structural and ideological determinants that constrain working-class students and socialize them for positions at the bottom of the heap. What the Brothers and Hallway Hangers demonstrate quite clearly, however, is the open-ended manner in which individuals and groups respond to structures of domination. Although there is no way to avoid class-based constraints, the outcomes are far from predefined. As posited by Bowles and Gintis, the fairly rigid structural correspondence between the educational and economic systems is simplistic and overdetermined. As Giroux points out, human subjects are viewed from this perspective as passive role bearers shaped by the demands of capital. Student nonconformity and oppositional behavior are not acknowledged. "What is disregarded in the notion of 'correspondence' is not only the issue of resistance, but also any attempt to delineate the complex ways in which working-class subjectivities are constituted. ... We are presented with a homogenous image of working-class life fashioned solely by the logic of domination."[1] Bowles and Gintis pay scant attention to the active, creative role of individual and group praxis. Their work, like much social research, tends to treat categories such as the working class as undifferentiated monoliths. Although Bowles and Gintis break important ground by examining how the process of schooling reinforces relations of dominance and inequality among classes, their theory ultimately is too crudely deterministic to capture the complexity of social reproduction.

Paul Willis approaches the issue of social reproduction from the other end, so to speak: He begins with the lads themselves—with their concrete lived experiences and complex, often contradictory attitudes. To his credit, he goes to great lengths to understand the cultural dispositions and practices of the lads on their own terms before linking his ethnographic material with the structural requirements of capitalism. Willis resists the temptation to force the link between culture and structure in a false, facile manner. His ethnography does uncover the local and embedded manifestations of larger socially reproductive forces, but only after a long detour into the lived culture of the lads. For Willis, that is the only route that will work. And it does work stunningly in his story of how the lads simultaneously resist and collude in their class subjugation. But by considering only the nonconformist lads in his study, Willis is hard-pressed to illuminate the purely institutional mechanisms that constrain the social mobility of working-class individuals. And his insistence on the autonomy of culture means that his actual account of how the lads end up in manual labor occupations is remarkably free of attention to structurally embedded constraints.

The interface between the cultural and the structural is critical to our understanding of social reproduction. To capture this relationship, the agency-structure dualism must be bridged by an analysis of the interpenetration of human consciousness and structural determinants. Macro models that demonstrate the extent to which status is inherited and quantitative studies that measure how educational, occupational, and income structures mediate the effect of class origins are not enough. Such projects merely set the context for beginning to wrestle with the real issues of how social structures capture agents' minds and control their attitudes and how individuals resist and succumb to the inertial pressure of structural forces. Aspirations provide a conceptual link between structure and agency in that they are rooted firmly in individual proclivity (agency) but also are acutely sensitive to perceived societal constraints (structure).

According to his disciples, Bourdieu's concept of habitus dissolves the distinction between structure and agency and points the way forward.[2] The habitus, as understood by Giroux, comprises "the subjective dispositions which reflect a class-based social grammar of taste, knowledge, and behavior inscribed in ... each developing person."[3] In Bourdieu's scheme, habitus bridges the perennial poles in social thinking: micro and macro, agency and structure, volition and constraint, internal and external. (Interpreting Bourdieu, Wacquant states that habitus "effects, from within, the reactivation of the meanings and relations objectified 'without' as institutions."[4]) Basically, Bourdieu believes that people absorb from their social universe values and beliefs that guide their actions. Like the basketball player who instinctively cuts to the hoop to receive a pass, people do not stop and think about their actions, nor can they explain why they undertook them. They learn to act and react not from explicit teaching but from experience, from thousands of street games, from subtle cues on the court, from "clicking" with their teammates. As Richard Jenkins relates, "The power of the habitus derives from the thoughtlessness of habit and habituation, rather than consciously learned rules and principles. Socially competent performances are produced as a matter of routine, without explicit reference to a body of codified knowledge, and without the actors necessarily 'knowing what they are doing.'"[5]

Habitus is a clever concept, but it is also a slippery one. I have yet to discover from Bourdieu's own writings *how* the habitus mediates between structure and practice. Clearly, objective and external constraints from above shape the habitus, which then shapes the practices of agents below. Clearly, causality also runs in the other direction. But just how does this dialectical process work? Does the habitus merely dispose individuals to act in certain ways, or does the habitus virtually guarantee structurally prescribed and socially reproductive outcomes? Depending on how it is mined, Bourdieu's mass of empirical and theoretical work provides different (and confusing, if not confused) answers to these questions.

On the issue of aspirations, Bourdieu and Passeron's theoretical formulations in *Reproduction in Education, Society and Culture* imply a circular relationship whereby objective probabilities are internalized as subjective hopes that reinforce structures of constraint.[6] Working-class individuals develop depressed aspirations that mirror their actual chances for social advancement, and then these stunted aspirations effectively seal the social immobility and continued subjugation of the working class. But a closed loop between structure and agency is incompatible with the findings of the present study. The Brothers, whose objective life chances were originally lower than those of the Hallway Hangers because of racial barriers to success, nevertheless nurture higher aspirations than do the Hallway Hangers. By emphasizing structural determinants at the expense of mediating factors that influence subjective renderings of objective probabilities, Bourdieu and Passeron presume too mechanistic and simplistic a relationship between aspiration and opportunity. Their theory fails to fathom the numerous factors that lie between and mediate the influence of social class on individuals.

Fieldwork with the Algerian proletariat and the French bourgeoisie, on the other hand, prompts Bourdieu to acknowledge how complex and contingent the relationship between objective life chances and subjective aspirations can be. Although Bourdieu never gives an adequate sense of the internal structure of the habitus, his varied empirical work suggests that, although habitus is primarily a function of social class, other factors can be incorporated into it. For example, he differentiates people not only by class and gender but also by whether they come from Paris or not. On my readings, habitus is constituted at the level of the family, and factors such as ethnicity, educational history, peer associations, neighborhood social ecology, and demographic characteristics (e.g., geographical mobility, duration of tenancy in public housing, sibling order, and family size) are all constitutive of the habitus. Bourdieu himself alludes to the interplay of mediations within the habitus: "The habitus acquired in the family underlies the structuring of school experiences, and the habitus transformed by schooling, itself diversified, in turn underlies the structuring of all subsequent experiences (e.g., the reception and assimilation of the messages of the culture industry or work experiences), and so on, from restructuring to restructuring."[7] When understood along these lines, the concept of habitus becomes flexible enough to accommodate the interactions among ethnicity, family, schooling, work experiences, and peer associations that have been documented in this book. Indeed, Bourdieu's notion of habitus is quite helpful in understanding the Brothers and the Hallway Hangers. As Bourdieu predicts, the habitus discreetly integrates individuals into a social world geared to the interests of the ruling classes; habitus engenders attitudes and conduct that are compatible with the reproduction of class inequality.

From Ethnography to Theory

Once we descend into the world of actual human lives, we must take our theoretical bearings to make some sense of the social landscape, but in doing so we invariably find that the theories are incapable of accounting for much of what we see. The lives of the Hallway Hangers and the Brothers cannot be reduced to structural influences or causes; although structural forces weigh upon the individuals involved, it is necessary, in the words of Willis, "to give the social agents involved some meaningful scope for viewing, inhabiting, and constructing their own world in a way which is recognizably human and not theoretically reductive."[8] We must appreciate both the importance and the relative autonomy of the cultural level at which individuals, alone or in concert with others, wrest meaning out of the flux of their lives.

The possibilities open to these boys as lower-class teenagers are limited structurally from the outset. That they internalize the objective probabilities for social advancement to some degree is beyond question. The process by which this takes place, however, is influenced by a whole series of intermediate factors. Because gender is constant in the study discussed in these pages, race is the principal variable affecting the way in which these youths view their situation. Ethnicity introduces new structurally determined constraints on social mobility, but it also serves as a mediation through which the limitations of class are refracted and thus apprehended and understood differently by different racial groups. The Brothers comprehend and react to their situation in a manner entirely different from the response the Hallway Hangers make to a similar situation; ethnicity introduces a new dynamic that makes the Brothers more receptive to the achievement ideology. Their acceptance of this ideology affects their aspirations but also influences, in tandem with parental encouragement, their approach to school and the character of their peer group, factors that in turn bear upon their aspirations.

If we modify the habitus by changing the ethnicity variable and altering a few details of family occupational and educational histories and duration of tenancy in public housing, we would have the Hallway Hangers. As white lower-class youths, the Hallway Hangers view and interpret their situation in a different light, one that induces them to reject the achievement ideology and to develop aspirations and expectations quite apart from those the ideology attempts to generate. The resultant perspective, which is eventually reinforced by the Hallway Hangers' contact with the job market, informs the boys' approach to school and helps us understand the distinctive attributes of this peer group. Thus, although social class is of primary importance, there are intermediate factors at work that, as constitutive of the habitus, shape the subjective responses of the two groups of boys and produce quite different expectations and actions.

Having grown up in an environment where success is not common, the Hallway Hangers see that the connection between effort and reward is not as clearcut as the achievement ideology would have them believe. Because it runs counter to the evidence in their lives and because it represents a forceful assault on their self-esteem, the Hallway Hangers repudiate the achievement ideology. Given that their parents are inclined to see the ideology in the same light, they do not counter their sons' rejection of the American Dream.

A number of important ramifications follow from the Hallway Hangers' denial of the dominant ideology: the establishment of a peer group that provides alternative means of generating self-esteem, the rejection of school and antagonism toward teachers, and, of course, the leveling of aspirations. In schematizing the role of the peer group, it is difficult not to appear tautological, for the group does wield a reciprocal influence on the boys: It attracts those who are apt to reject school and the achievement ideology and those with low aspirations and then deepens these individuals' initial proclivities and further shapes them to fit the group. But at the same time, the peer subculture itself, handed down from older to younger boys, is the product of the particular factors that structure the lives of white teenagers in Clarendon Heights.

In addition to the peer group, the curricular structure of the school solidifies the low aspirations of the Hallway Hangers by channeling them into programs that prepare students for manual labor jobs. Low aspirations, in turn, make the Hallway Hangers more likely to dismiss school as irrelevant. Once on the job market, the Hallway Hangers' inability to secure even mediocre jobs further dampens their occupational hopes. Thus, although each individual ultimately retains autonomy in the subjective interpretation of his situation, the leveled aspirations of the Hallway Hangers are to a large degree a response to the limitations of social class as they are manifest in the Hallway Hangers' social world.

The Brothers' social class origins are only marginally different from those of the Hallway Hangers. Being black, the Brothers also must cope with racially rooted barriers to success that, affirmative action measures notwithstanding, structurally inhibit the probabilities for social advancement, although to a lesser degree than do shared class limitations. What appears to be a comparable objective situation to that of the Hallway Hangers, however, is apprehended in a very different manner by the Brothers.

As black teenagers, the Brothers interpret their families' occupational and educational records in a much different light than do the Hallway Hangers. Judging by the Brothers' constant affirmation of equality of opportunity, the boys believe that racial injustice has been curbed in the United States in the last twenty years. Whereas in their parents' time the link between effort and reward was very tenuous for blacks, the Brothers, in keeping with the achievement ideology, see the connection today as very strong: "If you work hard, it'll pay off in the end" (Craig). Hence, the achievement ideology is more compatible with the Brothers' attitudes than with those of the Hallway Hangers, for whom it cannot succeed against overwhelming contrary evidence. The ideology is not as emotionally painful for the Brothers to accept because past racial discrimination can help account for their families' poverty, whereas the Hallway Hangers, if the ideology stands, are afforded no explanation outside of laziness and stupidity for their parents' failures. The optimism that acceptance of the achievement ideology brings for the Brothers is encouraged and reinforced by their parents. Thus, we see how in the modified habitus ethnicity affects the Brothers' interpretation of their social circumstances and leads to acceptance of the achievement ideology, with all the concomitant results.

Chief among these results is a positive attitude toward education that influences the Brothers' relations with teachers and reaction to the curricular structure of the school, thereby making it less likely for the boys to select a future in manual work via a vocational program. Their validation of the achievement ideology also affects the ethos of their peer group, which in turn influences each individual's orientation toward school as well as his aspirations. Because their contact with the job market has been minimal, the Brothers have yet to undergo experiences that might upset or alter their perspective. Once they graduate from high school, the Brothers probably will need to temper their aspirations as Juan has done. Whether they begin to question the achievement ideology and the openness of American society or whether they reproach themselves for frustrated ambition remains to be seen. From a political perspective this is an intriguing question, but from a sociological angle what is equally fascinating is the way ethnicity mediates the limitations of class, thereby creating a refractive effect that catalyzes the Brothers to construct meaning out of their existence in an entirely different manner from the Hallway Hangers.

A fundamental aspect of habitus (but hidden in this book because of its constancy) is gender. As boys, the Hallway Hangers can inhabit a subculture whose values receive a good deal of validation from the dominant culture. The cultural inversion employed to turn "bad" into good is based on a valuation of machismo taken to the extreme. Being tough, "cool," and defiant all derive from an overstated pride in masculinity, an ideal portrayed by a whole series of Hollywood actors. The Hallway Hangers exaggerate and manipulate this ideal, investing it with new dimensions until it is so distorted that John Grace can embody it. Lacking in nearly every category that defines success in America, the Hallway Hangers latch onto and inflate the one quality they still have: their masculinity.

Girls from Clarendon Heights experience and manipulate the structural forces of class, race, and gender in their own ways. Although we have no original empirical material to inform our analysis, a rich ethnographic study, undertaken by Jane K. Rosegrant in Clarendon Heights itself, offers us invaluable information on how lower-class girls understand their circumstances and what types of action proceed from these interpretations.

Rosegrant delves into the life histories of five women from Clarendon Heights in an attempt to determine the combined importance of the "distinct, yet intertwined threads of influence"[9] of class and gender on their lives. Although small, her sample cuts across racial lines, encompassing three whites, one black, and one Latina. These women and their daughters are subject to even more structural limitations than are the boys in this book because they have to contend with patriarchy as a mode of domination as well as class and race. Women in Clarendon Heights face a future that holds out little promise. Resolution of the structural forces acting on girls in Clarendon Heights, however, is radically different than for boys because, among other things, girls can realize a goal that seems to promise them freedom from the forces by which they, like the Hallway Hangers, feel trapped.

It is at this juncture that the "mothering option" raises its head. As teenagers, the women of this study ... underwent the same hardships and lived the same stigma that their brothers felt. Certainly they knew their families were poor, that they were living different lives than the ones they saw depicted on T.V., and that somehow it was their parents'—especially their father's—"fault" that they were in this position. They certainly felt bad when they did poorly in school and they did not look forward to the jobs they would hold in their lifetimes—work at least as dull as that for which the boys were headed. However, the girls could react to these pressures and find a respite from them, that the boys could not. Within the mainstream of our society, a clearly defined and lauded path existed which they could follow. Thanks to this "escape route," the girls were not forced to cope with an overwhelming image of themselves, either personal or societal, as failures. No matter how poorly they performed in school, or how dismal their employment outlook might have been, they had a route to respectability. The importance the aspiration to mother had in their lives can not be overestimated. In the midst of their often tumultuous childhoods, it gave them something concrete to cling to. Unlike their fathers, brothers and boyfriends, they were headed for a future they desired, one of which society supposedly approved. They could be mothers, and nothing and no one could keep them from realizing this goal.[10]

Rosegrant's finding is substantiated by the daughters of these women as well. When she asked these adolescent girls to what jobs they aspire, they were all indifferent about their future work roles but were unequivocal in their desire for children, despite their mothers' advice to the contrary. The response from eleven-year-old Sara is especially instructive: "Me? No, I want to get pregnant when I'm sixteen. Get an apartment, have a baby." One girl whose performance in school is exceptionally good nevertheless states, "I don't wanna go to college; I wanna have four kids."[11] While the Hallway Hangers attempt to escape the forces bearing upon them through the protection of their peer group with its celebration of masculinity, the girls look to parenthood and maternity.

As we might expect, however, the relief that mothering seems to hold out is largely illusory. Although none of the women in Rosegrant's study regretted having children, they all came quickly to the painful realization that being poor and a parent (usually a single one) is fraught with inestimable difficulties. As important as the practical burdens motherhood imposes is the denial these women felt when they failed to receive the respect that had been promised them. "If the Hallway Hangers of MacLeod's study felt betrayed by society as teens coping with school and work, these women come to feel this betrayal as young women coping with motherhood. They had done what they understood they were supposed to do—either willingly or by default—but society seemed to be reneging on its part of the deal."[12]

If motherhood, in spite of its promise, offers no relief from the structural forces impinging on lower-class girls, neither can girls expect consolation from a supportive peer group. Whereas the boys can construct a subculture offering alterna-

tive ways of maintaining some self-respect and dignity, the girls have no such avenue open to them. Consider the conclusion Anne Campbell draws from her
extensive research on the lives of girls in New York street gangs.

> For these girls, there was no escape in the gang from the problems they faced: their
> female role could not be circumvented, their instability remained and was magnified,
> their isolation was covered by a rough veneer. The gang was no alternative life for
> them. It was a microcosm of the society beyond. Granted, it was one that had a public
> image of rebellion and excitement and offered a period of distraction (discussions of
> gang feuds and honor and death). But in the end, gang or no gang, the girls remained
> alone with their children, still trapped in poverty and in a cultural dictate of woman-
> hood from which there was no escape.[13]

Denied the camaraderie and solidarity that "male bonding" affords the boys,
girls in Clarendon Heights fulfill the roles that patriarchal society defines for
them, particularly the role of "girlfriend," which effectively keeps them divided,
dependent, and subordinate. Nonconformist girls may well drop out of the race
but without the solace of a closely knit peer group that has modified definitions of
success. In such a predicament, it is no wonder that the option of motherhood
seems attractive.

Another case that demands our attention is the situation of blacks at the very
bottom of the socioeconomic strata who react to their predicament in much the
same way as do the Hallway Hangers. What aspects of their habitus produce an
outcome so different from that of the Brothers? Across the city in the projects
housing mostly black and Latino families, one finds an abundance of black
youths "hanging" in doorways, pessimistic about the future and cynical about the
American Dream. Because they share with the Brothers the three main structural
variables of social class, race, and gender, we must look to other factors making
up the habitus to understand the differences between the Brothers and their black
peers across the city.

For a start, their family occupational and educational histories are slightly
more desolate, and there is often a more extended stay in public housing (two or
three generations). Living in a neighborhood where black failure (by conventional criteria) is ubiquitous, these boys are likely to view the economic gains of
the civil rights movement as illusory. For them affirmative action is a token ges-
ture that has little bearing on their lives—when the deck is stacked against you,
being dealt one face card hardly guarantees a winning hand. Because they view
the conditions that contributed to their parents' demise as largely intact, the ethnicity variable does not have the same refractive effect it has for the Brothers.
Without the ambiance of improved life chances, the achievement ideology rubs
harder against the grain of these boys' experiences, thereby spurring them to reject the dominant ideology, disassociate themselves from school, and organize
themselves into peer groups with an ethos much different from that of the Broth-

ers. Because these project youths see the path to conventional achievement as blocked and because they are susceptible to racially rooted negative judgments by the dominant culture, it should come as no surprise that they form protective peer subcultures whose evaluative criteria are much like those by which the Hallway Hangers measure success. To be bad is to be successful, at least in the limited sphere of one's peer group. Despite the class, race, and gender variables these boys share with the Brothers, the internal structure of their habitus is substantially different and gives rise to different expectations and actions.

This schematization of intermediate factors between the structural determinants of social class and individual social actors explains a great deal of the empirical material this ethnographic inquiry has uncovered. This depiction of the social landscape inhabited by lower-class teenagers accommodates both the Hallway Hangers and Brothers as well as other social groups about which we have limited empirical data. We also should be able to locate and make sense of the situation of individuals on this social map.

Individuals in the Social Landscape

Boo-Boo and Derek pose an interesting challenge. Not only do they share the variables of class, race, and gender, but these two boys are also from the same family, yet have completely different outlooks on their futures. Because the boys have different fathers, their early home lives were somewhat varied. The crucial point of divergence, however, was Derek's acquisition of a federal scholarship to attend Barnes Academy after third grade. Enrollment at a prestigious private school not only objectively raised Derek's chances for success by providing him with a superior education and new opportunities—it also meant an entirely different form of socialization than that which Boo-Boo and other boys from the neighborhood were undergoing at the local grammar school. Derek was in white, upper-class educational environs for most of the day and spent most of his free time with his Barnes Academy friends. Thus, the two brothers had radically different peer associations. While Derek was spending his summers sightseeing around Texas, Mexico, and Martha's Vineyard with a rich friend and his family, Boo-Boo was hanging in the project with the Hallway Hangers. Both boys, although hesitant to speak about each other, draw attention to their different peers as an important source of variance between them.

JM: How'd you end up hanging with Frankie and them?

BOO-BOO: When I was in school, they was in school. My brother went to Barnes, started hanging with other kids. When he started hanging down here, Juan and Craig were around.

(in a separate interview)

JM: Why do you think your brother hangs with them [the Hallway Hangers]?

DEREK: I don't know. ... I only started hanging with Super and Mokey and everybody a couple of years ago. Before that, I hung up by Mirror Lake with the guys from Barnes.

Thus, although the main variables of class, race, gender, and family are the same for Boo-Boo and Derek, the differences in other factors making up the habitus, especially schooling and peer associations, readily account for the existing disparity between the brothers.

Billy, the boy who has won a scholarship to attend college, also presents us with a challenge, for he used to be indistinguishable from the Hallway Hangers. He is still friendly with Jinks, Slick, and Frankie and speaks matter-of-factly about his early years in high school.

BILLY: I was getting high with them [the Hallway Hangers], having fun with them, cutting classes. ... We all hung together. We all used to go out during lunch, about ten of us, get smashed. I'm serious. We'd come back hardly able to stand up and go to shop [Oc. Ed.]. ... I used to smoke dope every single day. I swear to God, I don't think I went one day without smoking. Then I just went home, went to sleep, wake up, get high, go to sleep.

Billy's family background is similar to that of the other boys as well. Neither parent graduated from high school or worked regularly. But the death of his father and separation from his mother altered his family in a drastic way and thus instigated a reorientation of other intermediate factors that resulted in an outcome far different than that for most of the Hallway Hangers.

The upheavals in his family situation coupled with the brutal murder of his best friend somehow touched off a spark in Billy to buck the odds and "make something" of himself. "I want to become successful in life. I wanna be someone, y'know? I don't wanna live in a housing development or anything like that." In keeping with his suddenly high aspirations, Billy embraced the achievement ideology at the same time his peers were coming to reject it. "Do I have an equal chance to make it as some richer kid? Yeah, I have an equal chance as anyone does. You can be the smartest person if you want to be, unless you have some disabilities, cuz all it takes is hard work and study."

Having chosen Oc. Ed. in eighth grade because "it was the thing to do back then. All my friends, all people from where I live—that's where everyone was," Billy began to work hard in school. He gradually drifted away from the Hallway Hangers, stopped smoking marijuana, and earned a spot on the high school hockey team as the varsity goalie. This, in turn, led to a whole new set of friends with different values and a different lifestyle, a change about which Frankie comments.

FRANKIE: Yeah, Billy figured what the fuck, man. He said, "Hey now I got a chance to fucking do something," and he did it. Good luck to him, y'know. I think he pulled a good move cuz he used to get high and shit all the time. ... Now he started playing hockey, y'know, and met a lot of kids on the team, ended up hanging with them. That's good, y'know. Hang with them and these dudes are all the time trying to get good grades. Y'know, Billy said, "What the fuck, I'll check this out."

Jinks and Chris see Billy in the same way.

JM: Do you think any of your friends will go to college?

JINKS: I think one might.

CHRIS: Billy?

JINKS: Yeah, that's about it.

JM: Does he still hang with you guys at all?

CHRIS: No, and that's the only reason [that he might make it to college].

JINKS: He used to hang with us.

CHRIS: He used to fuck up.

JINKS: Like eighth grade, ninth grade. Then he just started going to school, doing all his work, started being by himself.

CHRIS: I think because his father died, mostly. He just said, "I wanna do something good with my life."

Billy won a scholarship and plans to attend a small, liberal arts college next year. He may well "make it" and leave behind his old friends, the Hallway Hangers: "I think I'll come back five years from now and I'll see eight out of ten of them still hanging in doorway #13, bummin' money, doing nuttin'."

Because his life illustrates the interplay among family, school, and peer group, Billy is a perfect example of the importance of mediating variables in the habitus and the complex relationships that exist among the various factors. If one variable is changed, it upsets the balance of the habitus, and the consequences can ripple through the other intermediate forces, changing all the interactions to mold a different outcome. Billy had some distinctive familial experiences that altered his aspirations. Changed aspirations led to new attitudes and behavior (in particular new interactions with peers and school), which led in turn to further alterations in expectation and action. Instead of hanging in doorway #13 next year, Billy expects to be settled on a college campus.

Cultural Autonomy Within Structural Constraints

By taking as our starting point the peer cultures of Clarendon Heights and working upward from ethnography to analysis, we have discovered how a number of factors mediate the influence of social class on the individual actors at the cultural level. As long as Bourdieu's concept of habitus is fleshed out empirically and deepened theoretically to accommodate these factors, it is a valuable descriptive device for understanding the social world of Clarendon Heights. Individuals, with their distinctive assets and character traits, have a good deal of autonomy. But although we can in no way predict with confidence the precise effect a particular change in habitus will have on people, the factors that frame their existence and from which they derive meaning go a long way toward explaining their outlooks and behavior patterns.

Structural features of class, racial, and gender domination permeate American society, but this book has been concerned especially with class-based constraints embedded in the educational system. The school's valuation of the cultural capital of the upper classes and its depreciation of the cultural capital of the lower classes are the most important mechanisms of social reproduction within the educational system, but the discriminatory effects of tracking and of teachers' expectations also inhibit the academic performance of lower-class students. No matter how students from the lower classes respond, the dynamic of the race for the jobs of wealth and prestige remains unchanged. Although a restricted number of individuals of working-class origin may overcome the barriers to success, the rules of the race severely limit and constrain these individuals' mobility.

My analysis of the aspirations of the Brothers and Hallway Hangers shows clearly the autonomy individuals possess in their response to this received structure of domination. How poor youths react to an objective situation that is weighted heavily against them depends on a number of mediating factors and ultimately is contingent. The Hallway Hangers' leveled aspirations demonstrate the extent to which structural constraints can impinge directly on individual attitudes. Confronting what they regard as a closed opportunity structure, the Hallway Hangers attach very little significance to their own occupational preferences in formulating their aspirations. Thus, we see how structure can reach into human consciousness to encourage dispositions that ensure the reproduction of class inequality. With respect to the Hallway Hangers, Bourdieu's perspective is vindicated.

The higher occupational aspirations of the Brothers, on the other hand, indicate that the connection between objective structure and subjective attitudes is

tenuous; ideology can cloud, distort, and conceal the mechanisms of social reproduction. Although structural determinants shape the aspirations of the Hallway
Hangers, the Brothers attest to the power of ideology to mold perceptions. Cognizant of no external barriers to success, the Brothers consistently affirm the
achievement ideology and the actuality of equality of opportunity. High aspirations may result from a capitalist society's contradictory need to present an ideology of openness and equal opportunity at the same time that the underlying
structure of class relations is maintained. However, the Hallway Hangers prove
that ideological hegemony is not a fait accompli; such hegemony often is contested and is realized only partially.

Although individuals can interpret and respond to constraint in different ways,
they must still face the effects of class domination. As Giroux reminds us, "While
school cultures may take complex and heterogeneous forms, the principle that remains constant is that they are situated within a network of power relations from
which they cannot escape."[14] Cultural practices operate within the limits defined
by class, gender, and racial barriers. In terms of the immediate perpetuation of
class inequality, it matters little how lower-class teenagers respond to the vicissitudes of their situation. No matter how clearly they understand their lives, no
matter what cultural innovations they produce, no matter how diligently they de-
vote themselves to school, they cannot escape the constraints of social class. Con-
formists accept the ideology and act within the system but come up against the
barriers of class; only a few break through. Nonconformists balk and do no better;
in effect, they withdraw from the system, never test its limits, and generally find
themselves in worse shape.

Structuralist theories are of value because they can show quite clearly why the
end result turns out to be much the same, but in doing so they often obliterate human agency by ignoring "the complex ways in which people mediate and respond
to the interface between their own lived experiences and structures of domination
and constraint."[15] Culturalist theories give us a sense of the texture of individual
lives but too often fail to contextualize attitudes and behavior as responses to objective structures. Giroux's insistence on a dialectical treatment of subjectivity
and structure is correct: "Determination and human agency presuppose each
other in situations that represent a setting-of-limits on the resources and opportunities of different classes. Men and women inherit these pre-defined circumstances, but engage them in a 'process of meaning-making which is always active'
(Bennett 1981), and leaves their results open-ended."[16]

The results may be contingent, but neither of the outcomes documented in this
study is positive. It is an open question whether the Hallway Hangers or the
Brothers are worse off. The Brothers' mobility is defined by structural constraints
that probably will result in the boys' entry into the stable working class. Because
the institutional mechanisms of social reproduction hinder rather than block the
Brothers' mobility, one or two of the Brothers may even break into the middle
class. However, unaware of the constraints (but subject to their effects), the
Brothers are prone to blame themselves for their plight. The Hallway Hangers, in

contrast, see through the ideology, perceive the constraints, and realize the futility of high aspirations. They salvage some self-esteem but in the process forfeit any chance for individual social advancement. In a sense, cultural innovations like those of the lads or Hallway Hangers aid the process of social reproduction because nonconformists often relegate themselves to the bottom of the pile.

From a wider standpoint, however, the Hallway Hangers, who see with a certain crudity the true workings of the system, pose a threat to the stability of social reproduction. But as we have seen, the counterhegemonic elements of the Hallway Hangers' perspective are divested of their political potential; the Hallway Hangers' racism, among other factors, impedes the formation of any sort of critical consciousness.

Although the Hallway Hangers' capacity to see through the dominant ideology is not politically empowering, it does allow them to maintain some semblance of a positive identity. In puncturing the achievement ideology, the Hallway Hangers invert the dominant culture's definitions of achievement. Whereas the conventional American example of success might be J. Paul Getty, self-made millionaire, Frankie holds up as an example John Grace, bartender being tried for attempted murder. By turning the achievement ideology upside down, the Hallway Hangers reject the official, authorized interpretation of their social situation; in so doing, they become free to create their own cultural meanings. Because they see the spoils of economic success as beyond their reach, the Hallway Hangers invert the dominant ideology in a way that gives them access to "success," albeit in forms the dominant culture recognizes as failure.

My finding that the Hallway Hangers reject the official ideology and my speculation that the poorest members of the black community do the same makes a good deal of sense. We would expect those clinging to the very lowest rungs of the socioeconomic ladder to reject the achievement ideology, for although all other segments of society can use the dominant ideology as a means to feel superior to whomever is below them, poor whites and blacks have no one to look down on. Even those only marginally better off can and do use the achievement ideology as a means of self-validation. As public housing tenants, Clarendon Heights residents routinely are depicted as irresponsible, morally lacking, and indolent by the city's other inhabitants. Consider the light in which an auto mechanic living in a working-class neighborhood across the city sees Clarendon Heights residents: "These people are fucking animals. ... I know what their habits are like; they won't stop at anything to rip you off. Fucking sponges, leeches, they are. They'll suck the blood out of anyone, anything. They suck it out of my pay check every week. ... At least I work for my money."

Willis writes that the working class does not have a structurally based vested interest in mystifying itself.[17] But, in the United States at least, the working class is so fragmented that only the very lowest strata have no use for the dominant achievement ideology. For the poorest segments of the population, both white and black, the only defense against the ideology is to turn it on its head and attempt to salvage as much dignity as possible via the redefined criteria for success.

This is a struggle that will never be completely won, for the judgments of the dominant culture are capable of piercing the thickest individual or collective shells. Willis captures the issue in *Learning to Labor*: "One of the time-honoured principles of cultural and social organization in this country as it is enacted and understood at the subjective level is that of 'them' and 'us.' That the term 'them' survives in 'us' is usually overlooked. ... Even the most 'us' group has a little of 'them' inside. ... Ideology is the 'them' in 'us.'"[18]

The poorest black and white people in America, who are fodder for the rest of society's hunger for social superiority, ironically turn on each other to fulfill the same function. The Hallway Hangers continually strive to convince themselves of their superiority over "the niggers." We might expect that poor blacks vaunt themselves over the "white trash" living across the city. The more effective means of maintaining a measure of dignity and self-respect, however, seems to be the inversion of the dominant ideology, a cultural response to class domination by those at the bottom of American society.

The interaction between the cultural and the structural that I have posited— that class-based institutional mechanisms set limits on mobility, thereby ensuring social reproduction, while cultural innovations can be at once both functional and dysfunctional for social reproduction—fits the ethnographic data. By ignoring the cultural level of analysis, determinist theories cannot account for the distinctive cultural practices and attitudes of lower-class individuals; nor can these theories explain how such practices can contribute to and threaten social reproduction. Culturalist theories seldom manage to connect the micro processes they document to the macro forces that constrain working-class individuals.

By striving to understand the world of the Brothers and the Hallway Hangers on their terms, this book has managed to uncover some important mediating factors that influence individuals at the cultural level. It is to these factors that deterministic theories must pay more attention. In addition, theorists such as Bowles and Gintis and Bourdieu must recognize individuals' capacity for reflexive thought and action—in Willis's words, their potential "not only to think like theorists, but act like activists."[19] Individuals are not passive receivers of structural forces; rather they interpret and respond to those forces in creative ways. In asserting the autonomy of the individual at this cultural level, however, we must not lose sight of structural forms of class domination from which there is no escape. To paraphrase Marx, we must understand that teenage peer groups make their own history, but not under circumstances of their own choosing.[20]

Notes

1. Henry A. Giroux, *Theory & Resistance in Education* (London: Heinemann, 1983), p. 85.

2. Loïc J. D. Wacquant, "Sociology as Socioanalysis: Tales of *Homo Academicus*," *Sociological Forum* 5 (1990):684.

3. Giroux, *Theory & Resistance,* p. 89.

4. Wacquant, "Sociology as Socioanalysis," p. 684.

5. Richard Jenkins, *Pierre Bourdieu* (London: Routledge, 1992), p. 66.

6. Pierre Bourdieu and Jean-Claude Passeron, *Reproduction in Society, Education and Culture* (London: Sage, 1977).

7. Pierre Bourdieu, *Outline of a Theory of Practice* (Cambridge: Cambridge University Press, 1977), p. 87.

8. Paul E. Willis, *Learning to Labor* (Aldershot: Gower, 1977), p. 172.

9. Jane K. Rosegrant, *"Choosing Children"* (Thesis, Harvard College, 1985), p. 120.

10. Ibid., pp. 125–126.

11. Ibid., pp. 133–134.

12. Ibid., p. 127.

13. Anne Campbell, *The Girls in the Gang* (Oxford: Basil Blackwell, 1984), p. 266.

14. Giroux, *Theory & Resistance,* p. 63.

15. Ibid., p. 108.

16. Ibid., p. 164.

17. Willis, *Learning to Labor,* pp. 122–123

18. Ibid., p. 169.

19. Paul E. Willis, "Cultural Production and Theories of Reproduction," in *Race, Class, and Education,* ed. Len Barton and Stephen Walker (London: Croom Helm, 1983), p. 114.

20. Karl Marx, *The Eighteenth Brumaire of Louis Bonaparte,* in *Selected Works* (New York: International Publishers, 1968), p. 97.

PART TWO

Eight Years Later: Low Income, Low Outcome

9

The Hallway Hangers:
Dealing in Despair

HEY JAY, WHAT THE FUCK brings you back to the Ponderosa?" Greeted by Steve in July 1991, I surveyed a Clarendon Heights that had changed considerably since 1983. Steve jerked his thumb over his shoulder at a group of African American teenagers lounging in the area outside doorway #13, previously the preserve of the Hallway Hangers. "How do you like all the new niggers we got here? Motherfuckers've taken over, man." I asked Steve about Frankie, Slick, and the other Hallway Hangers. "I'm the only one holding down the fort," he answered. "Me and Jinks—he lives in the back. The rest of 'em pretty much cut loose, man."

Indeed, the Hallway Hangers' clique has broken up. Of those who have moved out of the neighborhood, only Slick and Shorty occasionally return to hang in the Heights. Although physically Clarendon Heights looks much the same, the surrounding neighborhood is slowly being transformed by gentrification. Students and young professionals have moved into the area, displacing Italian and Portuguese families. Ice cream parlors and posh restaurants that cater to the new clientele are replacing the pawn shops and family-owned five and dime stores. The vacant lot across from Clarendon Heights, once strewn with battered cars around a sagging basketball rim, is now the site of a smart office building. "Smile, you're on candid camera," Steve announced, pointing to small video cameras mounted on the office walls and trained on the area in front of doorway #13. "The cops've gone high-tech on us. But shit, it's too hot to deal out here now anyways, with all the spooks takin' over."

Later in this chapter I probe the siege mentality and racism of the Hallway Hangers, explore how their identities are formed around the axes of race, class, and gender, and recount their experiences of work. In their mid-twenties, the seven Hallway Hangers should be in the labor force full time. Most of them aren't: They are unemployed or imprisoned, or are working sporadically either for firms "under the table" or for themselves in the drug economy. Before considering these issues closely, I briefly sketch the fate of each young man since 1984.

155

Since 1984 Stoney has moved from pizzeria to pizzeria and from prison to prison. When I saw him in September 1987, Stoney was depressed. "I've been in and out of the can since you left, but it's been for stupid shit—not going to drug or alcohol classes, drinking in public, ignoring court summonses, possession—shit like that." Later that day he went to the courthouse and asked to serve a suspended six-month sentence for possession of cocaine. Hoping to cleanse his system of drugs, Stoney thought jail would do him good. When I visited him a month later in the county jail, he was miserable and could hardly believe his stupidity. Stoney is still dependent on valium and, according to friends, has tried to take his own life several times. In 1988 he robbed a convenience store with a tire iron and spent two years in jail. He got out, found his girlfriend and two children living with another man, acquired another pizza job, fell in love, sold his belongings, and moved with his fiancee to the South where she had lined up a job. Stoney found work but her job fell through, and three months later they were back in town. Stoney was soon arrested another time for armed robbery, again after drinking and dropping valium. He held up a pizza deliveryman, took $40 and a large pizza, and was sentenced to the maximum security prison for up to five years. Due to overcrowding and good behavior, he had minimum security status when I visited him in 1991. Remarkably healthy and upbeat, he looked better than I'd ever seen him. Stoney still hopes to own a pizza parlor. "Things haven't gone good," he said, "but it'll get better. I hope so anyway."

Steve has also been in and out of prison five times over the past seven years, mostly for violating restraining orders and beating his girlfriend. The father of two children, Steve admits that paternity "didn't faze me—I was a kid still." Apart from occasional babysitting, Steve offers little financial or moral support to their mothers. He cycles in and out of construction jobs and has dealt crack to supplement his income. Steve seems to have progressed from "the stereotypical project youth ... constantly on the lookout for a free ride" to the stereotypical hood whose violent existence seems completely unanchored. Many people around Clarendon Heights consider Steve "crazy." Stoney, whose jaw was broken by Steve in a street fight, says, "Steve's a maniac. He's got a big heart, but he's a fuckin' maniac."

Shorty could easily wear the same label, having spent ten days in a state psychiatric hospital after attacking a police officer. In another fight in front of Clarendon Heights, he stabbed a boy named Rico in the stomach with a hunting knife. The boy went into a coma and Shorty was charged with attempted murder. Then Rico recovered, and upon discovering that Shorty was actually a distant cousin, he dropped the charge. Shorty ended up doing thirteen months, and when he refused to attend Alcoholics Anonymous (AA) classes after his release, he served another six. Shorty worked a few construction jobs before getting stabbed himself a few blocks from Clarendon Heights. He was in the hospital for fourteen days after his spleen was removed and his bladder repaired. True to form, Shorty refused to identify his assailant, even under intense police pressure. He still lives with his mother, works sporadically, and likes crack cocaine.

JM: What about women? Steady girlfriend or ...

SHORTY: Yeah, got one girl. I stay with her. I don't go around fuckin' other broads. Maybe, maybe once in a while, once in a while I'll go out and grab another piece of ass, but I don't like to because I don't wanna catch no fuckin' AIDS. You gotta watch where you're poking your hose these days, you know. Fuck that.

Shorty's existence may seem unsettled but he finds it surprisingly composed. Asked if things had gone as he expected over the past seven years, Shorty replied, "No. I thought I'd be in jail for fucking life. Murder. I'll tell ya one thing, I didn't think I'd slow down like this."

Chris failed to slow down in pursuit of his teenage aspiration to be a big-time cocaine dealer. In 1984 he was moving up in the drug underworld of the city, expanding his clientele to other neighborhoods and to a nearby city. But as his market grew, so did his own appetite for drugs until, according to Jinks, "he became his own best customer." Having lost the trust of his suppliers, Chris increasingly turned to theft to support his heroin and cocaine habits. When I saw him in 1987 he had already been jailed several times and was awaiting trial on a breaking and entering charge. "I fucked up, Jay, that's all. Cocaine did it to me. What can I say? I'm at rock bottom and I'm fucking embarrassed for you to see me like this." But Chris was not at rock bottom in 1987 because he has sunk considerably since then. When I interviewed him in jail four years later, Chris described how he and his girlfriend Samantha had been homeless for the past several years, moving from one "base house" to another when kicked out by other addicts, sleeping in hallways and on the street. He recounted how he robbed friends and family and then resorted to increasingly risky theft: stealing radios and tape decks out of cars, breaking into dormitory rooms and houses, passing stolen checks, and finally sticking people up. Chris has been imprisoned six times, most recently for holding up three college students with a stick beneath his shirt in an effort that netted him $97 and probably seven years behind bars. Samantha cannot visit him because she jumped bail, and his family will not accept his collect calls. "Jay, I wanna have a normal life so bad. You don't know how bad I'm aching inside. I just want so bad to have a normal life."

Boo-Boo, the other black Hallway Hanger, is also in bad shape. In 1985 he began working at a car wash for $4.30 per hour. "It was a shit job for shit pay, but what else could I do?" After fourteen months and only a fifty cent pay raise, Boo-Boo quit. He hung in Clarendon Heights and did a stint in jail after a drunken joy ride. After his release Boo-Boo was in high spirits. He was in love and had somehow been accepted into the army despite his record. On June 4, 1987 he was married and on June 8 he was inducted into the armed forces. But on July 15 he was given a medical discharge for bunions growing on his feet. Two weeks later, at his wife's insistence, their marriage was annulled. Shortly afterward, Boo-Boo met Ginger, a young Italian woman, and eventually moved in with her family in a housing project across the city. They moved out when Ginger gave birth, and another daughter was born a year later. In 1990 the Department of Social Services took custody of the girls because, according to Boo-Boo, their basement apartment was often flooded and perpetually damp, and because "the kids weren't being looked after right." Boo-Boo and Ginger moved to a nearby city and became enmeshed in the crack cocaine racket. They emerged unharmed, but since then Boo-Boo's family and personal life have completely crumbled.

Slick was also struggling in 1987 when I visited him in jail. He had joined the marines in 1984 but was discharged several months later. He worked under the table as a construction laborer, landed a permanent job with a roofing company, and was making over $10 per hour when he was arrested for disorderly conduct after a brawl. As part of his probation, Slick had to attend weekly AA meetings for several months. He missed the final two sessions and was sentenced to six months in the county house of correction for violation of probation. Once out of jail, Slick settled back into his roofing job and began to supplement his wages by dealing cocaine. He and his girlfriend Denise rented a condominium until Slick bailed out of the drug racket. Sitting in their current ramshackle apartment, Slick spoke of his determination to stay straight.

SLICK: What you do, you make money. You make the legal money and you make it and you make it and you make it. You just don't give in, man. Cuz I don't wanna go back to doing illegal things, know what I'm saying? ... Lemme tell you what a good job is right now. Working five days a week, forty hours a week, working steady. That's what a good job is right now. Cuz there *ain't* no jobs out there right now. And a good guy, a good provider, is a guy that comes home with his paycheck every week and does the right thing. Doesn't go out drinkin' and druggin' and fuckin' going crazy and shit. That's a good person. That's what a lot of these people, myself included, are looking for. Just for something that you can say, "Hey look, I work my forty hours a week, I work hard all week, I take care of my kids, I take care of my family, y'know, I'm doing it the right way. Know what I mean?

Slick currently earns over $12 per hour, far more than the other Hallway Hangers. Still, the work is irregular: Slick gets laid off nearly every winter.

After "bouncing from job to job, just gettin' by, keepin' myself occupied, staying away from trouble," Jinks jumped into drug trafficking. Like Slick, he managed to climb out again, still intact, and currently has a steady job in a warehouse. Jinks lives in Clarendon Heights with his girlfriend and their six-year-old son. Apart from Steve, he seldom sees the Hallway Hangers.

JM: When you look back on the heyday, back in high school as teenagers, how do you look back on it?

JINKS: It's, say, confusing. I can't say I'd want to change the way it was, but I can't say I'd want it to be the same way. You know, because we were all so close back then. But we all went our separate ways. And if we were as close as we thought we were, we wouldn't've parted our ways. No matter what happened to us, each havin' our own families, we would always still be the same people we were and be that close. Which we're not.

Now twenty-five, Jinks fears his successors hanging around doorway #13. "I don't feel safe not knowing this kinda kid standin' out front. I don't know one of them. I don't feel safe." This is more than caution bred by age. Jinks fears the new hallway hangers because they are black.

When Frankie moved out of state with his mother in 1984, he came back every weekend to hang with his friends. Now he lives within a mile of Clarendon Heights but hardly ever stops by. Frankie is a changed man. He touches neither drugs nor alcohol, attends weekly AA meetings, sees counselors regularly, receives motivational training, and prays "every morning and every night—and a few hundred times during the day." This metamorphosis occurred in 1989 when Frankie perceived that his substance abuse combined with his violent temper could prove fatal. Now Frankie lives quietly with his son, his girlfriend, and her family. Despite this internal revolution, Frankie is unemployed.

Taken individually, the Hallway Hangers are easily seen as simply losers, the relative success of Slick, Jinks, and Frankie notwithstanding. The Hallway Hangers are alcoholics and drug addicts. They fight, they steal, they deal crack. They treat women as objects and victimize people of color. They can't stay out of jail, much less hold down steady jobs. In short, the Hallway Hangers seem to have screwed themselves. But once we widen the camera frame beyond individual portraits, we begin to see the background factors that influence the Hallway Hangers' lives and push them toward self-destructive behavior. The social and economic structure, often obscured and ignored, determines the opportunities, influences the attitudes, and affects the actions of the Hallway Hangers. Their story is not just a narrative string of personal failures. Rather, their personal biographies are inextricably linked with the changing structure of the economy. Even when the Hallway Hangers straighten up, as Frankie has, they are hard-pressed to make progress. The racism, sexism, substance abuse, violence, and criminal exploits of the Hallway Hangers are all tied to their subordinate position in the class structure and their quest to fashion identities as poor white men. This is not to say that they are absolved of responsibility for their attitudes and actions, nor that crime ceases to be criminal if committed by someone clinging to the bottom rung. But to understand what has happened to the Hallway Hangers between 1984 and 1991, we must examine their collective experience on the legitimate labor market and in the underground economy, and then we must strive to fathom how they understand and project themselves as lower-class American men.

On the Job

The Hallway Hangers have faced a job market completely different from the one their fathers entered as young men. With the restructuring of the U.S. economy—the shift from manufacturing to service employment—masses of traditional blue-collar jobs in industrial production have vanished. As markets and corporations have become internationalized, many American industries have reduced their labor and production costs by replacing workers with machines and by moving operations overseas. America's northern cities, hard hit by deindustrialization, now rely more on jobs devoted to the processing of information than on the production and distribution of goods. Clarendon Heights residents work in a city dominated by the economy of the service sector—administration, finance, and information exchange. In 1980 information-processing industries provided more jobs in the city than did manufacturing, construction, retail, and wholesale industries combined. In the mid-1950s, by contrast, jobs in the more traditional urban industries outnumbered data-processing employment by a margin of three to one.[1] By 1988 manufacturing jobs accounted for only 6 percent of all wage and salary jobs in the city.[2] Urban industrial transition is part of a larger national trend. Of the 23 million positions created between 1970 and 1984 across the country, 22 million were in the service sector, and today more than three-quarters of all employment is in the service industries.[3]

The rise in managerial, professional, technical, and administrative jobs, coupled with the precipitous drop in blue-collar employment, has landed high school dropouts in desperate straits. The number of jobs in the city held by those who did not complete high school declined by 59 percent between 1970 and 1980. Even those who finished high school have been stranded: Jobs held by high school graduates also dropped by 29 percent. Conversely, the quantity of jobs for college graduates grew by 71 percent.[4] In short, the new postindustrial economy has reduced opportunities for undereducated inner-city youths to a trickle.

The shift from a manufacturing to a service-based economy means that for the working class there are far fewer jobs with good wages, fringe benefits, and opportunities for advancement. Jobs in the service sector tend to be polarized between high-salaried, credentialed positions (such as those for attorneys and stockbrokers) and low-wage, menial positions that offer little security (such as those for janitors, security guards, and fast-food cooks). Many service jobs pay little more than $5 per hour, whereas workers in unionized manufacturing industries have often made two, three, and even four times that amount. Between 1979 and 1987, 50 percent of all new jobs created in the United States were at or below the poverty level, only 38 percent were at the middle-income level, and a mere 12 percent were at the high-wage level.[5]

The occupational histories of the Hallway Hangers between 1984 and 1991 reflect the shift from a manufacturing- to a service-based economy. They have been employed as janitors, garbage collectors, cooks, caterers, couriers, cleaners, carpet layers, landscapers, inventory keepers, movers, packers, plumbers' assistants, groundsmen, soldiers, and store clerks. They have worked at car washes, junkyards, hotels, and restaurants. Although the Hallway Hangers have labored in the construction industry, most of these jobs were "off the books" and approximated service work rather than traditional blue-collar employment in terms of earnings, job security, and working conditions. And, as noted, the service sector tends to pay low wages, offer few opportunities for promotion, and encourage high turnover. The experiences of the Hallway Hangers bear this out.

Few of the Hallway Hangers have held stable jobs. Even Jinks, who has had his current job for over three years, has worked for nine different employers since February 1984. Frankie has held twelve jobs. Despite having been incarcerated for most of the period under consideration, Shorty and Stoney have had thirteen jobs between them. Boo-Boo has held six jobs in between periods of unemployment. In previous decades, most American youths, preoccupied with their peer group and prospective sexual partners, went through a period of labor market experimentation and adjustment before they settled down into a career job.[6] Many of the Hallway Hangers, however, have failed to hold a steady job even in their midtwenties. Although some of this turnover can be attributed to their behavior, much of it stems from the nature of the jobs the Hallway Hangers have held. Slick, Steve, and Shorty, for instance, have all been routinely laid off from their construction jobs during the winter months. Similarly, seasonal swings have forced Jinks to switch from one hotel job to another: "It would get slow around Christmas time. They were cutting my days from working five days to two days. ... I skipped around, I jumped to three different hotels. Hey, you gotta pay for those Christmas presents." Shorty had two stints working for the city but was laid off just before qualifying as a permanent employee. Recent research suggests that the Hallway Hangers are not atypical. Paul Osterman's 1992 study shows that roughly a third of all high school graduates, and even more high school dropouts, fail to find stable employment by the time they are thirty.[7]

All of the Hallway Hangers have worked "under the table." Steve, Boo-Boo, Frankie, Shorty, and Jinks have worked in construction illegally. Most of Stoney's jobs at pizza places and Boo-Boo's two most recent jobs—at a scrap yard and a moving company—have been "off the books." Shorty's most recent employer, the owner of a liquor store, paid him cash.

SHORTY: The job in the liquor store, ha: five bucks an hour. But I needed the money. Anything goes, y'know. ... I stayed there for five months. I asked him for a dollar raise, y'know, cuz I was doin' everything. I was doin' the inventory, the shipping, receiving, cash registering, sayin', "I can't be doin' all this shit. Give me some more money." Y'know, he wouldn't give it to me, so I left.

JM: Do you like working under the table, or would you prefer to get a check?

SHORTY: At first I liked getting cash. No paperwork or taxes to worry about. Like he's doing me a favor, y'know? But really, I'm the one getting fucked. No fucking Social Security when I'm an old geezer, no unemployment when I get laid off. And no help if you get hurt, no what's it called—workmen's compensation. It's better to get a regular check. I was working carpentry for a real estate company. It was under the table. But then we went on the books because they had too many guys workin' for them.

JM: Did you have to take a pay cut when you went on the books?

SHORTY: No, I got a raise.

JM: Have you ever insisted on being paid by check?

SHORTY: What're you, fuckin' nuts, Jay? "Excuse me, mister, could I have a check, please?" I'd be on my ass at home the next day watching *General Hospital,* cuz there's a hundred and fifty fucking guys ready to work in my place.

Shorty suggests that "off the books" employment outside the framework of public regulation benefits employers while hurting workers, and that a reserve army of unemployed people further undermines the position of employees. All of this is confirmed by Saskia Sassen, whose New York study indicates that the growth of the informal economy represents a structural feature of the postindustrial city.[8] Working "under the table," the Hallway Hangers, like so many other inner-city residents, sell their labor in a market unfettered by laws, job descriptions, or institutional constraints. Job security is nonexistent, as Shorty underlines by saying *when* rather than *if* he is laid off. Under such conditions, unprotected by the laws that the working class fought to institutionalize, a human being's labor is most nearly reduced to a mere commodity.

The hourly wages of the Hallway Hangers have ranged from $3.65 to $12.50 but most of their jobs paid between $5.00 and $7.00 an hour. Again, their experience is connected to larger economic trends. Over the past two decades, the real annual earnings of young adult men have deteriorated by 31 percent.[9] In contrast to most of the Hallway Hangers, who have been stuck in entry-level positions, Slick has more than doubled his earnings.

SLICK: When I started roofing I was making six dollars an hour, and now I make twelve-fifty. I went from a laborer to assistant foreman over about a six-year period of time with the same company.

JM: So although you usually get laid off in the winter, you're bringing in good money, now.

SLICK: Yeah, I bust my ass, but bills are still breaking my back.

JM: Tell me about them.

SLICK: I pay child support for my two kids, that's the first priority. Then five hundred dollars a month for rent. We gotta have a roof over our head. [Slick lives with his girlfriend Denise and Sean, their infant son.] And this month I gotta pay three hundred dollars for Sean's christening. I gotta pay for the DJ and the hall—that's three hundred and fifty dollars. Then I got Denise's father's birthday this month—that's gonna cost us at least another hundred and a half. Then I got her cousin's christening this Sunday. That'll probably cost us half a yarder—fifty bucks. Plus all the photos of Sean. Not to mention the little stuff like eating, like food shopping and shit. It adds up like crazy. You work longer hours, know what I'm saying? But there's only so many hours in a week. And I didn't count the phone bill, the electric bill, the heating bill.

Most of the Hallway Hangers have earned roughly half of what Slick currently makes. Only Jinks, who makes $8.93 an hour after three years with one company, has also been able to set up a household with his girlfriend. The rest of the Hallway Hangers have lived with parents and friends, or have been incarcerated or homeless. All of them have worked for an hourly wage rather than a salary. None has owned a car.

Slick and Jinks are not the only Hallway Hangers to have received raises. Shorty's account of one of his "under the table" construction jobs has an interesting twist.

SHORTY: I started off at five dollars an hour, I was just a laborer, y'know, sweepin' up and shit after the carpenters. I stayed there about a year and I was making nine bucks an hour, carpenter's helper. They were paying me good. Then they just laid everybody off because we finished. What they were doing was makin' all them old buildings into condos, moving ... all the poor people out. That's why all the kids, they started bringing all the fuckin' condos down and smashin' the windows every night. We go and put up nice siding and something like that, and they'd go buy fuckin' paint and throw it on there and everything, cuz they were moving all the poor people out and and movin' all the yuppies in and shit.

JM: So what did you think of that?

SHORTY: I thought it was wrong, y'know, but hey, I was getting paid for fuckin' work, y'know. Gotta make some money. Shit, the way I look at it now, those kids were helping me by trashing our work. Cuz I woulda got laid off sooner. But at the time I was pissed off. Come and see your work all fucked up each morning.

Frankie was also promoted in one of his early jobs when he was living out of state with his mother.

FRANKIE: I went in as like a dockperson, y'know, just unloading trucks, and I ended up doin' pretty well. It was a friend of a friend that helped me out. I ended up going from a dockworker to a shipper to a material control specialist. I was sittin' on a computer all fucking day.

JM: Tell me about how you were able to move up.

FRANKIE: Actually, it was because I knew this guy. A lot of it was luck. It was this guy who drank and couldn't make it in on Saturdays. I had to replace him, and they threw me on a computer, because they were so far behind. And they noticed I caught on real quick, and they sent me to school. I moved to shipper within six months and after that, I'd say within another six months, I became a material control specialist. What I was doin', I was keepin' a computerized inventory for them. They sent me to a few courses, y'know.

Frankie is the only Hallway Hanger to have received any formal training on the job.

The Hallway Hangers have generally worked at jobs for which few skills are required and few can be learned: dead-end jobs with little opportunity for advancement and little reward for seniority in the form of higher pay or a better position. Boo-Boo's experience, for example, contrasts with Frankie's.

BOO-BOO: I worked for this moving company. I worked for them awhile, then I quit. I was gettin' ten dollars an hour, under the table. It was good. I was makin' like a hundred dollars a day. It was excellent. I was doing all right then.

JM: Why'd you quit?

BOO-BOO: Well, he started to get this attitude where, instead of promoting me, he was demoting me. First I was makin' ten dollars an hour, then he brought it down to seven-fifty, and I was takin' it for a while. But then, y'know, you move pianos, you move everything, anything, you name it, we're moving it. Big giant copy machines. All kinds of stuff. If anybody's working a job, working hard, doing a good job, and they're getting ten dollars an hour, you never get demoted. I've never heard of anyone getting demoted. Taking money away, cuz he said he was losing money. It was a self-made business, his own business. He made it himself. He has like three trucks. He owns his own house. Nice new

Volvo. He was just getting real cheap about everything, so I just like broke loose. I said, "Sorry, dude, I can't work for you anymore." I just quit.

Most of the Hallway Hangers' jobs have been with small firms, which have a high chance of failure and are especially susceptible to downturns in the business cycle. Jinks did renovation work for a year and a half "til the company went bankrupt on me and left out owing me twelve hundred dollars. How could I afford to fight it in court?"

Jobs in the service economy, especially with small firms, are seldom unionized. Of the Hallway Hangers, only Frankie has been in a labor union. He worked on a catering crew with clear lines of advancement and managed to move up.

FRANKIE: I ended up getting in a hotel/restaurant union. I started off as what they call a runner and within two days I went from becoming a runner to general service in the catering crew.

JM: What's a runner?

FRANKIE: A runner was just you run supplies from the kitchen to the entrees. And I ended up becoming general service for the catering within two days. From a runner to general service was like a buck-fifty raise within two days. And within the month I got another two-fifty raise because I became a steward on the crew. It was a union job with union rates and I was getting merit raises, too, y'know. I was makin' good money there. I was gettin' three squares [meals] a day. And the overtime was great. It was great. I was working hard, but it was also a learning process.

Frankie credits the union for helping to ensure a decent pay scale, opportunities for promotion, and a measure of job satisfaction. But he is most indebted to the union for the personal support it lent him. When in 1989 Frankie approached his shop steward about his addiction to drugs and alcohol, the union arranged for thirty days of residential treatment and then for placement in a halfway house. Back on the job, Frankie got into a fist fight when two colleagues ridiculed his temperance. He was fired and decided not to appeal against his termination.

FRANKIE: I just said, "Fuck it. There's so much booze around here anyway." And I left the job, y'know. I'm kickin' myself in the ass over that. But I just couldn't do it. So I left there. An' I tell you, I haven't been drinking in—it'll be two years next Thursday.

Jinks has worked at hotels as a cleaner and with banquet set-ups and convention services. He explained that none of his jobs were unionized, "but all the hotels around here, they keep competitive with the union wage, so they avoid everyone going into unions." Jinks made up to $6.95 an hour but kept having his work-week reduced during the off-season. Also, he hated his work hours.

JINKS: I worked the graveyard shift, 11 P.M. to 7 A.M., at one hotel, and then at the Marriott was swing shift. I would work one during the day, one at night. Same thing with the Hyatt Regency, was no set hours. It was whenever there was work to be done, I'd work.

Still, unlike most of the Hallway Hangers, Jinks received some employment bene-fits. "If anyone else out here [Clarendon Heights] gets sick, they're fucked, but I've gotten health insurance with most of my [hotel] jobs."

As with hotels, restaurants, and small businesses, the construction industry can be devastated by recession. In fact, in the years after the bottom fell out of the lo-cal economy in 1989, 45 percent of low-level construction jobs were lost.[10] Since then, with the exception of Slick, the Hallway Hangers could not even rely on ca-sual work as day laborers. As Steve complains, "Nowadays, man, it's fuckin' tough [to get a job]." Slick concurs: "There *ain't* no jobs out there right now." By saying "nowadays" and "now," Steve and Slick emphasize their current difficulty finding work. The recession exacerbates the more permanent bias in the labor market against the unskilled. Between 1980 and 1990, the unemployment rate in the city for high school dropouts rose from 19 to 35 percent. For high school graduates the unemployment rate increased from 12 to 18 percent.[11] Unemployment, always a problem for the Hallway Hangers, has taken an especially severe toll since 1989. Shorty, Steve, and Boo-Boo have all had long bouts of unemployment, and none have qualified for unemployment benefits because their work has been "off the books."

Unemployment has been particularly difficult for Frankie to accept. Having quit drinking and doing drugs, he has been trying to turn his history of substance abuse into an asset on the job market. Frankie still attends Alcoholics Anonymous and Narcotics Anonymous meetings regularly and seldom visits Clarendon Heights, where he is now known as "preacher" for his sermons on the evils of al-cohol and drug abuse. Unemployed, he is currently studying part time and hopes to work as an apprentice in building maintenance, learning about heating, venti-lation, and air conditioning. His tuition and part of his training wage will be paid by a government agency for the disabled. As a recovering alcoholic, Frankie is eli-gible for its programs. He has also learned job application and interviewing skills, and sees two personal counselors regularly. The irony is that Frankie held down a number of jobs while addicted. "It's fucked up," he says. "Now I'm sober and I've got all this help, and I'm unemployed." Indeed, that so many of the Hallway Hangers could do their jobs while drunk or stoned says something about their at-titudes toward work, but perhaps even more about the types of jobs they have held.

The Hallway Hangers have relied almost exclusively on one means of landing their jobs: connections. It was through his brothers that Jinks was offered a job laying carpet. And his mother, a long-term employee at the Hyatt, found him his first hotel job. Steve and Shorty secured construction jobs through friends, including Slick. After describing how scarce jobs are, Steve added, "I'm lucky I know a few people, that's about it." Shorty also found other jobs by exploiting personal contacts. "I got connections," says Shorty. "Look at my brothers; they're both cops. They know a lotta politicians." When he ran out of contacts, Shorty had no success on the labor market. "I went to a lot of places and filled out applications, but nobody called me. Fucking nobody." Boo-Boo also secured his position with the moving company through a Clarendon Heights friend. Frankie was offered nearly all of his twelve jobs through connections.

FRANKIE: The job on the catering crew was like the only job I actually went and applied for. Everything else was handed to me.

JM: How did that happen, those connections?

FRANKIE: I come from a big family, a pretty well-known family. Just from the local bars, y'know, that's the way it works. That's the bottom line. ... Politicians, guys I knew who were already working for the city or for the state. Thing is, I've burned a lot of those bridges now."

What success the Hallway Hangers have had on the job market seems to have been achieved almost exclusively through informal networking.

The networks to which the Hallway Hangers have access, however, are inferior to those of the more affluent—a point that Jinks well understands.

JM: Have you found in your own working career that connections have been helpful?

JINKS: Yes, the jobs I used my connections for, my mother, that was helpful. But even now, where I work now, I see my boss's son works for him, okay. He has this kid who graduated from college, he's a salesman. The kid shows up maybe one day a week, he does absolutely nothing. He's a complete moron, and he can do as he pleases because his father's the boss. Because he's got money it makes everything he does right, y'know, whether it be wrong or right. He can't do no wrong. I see it at my job and everywhere else, and it's just all over the world.

Jinks's mother helped him get entry-level jobs in hotels, and his brothers helped Jinks get a job laying carpet for a daily wage of $35. For that he is grateful. But Jinks is also aggrieved that middle-class youths, by virtue of their more privileged background, have access to superior social networks and hence better jobs.

Frankie has had a similar experience, not uncommon in small firms where managerial control in the workplace tends to be informal, unstructured, and concentrated in the hands of family members.

FRANKIE: I also became a material control specialist for a hearing aid company. … I left there—it was a family-oriented business and they brang in their son, but he's a high school kid, y'know, and (he says this incredulously) he became my *boss*. And here he's only a junior in high school. I couldn't accept that. His mother was the personnel director, his father was the general manager, his two brothers were the other two managers, so they were weaning this kid in. So I went, y'know, my old method I woulda just left. But I went and had a discussion with his old man. I just told him, "I just can't find myself taking orders and shit from this kid." He said, y'know, he didn't blame me. But he also said, "You realize this is my son?" So I told him okay, I told him I'd hafta leave.

JM: Was it just the idea of having the kid as your boss, or was it how it worked out in practice, was the kid an asshole? ·

FRANKIE: He was an asshole. He didn't know the job, but he was trying to change standard operating procedures to his way. "I think it'd be better this way." And I'd say, "No, it's not, and this is why." Simple. He'd say, "Well I don't care why." It was just a lot of that on a daily basis. What I felt was my old behavior, y'know, the old project self coming out of me, and I was gonna fucking whack the shit out of him, is what I was gonna do. But I know I was the only one gonna get hurt out of that. I finally learnt, I ain't gonna lower myself to this kid, so I gave two weeks' notice. I left but then I was unemployed for *a while*. … And it's been tough. Cuz, y'know, the economy fucking sucks.

For Frankie, the cost of maintaining his pride has been the trial of extended unemployment.

In fact, Frankie's job at the hearing-aid company had already been straining his sense of self.

FRANKIE: It was just a desk job, y'know, and that's not me. I'm not a desk job guy. It was a good job if you could sit at a desk for eight hours a day.

JM: What was it about the desk job that … ?

FRANKIE: I just, it's just not me, man. You know me, I'm hyper. It was a lotta things. People's mothers, I remember these two ladies, they useta kill me. All they did was talk to me about how their sons hung out with little troublemakers and punks and all that. And just the office atmosphere, I'm not big into gossip, never was and never will be. Just not able to leave these people, y'know? At least if you work in a warehouse or somethin', y'know, "I gotta go do something." You can only go to the bathroom so many times in an office (*laughs*). I'm just too hyper, man. I just couldn't sit there. Y'know, they wanted me to wear a shirt and tie, and I'm a jeans and dungarees guy. That's just not me, y'know. Yeah, so I left there in August '90 when they brought their son in.

The humiliation of working under an incompetent youngster, combined with the passivity and social relations of white-collar work, spurred Frankie to quit the job.

The Hallway Hangers have been trapped in what economists call the secondary labor market—the subordinate segment of the job structure where the market is severely skewed against workers. Jobs in the primary labor markets provide wages that can support families and an internal career structure, but the rules of the game are different in the secondary labor market. Wages are lower, raises are infrequent, training is minimal, advancement is rare, and turnover is high. Neither seniority nor education provide much of a return for workers in the secondary labor market.[12]

Whereas many youths begin their working careers in the secondary labor market and then break into the primary sectors, the Hallway Hangers have been confined to the secondary sector. Slick, the highest paid among them, still struggles to support his family and will be laid off as soon as the snow flies. Jinks's warehouse job has provided more security than his hotel jobs but offers little scope for advancement and little job satisfaction. Frankie, the only one to receive formal training on the job, has been unemployed for several months, despite having undergone state-sponsored training to improve his job prospects. These have been the success stories. The remainder of the Hallway Hangers have eked out a subsistence wage on the margins of the American economy. When they have managed to find work, it has tended to be "off the books." Asked what his best job has been over the past seven years, Boo-Boo answered, "The one at the junkyard." He made $5 per hour "under the table." Although their experiences on the job market have been varied, the Hallway Hangers have generally held menial, dead-end jobs in the secondary labor market.

Working the Street

When the legitimate job market fails them, the Hallway Hangers can turn to the underground economy. Since 1984 almost all of the Hallway Hangers have at least supplemented their income from earnings on the burgeoning, multibillion-dollar drug market. The street economy promises better money than does conventional employment. It also provides a work site that does not demean the Hallway Hangers or drain their dignity.[13] As workers in the underground economy, they won't have to take orders from a boss's arrogant son, nor will they have to gossip with office colleagues and strain to camouflage their street identities. They won't be asked, as Boo-Boo was, to take a 25 percent pay cut after several months on the job. Still, the informal economy is hardly a mecca of opportunity. The risks are serious and, in many cases, have been undertaken by the Hallway Hangers only when other options have been played out. After being cheap labor fodder for firms intent on avoiding unions and even the minimal obligations of a bona fide payroll, many of the Hallway Hangers have been unemployed but barred from the unemployment line. Ineligible for benefits and desperate for income, they have moved from outlaw "under the table" employment to illegal jobs dealing drugs. For most of them, the experience has proved as unsatisfactory as their work in the formal economy.

While there has been a shift in the U.S. economy in the past twenty-five years from manufacturing to service jobs, an even more dramatic change has occurred in the Clarendon Heights drug economy over the past ten years. In early 1984 marijuana was still the most popular drug in Clarendon Heights. But with U.S. drug policy concentrating on interception at the borders, the price of marijuana has skyrocketed while the cost of cocaine has come down.

FRANKIE: Cocaine's getting cheaper. Now you can get a quarter [gram] for fifteen bucks. ... Pot's outrageous nowadays. I mean, jeez, you're paying a hundred and eighty bucks for an ounce. When I first started smoking pot, it was forty bucks, you get a four-finger ounce. Pot's too high. It's too big to smuggle. C'mon, y'know. Seventy thousand dollars of cocaine you throw in your suitcase. You need a fucking truck for the pot.

(*in a separate conversation*)

SHORTY: Weed's too expensive. ... You used to get a joint the size of your pinkie for a buck. Now you pay five dollars for a pinner. You get a couple of pieces of leaves, two twigs, and about ten seeds, and you're paying five bucks for it. ... The cheapest thing is coke. Everybody and their mother's doing coke now.

As in the rest of the country, cocaine became much more prevalent in Clarendon Heights during the mid-1980s. In 1984 all of the Hallway Hangers enjoyed snorting powdered cocaine for its intense, euphoric high. Chris would occasionally dissolve the powdered cocaine into an injectable fluid and "shoot it up."

Then came the biggest change in the local drug economy: Cocaine began to be marketed in its unadulterated "base" form known as "crack." Prepared and distributed in small crystalline quantities, crack sold for as little as $5, far less than the minimum price tag for powdered cocaine. And crack is easily smoked. Absorbed into the bloodstream through thousands of tiny capillaries in the lungs rather than through the nose's mucous membrane, crack cocaine provides a more intense high. And whereas powder can be "cut" and significantly adulterated, base or crack is purer and more addictive.

JINKS: Crack, it's cheaper to buy [than powdered cocaine]. The high is better than just snorting coke, but it don't last as long. Everyone enjoys it more, but the only problem it's more addictive. You get addicted quicker to it. ... It's a good high, but then after you're comin' down and you have no more money and you can't get no more, it's depression. It's even worse than comin' down from snorting it. You're like, "Wow, where did all my fuckin' money go?" And if you have anything in your pocket, you'll go give it to the dealer to get more crack.

(*in a separate interview*)

FRANKIE: Coke is faster-paced [than marijuana], it's more addicting and you need a lot more, and people realized that. That's why they developed crack, cuz it's even more addicting. ... Everybody's out there to get their own, man, if you're hooked on the shit. I know personally, you take that first hit, and it feels fucking great. But after that, you're just chasing, man, feel like shit the rest of the time. And, y'know, you'll do whatever it takes to fuckin' get high.

The advent of crack capitalism in Clarendon Heights has changed the nature of dealing. Buyers no longer come into doorway #13, sample the merchandise, haggle over the price, and make their purchase. The transaction is now furtive and impersonal as money and pre-packaged drugs change hands swiftly. The large volumes of cash and the desperation of addicts make the threat of predatory violence from customers and competitors as worrisome as police detection. "It's a fucking drugstore out here," relates Steve. "Twenty-four hours a day." Indeed, before the police cracked down, a convenient "drive-through" dimension had been added to the business. Customers placed their order at the curb, drove around the block, and picked up their drugs on the return pass.

The Hallway Hangers report that by dealing full time they could make up to a thousand dollars a week. Some worked as street sellers; others worked out of their homes and out of bars. Chris, Slick, Jinks, and Frankie have all dealt intensively on a full-time basis, but none of them was able to stay in the drug business for more than a year. The other Hallway Hangers—Steve, Shorty, Boo-Boo, and Stoney—have peddled drugs sporadically over the past seven years to supplement their incomes.

If the Hallway Hangers can make so much money in the drug economy, why don't they make a career of it? All of them understand the risks. Three young men on the fringes of the Hallway Hangers have been killed over the past five years, and the Hallway Hangers themselves have lost their youthful sense of immortality.

Many of them have been pushed out of the underground economy by teenagers who are willing to take more risks.

FRANKIE: There's a lotta quick money to be made, so they're cliquin' up, they're becoming cliques, gangs, whatever you wanna fucking call 'em. And, y'know, they don't care about dyin', so they saying. That's the coke talkin', and I know that. But, y'know, it's the image they have to put out.

When Slick dealt full time he and his girlfriend Denise lived in a condominium. A year later he bailed out because of the risks.

JM: How did you go back to eight dollars an hour if you know you can make ...

SLICK: Two hundred dollars a day ...

JM: On the street?

SLICK: Yeah. You gotta remember, you gonna get caught. People, kids on the street, guys, they don't think far enough ahead. They thinkin' for now, what can I do right now. Don't forget when you're sixty-five and don't get no Social Security, what you gonna do then, still sell drugs? Sometimes it does pay off, though.

JM: Can it pay off over the long term if you play your cards right?

SLICK: Can it pay off? Yeah, it can. But there's not too many people out there who can do it, y'know. It takes a lot of organizational skills. You can make a go, but then you gotta worry about getting caught, you always gotta be looking over your shoulder. Worry that someone's gonna rat you out. And that's a big worry, believe me, every night. Every time you see a police officer, thinking, is he gonna be grabbing me on something. You always gotta look out. You always gotta worry about it. This is my second son. Before he was born, before I started working steady, I was making whatever money I could, but I knew when to stop, you know what I mean? You can't, I knew when not to go too far, knew when I was pushing it.

Jinks very nearly pushed it too far and, like Slick, hates to consider what that would have meant for his child.

JINKS: I was runnin' with this guy. I was sellin' for him. I had five pounds of pot. I had it in three different houses. I would go with him to pick up a kilo of cocaine. Go with him, break it up on the scale into ounces. I was making money. It was a quick cash flow.

JM: During that time, how much would you bring in on a good week?

JINKS: On a good week a couple of thousand dollars, easily.

JM: So how would you discipline yourself from getting used to making that kind of money to go back to a steady job?

JINKS: See, I got, I got a scare of my lifetime because the kid I was dealing with was with a few other people, and they got arrested for murder. And they doin' big time in jail now. They got convicted. That was enough to put fear in me.

JM: You could've been with them?

JINKS: Exactly. Because I was goin' everywhere with this guy. I mean, I was seeing machine guns, hand grenades; this guy had everything. And he would've done anything for me. And I was the same way. I would've done anything for him. So I looked at it as I could've been in that position.

JM: Did you just stop completely?

JINKS: Yes, yes, I did away with it all.

JM: Right, and so lookin' back on that ...

JINKS: It's a scary thought, it's a scary thought. I look at it: There was two paths I could've took. I took the right one. If I took the wrong one, I could be dead right now, or I could be behind bars for the rest of my life, never have the chance to see my son grow.

Apart from the risks of violence and arrest, the Hallway Hangers perceive the impact that cocaine addiction had on their profit margin.

JM: What happened with your dealing?

FRANKIE: Well, for one thing, my connection got popped [arrested]. But another thing is that my habit grew. I was kinda losing money cuz I was doing more. And the people working for me, they were coming up with some *serious* stories, y'know, "This happened ..." Cuz I know today their habit grew. It became a losing business for me. Just due to addiction. ... I useta have a quarter gram of coke last me a night. Towards the end, y'know, that wasn't even a hit.

Addiction also cut into Steve's illicit earnings in the cocaine trade.

STEVE: I was sellin' the shit for a while. I got heavy into that.

JM: Just marijuana, or coke?

STEVE: Coke. I got too heavy ...

JM: That's where the money is?

STEVE: Yeah, but it's not worth it either. You do more than you sell, for Chrissakes. You get caught up in it.

"Getting caught up in cocaine" is a recurrent theme among the Hallway Hangers.

FRANKIE: I got violent, man. And I know today the coke had a lot to do with it. I never really did coke before, cuz I seen what it did. But then I just got caught up in it. It made me violent, between that and the booze. When I useta just drink, I'd get drunk, I'd go home, and I'd pass out. When I drink and do coke, I stay up. I get crazy. And coke enabled me to drink more. It also changed my attitude. You get low on your coke, you start thinkin' where the next shit's coming from. You do anything to get it. Rob, steal, beat the shit outta someone, do what you gotta do. I know that's what I did. ...

I was all over, man. I tell ya, I'd be in an apartment on Juniper Street one day and I'd be gettin' high with fuckin' two Colombians in the suburbs at four o'clock in the morning the next night. And don't know these two fuckers from a hole in the wall. It was sick. It put me in situations that. ... See, one thing I was brought up, be careful who you're with, keep your mouth fucking shut, and just go about your business. I started doing coke and I started searching for these crazy fucking people cuz I knew they had coke and I knew I wanted it. I was around people I didn't like, man. I knew they were snitches, they were no good; but they had coke, so I would buddy up with them, y'know? Something that totally goes against my grain, what I was taught. So yeah, it fuckin', it even lowered my street values, which is, y'know, pretty incredible. ...

I know what it is like to be strung out on fuckin' coke and to think, I mean, I've thought of suicide, homicide myself, on coke. ...

I did controlled thieving and shit like that, y'know? In the end, I'd deal the coke but I'd just deal it so I'd have some for me. I wouldn't deal it to make money. Y'know, I'd go grab an eight-ball off one guy and sell so much and have the rest for me. And then I'd just take it. Fuck up people, y'know? Fuck it. I was entitled to it, so I thought.

Boo-Boo also got caught up in the cocaine racket—with near-fatal consequences.

BOO-BOO: I got caught up in all this bullshit. Drugs and shit, cocaine. I was caught up in drugs from November of '90 til the first of June [1991]. I got caught up in the drugs. I moved to Raymond and I started meeting all kinds of people, cuz my sister lived there. One night, they just come over and they had coke and stuff like that, and they said, "Do you mind?" Cuz they were smoking it.

And a kid come out and said, "Do you want to try it?" And that it would be good. So I did it, and it was, tsph, just caught up in it. I was just caught up, I could feel it coming over me.

JM: It's a good high?

BOO-BOO: Yeah. Excellent. So I just got caught up in it and it was like an everyday thing. It was like I didn't care about anything. Well, I cared, but that's what I wanted to do almost every day, get high and get high and get high and get high (*trails off*).

I never really had money. I was never really buying it. It was just like people coming over, people would ask me where they could get it and I was getting it for them. It was just craziness. ... At the beginning, it just started off with one day them coming over and they got like twenty dollars' worth of stuff and we sat there and we like smoked it, and it just, it just, y'know, they'd come back the next day and they'd have more, and I'd go out and I'd like snooze around just to get a little more higher and stuff like that. Sometimes we'd be up all night, til the next morning, smoking and smoking and smoking and smoking. Not caring. Just started not caring about anything, really. ... They'd all come up to our apartment. It was one of the biggest drug streets in Raymond. The people upstairs on both sides, they sold it. They sold it across the street, down the street, around the corner. It was, it was just everywhere.

JM: So were you able to make some money that way?

BOO-BOO: I was making a little bit of money, then one time I got caught up with this guy who gave me some stuff to sell, and I didn't.

JM: Smoked it all?

BOO-BOO: All of it. He tried to shoot me twice. ... He gave me three hundred and forty dollars worth of stuff, worth of rocks all made up. He told me I could keep seventy dollars for myself and sell the rest. I said fine. So what I did is, like a fool, I smoked one of them things, and it was history. I sold some, but then I spent that money on more. Screwed up. He almost shot me. Came to my house like three days later with a nine millimeter, and he was gonna shoot me. He had the gun out. I just had to beg him, told him I'd get the money for him. I tried to get up the money. I got up some of the money for him, but I didn't get it all. And then one day I was out and still getting high and he saw me, pulled the gun on me again. I was lucky, man. ... Drugs will fuck you up.

Of all the Hallway Hangers, it is Chris who most dramatically illustrates how "drugs will fuck you up." Interviewed in 1991 as he awaited trial for three armed robberies, Chris described his tight downward spiral.

CHRIS: It's been crazy. I know it. I can see what I've done to my mom, what I'm doing to myself. I can see it, but I can't fucking seem to do anything about it. I've got the habit and I can't kick it. Freebasing. I'd just do what I had to to take care of business. I'd leave Samantha sleeping in a hallway and go out and do whatever I had to so we could get our next smoke. Break into houses and take money, cameras, VCRs, stereos, mountain bikes, clothes—whatever shit I could find. And then sell them on the street for next to nothing. Cuz these motherfuckers *know* you're desperate. Man, I've taken fifty bucks for a stereo I know is worth more than a thousand. But it don't matter, cuz whatever I got would be smoked up. I stole five hundred dollars out of a guy's wallet. It was on his dresser and his keys fell right by his fucking head. Dude didn't wake up, though. I took his mountain bike—it was right by the door—and rode back to where Samantha was spending the night in this base house. I sold the mountain bike by ten o'clock for a hundred bucks. By noon we were broke. Went through that six hundred bucks in a morning. You do a hit, next thing you know, you're broke. ... Man, I stole my sister's jewelry, all kinds of shit. Now look at me. No socks, no deodorant cuz I don't have no money. Shittin' in a fucking bucket in here, no lie. What the fuck kind of life is this?

Awaiting trial, Chris has checked into the jail's detox and drug-rehab program, the first move he has made to deal with his drug problem. Even so, Chris speaks with a subdued desperation, has little hope for the future, and feels desperately lonely.

Denied conventional careers, the Hallway Hangers have turned to the underground economy. Peddling drugs holds out the prospect of fast money and respect on the street. But a workplace that offers more dignity than jobs in the formal economy turns out to be fraught with danger. And for drug entrepreneurs, distribution has a way of turning into consumption, especially of crack cocaine. The Hallway Hangers have quit the drug business, but not before some were sucked into a downward spiral fueled by their own addiction, of which Chris is only the most spectacular example. "Caught up in" the cocaine racket, the Hallway Hangers have generally lost rather than gained autonomy and independence in the informal economy.

The allure of a career in the underground economy makes sense only when measured against the competing option of an underpaid menial job in the secondary labor market. Unemployment is the most powerful incentive. Frankie dealt intensively when he was jobless after returning from out of state in 1988. Laid off from his hotel job, Jinks renewed a friendship with a big-time player in the drug world and began dealing for him. And Slick turned to the drug economy in 1990 when his construction job was one of thousands threatened by the local economy's steep slide. In neighborhoods like Clarendon Heights, there are few career alternatives to crack capitalism.

For the Hallway Hangers drugs are a form of recreation as well as a form of work. Asked about their abuse of drugs and alcohol, Stoney replies, "It's a form of recreation. That's our recreation. Rich kids might go skiing or snow-mobiling or go on vacations. We get high." The Hallway Hangers do not have the resources to "get away from it all" through conventional leisure pursuits, so they use drugs to escape the boredom, powerlessness, and despair that poverty breeds.

Stoney implies that the attraction of drugs for the Hallway Hangers can be understood only against the backdrop of class exploitation; Slick makes a similar point from a different angle.

JM: Why did you, not you particularly but the whole group of you, use drugs so heavily? What was the allure of drugs for you guys?

SLICK: Escape.

JM: From?

SLICK: From the way you are. You know what I mean. You use drugs, you get a sense of fucking balls. You know what I mean? You're not yourself. You're somebody that you really want to be.

Drugs, says Slick, promise power and self-actualization, which are otherwise beyond the Hallway Hangers. After five years of living among and learning from crack dealers in East Harlem, anthropologist Philippe Bourgois agrees. Bourgois argues that drugs provide an illusory escape from oppression. "Instantaneously," he writes, "the user is transformed from an unemployed, depressed high school dropout, despised by the world—and secretly convinced that his failure is due to his own inherent stupidity and disorganization."[14] But the "born-again metamorphosis" offered by substance abuse, especially crack, energizes the user for only a matter of minutes at most. And as Slick has learned from hard experience, drugs do not provide power—only a fleeting "sense" of it. Moreover, the dependency and instability that drugs often bring in their wake only compound and thicken the debilitating effects of poverty from which drugs are meant to offer an escape.

Drug dealing is the most popular way of generating income in the underground economy, but it is not the only way. Theft was an important element in the early criminal careers of the Hallway Hangers; they stole bicycles and cars, broke into local stores and factories, and often sold the stolen merchandise on the underground market to pay for teenage necessities like sneakers and six-packs. Chris continued to steal to support his cocaine habit; and Frankie, until he quit doing drugs, would rob or extort money and drugs from younger, less experienced criminals. But the link between drugs and crime works differently for Stoney. Rather than robbing in order to get high, Stoney seems to get high in order to commit mindless robberies.

STONEY: It's the valiums, man. They make me do crazy shit but I can't seem to
leave them alone. I'll do ten or fifteen of 'em and then drink to get the high. Af-
terwards, I can't remember what I've done, won't remember a thing.

As noted earlier, Stoney was convicted of attempting to rob a convenience store
with a tire iron after taking ten valiums and drinking on top of that. "It's a stupid
high; it's a fuck-up high," Stoney admits. "It depresses you." Several months after
his release from prison, he was arrested again for armed robbery—again, after
drinking and dropping valiums. This was the time he had held up a pizza deliveryman for forty dollars and a large pizza.

By contrast, Boo-Boo turned to robbery for strictly economic reasons, two
years before getting involved in serious drug abuse. He was living with his
girlfriend Ginger and their two children in a dilapidated basement apartment because Ginger had not received a subsidized housing voucher.

JM: When you were unemployed, how would you hustle up the money and stuff?

BOO-BOO: Whaddya mean?

JM: How would you get, y'know, how would you survive?

BOO-BOO: Well, my girlfriend got her check and stuff like that. ... And me and
some friends, we robbed a night deposit thing one night. Made three thousand
dollars. Got caught up in that. We did that a couple of times. ... I did it cuz I
needed, our bills were all screwed up and stuff. We were behind in rent, and I
needed food and my kids needed clothes, and Ginger wanted all kinds of stuff
for the house and stuff like that. So I went, me and this kid, we made good
money. ...
   See, any business on this whole street, they always, they hafta, either they
have a safe in the store, or they have to take the money to a bank, either way. So
after like seven o'clock or so, you just sit out there, just watch 'em for one week,
and then the next week, you go and just take it, and run. It's like snatching a
pocketbook or taking a newspaper. Y'know, it's easy.

JM: And you'd have a car nearby where you could get up outta there?

BOO-BOO: No, just run a coupla blocks, hop into a cab (*chuckles*), and go home. I
did it twice. One time we went and robbed in Jackson Square and they had
these big giant bags with a whole bunch of small bags in them. They were all
checks, we had like a million dollars in checks.

JM: Were you able to cash any of them in, or ...

BOO-BOO: No, we just threw 'em in the river, got rid of them. ... I got away from
that, though. Cuz if you get caught, it's federal stuff. I got away from that.

Boo-Boo has turned to theft when unemployed and under severe financial pressure. Other Hallway Hangers have also chosen economic crime or "off the books" employment when decent, aboveboard jobs eluded them. Some have resorted to dealing drugs after losing legitimate jobs. Others have dabbled in the drug economy to supplement their wages from jobs in the formal sector. In general, the underground economic initiatives of the Hallway Hangers have been undertaken when these young men have been deprived of legitimate economic opportunities.

However, the entrepreneurial criminal careers of the Hallway Hangers have not been governed by economic rationality alone. The Hallway Hangers are not cool cost-benefit analysts. Their actions on the job market, both aboveboard and below, are inextricably linked with their emergent social identities, with their sense of who they are. The Hallway Hangers experienced school together—they developed rituals of resistance, indulged in the joys of alienation, and collectively projected identities they considered superior to those of other students and school staff. In a sense, the street is an extension of their schooling. The underground economy allows scope for collective experience and expression, whereas the new service economy does not. The cultural experience of working in a service-sector job is completely different from the interpersonal dynamics of working on the shop floor in a factory. In the factory, aspects of working-class and street culture are assets. One can afford to be tough, macho, quick-witted, verbally sharp, and resistant to authority; collective identity and solidarity, formed at the point of production, are encouraged and given expression by unions. The Hallway Hangers, in contrast, tend to experience the job structure as atomized individuals. Their work sites allow little space for resistance. Whereas the new service economy pays poorly and severely circumscribes cultural identity, the underground economy pays well and seems to offer scope for collective expression and resistance to authority.

And yet, in reality, cocaine capitalism, far from creating conditions in which the collective identity of the Hallway Hangers can flourish, further fragments their peer group.

JM: You guys used to be tight. Tell me about how that started to change and why.

FRANKIE: You want my theory?

JM: Yeah.

FRANKIE: I believe it was cocaine that separated a lot of us. You start out doing cocaine, y'know, you share it. You start getting a little hooked on cocaine, you start hiding it. You don't wanna be around people. You don't wanna share. It's a sick drug, man. It does a number on you. A couple of people went in and outta jail. So between goin' in and outta jail, and drugs and women. I know for me I clung onto a woman. It's a combination of a lot: between jail and cocaine, I know cocaine definitely separates people. You fucking grate on each other. You begin hating each other, y'know? Between women, coke, and jail. lotta guys were in jail, lottta guys were just fucked up, man. People took their outs. A few went jail, some went drugs—that's about the only two routes we went, I guess.

Marginalized more than ever by the shift from manufacturing to a service economy, the Hallway Hangers turn to the underground economy for financial gain and cultural affirmation. They find neither. Drug distribution in pursuit of profit easily turns into costly drug addiction and desperate, self-destructive behavior. Drug dependency also weakens their friendship ties and further dissolves their peer group.

Prison, of course, provides ample opportunity to develop a collective identity around resistance. Chris, Stoney, Shorty, and Steve have been incarcerated for most of the period since 1984, and Slick has also done a stint behind bars. The Hallway Hangers have shared a common experience in prison, which, like school, provides a clear institutional structure to challenge.

SHORTY: We were all up there, man, at one time—me, Steve, and Slick in '87 and '88. Steve's like, "I love it up here." Hell, we were sayin', "If the judges could see us now, eh? We're in here, we're drinking home brew and smokin' dope, getting high. Don't have to pay no rent, no electricity, we have to pay for no food, sittin' here living it up. If the judge could see us now, right?"

The Hallway Hangers were able to create and exploit spaces even within the "total institution" of prison to celebrate their little victories and make life bearable, but the conditions of incarceration remained unchanged, as Shorty articulated in his next breath.

SHORTY: It sucks, y'know, it sucks. You don't like to have someone getting paid eight dollars an hour to tell you what to do. And the screws will fuck you over. Lock you up for ninety days. Locked up all day long. They don't let you out for chow or nothing. They slide your chow under the door. They only let you out on Wednesdays and Saturdays to take a shower—they give you fifteen minutes. … I've got sick of doing fucking time. Sick of fuckin' gettin' in a fucking cell. A dog has more room in a fucking kennel than two guys have in a cell. You got two guys in a fucking cell. It's a hundred and fucking eight degrees. Fucking, one farts or something—it smells for twenty-four hours. No fucking circulation in the fucking thing. No AC. Fuckin', in the winter you freeze. All fucking holes in the window. You get some fucking asshole that's working. You wanna make a phone call cuz somebody's sick in your family, and he's being a prick to you, "Fuck you, you ain't gettin' a phone call." You wanna kill him.

The social relations and physical conditions of prison life combine to create an extraordinarily oppressive situation.

Stoney detests prison life. "I hate it, I can't stand it," he declares. "It's the physical aspect and the psychological aspect: I don't know which fucks you up more." However, after six stints in prison, Stoney is becoming "institutionalized"—dependent on prison life. Recall that in 1987 he requested to serve a suspended six-month sentence.

STONEY: It's weird, y'know, when I did these dumb robberies I was high, really fucked up. But I was also like, fuck it, I'll go back to jail if I have to. It's weird, but I kinda feel safer in prison than out there. It's hard to believe. But that's the way it is.

Stoney's absurdly inept armed robberies may have stemmed from a longing, conscious or unconscious, for the security of prison life.

Shorty thrived in prison, at least from an entrepreneurial point of view. He made and sold knives, peddled drugs, and helped run a gambling operation.

SHORTY: They raided my cell; they thought I had weed. I did have weed, I had twenty-two joints—they couldn't even fucking find it. It was underneath my pail. They took down my curtains, everything. They found sixty-four football cards. I had homemade football cards. They busted me for racketeering (*laughs*). I had football cards and lottery sheets. I used to take the numbers and run the betting on the games. ... I know how to make some real nice ice picks. From the headphones of Walkmans, you know the metal piece that goes through there? I used to go to people's cells and rip them off, steal their fucking shit. Take it, rip it apart, get the metal piece and put two of them together, and I'd put tape around 'em. Get tape from either a guard or from fuckin' some of the maintenance workers. Put the tape around it and file it on the ground, out to a ice pick. Some nice ones I made in there, baby.

JM: You'd make money that way?

SHORTY: Yeah. I was selling 'em for five packs.

JM: Cigarettes.

SHORTY: Yeah, cuz one day we were s'posed to have a racial riot, us and the blacks. It never happened, but I still made a lot of money on them.

Ultimately, the Hallway Hangers are themselves hurt by the racial hatred they sow. But prison is one place where Shorty has actually managed to squeeze some short-term profit from racial antagonism.

Incredibly, none of the Hallway Hangers have been arrested on drug charges since 1984. And although Chris and Stoney have been convicted of robberies, no other Hallway Hanger has been convicted of an economic crime. The Hallway Hangers have been caught perpetrating violence rather than committing economic crime. They have been arrested for assault, assault and battery, assault on a police officer, assault with a deadly weapon, violating restraining orders, mayhem, and attempted murder. This pattern contrasts sharply with that found by Mercer Sullivan in his study of young offenders in three Brooklyn neighborhoods. Sullivan found that white, Latino, and African American men all moderated their street fighting as their careers in economic crime unfolded. Moreover, their forays into economic crime more often resulted in arrest than did their street violence.[15] Why do the Hallway Hangers intelligently and calculatingly bow out of dealing drugs as the risks mount, yet succumb to the temptation of mindless violence? In fact, the violence of the Hallway Hangers is neither mindless nor random. It's not about money. It's about something more important to these young men: protecting and projecting their identities.

Producing Themselves

The Hallway Hangers' violent crimes are tied to their identities as men—specifically, as white men. Street fighting is about maintaining one's status, and for the Hallway Hangers this status is defined in relation to, and usually at the expense of, people of color. Back in 1983 Slick made that connection explicit: "If you have a fight up the high school, you're considered bad ... especially if he's black, around this way." Eight years later, the Hallway Hangers are still at it—and these incidents involve not just hotheads like Steve and Shorty but Frankie and Slick as well. A telling fact emerges from these incidents: Most of the victims have been black.

Shorty was lucky to be convicted of only disorderly conduct for assaulting two African Americans with a knife.

SHORTY: I got arrested in front of the projects. For disorderly conduct. I was chasing these two black guys—I had 'em in the cellar [actually a large stairwell outside a basement office near doorway #13] with a knife, chased 'em into the cellar. I was about to stab them when all the cops jumped on me and shit.

Slick was also imprisoned after fighting with black youths. "The reason I went to jail," he relates, "was because I threw them two niggers off the porch." Frankie was charged with attempted murder, his victim a Latino youth.

FRANKIE: I almost killed this Spanish guy, I beat him with a baseball bat. I remember sittin' in the jail cell and the cop told me the guy died. It was Martin Luther King weekend, so I had a few days to think about this guy being dead. Then this cop told me that he was okay. He wasn't okay, but he wasn't dead, y'know. He ended up being in the hospital awhile, about a month or so. He ended up having a broken jaw, broken ribs, broken eye socket, broken shin. ...

He had bumped into my girl. It was a fight, y'know? He had a knife. I had a bat. He lost. I only got a year's probation cuz he was trying to stab me, too. Hey, I was protecting myself.

Six months later Frankie and Steve were charged with assault and battery, armed robbery, and malicious destruction. Their victim was a Haitian cab driver. Frankie and Steve, both on probation, faced ten years in state prison until the case against them fell apart when the unlicensed driver failed to appear in court. All of these confrontations took place in front of Clarendon Heights.

It appears that the Hallway Hangers, lacking the traditional marks of working-class manhood—blue-collar breadwinning jobs and households of their own—have tried to shore up their masculine identities through highly public displays of violence. This violence is not directed indiscriminately; the Hallway Hangers lash out at those by whom they feel threatened: black men. They seek to regain a sense of male power by asserting their dominance at its most basic level—raw physical violence. In his study of youth unemployment, Paul Willis warns that without the social and cultural identity afforded by a job, young men may resolve their "gender crisis" through an "aggressive assertion of masculinity" and a "physical, tough, direct display of those qualities now 'automatically' guaranteed by doing productive work." Such aggression, Willis adds, "may also deepen some of the brutalities and oppressions experienced by working-class women."[16]

Indeed, some of the Hallway Hangers have directed their animosity and violence against women. Steve was jailed once for ransacking his girlfriend's apartment and destroying much of her property. He has also been arrested for violating restraining orders and beating his girlfriend. Shorty's claimed conversion to monogamy came not out of feelings of fidelity but out of a fear of AIDS, and his confession of lapses underscores his own frankly exploitative attitude toward women. In contrast to the other Hallway Hangers, Steve admits to carrying on several casual sexual relationships simultaneously. I stayed with Steve for several days in 1991. He was an exceptionally solicitous host, constantly asking after my needs. This generosity contrasted sharply with his attitude toward women. Arriving back at his mother's Clarendon Heights apartment one evening to find the door locked, I joined a teenage girl sitting on the stoop. She was waiting for Steve to return and walk her home. "He's just gone around the corner to call his son's mother," she smiled. We waited an hour and then I drove her home. Back at his apartment later that night, I asked him what happened. "Yeah, I was s'posed to walk her home, but I saw Shorty and we went for a few beers and then bought us a couple of gems [crack crystals]. She's pretty fucking nice, though, huh? Only fucking fifteen, though." Then, laughing, "I fucked her on your bed. Sorry about that." Sexual exploitation, underlined by postcoital disregard, seems to feed Steve's sense of masculine superiority and dominance.

Whereas other Hallway Hangers may have physically abused their partners (Shorty is rumored to have beaten his girlfriend), Jinks set upon the police in a

public display of violence. When police officers used excessive force while arrest-
ing his disabled brother, Jinks "went a little crazy and attacked the cops." Boo-Boo
has also been arrested for assaulting a police officer. Taking on the police, potent
symbols of power and authority, may dramatically improve one's masculine credibility among Clarendon Heights peers, but it's also the one violent street crime
that's unlikely to go unpunished, and most of the Hallway Hangers shy away from
police confrontations.

In one extraordinary incident, Shorty managed to combine racial hatred with
violence against women and the police.

SHORTY: I lived with this girl, I was with her for about fucking six months, then I
went to jail. And she was with a nigger when I come out. I got outta jail and
fuckin', I went crazy when she was with a nigger. That was my worst nightmare.
I told her, I says, "Hey, I know I'm gonna be away for a while." Says, "Do what
you gotta do," y'know? "If you gotta get fucking laid, get laid," y'know?
(*groans*). But then when it was a fucking nigger, she's lucky she's livin' and I'm
lucky I'm not doing a fucking murder beef. I almost threw her out the third-
floor window. Instead, I tore the door off. Took a knife, cut apart the whole
power set, tore the fuckin' fridge doors off, threw them out the third-floor window. Threw the stereo, threw the TV, everything out the window. I almost did
big time for that. The cops come up sayin', "Shorty, calm down." I said, "Boff
(*smacks fist into palm*). Fuck you." I bit three fucking cops, assaulted about
eight of 'em. I was in tip-top fucking shape. I went in jail weighing 238 pounds,
I come out weighing 155. The cops all started jumping on me, hitting me with
billy clubs. I was still fightin' 'em, kept fucking fightin' and fightin', and then
they finally just kept whacking me with the clubs, and I was knocked out.

This incident illustrates the desperation and futility of the Hallway Hangers' contorted efforts to preserve a sense of personal and social ascendancy amid a tangle
of racial, gender, and class issues.

Shorty's story highlights the connection between the Hallway Hangers' racism
and the imagined threat of black sexual superiority. Recall that in 1983 Frankie
concluded that two white girls provided Chris with cocaine because "they want to
suck his black cock, that's why." And when Shorty's girlfriend slept with an African American, Shorty seems to have considered it a direct challenge to his manhood and responded with an orgy of violence. For Shorty, this "worst nightmare"
represented the most extreme incursion of black power into his world. For the
white Hallway Hangers, perceived black ascendancy haunts them in Clarendon
Heights, in the underground street economy, and on the legitimate labor market.
Now, it seemed to Shorty, blacks were superseding him in the bedroom.

The Hallway Hangers are obsessed with the number of African American residents moving into Clarendon Heights and allegedly taking control of the neighborhood.

JINKS: They're movin' more black families and foreign families into this place than white families. A white family moves out, a foreign family moves in. Now you tell me there's no white families out there on the housing list. It's just discrimination. ... It's been a lot more drugs comin' around here. ... The violence has gone up around here. I mean, there's been a few shootin's around here.

JM: There's always been shootings.

JINKS: Yeah, but I mean the shootings were not people shootin' each other, just, y'know, one black dude shootin' another black dude over a sale or over turf. Now it's over drugs, the shootings out here. Before there was a solid reason behind the shootings. Now they're all out here sellin' the shit. Now it's drive-by shootings. I don't want my kid to be out there.

JM: Who's "they," when you say "they"?

JINKS: I mean all the black kids. They sit out here twenty-four hours a night sellin' crack. Now you got black people out here who you don't even know who the hell they are. I don't feel safe at all.

Frankie also contrasts the mythological golden years of Clarendon Heights with the way things are now.

FRANKIE: Lemme tell ya, when I grew up in Clarendon Heights, even though it was a bad place to a lotta people, to a lotta the outside people—even, y'know, cops wouldn't come down there—but within the community we were tight. Everyone knew their next-door neighbor, everybody looked out for each other. Cuz we were tight. I look at it today and now you've got niggers from the East Side, from Riverside, y'know, niggers from all over. No one knows each other. Before everybody knew everyone, and everybody took care of everybody. Now everyone's out for themselves.

JM: What's the cause of that?

FRANKIE: I believe the fuckin' black culture is a major reason for that. Y'know, I still suffer from Archie Bunkerism, but, y'know, that's just somethin' that's been inbred inta me. But that's [black culture] got a lot to do with it.

JM: Because ...

FRANKIE: Because they're fuckin', they have no fuckin' values in life. They don't respect themselves, how they gonna respect others? And I honestly believe that. And the reason I honestly believe that is cuz I know. I've seen it. I've seen 'em all my life. I was always brought up to respect women, respect older people, and never rat on anyone. I look at the niggers and they don't respect their own mother. They have no respect, no respect for themselves.

The Hallway Hangers attribute problems that they themselves inflicted on Clarendon Heights for a number of years to new black residents and their friends. Clearly, they feel threatened by the rising tide of blacks in the neighborhood. In fact, the proportion of racial and ethnic minorities living in Clarendon Heights has increased substantially, though not as dramatically as the Hallway Hangers suggest. Whereas minorities accounted for roughly 35 percent of the project's residents in 1984, they made up nearly 60 percent of that total in 1991.

It's not the sheer number of African Americans in Clarendon Heights that bothers the Hallway Hangers as much as the sense that whites are losing control of the neighborhood. To the Hallway Hangers, black youths have the temerity to congregate in front of the housing project and outside doorway #13, hallowed space that the Hallway Hangers inherited from their elders and bequeathed to their younger peers but that is now lost forever to blacks who "don't know their place." The racism of the Hallway Hangers has a strong territorial dimension. Fears of invasion and displacement are powerful themes that point to the role of an imaginary territory in the social identities of these young men.[17]

Shorty's racism and its violent expression are evoked by black challenges to his status and sense of self. He works himself into a frenzy describing how "young, wise, cocky little niggers" around Clarendon Heights fail to show him the deference he deserves.

SHORTY: It's nothing but blacks there [Clarendon Heights], man. Some of 'em have no respect. One night I was there, I was looking for this black kid, Super. I was gonna buy a couple of lines off him, right? Fuckin' two of them niggers givin' me a hard time, started laughing and shit while I was walkin' away. They were real wise, about sixteen or seventeen years old. I went back there, slapped one of 'em in the face, and said, "Who the fuck you think you're talkin' to?" Y'know? They got real cocky attitudes.

The Hallway Hangers, without the trappings of conventional success, always had their self-esteem invested in their tough street identities, but now even that street credibility is being eroded by assertive young blacks in their neighborhood. The incident recounted by Shorty began with the humiliation of having to search out a black youth to buy cocaine, a commodity whose local distribution the Hallway Hangers had hitherto controlled. Indeed, young African Americans have successfully challenged white control of the drug trade around Clarendon Heights, fueling the Hallway Hangers' resentment of blacks. "I was selling drugs," recounts Shorty. "We stopped sellin' cuz it was gettin' too hot. As you've noticed with all them niggers around sellin' 'em now."

The Hallway Hangers resent black competition in the drug trade but also on the legitimate job market. Chapter 7 explored how the racism of the Hallway Hangers retards class consciousness. Their feeling of being victimized by class exploitation is undermined by their conviction that affirmative action and blacks are the real problems. What begins as a rudimentary but promising perception of their condition is derailed into a strident racism that contributes to the oppression of other members of their social class and, ultimately, to their own continued subjugation. This tendency is even more dramatically illustrated by the recent research detailed here. The Hallway Hangers trace their problems as adults, particularly their employment problems, to "reverse discrimination." Jinks, the only white Hallway Hanger who empathized with blacks back in 1984, takes quite a different attitude in 1991.

JINKS: Nowadays, you know who's the minority, right? The white American. You go to find a good job nowadays, you gotta be black, Puerto Rican, Indian, something to get anywhere. You're either overqualified or you're underqualified. And they give it to someone who don't know what the hell they doing. ... That's how backwards this whole world is. It's so screwed up; you have double standards. That's what this world's full of is double standards. It ain't gettin' any better. It's gettin' worse as years go on. ... Don't get me wrong, it's not stereotype niggers; it's Puerto Ricans, it's all these immigrants who come over off the boat. They can't speak much English but they can sign their name and get their paycheck every week on a good goddamn job that someone who worked their ass off all their life should be able to get. ... It's not just the blacks. Minorities are taking over this fuckin' city. ... I'm a typical American. I get no breaks in life. All I do is bust my ass. Everything that I should have a fair shot at, they say, y'know, "equal opportunity employer." But it's not equal opportunity employer, because they've got standards that say that they have to have so many blacks, so many minorities working for these companies. They have to be promoted before you; they have to get a shot at the job before you. They're entitled to it before you.

For Frankie, the Hallway Hangers are victims on account of their racial and gender identity. They are exploited as white men.

FRANKIE: Well, I look today, and if anyone shoulda had a chance to make it, it's fuckin', it's black people. They got a chance to make it. Cuz there's fucking quotas to be filled. I look today, y'know, I honestly believe the most discriminated person is a fucking white male between the ages of twenty and forty out there on a fucking job. Especially if you want any decent job—post office, public transportation job.

Here Frankie not only scapegoats African Americans, he also contrasts his occupational prospects with those of women.

Shorty takes the New Right rhetoric about white males as the new disadvantaged "minority" and gives it a sharp, characteristically perverse twist. Note the way he moves from seeing African Americans as a neighborhood menace to viewing them as an occupational threat, linking the two with a bizarre theory of impending racial Armageddon.

SHORTY: Those young niggers taking over this place can take their guns and all that kind of thing, none of that shit scares me. I'll stick it up their fuckin' arse. They better shoot me in the head, you know what I'm sayin'? Serious, I hate fucking spooks. I can't stand fucking niggers. I hate 'em.

JM: What does that go back to?

SHORTY: That goes back to like what Charles Manson said, there's goin' to be a fuckin' racial riot, racial fuckin' war, that's what's goin' to happen, believe me. Blacks against the whites, it's happening. We're the minorities now. Can't get a fuckin' job. Fucking all the projects around here in this city, all the maintenance guys, they're all fuckin' blacks and Puerto Ricans. They ain't hiring whites around here; you gotta be black, black or fucking spic. We're the minorities.

In 1984 Shorty was clear about where to lay the blame for his brother's unemployment: "It's cuz of the fuckin' spics and niggers." Seven years later, he traces his own employment problems to the same source: racial and ethnic minorities. And now Shorty, along with Jinks and Frankie, claims minority status for himself as a white man.

In a sense, the Hallway Hangers *are* a minority, not by virtue of their race or gender but on account of their social class. Minority status is fundamentally determined by a lack of power rather than by numbers, and as members of a particularly disadvantaged stratum of the working class, the Hallway Hangers are certainly lacking in power. But the class dimension of oppression eludes the Hallway Hangers. The job Shorty covets is in building maintenance, the lowest rung in the City Housing Authority's vast job structure. Shorty does not resent the virtual exclusion of people with working-class roots from senior supervisory positions and even from middle-level management and social work jobs. But he is prepared to wage war with racial and ethnic minorities, oblivious to the fact that he is fighting fellow victims over virtual crumbs.

Of the Hallway Hangers, now only Jinks explicitly critiques class injustice. He insightfully describes how differences in cultural capital handicap the poor and perpetuate social inequality.

JINKS: We have not been given all the gifts we need to live a happy life. We have to get by with what we have. ... A lot of people from this area are not well-spoken people, their grammar is not great. They grew up in the streets, hanging in the streets. They talk street slang. They don't know how to present themselves in an appropriate way, where people who come from high-class families, they're taught right away, you gotta be, do this, do that, do this, and they get the breaks because their parents know people. They know people, they got connections. That's how they got somewhere. You gotta have connections to get anywhere in life. If you don't know anybody, there's no one out there who's gonna just come to you and say, "Gee, you look like a good kid. Why don't I do this favor for you." It don't work like that.

Jinks recognizes that inequality is formed by the chasm in earnings and experiences between workers and capitalists.

JINKS: One of my bosses, when I started workin' for him, he owned three companies. He was part-owning the one I work at. He doesn't never work. All he does all day is sits at his house and picks up the telephone. He must make a hundred thousand dollars a year just on the telephone.

Jinks also resents the preferential status and treatment that his boss's son enjoys at work, an injustice he sees "at my job and everywhere else, and it's just all over the world."

Jinks's comments notwithstanding, the Hallway Hangers generally fail to articulate a sense of class consciousness. Where, after all, would they get the resources to construct a sense of self that highlights social class? Certainly neither mass culture nor the media speak of class, and the Hallway Hangers' own experience of work has failed to instill a class identity. Only Frankie has been in a labor union, and in spite of his humiliating experience working under his boss's son, he fails to consider class injustice as constitutive of his plight. Instead, and against all the evidence, Frankie insists that as a white male he is handicapped by his race and gender. This sort of contorted explanation for the Hallway Hangers' failure to get ahead attests to the utter absence of a class-based ideology in the United States.

The Hallway Hangers' views point to the power and pervasiveness of the achievement ideology—the widespread belief that everyone has equal access to the American Dream. But they also point to the pressure being exerted by New Right ideology.[18] The New Right refrain that "reverse discrimination" victimizes white men meshes powerfully with the Hallway Hangers' sense of territorial displacement. In a way, New Right ideology rescues the achievement ideology. The Hallway Hangers feel exploited. As Jinks says, they bust their ass but get no breaks. But instead of questioning the achievement ideology, they adopt a peculiar version of it: "If only racial bias against whites was removed, then rewards would be based on merit and hard work, and we would prosper." The Hallway Hangers know they are oppressed, but under the combined sway of the achievement ideology and New Right rhetoric, they articulate their feelings of exploitation in the idiom of racial rather than class exclusion.

The Hallway Hangers forge their identities in terms of race and gender. Feelings of racial and male supremacy buttress their sense of self, since the psychological solace of conventional success eludes them. But their racism and sexism siphon off their rage and blind the Hallway Hangers to the reality of class injustice. African Americans are seen as a sexual and economic threat, and therefore as a challenge to the Hallway Hangers' masculine identities. Their male pride already suffering from their inability to secure good jobs and independent households, the Hallway Hangers aggressively assert their masculinity in displays of street violence usually directed against blacks and perpetrated in and around Clarendon Heights.

The African American threat is felt at two levels: at a private individual level and at a public communal level. Frankie tries to articulate a communal identity of white working-class fraternity, of an interdependent, protective community of which he is a part. Violence against blacks shores up the Hallway Hangers' individual masculine identities but also becomes part of an effort to defend a mythological community that they believe is disintegrating.[19] Viewing his girlfriend as an extension of himself, Shorty sees the black man in her bedroom as an incursion into his private territory and also as a threat to his public persona. His violent reaction became a public event, despite the fact that domestic abuse seldom comes to light. Other Hallway Hangers may dominate their partners privately, perhaps through physical brutality. But whereas in 1984 the Hallway Hangers were typically involved in short-term casual relationships, all but Steve and Boo-Boo are now seriously involved in avowed monogamous partnerships. All except Chris are fathers, and four of the Hangers have two children each. For many of the Hallway Hangers, fatherhood has become a key element in their identities.

If the Hallway Hangers have attempted to shore up their sense of self through exaggerated displays of masculinity, fatherhood has pulled in the opposite direction by prompting many Hallway Hangers to rethink what manhood is all about. Jinks lives with Beth, his girlfriend of eight years, and their five-year-old son Mark.

JM: What was your reaction when you found out you were going to be a father?

JINKS: I was shocked. I was seventeen and she was sixteen. The first reaction was she wanted an abortion, but her mother would not let her get one.

JM: What about you?

JINKS: Me? I didn't wanna be a daddy either at the time. I knew it would take all my freedom away. But then as she started carrying it, I got more excited about it. I got more and more excited about it.

JM: I notice you spend most evenings with him. Do you get any shit from the guys for doing that?

JINKS: No, no. They more or less respect me for it.

JM: Why is it that some people will take that kind of responsibility and others don't? I mean, Steve babysits his kids sometimes, but he doesn't seem to feel much responsibility for them.

JINKS: It's like, it's like they try to hide their true feelings that they have in their heart. They have to put out a macho image. It's like they're afraid of somebody actually knowin' what they feel inside.

The tension between their macho street image and the tenderness and devotion demanded by parenthood is felt by other Hallway Hangers as well. Several visits to Slick's home reveal that he dotes on his baby son, and partly because his girlfriend Denise has reverted to her cocaine habit since giving birth, Slick undertakes many household and parenting chores.

SLICK: See, my father screwed on us when we were kids. I always said I'd never do that to my children. I like being a father. I love my kids. I love them more than anything in the world. You try to, all you want to do is do the right thing for the kids. You want to be able to hear him say, "Yeah, my dad was there for me." That's it. They don't have to say anything else good. They can say I was an asshole. I don't care about that. I just don't want them never to be able to say that I wasn't there when they needed me. Cuz that's one big thing I hold over my father. I don't believe in a father that's not paying attention to their children. ... I see my three-year-old at least twice a month, and even that's not easy cuz I don't get along with his mom too well anymore.

JM: Why is it that some people having children will really ...

SLICK: It tries to make you do the right thing?

JM: Yeah.

SLICK: And some people it just doesn't affect 'em?

JM: Yeah, they don't take real responsibility for the kids.

SLICK: They don't want to get hurt. Who the fuck wants to get hurt? It means turning your life around, and that ain't easy. You're scared of yourself, because you know you can't do the right thing. You don't think you can. Scared of the peer pressure. That you're called a pussy by some of your quote, unquote friends. Wanna know why you're staying home all the time. I got my own brother saying it. But hey, lookit, I got responsibilities.

Embracing the role of father "means turning your life around," a complete reorientation of identity, according to Slick. Earlier in our discussion, Slick catalogued the marks of street credibility—drugs, money, clothes, cars, women—and then abruptly changed tack to undermine their significance and the image they convey.

SLICK: You get drugs, you have money in your pocket. You have money in your pocket and you have women. Gotta have the fancy car, gotta have the clothes. Gotta look good if you're to really be someone. So that's how that goes. That's why everybody's trying to live up—was or is—trying to live up to an image of being a tough person. What I'm trying to say, the whole thing is, the way I try to see it is you can be a tough person but you can also be a nice person. Don't have to be an asshole, goin' around fucking whackin' people to show who you are. You don't need to go through that nonsense bullshit anymore.

In forging his identity Slick is softening up his uncritical affirmation of masculine toughness and molding it into a new form of self-identity with fatherhood at its core. Frankie seems to be undergoing a similar process.

Frankie says that he returned to the city in 1987 and moved in with his girlfriend's family in order to spend time with his baby son, but admits that he "went right back to the boys. Except we were older now. We were barroom drinkers. We moved from the streets to the bars."

JM: Tell me about the impact of fatherhood on you.

FRANKIE: It was '86. I dunno. It was a lotta responsibility. I was confused. It definitely wasn't planned (*laughs*). It was scary. I was the first one of us to have a kid. It was a lotta responsibility, but I didn't take a lot at first. I was too busy gettin' high. It was different for her, y'know, cuz she had to stay in the house. I wouldn't stay at home. I'd say, "Fuck you, I'm goin' to the bar." Yeah, at first I didn't really take much responsibility. I knew I had a son, this and that, but no responsibility. I mean, I paid my money, but I still went and played my game.

Today, today it's great. Six years ago, I was his father. But until like two years ago I became his daddy because I never spent time with him. But the past two years I have. ...

I used to be a tough guy back in '84, man. I was the toughest motherfucker you've ever seen—in my own mind. I look back and I remember that: We were all tough. I believe I'm a tough guy now. Not drinking. Not doing drugs. Being a decent dad.

Frankie and Slick redefine what it is to be tough, and, as with Jinks, their personal reorientation has been largely catalyzed by their experience of fatherhood.

There is no denying the dominance of machismo culture among the Hallway Hangers. Yet under the sway of fatherhood, that dominant sense of masculinity is being challenged. Several of the Hallway Hangers are beginning to define their masculinity in new ways by allowing fatherhood to foster nurturing and caring capacities in them. Like class and race, gender is socially constructed and hence subject to change.[20] Underemployment and joblessness undermine the traditional masculine identities of the Hallway Hangers. Yet as men spend more time helping to rear children in changing economic circumstances, counterhegemonic male identities may be formed. Physical toughness, breadwinning, and the mere fact of paternity are still the most potent symbols of manhood, but it is instructive that even hardened Hallway Hangers are beginning to subscribe to and articulate roles that run counter to male machismo.

Parenthood has certainly wrought changes in Boo-Boo's outlook.

JM: When was your first child born?

BOO-BOO: It was January 31st, 1989, that Natasha was born.

JM: So what effect did that have on you?

BOO-BOO: Oh, I loved it. It was excellent. It was beautiful. She was beautiful. I was there when she was born and everything. It was excellent, it was great. I was at the junkyard and then we moved and I was working for the moving company, so I had money, I was takin' care of business and stuff. I just wanted to be a family man. I stayed home. I'd take care of my daughter while Ginger was out running in the street. I liked it a lot. I was taking care of her more than Ginger. They'd wake up in the middle of the night and I'd be the one to wake up with her and make her bottles, change her, do whatever needed to be done. Jesus Christ, our kids are beautiful.

Boo-Boo has felt the joy of fatherhood, but he has also experienced the pain and devastation of loss. First he and Ginger lost custody of their children. Then came the real disaster. Ginger and Natasha were diagnosed with Acquired Immuno-deficiency Syndrome (AIDS), Boo-Boo and Connie as HIV positive. Natasha died in July 1991.

BOO-BOO: I was there in the hospital and everything when it happened. I still don't understand it. I mean, I know she's gone and everything, but I don't understand it. I still see her. I see her in the casket in my eyes. I can see her. I can still see her.

Numb with grief and pining for Natasha, Boo-Boo was struggling to face Ginger's impending death in August 1991. He often traveled twenty miles to visit Connie in her foster home. "In a while," he said quietly but matter-of-factly, "I'm gonna be all alone. Ginger's dying and probably this little girl, too."

Boo-Boo's sense of solitary suffering, of being alone in his affliction, is important. He has no support systems or informal networks to help him cope with either bereavement or his own medical condition. Whereas the gay community cuts across class lines and can flex its financial muscle to mobilize resources and organize support for those who are HIV-positive and have AIDS, those at the bottom of the pile without the wherewithal to tap into those support systems are largely left to fend for themselves. Ginger probably caught the AIDS virus from an infected needle. Drug abuse and AIDS are intertwined killers that hit the inner city with particular ferocity in the latter half of the 1980s and into the 1990s. Alone, AIDS is lethal and drug abuse is dangerous. Linked by infected needles, they have wrought human tragedy on a massive scale. In Clarendon Heights, rumors about AIDS are rife. Before tracking Chris down in prison, I was told by ten people that he had died of AIDS. Like Chris, Boo-Boo was also under threat of another condition that reached epidemic proportions in the 1980s: homelessness. Boo-Boo has no place to go once he exhausts his dwindling welcome at Ginger's uncle's home. Still, he refuses to let hope be altogether eclipsed. "I just need someplace where I can base myself with a job and a place to live. ... I'm just trying to make it on my own."

Boo-Boo struggles on, as do the rest of the Hallway Hangers. But that is largely what they expected to be doing back in 1984. Whereas the Hallway Hangers were cynical and pessimistic, the Brothers believed in the American Dream and placed their faith in education. Has that faith been rewarded?

Notes

1. John D. Kasarda, "Urban Industrial Transition and the Underclass," *Annals of the American Academy of Political and Social Science* 501 (1989):28.

2. Andrew M. Sum and Joseph Franz, "The Geographic Locations of Jobs by Employed High School Graduates" (Unpublished paper, 1990), p. 3.

3. U.S. Bureau of the Census, *Current Population Reports,* Series P-60, No. 146 (Washington, D.C.: Government Printing Office, 1985), table 40. Cited in Loïc J. D. Wacquant, "Redrawing the Urban Color Line," in Craig Calhoun and George Ritzer, eds., *Social Problems* (New York: McGraw-Hill, 1992), p. 13.

4. Kasarda, "Urban Industrial Transition and the Underclass," p. 31.

5. *New York Times,* 27 September 1988. Cited in Thomas R. Shannon, Nancy Kleniewski, and William M. Cross, eds., *Urban Problems in Sociological Perspective* (Prospect Heights, Ill.: Waveland Press, 1991), p. 104.

6. Paul Osterman, *Getting Started* (Cambridge, Mass.: MIT Press, 1980).

7. Paul Osterman, "Is There a Problem with the Youth Labor Market and If So How Should We Fix It?" mimeo (Sloan School, MIT, February 1992).

8. Saskia Sassen, "The Informal Economy," in *Dual City: Restructuring New York,* ed. John H. Mollenkopf and Manuel Castells (New York: Russell Sage Foundation, 1991), pp. 79–102.

9. Andrew M. Sum and Joanna Heliotis, "Declining Real Wages of Youth," *Workforce* (Spring 1993):23.

10. Andrew Sum, personal conversation, August 1993.

11. Bureau of the Census, Public Use Microdata Sample File, 1980 and 1990.

12. Richard Edwards, *Contested Terrain* (New York: Basic Books, 1979), pp. 163–170.

13. See, especially, Philippe Bourgois's "In Search of Respect: The New Service Economy and the Crack Alternative in Spanish Harlem" (Russell Sage Foundation Working Paper #21, May 1991).

14. Philippe Bourgois, "Just Another Night on Crack Street," *New York Times Magazine,* 12 November 1989, p. 94.

15. Mercer L. Sullivan, *Getting Paid* (Ithaca, N.Y.: Cornell University Press, 1989), pp. 108–113.

16. Paul Willis, "Youth Unemployment: Thinking the Unthinkable," mimeo (n.d.), p. 8. Cited in Lois Weis, *Working Class Without Work* (New York: Routledge, 1990), p. 191.

17. John Dickie first made this point in one of his incisive reviews of the manuscript.

18. For an account of how New Right ideology resonates with the outlook of white, working-class, male students, see Weis, *Working Class Without Work.*

19. I am indebted to Doug Taylor for this point.

20. I am grateful to David Webb for clarifying my thinking on the nature of gender. Webb himself is indebted to feminist theory. See S. Farrell and J. Lorber, eds., *The Social Construction of Gender* (New York: Sage, 1991), and J. Hearn and D. Morgan, eds., *Men, Masculinities, and Social Theory* (London: Unwin Hyman, 1990).

10

··

The Brothers:
Dreams Deferred

*I*N 1984 the Brothers hoped that by 1991 they would be on the way to middle-class prosperity. Although I considered these aspirations optimistic, I wrote in the first edition that "with a high school diploma, a positive attitude, and a disciplined readiness for the rigors of the workplace, the Brothers should be capable of landing steady jobs." If the Brothers were naive, so was I. My prediction that they would secure decent work was wrong, and so was my assumption that they could cash in on their credentials and attitude. Although they have certainly fared better than the Hallway Hangers, the Brothers have themselves stumbled economically in the transition to adulthood.

Shortchanged on the Labor Market

Even more so than the Hallway Hangers, the Brothers have been employed in the service sector of the economy. They have bagged groceries, stocked shelves, flipped hamburgers, delivered pizzas, repaired cars, serviced airplanes, cleaned buildings, moved furniture, driven tow trucks, pumped gas, delivered auto parts, and washed dishes. They have also worked as mail carriers, cooks, clerks, computer operators, bank tellers, busboys, models, office photocopiers, laborers, soldiers, baggage handlers, security guards, and customer service agents. Only Mike, as a postal service employee, holds a unionized position. Although their experiences on the labor market have been varied, many of the Brothers have failed to move out of the secondary labor market. Instead, like the Hallway Hangers, they have been stuck in low-wage, high-turnover jobs.

Consider Mokey. We left him in 1984 as a junior in the rigorous Fundamental School at Lincoln High. His only contact with the job market had been part-time janitorial work with his father. After another summer in Upward Bound, Mokey made the varsity football team in his senior year, worked part-time in a restaurant washing dishes, and graduated in 1985. He was unemployed for a few months before he found work as a stockboy in a large department store. Poor prospects of promotion and a paltry wage of $4.62 an hour prompted Mokey to quit the job and enter a nearby community college in January 1986. He was enrolled in a liberal arts program on a part-time basis for two semesters and then dropped out. "It wasn't doing me much good," he explained. "I couldn't seem to get motivated. I wasn't sure there was going to be anything at the end of the line."

Over the next four years Mokey worked at five restaurants, busing tables and cooking. Two of the restaurants laid him off when business dropped, two closed outright, and Mokey quit one job after getting burned twice in a cramped kitchen. He earned between $5 and $7.50 an hour at the restaurants, which included two exclusive ones. Mokey took pay cuts when he landed subsequent jobs delivering pizzas, stocking the shelves of a boutique, and moving furniture in a warehouse. Derek helped him get a job handling baggage at the airport, but Mokey was fired after a year and a half—unjustly in Mokey's view. When he was unemployed for an eighteen-month stretch, Mokey spent up to thirty hours per week working as a counselor in a youth enrichment program. He supervised children on camping, cycling, canoe, and ski trips, mostly on a volunteer basis. The responsibility, autonomy, and respect he was accorded in his youth work contrasted sharply with his other jobs.

Mokey left several of his jobs when it became obvious that they were not advancing his career. But quitting damaged his prospects even more. Mokey keeps careful employment records and understands that twelve jobs in seven years does not impress prospective employers.

MOKEY: I don't have a good job because I haven't been at a job more than a year. Cuz mostly I'm always leaving or getting laid off. One guy, one employer [said], "How come you haven't been at these jobs over a certain amount of time?" It's just that they weren't good jobs, the ones I quit. And it's not like I can help it when a restaurant closes.

Now, after six years on the labor market, Mokey has come full circle. He has been unemployed for a year, apart from ten hours of cleaning work with his father each week, the same part-time job he held in 1984. And yet his prospects are worse than when he started.

MOKEY: Oh, it's bad, it's bad to try and get a job. Cuz I would look for particular jobs so that I can stay at them. Like my parents told me to go for a job, doesn't matter what kind of job it is. So there was one week that I just said, "Oh, I'll go for anything." So I actually went to anything like gas stations and all different types of jobs, and they still weren't hiring. I mean, I'd go there, I went to a couple of interviews and they never called. ... It's frustrating. I look it up in the paper, I call them and they tell me to come in and fill their application. I go fill it out and they go over the application and then they tell me they'll give me a call if they're interested. So they don't call because they're not interested. ... You get frustrated. You're out there and you wanna do this and all these jobs say, "We're not interested." I call places and they've already had someone taken that position. Or when you get there, they tell you someone already taken your position. It's like, "Oh great. Come all the way out here and you already have the position filled." It is frustrating out there.

Mokey expected that diligent work would be rewarded with increased responsibilities, promotion, and pay raises. That's what the achievement ideology promises. Repeatedly disappointed, Mokey soon discovered that in a recessionary economy he would be lucky simply to keep a job. Now, even with dampened expectations, he can find no work whatsoever.

In contrast to Mokey, Juan has generally stuck with his jobs—but to little avail. For three years he worked at an autobody shop replacing windows. His hourly wage still below six dollars, he left to enter a community college but could not afford to stay. He worked for three weeks in a department store basement as a stockboy, was unemployed for a couple of months, then took a job at McDonald's. He began at an hourly wage of $4.50, moved up to $5.57 as a crew leader, and after two and a half years was taking home $7.50 as a swing manager.

JUAN: It was all right, but the pay wasn't good enough, for like bills. Then they started cutting all the hours off, cuz supposedly they wasn't doin', y'know, that much business. It made it tight for me, so I left there in '89.

JM: Could you move up any further? Or was that really the highest you could go, was swing manager?

JUAN: No, I coulda moved up further if I wanted to. But they wanted more [hours] than what they were paying. They want you to work for salary and put in so many hours if it's necessary, and I couldn't work thirty hours on salary and I get paid for twenty.

Juan painstakingly worked his way up to a salaried position, only to take home less pay for his troubles.

When he quit McDonald's, Juan used Derek's contacts at the airport to get a job as a customer service agent with a wage of $6.87 an hour. He was up to $7.50 when he was fired a year later.

JM: What happened?

JUAN: I came in a couple of times late. And they're very strict on timing. You gotta be there on time. If your shift's at 8:02, you gotta be there at 8:02, period.

JM: Was it a big blow when you lost that job, or ...

JUAN: Yeah.

JM: How'd you feel about it?

JUAN: I feel bad about it. Outta all the jobs I ever had, it was better because I was gettin' medical insurance in there, y'know? It was better than anything.

JM: Was it your fault you lost it, or was it just the circumstances, or what happened?

JUAN: Well, it was probably my fault cuz, y'know, I came in late a couple of times. Well, more than a couple of times. I came in late three times and I called in sick four other times. I mean, I can't blame it completely on myself, cuz everybody does it, and some of 'em will get away with it. I was doing all right, I mean, everybody lik'ded me and everything, and the only reason was that I came in late three times and called in sick four other times.

JM: During the whole time you were there?

JUAN: Yeah, during the whole time. Sooner or later something would happen, I'd have some kind of incident. And after the seventh time you call in sick or come in late in a year, you're terminated. There's no second chances. Up to seven and you're gone. You're history.

For the past two years Juan has worked at Jim's Tow. The work site consists of a trailer office and a large fenced-in area crammed full of cars, some just towed in, others in various states of disrepair strewn about the lot. I found Juan in the back, amid the rusted shells, painting the front fender of a red Toyota in a shade slightly brighter than the rest of the car.

JUAN: Can you believe this? Look at this, man. I told Jim it was the wrong damn color; it's not mixed right. "Go ahead," he said. "It's close enough. She probably won't even notice." But watch who'll take the blame when she comes to get her car (*shakes his head furiously and sighs*). If you're gonna do a job, do it right— that's what my mother always says.

JM: (*Laughing*) Mine, too.

JUAN: Yeah, well, I guess Jim's didn't. This is just stupid. Now the damn spray gun is clogged all up. I hate this job, can't stand it.

JM: What's the worst part?

JUAN: Always being disrespected. Just treated disrespectfully. My boss, Jim, the owner, he treats me as if I'm like dirt. ... He said he was gonna give me a raise. He said that six months ago and I still haven't seen the raise, not a penny. Y'know, I'm gettin' paid seven dollars an hour. I deserve for the work here— y'know, I do paint work, I do autobody work, I do mechanic work, and I do the driving, the towing—I deserve at least nine dollars an hour. But what are you gonna do? Life goes on.

As we talked, as if on cue, Juan was summoned by his boss. Standing on the back steps of the office about forty yards away, Jim bellowed Juan's name sharply several times. "See what I mean?" said Juan with a tight-lipped smile that quickly turned into a grimace. He shook his head and continued to clean the clogged paint sprayer, his back to his shouting boss. Finally, a few face-saving seconds after Jim went back inside, Juan got up, excused himself, and trudged toward the office.

Two weeks later, we talked again on the lot of Jim's Tow, this time as Juan worked on the carburetor of a Chevrolet Caprice. More upbeat, Juan still complained about his job.

JM: What are your hours like?

JUAN: Depends. Depends when he needs me. Last week I worked seven days, put a lot of hours in. Y'know, I need the money. I usually work six or seven days a week. Whenever he calls me, I'm here.

JM: You get overtime.

JUAN: Overtime? What's overtime? They've never heard of that around here. I told you, this isn't the greatest job in the world.

Whereas Mokey changed jobs rapidly in search of a bona fide career opening, Juan has stayed with his jobs. The result has been much the same for both young men: disappointment.

Derek graduated near the top of his class in June 1984. Three weeks later he was married and on his way to boot camp in the navy. After training in aviation electronics, Derek was stationed about a hundred miles from the apartment he rented for his wife, Faith, and their infant son in a working-class neighborhood near Clarendon Heights. Inexplicably, Derek's pay suddenly was cut off for two months. Already disillusioned with the navy, desperate to feed his child, and frustrated at his superiors' inability or unwillingness to rectify the problem, Derek went AWOL. Thus, the promising thirteen-year-old pupil at a posh private school ended up festering in a military prison five years later. Released with a lawyer's help, Derek endured three months of unemployment before finding a job as a ramp worker at the airport. He has been there now for seven years and makes $7.50 an hour.

Derek may not earn much, but he enjoys his job. He interacts easily with fellow workers, having carved out a social space within his workplace that gives him security, autonomy, and satisfaction. Indeed, he often refers to his "niche" in the airline industry.

DEREK: This is really my niche. I love being around airplanes, I love meeting people. I like the prospect of travel and I've been traveling a lot: every year I take like two or three trips, flying at a great price. ... I found my niche. I just like being outside, being around a lot of people, having fun, y'know, getting along, doing the job.

Derek's job satisfaction, however, has come at a price. His wage is low, especially after seven years in the industry. He often works the night shift from 9 P.M. to 6 A.M. Almost all of his moves within the company have been horizontal—from ramp leader in charge of loading and unloading the aircraft, to passenger service agent, to team leader responsible for overseeing the routine maintenance of the aircraft between flights, to aircraft cabin cleaner. When I spoke with him, Derek was cleaning aircraft interiors on the graveyard shift. One of the benefits, apart from the hourly wage differential of twenty-five cents, is the scarcity of management. "When I'm on nights, there's really not much management contact except that one supervisor for the total rest of the overnight shift. And that makes a big difference; everything's much more relaxed." Derek was recently offered a management position but refused to sacrifice or diminish his friendships by taking on a supervisory role.

DEREK: Management is very unrelenting. They'll demand that you get down harder on the employee and, I don't know how to explain it, I just don't work well with management because I don't consider management to be people oriented. It's like when I became an agent council representative—that's a person like if employees have problems with other employees and they have problems with management, I become like a middleman and say, "Okay, well here's how we can work this out," and that was pretty good because it's like I was still one of the agents and everyone looked at me as being an agent and not as a supervisor saying, "Okay, these are the rules; you have to abide by them, otherwise, y'know, you're out." And I enjoyed that a lot. I really enjoyed that a lot. Being a supervisor—that's definitely not for me. The pay really doesn't matter, it's not the most important thing, it's just being with the people, y'know, people who care, that's what it is.

Being a supervisor would divorce Derek from the rank and file and force him to bear down on his friends. He prefers to mediate rather than to dominate, even if it means sacrificing his career.

As comfortable as Derek is in the airline industry, he longs to exercise his knack for mediation as a police officer. "I consider a police officer to be more of a mediator, like a go-between person, you know, trying to resolve problems, and that's something I like doing." In 1989 Derek was offered a job as a policeman in the small town of Avon across the state.

DEREK: Right after I got out of the military I was looking into law enforcement but at the time I needed to make money so I gotten into the airline industry. ... The only thing that's ever been on my mind is law enforcement. It's something I've always wanted to get into, like taking the state police test, passed that.

JM: You got a ...

DEREK: I got a ninety-eight on that, I took the local police test here in the city and I got a ninety-seven on that. I was called for the Avon Police Department. I was like this close, inches from becoming an Avon Police because I'd gone through all their screening tests, then all the background checks, their psych evaluations, whatever, but I let Faith and a million other people talk me out of it. They figured you're gonna get shot, this'll happen, that'll happen, nobody likes the police anymore, and y'know, this was like two years ago and I dunno, I just let people talk me out of it. ... I just always thought being a police officer would be a nice prestigious career. ... I want to have some kind of gung ho career. Yes, that's it. If I couldn't be a marine, why not be a cop or something like that.

JM: The action, the adventure?

DEREK: Yeah, yeah. I like the guns, too.

JM: Now where did that come from?

DEREK: I dunno.

JM: You seem so gentle, y'know.

DEREK: Yeah, I am. My father had an unbelievable collection of guns. I don't know, me, my father, my grandfather, we're all exactly alike. We all like guns. I'm not too keen on the ocean like they are [Derek's father and grandfather were sailors], because I've just got this big fear of this giant shark coming up and eating me (*laughs*), but I'm exactly like they are: I like to travel a lot, I like to meet new people. I mean, I wanna be a world traveler some day, and I will be because I know if I want it *I will get it.*

The same sense of efficacy applies to his police aspiration.

DEREK: I will get into law enforcement. Because it's what I want. I've pretty much taken the stance from now on whatever I want I'm gonna get, no matter what. In fairness, but if I want something I'm gonna get it.

What Derek wanted more than anything else in 1991 was an apartment big enough for his family.

DEREK: Look at this place. It's big enough for two but not four. We knew that when we moved in. But rent these days, it's crazy. Crazy. We're doing okay, though; we're getting along.

JM: It's good to talk to someone who's a success story.

DEREK: I'm not really a success. It's just that nothing bad has happened, and I don't want anything to. I just wanna be in a position to avoid disasters.

More than I do, Derek understands the fragility of his relative prosperity.

In February 1984 James was studying assiduously, making up failed classes after school and intent on designing computer games as a career. The next year, however, he was expelled from school for excessive truancy.

JM: What did your father have to say about that?

JAMES: Let's just say I had a little chat with my father's fists. Then the next morning he woke me up at seven o'clock and put a newspaper in my face, pointing to a little ad. "This is where you're going today, buddy; now move!" It was a free course for a G.E.D.

James enrolled in a class made up mostly of adults for whom English was a second language; he took and passed the test four weeks later, receiving his high school equivalency diploma in the summer of 1986. With the help of a federal Pell grant and $2,500 in student loans, James immediately enrolled in a computer school. "I was lucky," he relates. "My parents paid most of the one thousand dollars that I had to pay. Because the total cost was like seven thousand dollars."

James landed a good job immediately after receiving his certificate in computer programming, although a connection proved as important as the credential.

JAMES: I had a friend who was a security guard at this massive bank, federal reserves, so he got me an interview there, like two days after I got out of school. I guess he had a guy in personnel who owed him favors. So they gave me a job as a computer operator there.

James worked nights from 11 P.M. to 7 A.M. for an annual salary of close to $17,000. A year later, another friend found him a more lucrative position at Citicorp out in the suburbs, also on the night shift.

JAMES: It was like ten thousand dollars more than I was making, but the only problem was the ride, right, like half an hour ride. I was like, "Yeah, for that much more money I'll take half an hour drive." So I gave my notice in, I went to Citicorp, got a car, and I worked for Citicorp for about one and a half years, and they had a layoff, they closed down my division. So there I was without a job. But Citicorp, they helped me get a job with another bank in the city. Another bank needed an operator, so I got a job there, only I had to take a pay cut of like ten thousand dollars, back down to eighteen thousand dollars a year.

Back on the night shift as a computer operator at a central city bank, James worked for a year before he was dismissed in June 1990. As James tells it, he was routinely victimized by his supervisor. Matters came to a head when he was forced to switch shifts and then was blamed for bungling the new operations he had not been trained to undertake.

JAMES: He just starts ripping into me, talkin' about I'm doing all this stuff wrong, blah, blah, blah, and if I don't like it, I can get outta here. And he's pointing in my face, and he's acting like he doesn't have any sense. So I got ticked off and I left. I walked out, and I said, "Hey, this ain't my shift, man." And I left, I went home. So I came back the next day and they had a book with the rules of the bank there, and one of the rules of the bank is that if you leave work without authorization, then you get fired, so …

JM: Have you been actively looking for work since then?

JAMES: Yeah, it's hard. It's been over a year now. Sending out résumés, going to different companies, filling out applications. I've been on interviews to banks out of state. … I've sent out an average of twenty letters a month. Nothing. So here I am sitting at home watching MTV.

James's heavy educational investment paid off at first, although he was actually overtrained for all his jobs. Qualified as a programmer, he worked as an operator. "Actually, what I'm doing is nothing—it's not even close to programming," he reported in 1987. "I just sit there, punch a few buttons, get paid." Job satisfaction was low, but pay was relatively high—until the economy began its nosedive. And James soon discovered that as wages shrank, so did job security.

Craig, too, has followed the prescription for occupational success by investing heavily in education. He attended a junior college after graduating from high school and then transferred to a large university. He struggled to pay his bills, and he struggled academically. To make ends meet, he had to work extensively during both academic terms and holidays. He finally graduated in 1989. Craig returned home saddled with over $10,000 in student loans and hoping to land an entry-level job in the business world. He was disappointed. Unemployed for over a year, Craig settled for a clerical job in a large store's credit department where he works the phone trying to recover delinquent bills for an annual salary of $17,000.

CRAIG: I just had to take the best job I could get. After a year, you get kind of desperate. I looked hard for a job in banking, preferably in investment. Nothing. In the end I accepted this sorry job.

JM: Do you use any of the skills you learned in college?

CRAIG: None. I don't know what kind of skills these are—detective skills, I suppose, or psychological skills. Actually, I'm pretty good at it. Half the time you hafta lie. It's just going after deadbeats who have moved out of state, trying to track them down. It's just a Joe Schmo job, but it's all I could get.

JM: Is there any room for advancement?

CRAIG: Not really. I don't see a future in this job. I'm looking for others. Hopefully, this is just to tide me over until I can get a good job. I don't want any old Schmo job.

Disappointed but not despondent, Craig is matter-of-fact about his current job and his continued inability to get a better one.

Mike, the only white member of the Brothers, graduated from Lincoln High School in June 1986 and enrolled in a state college. After several weeks, unable to acclimatize culturally and socially, he returned home. Following ten weeks of unemployment, Mike went to real estate school and got his license but has been unable to put it to use. He also took civil service exams for the positions of mail carrier, post office clerk, and firefighter. Meanwhile, he found a night job as a security guard for $7 an hour. Having applied to Eastern airlines for a job as a flight attendant, Mike was flown to Florida for an interview but failed to get the position. In August 1987 he landed a job as a bank teller. Combining a forty-hour week at the bank with twenty-four hours of security work, Mike brought in $550 a week. A year later he quit both jobs to begin work for the post office as a mail carrier and also signed on with a modeling agency. Mike's modeling career began to peter out when he pulled a stomach muscle, stopped working out regularly, and began putting on weight, but in 1991 his total earnings topped $36,000. He has owned a BMW and recently bought a Mazda sports car. "I'm making more money than most yuppies," Mike reports. Indeed, he is on the verge of purchasing a $138,000 house in a working-class suburb as an investment.

Mike is a relentless believer in the American Dream and in individual responsibility. To him, the Hallway Hangers have only themselves to blame for their failure.

JM: Do you ever see Frankie or Jinks or Slick or any of those guys around?

MIKE: No, I never see them. Those guys are fucking rejects. Trash. Fuck 'em. Fuckin' trash. You can make it. You can do whatever you wanna do. If you wanna be trash, you'll be trash.

The irony is that Mike landed the job at the bank only after he and Craig indulged in a little collective use of credentials. They doctored Craig's diploma to make it appear that Mike had received his associate's degree, a foray into white-collar crime about which Mike makes no apologies. "Hey, what was I s'posed to do? Be a security guard the rest of my life?" Mike, it seems, caught the 1980s mood of aggressive individualism and runaway greed. "Hey, that's what it's about. You've got to be cutthroat. You've got to be competitive." Whereas Wall Street bankers made millions of dollars with their scams, Mike made hundreds. When his BMW began to run ragged, he paid $400 to have it stolen, battered, and dumped as part of an insurance job. And as much as he rails against welfare fraud, Mike himself has continued to live illegally in his mother's Clarendon Heights apartment.

Super is one of the people against whom Mike fulminates for not having made more of himself. Since graduating from high school in 1986, Super has worked at U-Haul putting hitches on cars, cleaning trucks, and filling them up with gas. He moved on to Burger King for a couple of months before landing a job delivering auto parts. Making $4.50 an hour, he worked there for five months before being fired for turning up late.

SUPER: It weren't no good job anyhow. I dunno, man, I just found out real quick after I graduated that unless you go on to college or somethin' you just ain't gonna make it. … I just wanna make somethin' of my life, y'know, be a success. Not just be stuck in these dead-end jobs. I'd like to get married and have a family, but how'm I s'posed to do that on four and a half dollars an hour?

Eventually, Super got a job at a grocery store and stayed for three years. He unloaded shipments, stocked shelves, and drove a delivery van for an hourly wage that increased from $6 to $7 an hour.

An hourly wage of seven dollars, however, was peanuts compared to what Super began making in 1990 when he turned to crack capitalism. As Super tells it, his criminal career was catalyzed by the anger and betrayal he felt when the police planted marijuana on him.

SUPER: I was working at the grocery store, I just got my check and I was walking through the park to my aunt's house. That's before all this crack shit came up. People were selling weed mostly. I passed through the park there, at that time the park on Lee Street was kinda hot. A cop said, "Hey you, come here." And I kept walking. Y'know, I'd seen someone there and I started talking to him. I guess the cop knew the guy was selling drugs. He said, "Stop."

I said, "For what? I'm going, y'know, I'm in a hurry, what you want?"

He just run up to me and grabbed me. "You selling drugs, what's your name, you bought some drugs?"

I was like, "I don't know nuttin'. I just come here, I know the guy from school." Showed him my check.

He was like, "I don't give a shit. If you ain't gonna help me, I'm gonna fix you." Locked me up. Put me in the paddy wagon. I stayed in the paddy wagon for like a couple of minutes and he came back. "See this? This is yours now. You don't want to help me, this is yours." He had come back with a bag of weed. Cops nowadays are crookedy, just like the same as the drug dealers. They arrested me, put me in jail. The cops out there now, they get paid off, sell drugs. The world's crazy now. Anyway, I couldn't believe that happened. I wasn't even thinking about dealing at the time, I just wanted to work, stay out of trouble. ... I was against drugs and shit. I was against people doing that, y'know. I was on the side with the cops, y'know.

Super's story is credible. Dealing drugs was a radical change for someone who, apart from school skirmishes, had stayed out of trouble. And yet Super may be portraying his entry into the street economy in the best possible light.

Whatever prompted his career change, Super emphasizes that once he started dealing, he was able to advance quickly. The drug economy provided excitement and money, but more important to Super was the promise of promotion.

JM: Tell me about how you got into it and stuff.

SUPER: Well, I got into it, I was so bored, I had no money and just worked my way up. I had no money, was broke, flat broke. So I worked my way up. I had to have money. I worked my way up, worked my way up.

Super started off as a runner, delivering packets of crack to customers. Within a few weeks he was selling on the street, handling the money himself but turning it over to his supplier who would give him a cut. Now Super works for himself, exploiting the small spaces in the market left fallow by the big dealers, moving from neighborhood to neighborhood and even out of state. For Super, the informal economy provided a far better career structure than the formal economy.

The pay is also superior to what Super could make working a legitimate job. At his peak, Super reports that he could gross up to $3,000 during a good week of hard work.

SUPER: It's some long hours. Sometimes stay up all night. Long nights.

JM: People call you any time on the beeper?

SUPER: Turn it off sometimes, y'know. If I'm real tired, I'll just turn it off and go to sleep.

Super sells powdered cocaine but usually cooks it up into its more marketable crystallized form. Crack is better for business, but Super is haunted by the toll it takes on his customers.

SUPER: Crack. Crack. There's something in it that makes them want it more. That crack shit does it to you. It's a real bad addiction, real bad addiction. It's like poison. I dunno, it just does stuff to people, makes girls do shit they don't wanna do: sell their body, steal from their parents, leave their babies out on the street, all shit.

JM: Now what about you, do you use the stuff?

SUPER: No, I use no crack.

JM: How do you keep from doing that, if you're around it all the time?

SUPER: I dunno, just be strong inside, hold up. I have people that say, "Try it out." Uh-uh. I see what it does to other people. I really don't want to sell this shit; it's the only way I can make a living right now. Can't get a job, can't do nothing, so ...

JM: Have you tried, have you been, have you had trouble getting a job?

SUPER: Yeah, I tried, y'know. I don't want to sell drugs for the rest of my life or nuttin'. I just want to try to get myself a job and get myself back on the, back going, try to get myself an apartment, get myself a place ...

Super is torn by his moral culpability as a purveyor of crack but sees no alternative way of generating income.

Addiction does not eat into Super's profit margin as it did that of the less disciplined Hallway Hangers, who are now largely dependent on Super for drugs. But like his white counterparts, Super is preoccupied with the dangers of the retail drug trade. The police often search him, and he is plagued by predators and competitors.

SUPER: It's not a life to live, man.

JM: What are the biggest risks?

SUPER: Getting caught by the cops, having people trying to rob you, people shooting at you. Stick-up people coming round and robbing you. Listen, that happens, happens a lot.

JM: Did it happen to you?

SUPER: People tried a couple of times, got robbed, but they didn't get nothing. ... I've just been lucky, I guess. Had knives, guns pulled on me. I would just say, "Hey, you got your gun, just go on and use it. If you gonna shoot me, shoot me." Usually it's not worth it to them to shoot you. But as you can see (*grins to reveal several missing teeth*), I've got in some nasty fights. ... You gotta have a gun, too. You can get busted for that, too, but you have to have one, regardless. If you're selling drugs you hafta have a gun.

JM: What about close calls with the police?

SUPER: Yeah, plenty of close calls. But I never would have nothing on me. They come and frisk me down, never have nothing. All I have is money. Can't do nothing if you don't have it. Cops come over and just grab me. "Which one, is it this one?" I guess they been doing surveillance or something. But they only get me with money.

JM: Do you only deal in the projects or ...

SUPER: In the projects, all over. It's good to move around, not stay in one spot a lot. I slowed down for a while. I stopped selling for a bit, y'know, and right now I'm not out there like one hundred percent like I used to. I'm like twenty percent, trying to slow down. You can't be greedy. See, most guys, especially when they start, they'll be greedy. That's why they don't stay in business for long. I used to make good money when I started off, but now I slowed down cuz it's getting bad out there. Gotta be careful, real careful. Go up to cars, that's one thing you never do. You got narcotics agents out there now, they go and rent cars with out-of-state plates. Driver'll say, "Whatcha got on you? Whatcha got? Whatcha holding?" Soon as you pull it out, boom, you're arrested.

JM: So all you do is hang around and people know you and will approach you?

SUPER: You can tell who smokes and who doesn't smoke.

JM: How can you tell?

SUPER: Easy, by just looking at 'em. You can tell if a person doesn't look right, you've never seen 'em before, or this and that. "Uh-uh, I don't have nothing." Tell 'em I don't have nothing. ... When you're living a life like this, you can't trust no one.

JM: That must be hard. What about your girlfriend?

SUPER: I trust her, but I can't trust her too much either.

JM: How come, what can happen?

SUPER: You never know, you have an argument with your girl and she'll call the cops. If she knows too much it can hurt ya. Sometimes, y'know, you'll get people, dealers, they'll get mad and call the cops on you, shit like that. Wanna come and rob you. Hatch fights with people, y'know. People that I've known for a long time, arguing with me. I had to hurt 'em, almost. I've had shootouts, got shot at. Haven't been hit yet.

Super has not been seriously injured, nor has he been prosecuted for a drug offense, but he understands that it is only a matter of time. Still, he plows on, longing for a legal job. Over and over, Super underlines how the dearth of legal economic opportunity keeps him in the grip of the risky cocaine trade.

SUPER: Right now I feel myself kinda trapped. I wanna get out of here bad. I just need a job, job paying all right, reasonable money.

JM: What's reasonable money, what would that be?

SUPER: Nowadays with rent, know what I'm saying, so expensive, food—about eight bucks, seven bucks an hour. That means I could get myself an apartment, probably go back to school at night, work in the day.

JM: What do you see as the difficulties of getting out of here?

SUPER: Money.

JM: But you've been making it quick. I mean, do you see yourself being able to work two months for what you can make in a couple of days now?

SUPER: Yeah, I know it may seem crazy, but I think I can do it if I could just make the money. Making my money legit, I don't have to worry about cops bothering me. No one bothering me, I'd work hard for that; no one can take that from you. ... I don't want to live this life any more, I wanna try to get a job, I really don't wanna sell drugs to people, y'know, I don't wanna try to make people do bad, y'know, I don't wanna try to down no one or nothing. It's the only way I can make a living right now.

JM: Do you get pressured a lot from other people to stop dealing, or do they just not know what's going on—like family and stuff, parents, your aunt, other people?

SUPER: They know what's going on. They're telling me to stop, try and get a job or something. There's no jobs, y'know, that's the way it goes. They say if I keep doing this, I ain't gonna live that long, usually dealing drugs, living fast life, end up in jail or dead, which is true. I might get robbed, might get shot. What are you going to do?

JM: How long do you think you can keep going this way before you really end up getting, either getting in big legal trouble or getting hurt?

SUPER: I dunno. Never can tell. Chance it every time. Could happen today. Could happen tomorrow. Never know. ... I just wanna stop doin' what I'm doin', y'know? This life ain't the life to live, y'know? I dunno. I just feel if I keep going as I'm going right now, selling drugs, I know I won't be in jail, I know I'll probably be dead. I know that myself. I try not to think about it, cuz it gets to me.

Although the other Brothers feel less hemmed in than Super does, most of them have found the transition from school to work more difficult than they anticipated. The Brothers, after all, were no dropouts. While many of their peers were dawdling through school days courting girls, playing ball, and getting high, the Brothers toiled in the classroom. And yet rather than question their commitment to school, the Brothers, Super included, reaffirm it.

Sold on School

All of the Brothers graduated from high school. A high school diploma, they expected, would give them a leg up on the labor market. They had been told over and over by their parents, teachers, and counselors to stay in school, that they needed a high school diploma to get a decent job. This was good advice. As cities in the United States have shifted from producing goods to processing information, jobs for high school dropouts have largely evaporated. As stated earlier, the city in which Clarendon Heights residents work saw a 59 percent drop between 1970 and 1980 in the number of jobs held by those who did not complete high school.[1] And as African Americans, the Brothers would be especially hard-pressed to find jobs as high school dropouts. National data for October 1990 show that among sixteen- to twenty-four-year-old high school dropouts, only 57 percent of the whites were employed. But the figure for blacks is truly catastrophic: Fewer than 30 percent were working.[2] African Americans with little schooling do indeed become ensnared in the web of urban industrial transition. The answer, educators and economists agree, is for blacks to stay in school. And the Brothers, without exception, stuck it out and graduated from high school.

Across the country, more and more African Americans, like the Brothers, are staying in school. Whereas between 1970 and 1990 the percentage of white sixteen-to twenty-four-year-olds not enrolled in school and not high school graduates remained essentially constant (between 12 and 13 percent), there was a sharp increase in school attendance by blacks, for whom the corresponding figure fell from 26 percent in 1970 to 13 percent in 1990.[3] But although blacks are staying in school, their job prospects fail to show a corresponding improvement.

What the Brothers did not realize is that jobs in their city held by those *with* a high school education also fell by 29 percent between 1970 and 1980[4] and has shrunk further in the ensuing ten years, particularly for young African Americans. In 1980 the local unemployment rate for black male dropouts between the ages of twenty and twenty-four was 26 percent. In 1990 the figure was 25 percent for those *with* a high school education.[5] As high school graduates, the Brothers have barely improved their job prospects over those of black dropouts ten years earlier.

There is a large racial gap in unemployment and earnings among high school graduates as well as dropouts. Nationwide, the unemployment rate for white sixteen- to twenty-four-year-olds with a high school diploma in 1990 was 9 percent. For black high school graduates it was 26 percent.[6] If black high school graduates without jobs feel betrayed, many with jobs also feel let down because they earn so much less than whites. In the local labor market for men in 1989, white high school dropouts between the ages of twenty and twenty-four earned $9,294 per year. White graduates made $14,237. Black dropouts of the same age earned only $7,648 per year. And blacks with a high school diploma made a mere $8,856—less than white dropouts. A high school diploma improved the earnings of whites by 53 percent. The return for blacks was a paltry 16 percent.[7] For African American men, a high school education simply does not pay off as promised.

For the Brothers this fact was a rude awakening. Many now feel they were deluded about the value of a high school diploma but trace the delusion back to themselves rather than to a restricted opportunity structure clothed in an ideology of equal opportunity.

MOKEY: My diploma didn't do anything for me, job-wise.

JM: When you consider back to like your hopes back in high school ...

MOKEY: I wish I could start it over. ... I think I shoulda worked harder in high school. Because in high school I didn't do a lot. I shoulda been at a better college. I just was really lazy about it. ... I didn't know what kind of major I actually wanted to do. Y'see, when I went to high school, I actually told my parents I didn't want to go on the Fundamental program—that's like college prep—and at that time I thought I was more of like a technical person. And they had that

Oc. Ed. trade thing over there at the high school. It was more like I wanted, a trade program. I wish I actually went to, y'know, trade classes. My parents, they just wanted me to just learn the education, y'know, and not the trade.

Although he recognizes the limited utility of his diploma on the job market, Mokey still berates himself for being lazy in high school. He also implies that under the sway of parents who advised him to "plan to be a success and reach the highest goal possible," aiming high and undergoing a purely academic course of study may have been a strategic mistake. Channeling students into vocational tracks is an important mechanism of social reproduction. Mokey resisted this process, only to find that the impermeability of the class structure is such that he might have been better off with more modest aspirations and vocational preparation. Super agrees. But Juan does not, for he graduated from the Occupational Education program and contends that his vocational degree has been of little use.

JUAN: High school hasn't really helped me, my diploma. To tell the truth, it really hasn't. I thought for sure I would need my diploma. But who needs a diploma for this (*turns up his oil-stained hands*)? High school hasn't helped me. You're better off to go to one of those, y'know, ten-month trade schools, that's if you've got the money.

The Brothers have discovered that for African American men, a high school diploma of whatever variety often fails to secure even a toehold in the postindustrial urban economy.

When I spoke with a jobless Super in 1987, he was despondent. He felt misled, and like Mokey, he reckoned in retrospect that he should have pursued a vocational degree in high school.

SUPER: I ain't goin' nowhere out here on the streets, man. Nowhere but down. I got to get an education, go back to school. I'm thinkin' about goin' to a community college.

JM: Were you disappointed with the jobs you got after you graduated?

SUPER: Yeah, I found out real quick when I got into the real world that it was gonna be a lot tougher than I thought.

JM: You were led to believe it would be different?

SUPER: Yeah.

JM: Who by?

SUPER: Teachers and stuff, I guess.

JM: Did you believe them?

SUPER: Well, yes and no.

JM: How do you mean?

SUPER: Well, I could see some kids had graduated but didn't get good jobs. But I thought I still might cuz some kids do. But, y'know, those kids did Oc. Ed.— sheet metal or carpentry, like—and their teachers got them jobs in construction or somethin'. Now I see that you can't get no decent job with just a high school diploma. Now, I hear that it's tough even if you go on and finish college to get a job.

It is instructive that Super began by reaffirming his belief in the value of education despite his frustration, disappointment, and confusion.

Super has good reason to be confused. The Brothers entered an educational maze when they enrolled in high school. Whereas middle-class pupils are clued in to where they're going thanks to the cultural capital they inherited from their parents, working-class students are given very little guidance in negotiating critical turning points. How were the Brothers to know whether they would be better off in the Pilot School or the Fundamental School, in House B or Oc. Ed., in a college track or a general one? And their confusion continues upon graduation from high school. Which programs, degrees, and institutions are worthy of investment, and which lead down cul-de-sacs? Pseudo-colleges and training programs have become a veritable racketeering industry. Many seem to target very weak students, suck money from them and from federal assistance programs, and spit them back onto the streets without having appreciably improved their job prospects.

In fact, with the exception of Derek, all of the Brothers have pursued post–secondary school education, although only Craig has completed a degree program. Super studied electronics at predominantly black Rosebank Community College for several weeks.

JM: What happened?

SUPER: I just left it, couldn't study. Couldn't handle it. Too much stuff on my mind. Didn't have no job or nothing. Didn't have no money hardly. Not enough to go to school.

Juan lasted two months at a nearby, mostly white community college before quitting. "It was a pity, y'know, cuz I really enjoyed it. I had to leave to get some money." Mokey attended the same school's liberal arts program for two semesters. As noted earlier, his motivation was sapped because his studies weren't improving his employment prospects: "I wasn't sure there was going to be anything at the end of the line." In fact, a comprehensive evaluation of community colleges finds that there is often very little at the end of the line for students. Norton Grubb's study shows that men enrolled in community college certificate programs fail to improve their prospects, and that even community college degrees yield relatively few benefits on the job market.[8]

And yet Super is convinced that further education is the key to his future, and both Mokey and Juan would like to return to school.

(*in separate interviews*)

SUPER: I think if I go back to school then it'll help me to get a better job and move on in life. And probably get away from this place. Carve me something out of life. Make me a better man than I am.

MOKEY: I've been accepted to go back [to community college], cuz job-wise, over the last year, it's been really bad, so I was gonna go back to school. I was gonna go into school for electronics, cuz I wanted to go to school for technology and for engineering. But I didn't get my financial aid. Don't know why.

JUAN: If I had the money, I'd go back to school, back to community college. I need to do something. But there's no way now. I've got too many responsibilities.

Super, Mokey, and Juan have always been confined to the slow lane of the formal economy. Now, having stalled out completely, they see further education as the answer. What else could help them?

To be sure, higher education can be crucial for economic success, but high-caliber schooling is beyond most of the Brothers' means. James proved an exception. His parents made a large contribution toward his expensive computer training and supported him financially while he studied. And his schooling paid off handsomely until the economy slid into deep recession. But then, James got breaks that other young blacks cannot count on, as we shall see.

Other Brothers have had the opportunity to study at four-year colleges. The September after his high school graduation, Mike found himself in a rural state college studying management. His fellow students were also white but not of his background, and Mike braved the cultural clash for only a few months.

MIKE: I picked the wrong school. Maybe I should've gone to a junior college to break myself in. The people were different, goddamn airheads. All they could do was go out drinking, come back puking. My roommates were scared of me, so I wasn't that friendly. I kept to myself. And the girls—they were snobby as hell, I couldn't stand 'em. Plus, y'know, I was used to city life and there I was all of a sudden in the middle of the fucking woods, nowhere to go. ... I just didn't like it. It wasn't me.

As a residential student, Mike found that the college's alien cultural landscape placed too many strains on his identity.

Craig, by contrast, flourished in a junior college. In September 1984 I drove him to a small, rural, two-year college to which he had won a basketball scholarship. He talked apprehensively in the car about adjusting to the new social milieu. But as the star of the basketball team, Craig proved popular among the almost all-white student body. In two years he graduated with an associate's degree and transferred to a large out-of-state university. Yet Craig struggled at his new school. He was granted only a year's credit for his work at the junior college and had to live off-campus. He was cut from the basketball team. And he failed two subjects when a delay in his financial aid caused him to miss the first few weeks of the spring term.

To make ends meet, Craig worked between fifteen and twenty hours each week during term time.

CRAIG: At first I worked at an architecture firm. I messed up that job. It was tough to work it around my schedule, and I ended up not showing up a lot. What happened was I got disillusioned. I was just photocopying stuff. It was just a lot of busywork. I never got a chance to help design at all, never got close to it.

JM: How did you get that job?

CRAIG: Showed them some of my drawings. I guess they thought if I could draw, I could photocopy (*laughs bitterly*). Architects do a lot of copying. It's not what it's cracked up to be.

Working two jobs, Craig logged up to seventy hours each week during the summers. Still, he could not afford to buy the required textbooks.

CRAIG: Man, some of those books were so expensive it was incredible. I remember one called *Structural Dynamics* went for a hundred and fifteen bucks. There was just no way I could afford that. A lot of books I ended up getting from the library, but then that was tough because they'd be on reserve. You couldn't check them out.

Finding the compulsory physics courses too demanding, Craig switched from architecture to business. He graduated in August 1989 in good academic standing.

Unlike most of the Brothers, Craig now has a stable job. However, it took him more than a year to find employment. And after five years of college education, his annual salary is barely a third of the national median for male workers. Craig's experience notwithstanding, the Brothers retain a deep faith in the ability of schooling to boost their economic prospects. And of course further education does help them. But the effect is often marginal. Having graduated from high school, many have found that their diploma is not worth much on the job market. And this is no misconception. Statistics show quite clearly that for African Americans who have invested in a high school education, the payoff is often scant. Those who graduate from college do much better; but as Craig illustrates, even black college graduates from disadvantaged backgrounds are hard-pressed to parlay their academic credentials into economic prosperity. For Craig, as for most of the Brothers, the gap between aspiration and outcome looms large.

Aspiration and Outcome: What Went Wrong?

The discrepancy between aspiration and outcome is much larger for the Brothers than for the Hallway Hangers. In 1984 the Brothers had hopes of middle-class careers, of happy families, of nice cars, and of homes in leafy suburbs. Eight years later, they are for the most part living at home with their parents and struggling to make ends meet. The first edition of this book could only speculate that the Brothers' aspirations and expectations would be "cooled out" once they experienced the realities of the job market. The critical question here is whether they have begun to question the openness of American society or whether they reproach themselves for frustrated ambition.

Some of the Brothers maintain their faith in the American dream. Derek does not earn much, even after seven years at his airport job. He and his wife live with their two children in a cramped two-bedroom apartment. But Derek's affirmation of equality of opportunity is still unequivocal. He is particularly vehement when reflecting on those who have resigned themselves to menial jobs or unemployment.

DEREK: If you really want something in life, you gotta go for it because it's really not that hard to make money. If you really want something, you just gotta go for it. Too many people I know don't realize that; it's their own fault, I guess. ... If these people would really commit themselves, they could have anything they wanted. And I don't know of anyone who could tell me different. ... There are too many opportunities out there, too many people that are willing to do things for you. Hell, they can even get a federal loan and get something out of their lives, but they don't want it.

For Derek occupational failure can be attributed to lack of personal initiative and competence.

Mike agrees. "If you dig in, there are a lot of opportunities out there. You just have to go for them," he insists. The Hallway Hangers are "a bunch of lazy, loser, fuck-up bums." A friend is also branded a bum, but Mike reconsiders.

MIKE: Bobby, he's a bum. No, that's not true, he's not really a bum. He works hard but he's kinda lazy. He's in a dead-end job. He's not going anywhere.

JM: Is that his fault?

MIKE: Yeah, it's his fault. Who else's fault could it be?

According to Mike, and to most Americans, those who fail have only themselves to blame. There is no publicly accepted idiom that can be invoked to explain failure apart from personal responsibility; a structural explanation is a nonstarter.

Most of the Brothers have tempered their belief in the openness of American society. They blame themselves for failing to get ahead, but the social order also comes in for some criticism. As noted earlier, Mokey chides himself for being lazy, for failing to study hard enough, and for switching jobs too frequently. But he also notes the lack of opportunity.

MOKEY: If I did something for myself, did better in school, I think I woulda been in a better position. But I know friends right now, I mean, they're in the same predicament. One friend, he graduated from Madison College and he's still looking for a job. … Looking for a job now is really hard.

Similarly, Super blames himself for his condition but never loses sight of the larger context.

SUPER: I've been moving a lot man, that's probably the main reason why, you know, I can't get my head straight. It's like when I got out of high school, I had in mind going to school, I was doing good. I just fucked everything up.

(*later in the same interview*)

SUPER: I know I need to stop [selling drugs], but how can I stop? I mean, I gotta make money somehow, y'know? There just ain't any jobs, no jobs. You know that, right? Ain't no jobs. Y'know, there's just no jobs, ain't no jobs out there.

Super never shirks personal responsibility for his plight, nor does he absolve himself of moral culpability for dealing crack. Still, he understands that he has been constrained by economic realities over which he has no control.

Juan castigates himself. "I really screwed up, I just screwed up, I screwed up my life." And yet he also indicts the opportunity structure. Based on his experience in several jobs, Juan is convinced that the term *entry-level position* is often a euphemism. "They always tell you when you start a job that there's gonna be good chances of being promoted, of moving up. But it never happens."

James knows the vagaries of the labor market. He has tasted occupational success, but he has also been unemployed for over a year, in spite of his eagerness to work, his specialized computer training, and his work experience. His own work history has taught him the importance of structural constraints on opportunity.

JAMES: I've been on many job interviews to this very day that I know I was more than qualified for. They knew that I could do the job, but the way that the economics is, there's fifty other guys that can do the job. The other guy can do that job, his job, six other people's jobs, ten other jobs, he'll work for every day of the week for no pay. It's just, there's too many people without jobs. ... It's just the economic system is falling apart right now.

James is the only Brother to criticize the economic system explicitly and consistently, and thus to contextualize individual choice within a larger framework. Responding to a question about Super dealing drugs, James sympathizes with his friend's situation.

JM: Tell me about Super. What happened with him, cuz in high school he never did all that well, but he tried hard.

JAMES: What I can't understand is selling drugs and stuff like that. That never was him. I guess he'd say he's doing what he has to do to get by. Man, a lot of people's doing it. I can't really find fault in them, cuz they doing what they gotta do to get by. They payin' their bills and stuff. And the way that economics are now, man, a lot of people that wouldn't be doing that before, wouldn't do something like sell drugs, or sell stolen goods, wouldn't have done that before, they're doin' it now because, hey, they don't have jobs and you gotta support yourself, you gotta look out for your family, and you gotta look out for number one.

JM: So you don't really find fault with them individually?

JAMES: No, no, I find fault with the economic system. That there's so many people out of work that a lot of people are forced to do that. ... Yeah, a lot of people are forced into it. They're not just criminals because they want to be criminals. They're criminals because they need some way to survive, and they can't. ... That's where we go back to the economic system now. Nowadays, if you have a job you're doing good, the way the economics is now. ...

James is clear on this point: that the lack of economic opportunity more than anything else explains why the Brothers have failed to get ahead as they envisioned. But notice how often James says "now" and "nowadays." He seems to blame the recession, passing economic circumstances, for their situation. This reasoning is quite different from the sociological insight that inequality in the system is structural rather than just temporary, although both types of explanation may be at work in James's statements. Recession may actually mask enduring inequality by making economic injustice appear transitory. Instead of having their faith in the free market pricked, those on the sharpest end of economic downturns simply long for recovery along with everyone else. Unfortunately, the Brothers and Hallway Hangers have rather less to recover than do the rich. In bad times even more so than good ones, it may be difficult to discern that the rules of the game are structurally rigged against the disadvantaged. Clearly James is not alone in emphasizing the current rather than the continued obstacles these men face, and this fact may have important political implications.

Whatever the exact diagnosis, James is convinced that economic realities are at the root of the problem. Still, he does not spare himself.

JAMES: I left the first job that I had. I jumped at the chance to get more money. I
   was young and I didn't realize if I had stayed at the federal reserve until now, I
   had befriended enough people to go up a level. (*Clicks his fingers*) Y'know, I
   would've been somewhere now.

For James, as for social theorists, both individual agency and structural constraint are required to explain his occupational career, his current unemployment, and what he sees on the street.

Derek and Mike retain faith in the achievement ideology. Mokey, Juan, and Super second-guess their decisions and find fault with themselves but also begin to blame the larger socioeconomic order, a critique that James extends. Interestingly, rather than blame himself or the social order directly for the discrepancy between his hopes and his current situation, Craig critiques the aspiration itself.

CRAIG: I think when you're in college you get really unrealistic expectations of
   what kind of job you're going to get. You think it will be easy to land a decent
   professional job in the business world. You think that's what you're being prepared for. But the reality is different. You see, studying is not the same as working. They're two different things. Going to and graduating from a four-year
   school doesn't guarantee you anything. Every Joe Schmo out there has a four-
   year degree. That's nothing. It means absolutely nothing. Anybody can go to a
   little state school and come out with a degree. Everybody's got the degree. And
   everybody's got a résumé stuffed with decent jobs that's been done on a good
   word processor with a laser printer.

None of the Brothers would be more justified than Craig in feeling betrayed by the achievement ideology. But rather than complain that the goal posts keep being moved, Craig seems to hold himself responsible for misjudging the situation and nurturing unrealistic expectations. Only now does he realize that with the general inflation of diplomas, employment prospects cannot keep pace with educational qualifications.

Racism

In coming to grips with the disparity between aspiration and outcome, the Brothers do not cite racial discrimination as an important factor. Rather, as we have seen, several of them contend that employment opportunities are constricted. In this the Brothers echo recent sociological thinking that emphasizes factors other than direct racial discrimination to explain the economic subjugation of blacks. Sociologists show how industrial restructuring, for example, has taken an especially heavy toll on the job prospects of inner-city black men, for whom the new information-processing jobs, many of them located in the suburbs, are beyond physical and educational reach. Structural changes in the economy mean that African Americans like the Brothers face a deflated opportunity structure. Most of the Brothers understand this fact themselves.

The Brothers are also aware that informal social networks—connections—are an important occupational resource that they largely lack.

(*in separate interviews*)

SUPER: Nowadays, y'know, you go to look for a job, you call, they tell you they got a long waiting list, y'know? This 'n' that. Depends on who you know, too, if you can get a job.

JAMES: One thing that I didn't know in high school that I wish I had've knew in high school is that it's not what you can do, it's who you know. ... If you befriend the right people, you're gonna move up that ladder. ...

CRAIG: You need to know the right people. That's what I'm seeing. I'm trying to develop some connections because I'm finding that's what you need out here.

After several years of struggle, the Brothers understand the importance of contacts on the job market, an insight that contradicts the achievement ideology they took to heart in high school.

Again, the Brothers are in line with sociological thinking. Studies of labor markets show by and large that people do not get jobs through an impersonal, meritocratic process based on their "human capital"—their educational attainment and prior work experience. Rather, people obtain jobs by exploiting informal personal networks; they learn about jobs through word of mouth rather than from newspaper advertisements or employment agencies.[9] Family, friends, and acquaintances are invaluable resources for learning about job openings and for pulling strings to get hired. Here again we see the workings of cultural capital. Working-class whites are advantaged relative to working-class blacks. The Hallway Hangers have landed jobs through white ethnic networking, but these are networks from which the Brothers are largely excluded. Mercer Sullivan discovered the same dynamic in his study of three New York City neighborhoods: Working-class whites used family and neighborhood networks to get blue-collar jobs, whereas "the minority youths suffered ... from their lack of comparable job networks."[10] Similarly, young whites in Boston interviewed by Paul Osterman were able to use parents and relatives twice as frequently to find jobs as were young blacks.[11]

Mike actually makes the connection between race and informal social networks. Craig, he says, is without a good job because as an African American he lacks connections.

MIKE: I thought going to college would help Craig. But he came back and was without a job for about a year and a half before he got this job, which is shit. I think he'll be okay when the economy picks up. It's hard, him being black. I think it's because of his skin color. They don't wanna hire blacks. Especially in this city, it's like white kin. Craig doesn't have no contacts. He doesn't know anybody.

In Mike's mind, the fact that Craig cannot exploit occupational connections is racially rooted. The black Brothers do not articulate this link, although their belief in the importance of connections may reflect experiences of race- and class-based exclusion.

Most of the Brothers explicitly discount racism as a handicap in their occupational careers; being black, some suggest, can be an advantage on the job market.

JM: Did you find in the jobs you were trying to get, or in your studying or whatever, that discrimination was a problem? Did being black hold you back at all?

SUPER: No, not really, never look at it thatta way.

(*in a separate interview*)

JM: Do you think being black has hurt you in terms of getting a job?

MOKEY: I've never felt any probem being a different color to an employer. ... I really don't think the racial thing bothered, I never been bothered by it. I really never put racial into a job. Going for some jobs, maybe cuz I'm black that would help, like for the police force.

Similarly, Derek rejects any suggestion of racism and indicates that affirmative action can help with public-sector jobs.

JM: Have you ever felt that discrimination has held you back in any kinda way in any of your jobs?

DEREK: No. When I went for the police officer [position] in Avon, I could've gotten it cuz I was black, but I could've gotten it cuz I scored well.

Only Juan speaks of a direct experience of racial prejudice in employment. He takes personal responsibility for losing his airport job but then indicates that racism also played a role.

JUAN: Everybody comes in late, and the thing is, some of 'em get away with it, so I found it discriminating.

JM: Because you're black?

JUAN: I saw it like that, to be honest.

For the other Brothers, racial prejudice played no direct role in their employment or educational histories.

But racism, after all, is often a subtle phenomenon. It seldom rings with the clarity of the Hallway Hangers' vicious denunciations. James alludes to the subtle workings of racial domination, first in his schooling and then in his workplace. In neither case does he view the situation as overtly racist, but both contribute to the subordination of blacks. Within the computer institute James attended, there were two distinct educational tiers. Classes were unofficially segregated along racial, class, and age lines, and James believes that he got a crucial career break when he switched to the more advanced "white" classes during the day.

JAMES: I realized how the business world works because of the fact that when I went to computer school, they started me off at nights, in night school. Night school was all black people. There were no white kids in night school, okay.

JM: Why was that?

JAMES: I guess white guys, they didn't wanna go to school at night. Beats the heck outta me, I have no idea. All I know is that I was way more advanced than most of these guys that were in my class at nights, because I had been working on the computers in high school and I had a computer at home. So I was like well ahead of them. I was like up there with the teacher. So the teacher said, "Hey, I have a more advanced class in the daytime. Why don't you switch over to day class?" So I did. And um, well actually, I do know why most of the people in my class at night—all of them were black, well, black and Hispanic—because they were workin' day jobs and then paying to go to school at night. So he switched me over to the day course with all white kids. They were as young as me, cuz the night class was older people, older black and Hispanic people. The day course was young white kids, but it was like young white kids from the suburbs that their parents were paying for them to go to school. But that class was way more advanced than the night class. So we got a lot more out of it.

Unable to give up their day jobs, students of color seem to have received substandard education in the night class. And for James, who could afford to attend during the daytime, direct discrimination would have played a role when "they started me off at nights." The registrar probably did not consider it an act of overt racism when he or she placed James in the night class. On the contrary, based on James's skin color, accent, and posture, it probably seemed a "natural" and "sensible" thing to do. Perhaps it never occurred to the registrar to inquire about James's qualifications and ability. Unconscious discrimination and institutional racism, as much as the outspoken prejudice of the Hallway Hangers, contribute to racial oppression. Although James does not use those terms, he feels privileged to have received the standard of education that his white counterparts take for granted.

Schooling aside, James insists that he felt no direct discrimination in his various jobs but then hints that racial dynamics played a role in his termination.

JM: Were you treated any different in your jobs, did you feel any discrimination on account of being black?

JAMES: No! No. None. None whatsoever.

JM: You didn't feel the last one was racial, that he was up in your face ... ?

JAMES: No, he was another black guy. I felt from the last job, I felt there was more pressure put on us because our operations department was black. And that's what it was. He didn't want them looking at our department and going, "Oh, these dumb black people, they keep messin' up every time." And that's what they were basically doing, was saying every time something went wrong on their end, on the higher end, like the software technicians and guys like that screwing up, we were the ones who caught the blame: "Oh no, those dumb guys in operations; they don't know what they're doing."

JM: So did your boss used to say that to you guys?

JAMES: Yeah. He felt a lot of discrimination, and that's basically what pushed him to, that's really what pushed him to firing me.

In a different context, James affirms that "racism is everywhere" and that police brutality against blacks is widespread. Back on the subject of occupational discrimination, James contends that being black can be both a liability and an asset on the job market.

JAMES: There's been so many negative things said about blacks and everything, a lot of people are scared to hire blacks. It depends on what you're doing. There's a lot of affirmative action in different types of areas, like hospital work, in computer work, banks, stuff like that. So, basically, these places have to meet quotas anyway. So they gonna hire you because you're black anyway.

JM: So do you think you might have actually benefited?

JAMES: Because I was black? When I was in computer school, a guy told me that I would benefit more because I was black.

JM: Was he white or black?

JAMES: He was white. He was the director of our school. He said a lot of places have to hire blacks.

JM: Do you think he was right?

JAMES: Yeah, yeah. Most definitely. That's the reason why they hired me at the bank (*clicks his fingers*). They hired me that same day that I went in for the interview. Then the second job, they hired me right then. They had no black guys workin' there, no blacks at all. They hired me right on the spot because of the fact that I was black.

Affirmative action, of course, seeks to help redress historic patterns of employment discrimination. In both the public and private sectors, affirmative action plans do not involve quotas; even plans imposed by the judiciary in extreme cases require only good-faith efforts to reach hiring objectives and goals. Targeting of this type, which seeks merely to level the playing field for qualified racial minorities, is increasingly viewed as reverse discrimination against white men. The Hallway Hangers certainly subscribe to this notion, and some of the Brothers believe that black skin may be an asset on the labor market.

In fact, affirmative action appears to have done little for poor African Americans. Although studies indicate that the earnings and promotion prospects of middle-class blacks have improved,[12] the situation for black men on the lower rungs of the labor market is still abysmal.[13] This reality is borne out by the experiences of the Brothers. Although some of them believe the rhetoric that all blacks, themselves included, receive preferential treatment via affirmative action, only James is sure to have actually benefited.

Caught in Cultural Limbo

The Brothers are caught between a predominantly white bourgeois culture and a black subproletarian street culture. Earlier, James alluded to the portrayal of blacks and the fears of employers. In the past decade, black youth street culture has been so sensationalized and demonized that young black men are automatically invested with an aura of moral irresponsibility, social unworthiness, and cultural depravity in the minds of many Americans. Like other young black men, the Brothers have become symbols of danger and degeneracy.

JAMES: You walk outside onto the street, racism's everywhere. I see it on the phone. I'm talkin' on the phone with my girlfriend at night, and people lookin' at me, on the phone. It's like last night, I'm on the phone, and a white lady and a white guy, you could look and tell how they dressed they don't live around here, they're from the suburbs or wherever you wanna call it—Beverly, Chester, some uppity rich place, Beverly, Belmont, something like that. And they don't wanna ask me if they can use the phone because of the fact that they sit at home and they watch TV every day and they see how vicious these young black guys are. They just pull out guns and they just shoot people, and they kill everybody and they're robbing babies and they're doing all this stuff—they're selling drugs and all that.

The Brothers do not look like hoodlums. But neither do they look like they belong on the *Cosby* show. Because they do not immediately convey a mastery of middle-class culture, they bear the public taint of the "underclass," with all the racially coded characteristics that term has come to imply. In the popular mind, the Brothers are morally dissolute and criminally inclined if not downright dangerous.

The irony here is palpable. By any standards of youth conduct, the Brothers were (and with the exception of Super still are) veritable puritans. They have a strong work ethic. They are sexually responsible. They don't smoke. They don't use drugs. They drink only in moderation. They respect adult authority. The Brothers are not angels, but they sometimes seem to be, even in comparison to the well-heeled but hard-partying university students up the street who steer safely clear of the Brothers and their ilk.

The Brothers must negotiate complex racial and class dynamics, not least in relating to prospective employers. In a study of Chicago employers, Joleen Kirschenman and Kathryn M. Neckerman discovered that young African American men are often considered shifty, lazy, unreliable, dishonest, ignorant, and socially inept. In short, employers view poor young blacks in much the same way as do most Americans. Many proprietors conflate race and class. The owner of a construction firm, for example, observed that for people of color in general, "the quality of education ... is not as great as [for] white folk from the suburbs. ... And it shows in the intellectual capability of the labor force. ... The minority worker is not as punctual and not as concerned about punctuality as the middle-class white." Other employers made class distinctions among prospective black employees. Unless black applicants could somehow signal middle-class origins, they were tagged with the racial stereotypes associated with the "underclass." Home address was also a distinguishing mark to many employers. African American applicants from ghetto neighborhoods, especially those from "the projects," were assumed to be particularly deficient. Kirschenman and Neckerman conclude that although race is of greatest importance, it is often qualified by class and geographical space in hiring decisions.[14]

Caught in a class and racial no-man's-land between white middle-class culture and black lower-class culture, the Brothers face special problems on the job. The new service economy has transformed the social relations of the workplace. Laborers in the old unionized manufacturing jobs could "be themselves" on the shop floor, where they were physically distant from consumers and socially distant from their bosses. Service workers, in contrast, often have neither a physical nor a social space to themselves. This situation places extraordinary demands on young working-class blacks who are constantly rubbing elbows with supervisors and customers. Busing tables in a swanky restaurant, photocopying files in a corporate office, or working the register at a supermarket, young black men like the Brothers must overcome the wariness and unease of their mainly white, middle-class clientele and supervisors. The Brothers are honest, dedicated, and hardworking. But these qualities are not easily projected across the cultural and social divide that separates them from their employers. To their white bosses, they may come off as sullen, inarticulate, and distant. As Philippe Bourgois's penetrating ethnography discloses, the basic subjective job requirement in the service economy—a "good attitude"—conjugates with racism and subtle class dynamics. Skin color, hairstyle, apparel, vocabulary, inflection, posture, gaze, and gait become signs of dissonance and unsuitability. Being looked in the eye can make supervisors nervous.[15] Especially in small firms where control is exercised informally and interpersonal bonding becomes essential for job security, young blacks like the Brothers are at a disadvantage unless they can cultivate a style of social interaction that puts employers and customers at ease.

Some of the Brothers have managed this feat. Derek's hourly wage at the airport may be paltry, but in contrast to the other Brothers, he has mastered the social milieu of his workplace. Between flights, he banters playfully with fellow workers, most of them white—teasing, laughing, winking, jostling. Obviously well liked by his colleagues, Derek's enthusiastic personality is given full rein. His job allows him to assert his identity, whereas other Brothers are required to submerge theirs. This includes his racial identity, which comes easily to the surface. I told him he was looking good after we greeted each other at the airport. "Of course, I'm black," he answered grinning. "Shame about Curt here, though," he laughed, jerking his thumb at an older white worker and dancing quickly away.

DEREK: In my workplace I have fun. It's like people will sit there and call me nigger and I'll just sit there and insult their mother. That's how we are, that's our workplace, we get along so well, I know everybody there. We're all friends. I mean, I could walk up to one of my friends' mothers and start tickling them like I do everybody else. See, that's the thing, I treat everybody the same. And that's why I get along so well with everybody.

In contrast to nearly all the other young men in this study, Derek has a job that allows him to be himself.

Of course, Derek draws upon unique resources in order to master his workplace. As a youth, he attended the prestigious Barnes Academy, where he learned the social cues of a wealthy white environment.

DEREK: For the first couple of years I started going to Barnes, it was like myself, a guy named Teddy Cook, and one other black student and two black girls. I think we were like the only black people that I saw in that whole school—the lower school, the middle school, and the upper, which was considered the high school. And, y'know, that never bothered me, that definitely never bothered me, because if it did I would never have gone to Mexico for two whole summers with Mexican people and white people and sometimes I thought I was the only black person in the country but it was worth it for the experience. ... I never had any money [at Barnes] but I managed to get along with everybody. I can get along with anybody if I want to.

JM: Right.

DEREK: And it was really different. I mean, this kid—his mother owned seven private schools and they could do anything they wanted, just like that. One time we spent the whole month in Acapulco, at the Princess [Hotel], like I think that's the most expensive place, and for my birthday one year we went out on the beach and we went horseback riding, parasailing, and they threw this big cake in my face, burnt my nose, and it was, it was, it was really different. And that same summer we went, we came from Mexico City, we went up to San Francisco for a wedding, and we went to Austin, Texas, for a family gathering they had. Y'know, I really got a look at what the other side's like.

At Barnes Academy, Derek was socialized into affluent white culture. Traveling with rich friends, he learned to adapt to alien and challenging social circumstances. Both experiences, hardly typical for poor young African Americans, have helped him to negotiate and master the complex social currents in his workplace.

James never quite mastered the social relations of his workplace, but he learned to be bicultural: to play the game downtown and to be himself back in the Heights. But he found it difficult to keep his professional and street roles distinct. He was accused of acting white at home; and, conversely, he lost his job because when his boss began to "rip into" him, James failed to batten down his street pride and walked off the job.

JAMES: The environment that you grow up around has a lot to do with the person that you come out to be, but, it's like, I can operate on a street level and I can operate on a professional level. But a lot of people don't differentiate the two.

They don't say, "All right, I'm at work now, let me act professional." They go in and they have their same street attitude. Someone from the Heights going in with an attitude like that, you're not going to stay in a job like that, not in a professional-level job. And that's what I've learned really quick. I learned that two days after I started working at the federal reserve bank, that I couldn't go in with my tough-guy attitude. Cuz you just can't function, you can't function doing your job. You have to have a professional attitude.

JM: Do you ever let the professional attitude come out here, and then people get on you for acting different?

JAMES: Yes. All the time, all the time. I went with a girl the year before last, she says to me, "If you only knew how white you sound!"

I'm like, "How white I sound? What do you mean, 'How white I sound'? I sound like me, I sound like myself."

She's like, "No, you sound white."

And like my girlfriend now, I called her house for the first time, I didn't believe that it was her. She sounds just like a white girl because she has that professional voice. But that's what a lot of black people have to put aside, too. They have to put aside the fact that they think because someone acts professional, they're acting white. If you're acting professional, that's what's gonna move black people to a different level, is a lot of professional-acting black people. Then you won't see on TV, you won't see every day, "Oh man, these black kids, they're out there shootin' each other, sellin' drugs on the corner, doin' this," because you'll have a whole society of professional people.

JM: Are there the jobs out there that would allow that to happen?

JAMES: Well, the way the economy is right now—no. If there were jobs out there that would allow that to happen, I would have a job. Cuz it's not like I'm chillin' at home, not looking for a job.

James highlights the difficulty of being caught in limbo between black street culture and white bourgeois culture. To many of his peers, professionalism is a betrayal of black identity. But with the eyes of the wider culture in mind, James believes that professionalism will salvage the race's image because it contradicts their stereotypes.

It was only because James swam against the flow of racial and class domination that he learned to act professionally. If he had stayed in the computer class into which he was originally placed, attending evening classes with older people of color who were holding down jobs, he may never have developed the resources to act biculturally. James learned superior skills in the advanced day course with suburban whites, but he stresses the importance of being socialized into "business culture."

JAMES: From the moment that I got into that class, I realized how exactly the business world works. I looked around and I knew I had to develop a professional attitude.

As James himself contends, he was lucky. He was lucky to have been noticed by his teacher and lucky that his parents' financial support freed him from a day job. But why was he channeled into the night class in the first place? The practice of tracking, it would appear, is not limited to secondary school. More insidious still is the extent to which the Brothers have been hamstrung by the discriminatory appraisal of cultural capital in their working lives.

Derek and, to a lesser extent, James have developed personal skills that allow them to cope on the job. But Craig is the only Brother who immediately conveys an outward mastery of middle-class culture. His wardrobe, bearing, and walk prevent him from being instantly stereotyped as a member of the ghetto poor. Five years of higher education have schooled Craig in bourgeois etiquette and deportment. Telephone calls to the other Brothers invariably result in brief conversations with their mothers, televisions blaring in the background. But when Craig is out, the caller reaches an answering machine with a smoothly articulate message sandwiched between bars of soft jazz. And yet despite Craig's bourgeois bearing, Mike insists that one of Craig's problems on the job market is that he will not go further and submerge his racial identity.

MIKE: Craig hasn't got the contacts, but I'll tell ya, another thing is that he acts too black. He hangs out with black guys most of the time; I think I'm really his only white friend. Y'know, he's into black music, black ... he's just into that black thing.

JM: You think that's hurt him trying to get a job?

MIKE: Yeah, shit yeah. You think the guy's who's hiring, the personnel guy, you think he's gonna be into L L Cool J?

In Mike's view, distinguishing oneself from the stereotyped street culture of the ghetto poor is not enough to ensure a higher rung on the occupational ladder. African Americans like the Brothers must completely abandon their racial identity at the company door if they are to really get ahead.

If Craig has edged in one direction in the bind between a dominant bourgeois culture and a black street culture, Super has moved in the other. Super alludes directly to the cultural clash he felt with his boss at the grocery store.

SUPER: My boss, this lady, I had this lady boss who started getting on my nerves. We couldn't get along. She'd like smile at me all the time, y'know, but I could tell she hated me. Man, I didn't really like her either. She was so uppity. Really, she was a bitch. Her boss, the vice president who was cool, understood me, know what I'm saying?

Making his money on the street, Super doesn't have to deal daily with the silent humiliation of his boss's patronizing smile. Now he deals daily with the prospect of arrest, injury, and even death. Super has become enmeshed in a street culture where brutal violence and the crack plague feed off each other and intensify problems of poverty, AIDS, and sexual exploitation, leaving wasted lives in their wake. And yet this is a way of life that Super has embraced not because he is so different from the rest of us but because he is so similar. Super's goals are completely conventional: to have a place of his own, get married, and raise a family. Only he has to resort to criminal means to achieve them. As Robert Merton's brilliant analysis of anomie makes plain, when society encourages everyone to strive for the same lofty goals and then denies the poor the wherewithal to achieve them, criminality is the inevitable outcome.[16] Like the dealers befriended by anthropologists Philippe Bourgois and Terry Williams,[17] Super sells drugs because he is so committed to making the American Dream his own. Even as he despairs of his lifestyle, he is quite clear about its attraction: "It's not a life you want to live, but y'know, you want to be someone, make fast money, have respect."

Groping for the Good Life

All of the Brothers, like Super, are in search of respect. But respect does not easily come their way. Juan works but is denied a job description, set hours, overtime, job security, and decent pay. Yet what bothers him most about the job is "always being disrespected." Disdainful of manual work, Juan is unable to generate self-esteem from his employment. In 1984 he longed for a "clean job," a longing he still nurses.

JUAN: I don't like dirty jobs. I'd rather get a clean job.

JM: Whaddya mean, like a dirty job?

JUAN: You got dirt all over you. I mean, at a autobody shop, you got chemicals all around there. And like, you get out, your head's all painty, you smell like thinner. If you got to go to an appointment or something, you gotta go home and have a wash, take a shower. At least at McDonald's it's a clean job. A lot of grease, but at least you look a little presentable wherever you go, just about, y'know? Over there, you come out all dirty, pants all ripped, with twenty different colors.

JM: Why do you think that's important to you, y'know, to have a clean job?

JUAN: On a clean job you got a better chance of gettin' promoted. In a dirty job, they just have you there to do one thing and that's it. Who cares? In a clean job, they respect you cuz you look good, you present yourself good.

Again, respect eludes Juan, whereas many manual workers might regard their dirty work clothes as a badge of masculine pride. For them, as for Paul Willis's lads,[18] the "real work" of manual laborers is superior to the flimsy, ephemeral, and effeminate character of mental labor.

Mike is the only Brother who begins to articulate a working-class consciousness, although he earns far and away the most money. Much of his political analysis seems to stem from his union membership.

MIKE: I'm thinking about going to night school, get myself a degree in management, just in case the post office isn't around in the future.

JM: What, you think it might be privatized?

MIKE: Yeah, it could be. Maybe fifteen years or so. I want training just in case. I don't wanna be hung out to dry if they do privatize it. They might, too. I'm tellin' ya, the Republicans are fucking us over. Reagan fucked us over so bad. I'm tellin' ya, it's the blue-collar worker in America who's getting screwed. They don't care. They might hack us up, sell us off, break the union. There goes the working class. They'll sell the post office to their fucking friends is what they'll do. Sell us to their friends and fuck America. I just got a letter from the union telling us how Bush is fucking us up. The Republicans, they hate us.

JM: You're a big union supporter then?

MIKE: Yeah. Management will fuck you over, I know that much. Unions can do something about that, can protect us. In white-collar work you're fucked.

Mike is proud to be working class and proud to be "making more than most yuppies." But when he's "on the prowl," trying to pick up women, Mike poses as a lawyer. He has a steady girlfriend but often boasts of his nightclub conquests.

MIKE: I just like to go out for a bang, go out to clubs, see what I can find. ...

JM: What about your girlfriend?

MIKE: Miranda? I'm still with Miranda. We're pretty serious, actually. It's five and a half years we've been together. I'll probably settle down with her. We could be married in a year or two. I won't go out and fuck around when I'm married. There'll be just one woman then. ... Yeah, I know. It must sound shitty. But hey, it's our nature. All men cheat. Whaddya think? Before civilization, we didn't care about nothing. All we did was run around and plug up every hole we could find. It's just our nature.

Mike's frankly exploitative approach to women is the exception among the Brothers. Craig accompanies Mike on his forays into black clubs, but Craig is usually accompanied by his girlfriend. James and his partner are on the verge of engagement, although he'd like to wait until he's found a job.

JM: So do you ever think about marriage?

JAMES: (*Laughs*) The first time I ever saw her I thought about marriage. I've gone out with lots of girls before, and I never thought about marriage. I wasn't the type of person to get married. I never thought about it, it never entered my mind—marrying someone. I liked this girl from the beginning. She's just like, "Be yourself." Cuz all these girls, they want this phony attitude and guys'll walk around like Ice T: "Yo babe, yo babe." And y'know, that's what I was thinking, "Oh, what if I act like me and this girl doesn't like me? I want this girl really bad, er, maybe I should act like somebody else." She told me to just be myself. She said the onliest reason she wanted to talk to me is because I was looking nervous. Because I just wanted to bust out and talk to this girl. And she said I looked like I had words caught in my throat. Man, I love Tricia so bad. ... I have had girls that I have treated bad. I treat my girlfriend now like gold, man, cuz she's what I want out of life. If you're brought up the way we were brought up is you treat a woman with respect. And that's how every, to me that's how every man should act towards a woman. Girls in our family are like, if you're a girl, you're a jewel. It's like a diamond, okay. It's like you went to a coal mine and you got a diamond. ... Yeah, we've been talking about getting married. But without a job, what kind of husband would I be? I need a job, man, I need a job.

For James, as for so many inner-city youths, the economic basis of marriage has been undermined.

The other Brothers are more prosaic about their relationships. Mokey and his partner, together since high school, have also contemplated marriage and children.

MOKEY: I said no. It's not time. How could we? We're both living at home. We can't afford a place, there's just no way. It'd be crazy. But it would be nice, too, though ...

Super lived with a woman for two years and was engaged to be married before she left him.

SUPER: She goes with one of my buddies, now. I see them all the time. That hurts, man, that does, I gotta admit it, that hurts.

JM: What about Keisha, how long have you been seeing her? Are you two pretty steady or what?

SUPER: Yeah.

JM: But sort of informal, on and off kind of thing?

SUPER: Naw, steady.

Most of the Brothers are involved in stable relationships with women. And yet Mike, Craig, James, Mokey, and Super do not have children.

Juan does have children—two baby daughters born five months apart. Juan's pride in fatherhood is overshadowed by regret. There are constant problems with and between the two mothers, one Italian and one of African and Portuguese descent, as they vie for Juan's affection and commitment. Juan supports both children financially and sees them every week.

JUAN: I really screwed up. I just screwed up. I screwed up my life. Two children and two different mothers. Shit. I thought I didn't have much money before. Ha. Now I see life used to be carefree—not so many bills as with my daughters. Now I've got to work every chance I get. Except Sundays, that's my day with my kids.

JM: Were you surprised when you found out you were gonna be a father?

JUAN: It was so unexpected. What can I do? I had no idea, y'know? But I found it can happen. I'm proud of my daughters, I'm proud of them. It's not like I'd ever leave them stranded. They're the first two things in my life, besides my parents, y'know? I don't take no shit from nobody when it comes to my children. They wanna tell me, "Oh, you hafta work on Sunday."

"Uh-uh. Today's my day off, it's for my kids, and I'm taking them out," and out we go, y'know? They try to do that with me, my boss Jim does. "Naw, I gotta take off, take my daughter to the hospital."

"No, I need you here today."

"You need me here? My daughter needs me over there." I may not be able to pay my bills, but I feel a lot better being there for them. "You wouldn't want me telling you you hafta work and you can't see your kids, right?" It's just a hassle. You've got to put your kids first, that's how I look at it. I have no choice. Matter of fact, when you think of yourself, you get greedy. I can't think about that. Cuz I got kids. If you think greedy, you ain't gonna think about your kids. Everything you see: I want, I want. But what about your kids, what do they need? ...

Those are my kids. I'm never going to deny them. But like I say, I wish it had never happened. ... I'm hanging in there. I try not to look at the worst. It could be worse, so you keep fighting, keep a free mind, keep hoping. Sooner or later, someone's gonna do you the favor that you've done to them.

Juan tries to feel buoyant, but he is struggling to stay afloat. Under the combined weight of a job he hates and family responsibilities he can not properly fulfill, Juan seems to be slowly sinking. Hope is the only thing he can hold onto.

JUAN: Things will pick up though. Things will get better further down the road. That's the way life is: picks you up, puts you down. Things will pick up.

JM: How do you stay so hopeful?

JUAN: You've got to be hopeful. You've got to be hopeful or you wouldn't be able to face the grind, the ratrace. You live by the days. If you wake up, you wake up. Tomorrow's another thing. Today's enough reality, I don't need anymore. Every day's precious, so you live day by day. Got to, ain't got no choice.

Derek is the other father among the Brothers. He was married in 1984 just before entering the navy.

JM: You got married right out of high school. That always surprised me, you got married that quickly.

DEREK: She was pregnant.

JM: Right.

DEREK: I felt an obligation, a moral obligation. Y'know, if I do something wrong, I have to do something to correct it. I'm not exactly the marrying type cuz I'm still a person that believes I want to get out and do this and do that, but I can't. I don't regret having my kids, it's just I regret not taking more time to have fun and do the things I wanted to do. Cuz I provide for my kids. That's important. I've got saving bonds set up for them that's deducted from my pay every month. I have fun with my kids. We go kite flying, we go to outdoor concerts and listen to jazz music and everything like that, and I feel like I have a good rapport with my kids. Carlton just turned seven and Amy just turned five. We talk and have fun together. I dunno, marriage, that's just not for me. But it's working.

Derek and his wife, Maria, live with their children in a small, two-bedroom apartment not far from Clarendon Heights. Although Maria works at an electronics firm, the family cannot afford to buy a home.

Derek longs for the "good life" he tasted while traveling with his Barnes Academy friends. At the same time, he insists that he is quite satisfied and is adamant that money does not necessarily bring happiness.

DEREK: I've always wanted to succeed, I've always wanted to try and do something with my life. ... I've had the opportunities to see a part of the good life, y'know. If you want something you go for it, and it made a hell of an impression on me. It's like I've seen everything that there is out there to get and I wanna try and be a part of it before, before too long.

JM: Do you ever run into any of your old classmates from Barnes?

DEREK: As of recently, no. The guy I went to Mexico with, I haven't seen him for three or four years. I know they've gone on to college and they've gone on to whatever professional or nonprofessional jobs that they get along with. But every long once in awhile, I'll run into somebody.

JM: Do you ever see people who are on the fast track in banking or something, making lots of money, and think, "I could do that. I have the intelligence, I have the drive, I have the commitment, I have the responsibility," y'know. Do you ever think that or do you ...

DEREK: No. All the choices I've made in my life, y'know, I'm starting to take control. But I'm not gonna kick myself in the ass because I didn't do something someone else has done. Cuz I know if I wanted to do it, I could just try a little bit harder and do it. So. I'm pretty much happy where I am. Not that I'll change it. Like I said before, pay doesn't matter. What matters is being happy. Happy, happy, happy. I'm meeting my bills. I'm doing it. I just need a house, a better home for the kids. They shouldn't have to share a bedroom at their age.

Although his home is cramped, Derek has at least managed, with his wife, to set up an independent household. Apart from Craig, none of the Brothers have a place they can call their own. Mokey, James, Juan, and Mike live with their parents. Super has no fixed abode; he currently spends most nights on a couch in his aunt's public housing apartment.

JM: You're twenty-four now. When you were back in high school, what did you think you'd be as a twenty-four-year-old back then?

SUPER: Out of college, have a good job, my own apartment. Or probably my own business or something, y'know, doin' good, not doin' bad.

JM: When you look at the other guys you used to hang with—Craig, Mike, Juan, Mokey, Derek, James—how do you think they're doing?

SUPER: Most of 'em, they're doing all right. Y'know, a couple of 'em got apartments, jobs. But they're catching hell, too. A lot of 'em are. Got kids, rent to pay. They're catching hell. And most of those guys are living at home, living with mommy still. I mean, they ain't teenagers any more. That's kinda pathetic, when you think about it. But I ain't one to talk. At least the ones that are working, they're making their money legal, not like me. I haven't ate a good meal in a long time. Like, I used to eat every day, y'know, like a home-cooked meal.

Super has money to buy food. What he longs for in his unsettled life are the security and fellowship a family meal symbolizes.

Mokey, James, and Juan cannot afford to live on their own, much less support a family. Only Mike and Derek have health insurance. The signposts that have traditionally marked the transition to adulthood for young men—a stable job, an independent household, the beginnings of a family—have proved beyond the Brothers' reach. Hard as they try, the Brothers have simply not been able to work up a head of steam on the labor market. Unfortunately, their experience is all too typical for poor young adults, particularly African American men. A high school diploma, a bit of college, a positive attitude, and a wealth of ambition do not pay off as advertised. The Hallway Hangers can be dismissed by unsympathetic observers as self-destructive burnouts. The Brothers cannot. The Brothers have made mistakes, but they are generally conscientious men committed to the American Dream. They show quite clearly that our society is not as open as it purports to be. Given the modest gains of the Brothers, who can condemn the Hallway Hangers for turning their backs on a game that is also rigged against them?

Notes

1. John D. Kasarda, "Urban Industrial Transition and the Underclass," *Annals of the American Academy of the Political and Social Sciences* 501 (January 1989):30–31.

2. Paul Osterman, "Is There a Problem with the Youth Labor Market and, If So, How Should We Fix It?" mimeo (Sloan School, MIT, February 1992), pp. 14, 51.

3. Ibid., p. 27.

4. Kasarda, "Urban Industrial Transition and the Underclass," p. 31.

5. Bureau of the Census, Public Use Microdata Sample File, 1980 and 1990.

6. Osterman, "Is There a Problem," p. 51.

7. Bureau of the Census, Public Use Microdata Sample File, 1990.

8. Norton Grubb, "The Economic Returns to Post-Secondary Education: New Evidence from the National Longitudinal Survey of the Class of 1972," mimeo (School of Education, University of California at Berkeley, 1990). Cited in Osterman, "Is There a Problem," p. 36n.

9. In this connection, see M. Corcoran, L. Datcher, and G. J. Duncan, "Most Workers Find Jobs Through Word of Mouth," *Monthly Labor Review* 103 (August 1980):33–36; and

Mark S. Granovetter, *Getting a Job* (Cambridge, Mass.: Harvard University Press, 1974), pp. 5–11.

10. Mercer Sullivan, *Getting Paid* (Ithaca, N.Y.: Cornell University Press, 1989), p. 103.

11. Paul Osterman, *Getting Started* (Cambridge, Mass.: MIT Press, 1980), p. 143.

12. Soo Son, Suzanne W. Model, and Gene A. Fisher, "Polarization and Progress in the Black Community: Earnings and Status Gains for Young Black Males in the Era of Affirmative Action," *Sociological Forum* 4:3 (1989):309–327; William J. Wilson, *The Truly Disadvantaged* (Chicago: University of Chicago Press, 1987), pp. 109–118; Michael Hout, "Occupational Mobility of Black Men: 1962–1973," *American Sociological Review* 49 (1984):308–322; Richard Freeman, *Black Elite: The New Market for Highly Educated Black Americans* (New York: McGraw-Hill, 1976); Andrea H. Beller, "Trends in Occupational Segregation by Sex and Race, 1960–1981," in *Sex Segregation in the Workplace,* ed. Barbara F. Reskin (Washington, D.C.: National Academy Press, 1984), pp. 11–26.

13. Marshall I. Pomer, "Labor Market Structure, Intragenerational Mobility, and Discrimination: Black Male Advancement Out of Low-Paying Occupations," *American Sociological Review* 51 (1986):650–659; Soo Son et al., "Polarization and Progress"; Wilson, *The Truly Disadvantaged.*

14. Joleen Kirschenman and Kathryn M. Neckerman, "'We'd Love to Hire Them, But …': The Meaning of Race for Employers," in *The Urban Underclass,* ed. Christopher Jencks and Paul E. Peterson (Washington, D.C.: Brookings Institution, 1991), pp. 203–232.

15. Philippe Bourgois, "In Search of Respect: The New Service Economy and the Crack Alternative in Spanish Harlem" (Russell Sage Foundation Working Paper #21, May 1991).

16. Robert Merton, *Social Theory and Social Structure* (Glencoe, Ill: Free Press, 1949), pp. 131–153.

17. See Philippe Bourgois, *In Search of Respect: Selling Crack in El Barrio* (New York: Cambridge University Press, 1995) and Terry Williams, *The Cocaine Kids* (Reading, Mass.: Addison-Wesley, 1989).

18. Paul E. Willis, *Learning to Labor* (Aldershot: Gower, 1977).

11

··

Conclusion:
Outclassed and Outcast(e)

*O*NE AFTERNOON, WHILE HITCHHIKING to the city, I was picked up by a motorist in a BMW. The charitable middle-aged man chatted away for an hour about his teenage children. As we drove into the city and past Clarendon Heights, however, he peered at the young men lounging in the project's doorways, shook his head in disgust, and dismissed them as ignorant, lazy losers. That sort of causal simplicity is attractive: Losers lose; wanting individuals lead to wasted lives; poverty is self-generated. What we see on the streets, however, is actually complex. Once we push beneath the surface texts of individual lives, we discover the hard contours of structural inequality.

Our society is *structured* to create poverty and extreme economic inequality. There are simply not enough good jobs to go around. For every boss there are many workers, and the gap in their pay is unparalleled among industrialized nations. Chief executives of large U.S. companies made 160 times as much as the average blue-collar worker in 1989.[1] Indeed, while Juan, Mokey, Stoney, and Shorty struggled to survive on earnings of five dollars per hour, top corporate executives routinely raked in up to $5,000 per hour (including stock options and other income).[2] By 1993 the median pay package for the chief executive officers of the Fortune 1,000 largest companies was worth over $2.4 million. By comparison, the median annual earnings for everyone over fifteen years of age in 1992 was $17,696.[3] Our occupational structure is shaped much like the Eiffel Tower. There is little room at the top, a larger but still limited number of tolerably well-paid positions in the middle, and near the bottom a wide band of inferior positions (with no "positions" at all for the unemployed). This roughly pyramidal structure ensures that even if everyone excels in school and strives ceaselessly for the top, the great majority are automatically bound to be disappointed.

The occupational structure guarantees a vast divide between rich and poor. In 1989, 1 percent of the population owned 37 percent of the wealth and 10 percent of the population owned 86 percent of the wealth.[4] By the end of Reagan's second

term, 32 million Americans were living below the poverty level and the gap between rich and poor was at an all-time high.[5] Consider not only the sheer magni-
tude of inequality between winners and losers but also the fact that most losers
have had to play on a field slanted against them. The pyramid isn't shaken up and
recast from scratch for each generation; rather, families tend to occupy similar locations in the social division of labor over time. Families at the top of the class
structure can use their superior status and resources to stay there, while other
families, low on options, languish at the bottom. We are all born into a social
class, and most of us die in the one into which we were born. Although a few
working-class individuals with dedication and ability will rise to the top of the
heap, most (including many who are just as conscientious and able) will remain
close to where they started.[6]

    The United States has a remarkably stable class structure, albeit one that is ob-
scured by the rhetoric of classlessness. To be sure, social mobility does exist—just
enough to maintain the myth of America as the land of opportunity. Whereas a
completely closed society cannot maintain a semblance of openness, a society that
allows some mobility, however meager, can always hold up the so-called self-
made individual as "proof" that barriers to success are purely personal and that
the poor are poor of their own accord. And so most Americans, the denounced
teenagers often as much as the denouncer in the BMW, see poverty in purely individual terms rather than as structurally induced.

    This book shifts the emphasis from individual deficits to structural inequality.
Part One discloses that the roots of perceived individual pathology—unruliness
in school, alcohol and drug abuse, violence, and crime—actually lie deep within
the social structure. The leveled aspirations and behavior of the Hallway Hangers
cannot be understood apart from structural constraints on opportunity that in
their cumulative effect are all too forbidding. The Brothers, in contrast, refuse to
be cowed by the long odds. Spurred on by the distinctively American language of
aspiration that gushes forth from our television shows, our pop songs, and our
advertisements, the Brothers lace up their sneakers and "just go for it." But we
have seen that schools, even ones as good as Lincoln High, end up reinforcing social inequality while pretending to render it superfluous. The Brothers struggle
academically in school and are socialized for positions near the bottom of the
class pyramid.

    Part Two explores how the Hallway Hangers and Brothers fare in the structure
of the job market. The results are depressing. The experiences of the Hallway
Hangers since 1984 show that opting out of the contest—neither playing the game
nor accepting its rules—is not a viable option. Incarceration and other less explicit social penalties are applied by society when the contest is taken on one's
own terms. There is no escape: The Hallway Hangers must still generate income,
build relationships, and establish households. The stresses of everyday life have
led Stoney to "escape" by choosing captivity over life outside prison. Trapped inside the game, the Hallway Hangers now question their youthful resistance to

schooling and social norms. Granted the opportunity to do it over again, the Hallway Hangers say they would have tried harder to succeed.

But the Brothers *have* always tried, which is why their experiences between 1984 and 1991 are as disheartening as the Hallway Hangers'. If the Hangers show that opting out of the contest is not a viable option, the Brothers show that dutifully playing by the rules hardly guarantees success either. Conservative and liberal commentators alike often contend that if the poor would only apply themselves, behave responsibly, and adopt bourgeois values, then they will propel themselves into the middle class. The Brothers follow the recipe quite closely but the outcomes are disappointing. They illustrate how rigid and durable the class structure is. Aspiration, application, and intelligence often fail to cut through the firm figurations of structural inequality. Though not impenetrable, structural constraints on opportunity, embedded in both schools and job markets, turn out to be much more debilitating than the Brothers anticipated. Their dreams of comfortable suburban bliss currently are dreams deferred, and are likely to end up as dreams denied.

Poverty: A Class Issue

This book shows clearly that poverty is not a black issue. In absolute terms, most poor people are white, although a disproportionate number of African Americans are impoverished. Many of the black poor live in ghettos: urban neighborhoods that are racially segregated, economically devastated, socially stigmatized, and politically abandoned. As government and civic institutions have crumbled and the labor market has declined, the vacuum has largely been filled by "the blossoming of an underground economy dominated by the only expanding employment sector to which poor minority youths miseducated by public school can readily accede: the retail trade of drugs."[7] As a result, these enclaves of concentrated and pernicious poverty have become virtual war zones where terror, despair, and death are commonplace. To much of the American public, however, the state of the ghetto signifies not the gross inadequacy of the welfare state but its overgenerosity to a black underclass that is morally dissolute, culturally deprived, and socially undeserving. The underclass has been twisted into a racial rather than a class formation, and poverty has become a black issue.

By bringing the white poor into view, our story dissolves the mistaken connection between African Americans and behavior associated with poverty—crime, family disruption, substance abuse, and so on. The Brothers and Hallway Hangers fail to follow the script penned by journalists, academics, politicians, and policy analysts. Because criminality is almost completely confined to the Hallway Hangers, this study debunks stereotypes about the black poor. Even in the case of white youths, what appears to be a tangle of pathology and purely self-destructive behavior turns out to have an underlying social rationality. Far from being a distinctive breed apart, the urban poor are ordinary human beings struggling to cope as best they can under oppressive circumstances. Poverty is not a moral problem, much less a black moral or cultural problem.

The underclass debate in the popular media divides the poor along racial lines, focuses the spotlight on African American poverty, and largely ignores the socioeconomic context in which the drama is set. This book draws the white poor out of the shadows, widens the debate beyond race, and recovers the common class basis of exploitation that bedevils all the urban poor—black, white, Latino, Asian, or Native American.

Industrial restructuring—the decline of manufacturing, the suburbanization of blue-collar employment, and the ascendancy of the service sector—has hit all the urban poor. Real wages and job security have fallen dramatically, as the experiences of the Hallway Hangers and Brothers illustrate. Layoffs, seasonal cutbacks, closings, and abrupt dismissals have been widespread for both groups of men. The economic recession of the late 1980s has exacerbated the instability of the low-wage labor market, and so has the weakening of labor unions and the absence of government regulation—both matters of public policy. It may be that insecurity and volatility are structural features of the new urban economy.

The experiences of both the Brothers and the Hallway Hangers also indicate that "career tracks" are sparse for uncredentialed individuals. The jobs these men manage to obtain seldom lead to a sequence of ascending positions with increased wages, responsibility, and security. Movement, when it occurs at all, tends to be lateral or between firms but not along an occupational ladder. Disappointed, workers like Mokey and Jinks move rapidly between dead-end jobs, a strategy that ends up reinforcing irregularity because they become even less attractive to employers. Contrary to popular perception, none of the Hallway Hangers or Brothers shun employment in low-wage entry-level positions as working for "chump change."

JM: You're looking for a job now?

BOO-BOO: Yeah.

JM: And how's that going?

BOO-BOO: Not that good. Not that good at all. I just gotta keep on looking. I'd even work at McDonald's or something. Just so I can get some money together, just til I can find something a little bit better. ... I'll work at McDonald's if I have to. I need something. Sell newspapers, anything.

Boo-Boo's stated willingness to accept any job is no empty declaration: Among other places, he applied for work at car washes, grocery stores, and fast-food chains. Mokey, Shorty, and Slick echo Boo-Boo's willingness to accept poorly paid menial employment. What they and the others object to are so-called entry-level positions that lead nowhere.

Both groups of men have been stuck in the secondary labor market with low wages, infrequent raises, awkward working hours, minimal training, and high turnover. Only James has earned a family wage, and he was soon laid off. Only a couple of these men have held jobs with basic health and retirement benefits. Most cannot afford to own a car, let alone a home. Stable employment is the crucial pivot for social and cultural transitions into adulthood. Without it, many of these young men have been unable to contemplate settling down, marrying, or establishing households independent of parents. Their physical mobility has been minimal, and they have generally been excluded from leisure pursuits that most Americans take for granted. In short, the lives of both the Brothers and the Hallway Hangers have been severely circumscribed by their subordinate position in the class structure.

Racial Domination: Invidious but Invisible

Both the Brothers and the Hallway Hangers are victims of class exploitation, but the African Americans among them have had to cope with racial oppression as well. Sometimes this oppression is brutally direct, as Shorty and Boo-Boo's contrasting experiences attest. Shorty assaulted several police officers after ransacking his girlfriend's apartment, but he was let off.

SHORTY: I had fucking, I coulda' been doing at least twenty years for that, right there. Three counts of mayhem, I had like eight assault and batteries on police officers, each one carries two and a half years to four and a half years. Mayhem alone carries fifteen to twenty. I had three of 'em for biting three cops. Lucky my brothers were cops. If I didn't have no brothers that are cops, I'd be, I'd be doing at least forty fucking years right now.

JM: So no charges were ever pressed?

SHORTY: Yeah, they pressed 'em at first, but then I got 'em all dropped. The judges were pissed off about that; they didn't like that. None of the cops showed up to court. I fucking lucked out big time then.

Contrast Shorty's experience with that of Boo-Boo when he was stopped by the police for reckless driving.

BOO-BOO: I was drinkin' and drivin'; I was cheatin' on my girlfriend with this other girl, Josie, from the Heights. We were drivin' around. The cops, they beat me up and they called me nigger and black bastard and all this stuff, y'know. It was crazy. And they put me in jail. ... They broke my nose and cracked my jaw, y'know, and ripped all my chains off my neck and scarred up my arms and all that stuff like that.

Racial domination is seldom as graphic and straightforward as police brutality, although some police officers are openly racist. Standing in front of Clarendon Heights one evening, I was asked by an officer in a cruiser, "Seen a carload of niggers drive by just now?" Doubtless, Boo-Boo was beat up largely because he is black. Yet there is also a history of police violence against white residents of Clarendon Heights: In the 1970s a white youth from Clarendon Heights was beaten by police in front of the project and died in custody. Moreover, black police officers can be just as brutal as their white colleagues. Even police violence cannot be explained in purely racial terms. Racial oppression, though it often takes the form of direct discrimination, is also more subtly embedded in the social order.

As African Americans, the Brothers are not as connected as the Hallway Hangers to informal networks that can provide access to jobs. Consider a string of three jobs Frankie held when he returned to the area from out of state.

FRANKIE: Then I moved back. I had my son. So I come back down here. I tried a little floor-laying.

JM: How did you get in?

FRANKIE: Mutual friends, y'know. ... Got the floor-layin' job. That didn't kick out. So I started seein' people, y'know, that I knew, guys that had jobs, and I went on to a few city jobs and state jobs—they were real good jobs, but doin' my drinkin'—like I had one job as a custodian up the high school, and it was a real good job. And I screwed that up by drinkin'. Y'know, it's a job where you got so much to do and then you can slack. And my slackin', I was leavin' the premises, goin' to the bar and playing the dogs, y'know. I just got in the way of fuckin' goin' to the bar and goin' to the dogs. So I left that. And when I left that I got another job through the same guy—a politician—and I was over to the big convention center and they made me crew chief. I was over there, I was a crew chief, and I didn't have a fuckin' inkling of what I was doin'. They have a cleanin' crew, just Spanish guys. Y'know, they couldn't even understand me. So I didn't show up much, evidently. But I was still gettin' paid. They paid me hours I didn't work. Y'know, I did eighty hours one week, and I was lucky to have worked ten, y'know. These were set jobs. And I couldn't even hold them. I know why today: cuz I was drinking.

Apart from access to jobs, personal connections provided some job security for Frankie. During roughly the same period, Juan, Mokey, and James all lost their jobs on account of minor infractions of bureaucratic rules in their workplaces. Frankie's experience also underlines the poor prospects of promotion for people of color. When people like Frankie come in at a supervisory level, people like the Brothers and Frankie's Spanish crew are robbed of opportunities for advancement. It is instructive that Frankie was able to exploit personal contacts to secure employment in the public sector, the area where antidiscrimination policies should most improve the prospects of racial and ethnic minorities. If Frankie can leapfrog over others in government jobs, it is no wonder that industries with informal hiring and training practices are virtually closed to the Brothers. Jobs in construction are a notorious case in point.[8] Slick, Shorty, Steve, and Jinks have all landed jobs in the construction industry through informal social networks. Jobs like roofing are hardly prestigious, secure, or highly paid; nevertheless, they are jobs for which white ethnic networking has given the white Hallway Hangers an edge over their black counterparts.

Their exclusion from occupational networks handicaps the Brothers, but they also have special tensions to negotiate if they do manage to get a job. In the new postindustrial service economy, both the Hallway Hangers and the Brothers are in closer contact with supervisors and clients than they would be in manufacturing jobs. The members of neither group have much social space in which to express their class and cultural identities. Frankie finds it difficult to interact with young, bossy, bourgeois supervisors, gossiping middle-aged colleagues, and the upper-class consumers whom his catering job served. But the Brothers must also deal with racial prejudice that stereotypes them as hoodlums. The interpersonal experiences of black jobholders, especially those who do not convey a mastery of middle-class cultural conventions, are a special source of tension in service jobs. Busing tables in a posh restaurant, Mokey will find it more difficult than Frankie to put customers at ease simply because his black skin evokes so many stereotypes.

Whether the result of social tension in the workplace, reduced access to occupational networks, or straightforward discrimination, African Americans fare poorly on the job market. Unemployment is higher and wages are lower for blacks than for whites. Moreover, the economic returns for a high school education are substantially less. The labor market is far from color-blind. And yet the Brothers do not cite racism as a factor that holds them back. Perhaps race is so seamlessly woven into their identities and daily lives that it simply does not stand out. Deeply embedded in their consciousness and inscribed everywhere in the outside world, race is simply taken for granted as a suffusive and ubiquitous fact of life.[9] In this respect, Boo-Boo is the exception that reinforces the rule. For the Brothers, their blackness hardly bears comment. But Boo-Boo, an African American who associated with the Hallway Hangers nearly all of his life, fell in with an exclusively black crowd when he moved to Raymond. For Boo-Boo, race is an issue.

BOO-BOO: It was kinda weird for me in Raymond. All of a sudden all my friends were black. It was weird, cuz they're just, they're more different than white people cuz of the fact the way they carry themselves, the way they dress and stuff, dress and talking, just being black. Like when I go down to see, y'know, say Chub and all them [in Clarendon Heights], they're like, "Wow, Boo-Boo changed." Then, y'know, I just, I dunno.

JM: Is that kinda hard for you, to balance that out, or ...

BOO-BOO: It is kinda hard for me. I mean, I been around white people all my life and then for one, for like six or seven months, whatever how long it was, to just, to just change, I changed that quick. And then got caught up in the drugs and all stuff like that. It's just a big change. It was. Big change. ... I just can't handle, I don't really understand, I don't understand black people at all, really. Cuz I haven't been around 'em. They don't understand why I can sit there and listen to rock 'n' roll, Led Zeppelin and stuff like that, sit in the house and listen to Led Zeppelin and Black Sabbath. Call me white man, Uncle Tom or something. So that's the deal with it. ...

JM: You and Frankie and Slick and Steve and Shorty were really tight way back; how did that kinda break up?

BOO-BOO: Well, they'd get to drinkin' and they'd want to fight me and stuff like that. We never got into a fight, but they like started calling me a nigger and stuff like that. It didn't really bother me, but after a while, y'know, they're s'posed to be my friends, and all the time we'd been hanging around it had never came to my mind to call a white person a honky. I don't understand that. It's strange to me. I never called anybody anything like that in my life. I don't consider myself a nigger either. I just consider myself as Boo-Boo Taylor. Same as anybody else. So I just broke loose from that.

Having traversed the racial divide and negotiated the tensions on each side, Boo-Boo thinks in racial terms. Of the African Americans featured in this study, Boo-Boo alone emphasizes racial discrimination in the labor market. Asked whether he'd been actively looking for work, Boo-Boo recounted how a friend had directed him to a store that was taking job applications.

BOO-BOO: So we walk up there, and she said, "We're not hiring." And she said it in a bad way where it came down to me like she was prejudiced cuz I was black or something. Cuz why would she say that, why should she lie and say she wasn't hiring?

JM: Has that been a factor a lot, do you think?

BOO-BOO: It has been around here, yeah.

JM: Discrimination, in terms of you trying to get a job.

BOO-BOO: Basically, around here, yeah. It bothers me, but—it's part of life.

For the black Brothers, race is so much a part of life that it figures only tangentially in their expressed worldviews. But to say that race is inscribed in the social scenery is not to denigrate its importance. On the contrary, the experiences of the Brothers and Hallway Hangers since 1984 beg the question of whether race is a more fundamental cleavage than class in American society.

Race Versus Class: Can They Be Untangled?

On the face of it, race appears to have taken on heightened importance as these young men have sought jobs. Racial inequality seems to account for differences in outcome both between and within the two groups. Given their ambition, schooling, and skills, the Brothers could have been expected to leave the Hallway Hangers in the dust. They haven't. Indeed, the Brothers are only marginally better off than the Hangers. Moreover, the African Americans within each group have fared poorly relative to the whites. Of the Hallway Hangers, the two black members—Boo-Boo and Chris—are in the most desperate straits. And of the Brothers, the sole white member—Mike—has been far and away the most successful on the job market. Does race matter as much as (or more than) class in determining the economic fate of African Americans in Clarendon Heights?

The race (caste) versus class debate has raged with particular passion since the publication in 1978 of William Julius Wilson's *The Declining Significance of Race.* Wilson's title is misleading, for he argues not that racial-caste oppression has become less significant in absolute terms for African Americans, but that it has become less significant *relative to social class* as a determinant of life chances. Whereas all blacks faced a wall of direct racial discrimination in past eras, a chasm between middle-class and working-class blacks has opened up since the 1960s. The relative success and security of the black middle class contrast sharply with the plight of poorer blacks who are trapped in the secondary labor market and in blighted inner cities. Racial inequality results not so much from direct discrimination as from structural changes in the economy that marginalize the black proletariat. Class, Wilson argues, "has become a more important factor than race in determining job placement for blacks."[10]

Wilson's book unleashed a furious storm of criticism and debate that continues to this day. Sociology journals still feature articles that purport to measure the effects of race versus class. Statistical analyses typically use a complex series of regression equations to discover that black-white disparities in educational and occupational attainment cannot be explained by other variables, and so are vestigially ascribed to race. But the entire quantitative quest to measure the relative importance of race and class is founded on the assumption that race and class can be reduced to one-dimensional, quantifiable factors that can be isolated from one another.[11]

The present study shows quite clearly that neither race nor class can be reduced to abstract forces that mechanically manipulate people like electrons in a charged field. Rather, race and class (along with gender) are interwoven in variable patterns, and the resultant geometry is complex. Class and race work simultaneously, and each can magnify or mitigate the effects of the other. Part One disclosed, for example, how race introduces new structural constraints and also serves as a mediation through which the limitations of class are refracted. Largely because the Brothers are black, they accept the achievement ideology and act as if class and racial barriers to success don't exist. And yet for African Americans living half a mile away in a black housing project, black skin becomes a reason to reject the American Dream. Class and race interact with factors like a neighborhood's distinctive social ecology to produce complex patterns that defy quantification.

This ethnography, with its minute "sample" sizes, cannot measure the relative effects of class and race any more effectively than quantitative studies have done. There is nothing to guarantee that the occupational outcomes of the Hallway Hangers and Brothers are representative rather than mere accidents of the job market. What this study can do, however, is explore and elaborate how simplistic and static concepts of class and race can be deepened.

Ain't No Makin' It demonstrates that class and race each have objective and subjective dimensions, a distinction pressed by Pierre Bourdieu and Loïc Wacquant. Drawing upon and extending Bourdieu's theory of social space, Wacquant argues that

> both class and race lead a dual existence: each exists first in materiality, as objective differences that can be observed, measured in the form of distributions of efficient resources and goods; and second in subjectivity, as schemes of perception, appreciation and action, in the form of symbolic distinctions produced and reproduced via socially engrained dispositions.[12]

In other words, class and race introduce objective structural contraints that individuals must face. The bricklayer's child has barriers to overcome that the banker's child need never negotiate. And blacks face limits on opportunity relative to whites. These are real differences rooted in objective material conditions.

On the subjective side, individuals can make of these objective conditions what they will in forging their identities. The bricklayer's son may look across his high school desk at the banker's boy sitting in front of him, shake his head dismissively, and silently wager that the other can't change the oil in his Volvo. Or he may see in the banker's son an effortless ease with girls, grades, and teachers and shake his head despairingly at his own oil-stained fingers. Or he may do both, depending on the context—which peers are around, who the teacher is, and whether the class is algebra or technical drawing. Both attitudes are subjective articulations of class identity that are ultimately rooted in objective economic inequality. But neither attitude can easily be traced to that source. The subjective refuses to be reduced to a reflex of the objective.

There is a real tendency to collapse the objective and subjective dimensions of class into each other. As a youth worker in Clarendon Heights, I had to struggle to make any sense of what I was seeing on the street until Bourdieu, Bowles and Gintis, and especially Willis introduced me to the logic of social reproduction. Seeing how heavily structural inequality weighs on the Brothers and Hallway Hangers, I now tend to analyze the primary material in that light. Thus, when the young men acknowledge constraints on opportunity, I applaud them as "insightful," "discerning," "penetrating." And I judge their subjective interpretations by how closely they point to the objective limitations of social class. There is an implicit yardstick of truth and an implicit politics here, both provided by the social reproduction perspective. Reading the research data along this *evaluative* axis allows an assessment of the truth of individuals' views and also of their political potential. If those who are denied opportunities see their condition clearly, they are more likely to kick up a stink and change things. This is a crucial issue, and it deserves to be addressed.

At the same time, the primary data need to be analyzed along a *descriptive* axis that revolves around the question of identity. The task here is to describe the opinions, values, and actions of the men as they seek to make sense of their situations. Leaving aside the sociological accuracy of their views, the descriptive part of my task concentrates on how the Hallway Hangers and Brothers maintain their identities in their distinctive social and cultural contexts. The class identities articulated by the young men in Clarendon Heights cannot be reduced to the question of whether they discern structural constraints on opportunity. The descriptive axis sees class identity as just one more identity, constructed around images of space and common cultural reference points. In this view, there is a class ideology in the United States, but it has almost none of the socialist content and symbolism that working-class identity features in, for example, Europe. The Hallway Hangers' opinions are explained not only by the absence of the good or true ideology that the evaluative axis presupposes, but also by the presence of numerous other ideologies. Class identity is always articulated in historically specific circumstances and always incorporates ideological or imaginary components: a sense of community, status symbols, territories, rituals, and gender and racial inflections.[13]

In combining the descriptive and evaluative tasks, always a treacherous enterprise, Willis is relatively optimistic about the capacity of British working-class culture to penetrate the dominant ideology and to catalyze constructive social change.[14] The Hallway Hangers and Brothers give few grounds for optimism. Given the sway of the achievement ideology, many of their counterhegemonic views are penetrating indeed. But insightful opinions are of little use in isolation; there needs to be an ideological perspective and a cultural context in which their insights can be applied that leads to *positive* and potentially transformative rituals, symbols, territories, and political strategies.

In fact, the Hallway Hangers completely invert objective reality in their subjective rendering of it. Their racial and gender identities as white working-class men are actually assets on the job market, whereas their class background puts them at a disadvantage. But most of the Hallway Hangers see exactly the reverse: They complain not about class oppression but about discrimination against white men. Here again, the views of the Hallway Hangers point to the potency, pervasiveness, and persuasiveness of neoconservative ideology and the historical slough of class analysis in the United States. Perhaps the Hallway Hangers fail to see class as a variable because they grew up so ensconced in their own class culture. Just as the Brothers do not consider race an issue, the Hallway Hangers fail to see class as constraining.

Like class, race has an objective dimension rooted in the structure of opportunities.[15] Educational attainment, annual earnings, rates of employment, and a host of other measures confirm that African Americans are disadvantaged relative to whites. Yet race exists not just in material differences in power and resources but also in its subjective dimension—in individuals' minds as a category that shapes the way they view themselves and the social world. As with class, the subjective articulation of race seldom lines up with its objective dimension. Thus, although race is a central category by which both the Brothers and the Hallway Hangers understand themselves, neither group underscores the objective constraints faced by African Americans. Structural constraints on opportunity, whether rooted in race or class, are largely invisible to the young men in this study. The Hallway Hangers and the Brothers, like almost all Americans, tend to interpret their situation in individual rather than structural terms.

Structure Versus Agency: "No One to Blame but Me"

Every individual in this study holds himself acountable for his condition. Chapter 7 disclosed how the Brothers blamed themselves for their academic mediocrity. The Hallway Hangers were less self-critical but still reproached themselves for screwing up in school. Eight years later, for both groups, the verdict is similar. The previous chapter shows how the Brothers variously chastise themselves for being lazy, unmotivated, indecisive, unrealistic, overly opportunistic, fickle, and generally inept. Juan is straightforward: "I really screwed up." Super is equally succinct: "I just fucked everything up." The Hallway Hangers, it turns out, are also hard on themselves.

(all in separate interviews)

JINKS: I could kick myself in the ass, because if I stayed in school, I'd probably have a better job, and I'd be doing better in life right now.

CHRIS: I fucked up. I regret everything. I feel real bad about my mom. I just fucked up, man, fucked everything up. I'd like to regain back the trust of my family. Man, I wouldn't wish this situation on anyone.

STONEY: I was doing good for a while. Running this pizza place over in Medway. He gave me the keys, the boss did. I was running it, doing a good job, too. The money wasn't great but still. I ended up fucking the guy over. He vouched for me when I was in the pre-release center. I burned that bridge. About two months after I got out I said, "Here, here's the key, I'm fuckin' through, I'm sick of this." Shoulda stayed. Shoulda stuck it out. He might've given me more money, who knows? My judgment sucks sometimes.

FRANKIE: I know today I wasted a lot of my life. I had a lotta fun but I wasted a lot of it. Lotta guys went to jail, lotta guys were just fucked up, man. And I was fucked up in my own way.

BOO-BOO: I should never have got into drugs. I dunno, if I could do one thing, start all over again, I'd just go right back to school, I'd do my thing, wouldn't get tied up in all this bullshit I got tied up in.

STEVE: I've been fucking up big time, Jay, no lie. Going away [to jail] too much, man. Fighting with my girl. I left her, and she called up and said I was doing drugs and drinkin' and all that other shit. Which I was. Called my probation officer and ratted me right out. … I dunno, dude, I guess I've got no one to blame but me.

Both the Brothers and the Hallway Hangers hold themselves responsible for their plight. Like most Americans, they point to personal vices and individual shortcomings to account for their subordinate position in the class structure.

But this is not the whole story. We have already seen that, apart from Mike and Derek, the Brothers blame not only themselves but also the socioeconomic order for their failure to get ahead. James argues most forcefully that the economic system is also to blame. He acknowledges constraints on economic opportunity, holds the government accountable, and sympathizes with those who turn to illegal activity. But James also contends that lower-class culture prevents people from developing proper ambition.

JM: What do you think about the white kids at Clarendon Heights? Steve, Slick, Frankie, Jinks?

JAMES: They, er, gee, what can I say about that? They reached a certain level in their life and then they just stayed at that level. They just said, "Oh well, this is my life. This is what my life's gonna be." But it's all attitude, it's all if you wanna go farther than you are. They're gonna be in the Heights all their life. It's like back to, if you grow up in a certain environment, then that's what you gonna

live. That's what you're gonna live all your life. That's what you're used to. And
that's how their life is. It's the same as the Coopers next door. The Coopers next
door are always gonna be the same. They're never gonna change. Fifty years
from now a new set of Coopers will be the same exact as these Coopers. Because they've reached a certain level, and they're always gonna be at that level.
I'm not down on them, that's all they know. They're gonna just say, "I stopped
at that level." But you can't say that. You have to want more for your kids and
for your grandkids.

The idea that the intergenerational transmission of poverty is due, at least in part,
to cultural attitudes and behavior is also implied by Slick. Like James, Slick points
to macroeconomic constraints on opportunity, cultural deficiencies of the community, and individual shortcomings.

SLICK: I feel like I was robbed. I look at people and I say, y'know, I could be doin'
what this guy's doing. If I had a college degree or something. But how was I
gonna go to college? Know what I'm sayin'? I couldn't afford to go back to Latin
Academy. My par—, my mother couldn't, because we moved into this city. So
that robbed me of that deal, know what I mean? You've just got to deal with it
the best way you fucking can. Believe me, I was pissed off about it, and I still
think about it to this day. I shouldn't be this dirty. Look at how filthy I am,
working with my hands, blisters all over me and shit. I should be working at an
office with a tie and nice suit on.

JM: So what do you say to the rich guy who listens to this story and says, "Wait a
minute. He wasn't robbed. That was him. He could've, when he came to Lincoln High, he could've made it. It was the people he hung out with, or …"

SLICK: Nope.

JM: What do you say to him?

SLICK: What I say to him is, "Come down and learn for yourself, come down and
see for yourself what it's like." Because you take it—I was a perfect A student all
through my school years til I got yanked out of Latin Academy. When I moved
here it was like, I ain't never got beat up before. I was into school. I was into
sports and shit. I come here, get picked on, get my ass kicked all the fucking
time. Finally, I went from being an A student to being, you know, you gotta defend yourself. What are you gonna study, you can't read a book on how to, on
how to act like these people do. Y'know, you gotta treat an animal like a fucking
animal. That's how it goes.

In the next breath, Slick places the corrosive influence of Clarendon Heights culture within a broader context of class inequality. Slick challenges the apparent su-

periority of the rich who, he claims, would be lost in Clarendon Heights without the props and symbols of their social status.

SLICK: Tell a person like that to come on down. I'll let 'em stay at my mother's house. The rich people you're talking about. Let 'em stay there with the cockroaches and the junkies shooting up outside and see how they react to it. Without their little Porsches and their little Saabs. Y'know, let them survive for a little while.

Slick's passing reference to roaches touches on an important dimension of lower-class life often missed by outside observers: what Wacquant calls the "demoralization effects" of life in intense poverty and permanent material insecurity. Living in places like Clarendon Heights tends to eat away at a person's energy and insides over time.[16] Slick knows it is different elsewhere and begins to articulate a critique of class privilege. But like the others, he holds himself responsible for his condition.

SLICK: I personally should've finished high school, then went on to some sort of college, any kinda college. Then looked over my options and *planned* on what I was doing. *Planned* on having children. *Planned* on my career. Instead of things just happening.

Like social theorists, both the Brothers and the Hallway Hangers wrestle with the roles of structure, culture, and agency in the reproduction of social inequality.

It should be obvious from this study that all three levels of analysis—the individual, the cultural, and the structural—play their part in the reproduction of social inequality. Had Slick been born into a middle-class family, he probably *would* be sitting in an office with a suit and tie on. Had his peer group been into Shakespeare and square roots rather than beer balls and bong hits, Slick might not be so blistered and dirty. Finally, Slick would be in better shape had he made different choices himself. Although all three levels have explanatory power, the structural one is primary because it reaches down into culture and individual agency. The culture of Clarendon Heights—with its violence, racism, and other self-destructive features (as well as its resilience, vitality, and informal networks of mutual support)—is largely a response to class exploitation in a highly stratified society. Similarly, Slick's individual strategies have developed not in a social vacuum but in the context of chronic social immobility and persistent poverty. To be sure, individual agency is important. Causality runs in both directions in a reflexive relationship between structure and agency. Structural constraints on opportunity lead to leveled aspirations, and leveled aspirations in turn affect job prospects. Contrary to popular belief, structure is still the source of inequality.

Most Americans tend to ignore the link between individual behavior and cultural patterns on the one hand and economic inequality on the other, but neither Jinks nor Frankie fall into this trap. Both contextualize their peer group in a nexus of class injustice.

JM: When you look back on the heyday, back in high school as teenagers and the closeness you guys had, what d'you think brought you together that way, compared to other people?

JINKS: Probably because we all grew up together, we were all the same age. We all went to school together. We were spendin' most of our times together as a unit, most of the time in the day. We were spendin' more time together, all of us, than we were with our families. We went through the good and the bad together. Most of the times were bad. I mean, in the projects, it's not everybody's happy-go-lucky. Nine times out of ten you're strugglin' to get what you want. So it makes your friendships bond tighter. Because you gotta rely on other people to help you through whatever it is you need. We didn't have money. So we had to get by with whatever we could. And how I look at it, what we used to get by with was our friendship.

JM: What would you say to those people who drive by and look over and see us. You can almost see it in their eyes, in …

JINKS: Yeah, they're stereotyping right away: "Yeah, these kids are no good." But they should try to take the time out to understand us instead of right away, "He's a hoodlum because he lives in a project." I mean, there are a lot of people out here who are just like me—hardworkin'. They'll do anything for anybody. All they want is to be treated the way they treat people, y'know, with respect and kindness. They're not out there to screw anybody, but there are a lot of people, "Areas like this bring trouble."

Frankie also refers to class prejudice and, like Jinks, sees their peer group as rooted in the experience of growing up poor in a hostile dominant culture.

FRANKIE: Well back then, y'know, back then we were cool. We hung tight because, I know today, because we were looked down on our whole lives, man. From the projects. I believe, in my opinion, we were never invited anywhere. When we were places, y'know, people always knew: "Those are the kids from the projects." I would say we stuck together just, for a fact that, just, just to prove these people right. "You're right." We were from the fucking projects, and you didn't invite us to your party so we're gonna come anyways, just to fuck it up. And it was the generation before us, the generation before us, when my brothers and them were growing up … it was just our values, man: Stick tight. We were taught that you had to stick together, just from generation to generation. ... I grew up thinking I was a bad fucking kid. And I liked that. I liked being known as a bad kid. I look back there—there aren't any bad kids—there's a lotta kids that just had a fucking tough life.

Bad kids or bad circumstances? Frankie leads us right back to the theoretical impasse between structure and agency. To what extent are the Hallway Hangers and Brothers victims of a limited opportunity structure, and to what extent are they victims of their own flawed choices?

Is Super, for example, forced to deal drugs because he was born at the bottom of a class society that glorifies conspicuous consumption while denying the poor real opportunity? Or does Super simply choose to deal drugs because he can't be bothered to work his way up legitimately like everybody else? In short, to paraphrase the title of Diego Gambetta's book, was he pushed or did he jump?[17] Is Super *pushed* into crime by the forces of social reproduction? Or does he *jump* as a matter of individual choice? Certainly Super is *pushed from behind* by forces of which he is largely unaware. Super was handicapped in school by the effects of cultural capital, tracking, and teacher expectations. On the job market, Super's alternatives are limited by the sectoral shift from manufacturing jobs to poorly paid service positions and then squeezed further by racial discrimination embedded in the labor market. Thus, Super is pushed from behind by structural forces acting "behind his back" that propel him into the street economy. In addition, Super is *pulled from the front*, as it were, by structural forces that he sees and with which he wittingly struggles. Super is aware, for example, that the economy's recessionary plunge means fewer legitimate jobs are available and that his high school diploma is far less helpful than he imagined. He also believes that cocaine capitalism proffers more of a career structure than do legitimate jobs in the new postindustrial economy. Pushed from behind and pulled from the front by structural forces, Super's entry into the informal economy is nevertheless his own decision individually taken. Super *jumps* into the cocaine trade because he wants to. Super wants "to be someone, make fast money, have respect," and his decision is intentional and even rational. And yet the decision cannot be understood apart from the structural limitations on his options. In the end, perhaps the fairest account is that Super was *pushed into jumping*.

Structure and agency are inseparable. Individual agents like Super are always structurally situated, and thus human agency is itself socially structured. Social structures reach into the minds and even the hearts of individuals to shape their attitudes, motivations, and worldviews. Structural determination is thus inscribed in the very core of human agency.[18] Bourdieu's concept of habitus captures the interpenetration of structure and agency, but habitus is more a label for a site than an explanation of what goes on within it. Bourdieu neglects the actual process whereby external forces and internal consciousness wrestle with each other. Rather, he seems to imply that agents are unwittingly and unconsciously disposed to adjust their dispositions and practices to the external constraints that bear upon them. In Bourdieu's view, all this happens behind the backs of agents in the sense that it unfolds beneath the level of rationality, conscious deliberation, and intentional choice. And yet while pushed from behind by structural constraints of which they are unaware, the Brothers and Hallway Hangers are also pulled by forces that they actively and consciously manipulate. Although he claims otherwise, Bourdieu's notion of habitus fails to allow space for this kind of conscious, calculative decisionmaking. Habitus is an ingenious concept, and Bourdieu is surely correct to insist on a dialectical relationship between objective structures and internal subjectivities. However, Bourdieu never makes clear *how* the habitus engenders thought and action, and so his resolution of the agency-structure dualism seems more a sidestep than a solution.[19]

Still, by insisting on the inseparability of structure and agency, Bourdieu reminds us not only that structure is at the heart of agency but also that agency can reach to the heart of structure. The social universe people inhabit isn't simply received as a given from without; rather, it is produced and constructed anew by agents. As Wacquant explains, "The structures of society that seem to stand over and against agents as external objects are but the 'congealed' outcome of the innumerable acts of cognitive assembly guiding their past and present actions."[20] Structures are not fixed, binding, nor unalterable, yet they often appear so. Bourdieu unravels and picks apart the symbolic power that cloaks exploitative and oppressive relationships with an aura of inevitability and renders them fair, natural, and normal.

Now we begin to see why the Brothers and Hallway Hangers give no indication that they might be able to alter the structures that constrain them. Among them there is very little political or collective energy, or even a sense that change is possible. Of the Brothers, for example, James is critical of the economic system and government policy but never suggests an alternative to the policy he criticizes, much less an alternative to the economic system. Neither do the Hallway Hangers envisage the possibility of substantive change. As we saw in Chapter 9, Jinks complains about class injustice in his workplace but feels politically impotent.

JINKS: ... He's a complete moron, and he can do as he pleases because his father's the boss. Because he's got money it makes everything he does right, y'know, whether it be wrong or right. He can't do no wrong. I see it at my job and everywhere else, and it's just all over the world.

JM: But apart from just recognizing that, it doesn't seem to make you that angry.

JINKS: It does and it don't. At times it does, but there's a lot of things in this world that make me angry. If I was to let every little thing that makes me angry bother me, I would be upset twenty-four hours a day. I would hate the world. I just try to have a few beers, smoke a few joints, and laugh at the world. It's so fucked up, it ain't even funny any more. That's why I try gettin' the philosophy, Hooray for me, and fuck everybody else. Cuz no matter how hard you try, you're not gonna change it. I cannot worry about every little thing in life, okay, because there's too much out there to piss me off. And no matter what I do, if anything I try, it's not gonna change it. It's not gonna make it a better place for anybody.

JM: Most people say, y'know, this is the United States, it's a democracy. Is it impossible that we could vote into office people that would change things for the better?

JINKS: That's my philosophy. I don't even vote because all politicians are crooks. The only thing they can agree on is to give themselves a raise. What about the poor folk? I mean, how many people are out on the streets homeless? They cannot put money aside to help feed them and support them, right, but they can give themselves a ten, twenty thousand dollar a year raise. ... We're in a state of recession, right? Fine, the cost of living goes up. How come our paychecks don't go up? It's just, I look at it at times, the whole world's fucked. No matter what you do, you gotta come out losin'. You can try and try and try and never get anywhere.

These last comments highlight the deeply felt sense of powerlessness amongst residents of Clarendon Heights. In 1983 Jinks was adamant that personal ambition was pointless: "I think you're kiddin' yourself to have any [aspirations]. We're just gonna take whatever we can get." Now his pessimism extends to aspirations for social change as well. "No matter what you do, you gotta come out losin'. You can try and try and try and never get anywhere."

This is pretty depressing stuff. We might expect those who are suspicious of the chances for individual upward mobility to be disposed toward collective political action to transform society. But when political *and* personal efficacy is judged illusory, then resignation and despair are liable to take over. The human psyche, however, resists hopelessness, and the Hallway Hangers are cast back on individual aspirations to sustain them. Slick is angling to be a supervisor on his roofing crew. Frankie wants to qualify as a mechanical contractor and supervise a building. Boo-Boo still hopes to be a mechanic; and Stoney, to own a pizza parlor. Shorty's aspirations are untempered by reality.

SHORTY: I'm s'posed to be getting my settlement soon, for gettin' stabbed. It's called victim of a violent crime, y'know. And I'm s'posed to get like probably forty grand. I'm gonna give my mother some money, help her out with some of her bills, and I'm gonna go halfs with my brother. We're gonna buy a two-family house and rent it out, the whole thing, and I still live with my mother, y'know. We'll see how that goes, and if it goes good we'll gonna buy another one and then another one, and just keep buyin' real estate, that's the thing to get into. ... I will make money one of these days. Like to buy a nice fucking condo on Palm Beach. Next to the Kennedys' (*laughter*). No, I'm serious. I'm gonna make some money.

As implausible as Shorty's vision may be, his aspirations help to keep him going. Whereas the Hallway Hangers previously drew sustenance from their peer group, today they rely on their own individual hopes. The Hallway Hangers have slid into the system alongside the Brothers. Without their tight clique and its own definitions of success, the Hallway Hangers have become much more incorporated into mainstream culture. Far from celebrating their outcast status, they see retrospectively in 1991 that their youthful resistance dug them deeper into marginality.

Frankie articulates this point most clearly. Today, he wants and needs to see opportunity. His recovery program from drug and alcohol abuse is predicated on a sense of personal efficacy, on a can-do mentality that emphasizes control over one's destiny. Given his own recovery, Frankie is preoccupied with the toll that substance abuse has taken on the Hallway Hangers.

FRANKIE: There's a lot of sickness there and I see it. I see it today, y'know. Two years ago I was part of it, y'know, and today I'm not, and I can see. For once I'm on the outside lookin' in. It's changes and it's drugs—there's no other way to put it. That's the bottom line. And I just know that from experience.

JM: Do you see any causes even beneath the drugs? Like, I'm hearin' you say that a lot of your problems during that time and individuals' problems now is the drinking, is the drugs. Are there things, are there other things that have kept people back?

FRANKIE: The economy sucks. It's just bad, a lotta people just don't see a lotta opportunity, y'know? They just don't see opportunity in life, man.

JM: Is it that they don't see it, or is it that the opportunity's not there?

FRANKIE: (*After a long pause*) Back then, I would say it's, y'know, they'd probably think it's not there. I, I, some days I still don't think it's there, but it's there, man. Y'know, you only feel when you stop tryin'. My whole problem is I never began to try, y'know? And I'm sure maybe that's some of their problems, y'know? You gotta be willing to try.

JM: It's interesting to hear you say, y'know, that you gotta try, cuz I remember back then you would look at the black kids from around the Heights—the Dereks and Mokey and ...

FRANKIE: Your buddies.

JM: Yeah, right. You said they were chumps because they did try, because they tried in school and they were convinced that they would make it.

FRANKIE: Well, I look today, and if anyone shoulda had a chance to make it, it's fuckin', it's black people. ... But no, I look at it today, y'know, they were probably doing the right thing, y'know? But my motives were different then, you hafta realize. I know I realize that. My motives were fucked up back then.

JM: Has it paid off for them?

FRANKIE: I dunno. I don't see them. I dunno what the fuck they're doin'. I don't care (*laughs*). But I dunno. I haven't seen them. I know I wasted quite a bit of my life.

Here Frankie cuts to the crux of the matter. His confession that "my motives were fucked up back then" sounds like an admission that the Hallway Hangers' resistance ultimately proved counterproductive. Caught in the game and convinced that the rules are beyond changing, Frankie's only sensible option is to commit himself to the competition. Frankie wants to believe that the future is in his own hands, only "you gotta be willing to try." Otherwise, what is left to hang on to? But the Brothers have always tried, and unbeknownst to Frankie, they have failed to make it. And what does Frankie himself have to show for all his aspiration and application, his job counseling and vocational training, his sobriety and disabled status? Frankie is unemployed. But he is absolutely right to make the effort and seize what little opportunity may arise. What other choice does he have? As Rickey, a street hustler from the ghetto of Chicago's South Side, relates: "You know, like I said, it's a goo' feelin' sayin,' 'Hey, you can't make it but you try.'"[21] For Frankie, as for the Brothers, Hallway Hangers, and countless Rickeys across the country, hope flies in the face of crushing odds. The American Dream may be but a mirage. Still, it provides a vision toward which the thirsty may stumble.

What Is to Be Done?

The picture that emerges from this ethnography deviates substantially from the myth of America as the land of opportunity in which any child can grow up to be president. American society is not as open as we like to think; the ladder of social mobility is not accessible to all, nor are its rungs easy to grasp. Both the Brothers and the Hallway Hangers testify to the prevalence of social reproduction rather than social mobility. For many of those in the lowest reaches of the social structure, the American Dream is a hallucination.

Such a picture is troubling, for it shatters many of our illusions about the fairness of the American economic and social system. It also demands a political response that goes well beyond the offerings of contemporary American liberalism. Extending the welfare state will not fix the basic problem facing the Brothers and Hallway Hangers. Improving the material conditions under which they live—better housing, health care, child care, and social services, less restricted and larger welfare and unemployment checks—certainly would be a step in the right direction, but such measures leave the basic emotional encumbrance of lower-class life untouched. These boys, all of them, desperately want to be somebody, to make something of their lives. By denying them that opportunity, by undercutting their very aspirations and reducing them to hopelessness at the age of sixteen, or by trapping them in the secondary labor market and leaving them disillusioned but still dreaming at twenty-four, the economic and social system causes untold misery, waste, and despair. The ideology that permeates American society holds out the rags-to-riches story as a valid option, despite the fact that very, very few people can live it out. If the Brothers and the Hallway Hangers are to have the opportunity to fulfill their potential as citizens and as human beings, more will have to change in the American political and social landscape than the expansion of the welfare state.

In short, what is required is the creation of a truly open society—a society where the life chances of those at the bottom are not radically different from those at the top and where wealth is distributed more equitably. Rather than reaching for the dizzying heights of the Eiffel Tower, the occupational structure could be shaped more like an onion. The socialist vision of a transformed class structure that radically reduces social inequality may seem hopelessly out of touch, but there is no denying that the capitalist free market, left to itself, can neither protect the environment nor meet human needs. The market has a major role to play in a decentralized socialist economy—but as a servant, not as a master. A mixed economy combining public power and private ownership can channel market forces so they flow in the desired direction. Competition and incentives do not require capitalism's unconscionable inequalities. Yet the 1980s saw the resurgence of a smug and vainglorious capitalism that widened the gap between the rich and poor to an all-time high. The tide may turn, but Democratic policies tend to tinker with a system that is in desperate need of an overhaul.

Whose Welfare?

For all the public cry for curtailment of the welfare state, the fact is that the United States does not have a welfare system worthy of the name. Public housing is a case in point. Experience has proved over and over again in nation after nation that a free market economy simply cannot provide homes for people on low and moderate incomes. Private developers build for the rich, not for the poor. Yet public provision of low-income housing in the United States lags way behind that in other industrialized nations. In 1980 public housing accounted for roughly 1 percent of the American housing market; in England the figure was 46 percent and in France 37 percent.

Instead of building housing for the poor, the United States has directly and indirectly subsidized homes for the better-off. From 1937 to 1968, 10 million middle- and upper-income private housing units were built with help from the Federal Housing Authority, whereas only 800,000 public units were constructed with federal housing subsidies. Moreover, as Wacquant notes, what little public housing was built consists mostly of cheap, massive, public housing projects stacked in central cities that reinforce racial segregation and the concentration of poverty.[22] The 1980s housing policy was even worse: to cease building public housing altogether. Widespread homelessness has been the result, a condition with which Boo-Boo and Chris are acquainted. And because only the poorest and most troubled families qualify for public housing, even small projects like Clarendon Heights are socially ostracized and physically forsaken.

Far from being an exception, public housing policy typifies America's scant commitment to the poor. Cries for the rolling back of welfare ignore the fact that benefits have already been slashed from levels that were paltry to begin with by international standards. The real value of the standard public aid package has plummeted by half. At the same time, eligibility has been tightened. In any case, only 55 percent of those eligible for Aid to Families with Dependent Children (AFDC) nationwide actually received "welfare" in 1992. Fewer than a third of the jobless qualify for unemployment payments. Job training programs, revenue sharing, and urban development grants were all axed in the 1980s.[23] These government cutbacks, combined with the disastrous effects of deindustrialization, have marginalized the urban working class more than ever.

And still the politicians and the populace clamor for more cuts, claiming in utter ignorance confident knowledge of the world in which the urban poor live. Yet the lives of the Brothers and Hallway Hangers—their youthful passion and desperation as they struggle to cope with poverty and devise strategies to escape its grip—point in a rather different political direction than the nation is willing to look. I read the story of the Brothers and Hallway Hangers as a harsh indictment of American class society and as a sharp spur to work for its reformation.

Better Schools?

In Clarendon Heights I was not primarily a sociologist; I was primarily a youth worker. If sociological study drives us to acknowledge the degenerative effects of gender-, race-, and class-based constraints upon young people, then educational practitioners are left in a quandary: If the problems go beyond the kids, what can we do? "Better schools" has been the standard rallying cry for social reformers concerned about sustained economic inequality in the United States. If only poor children had access to quality education, opportunity for individual mobility would be equalized across social classes and the gap between rich and poor substantially reduced. But the problems with this approach are substantial. First, as we have seen, schools actually maintain and legitimize social inequality. Second, educational reform leaves the underlying structure of economic inequality untouched. Still, though no substitute for fundamental structural change, improved schooling could help countless individuals like the Brothers and Hallway Hangers.

My first recommendation is that the achievement ideology must be replaced with ways of motivating students that acknowledge rather than deny their social condition. When used to cultivate discipline by highlighting the eventual rewards of educational attainment, the achievement ideology is neither effective at drawing obedience and attentiveness out of students nor conducive to the development of a positive self-image among working-class pupils. The familiar refrain of "Behave yourself, study hard, earn good grades, graduate with your class, go on to college, get a good job, and make a lot of money" reinforces the feelings of personal failure and inadequacy that working-class students are likely to bear as a matter of course. By this logic, those who have not made it have only themselves to blame. Because it shrouds class, race, and gender barriers to success, the achievement ideology promulgates a lie, one that some students come to recognize as such. For those pupils whose own experiences contradict the ideology—and in an urban public high school there are bound to be many—it is often rejected, and rightly so. Teachers are left with nothing to motivate their students, and it is no wonder that "acting out," aggressive disobedience, and unruliness predominate. School officials can round up the offending students and label them "slow," "learning impaired," "unmotivated," "troubled," "high-risk," or "emotionally disturbed" and segregate them, but the problem is much more deeply rooted.

Teachers do not promote the achievement ideology because they want to make working-class students miserable. Nor are they intent on maintaining social order and cohesion in the face of class inequality by contributing to the legitimation function of the school. In my experience, most teachers are well-intentioned, hard-working men and women who are striving to do a difficult job as best they can. They parrot the achievement ideology because they think it will motivate students, because it probably does not contradict their own experiences, and because they believe it. Most middle-class Americans do. As Willis writes, "What kind of bourgeoisie is it that does not in some way believe its own legitimations? That would be the denial of themselves."[24] The equality-of-opportunity line of reasoning may have worked in the middle-class high schools from which most teachers hail, but its utility in an urban school serving low-income neighborhoods is diminished greatly.

If students like the Hallway Hangers are to be motivated to achieve in school, it must not be at the expense of their self-esteem but in support of it. Schools serving low-income neighborhoods must help students build positive identities as working-class, black and white, young men and women. Rather than denying the existence of barriers to success, schools should acknowledge them explicitly while motivating students by teaching them, for example, about historic figures who shared the students' socioeconomic origins but overcame the odds. Success stories can be important motivators so long as emphasis is put on the obstacles against which these figures prevailed. Teachers can also strive to include material about which the students, drawing on the skills they have developed in their neighborhoods, are the experts. If the school could believe in the legitimacy and importance of students' feelings, perceptions, and experiences as working-class kids, the students themselves might come to do the same, thereby giving them a positive identity and a dose of self-confidence as a foundation for further application in school.

If such measures were undertaken on a systematic basis, boys like the Hallway Hangers might feel as though they belong in school, that they need not choose between rendering themselves naked and vulnerable by stripping off their street identities or aggressively asserting their street culture in disruptive rebellion. One of the reasons the Hallway Hangers speak so warmly about the Adjustment Class is that in Jimmy Sullivan's classroom they were allowed to maintain their street identities. Even more important, these identities were vindicated and given legitimacy because the teacher himself embodied many of the attitudes, values, and traits esteemed by the culture of the Hallway Hangers. The Hallway Hangers saw in Jimmy Sullivan a bit of themselves and in themselves a bit of Jimmy; because of the status and authority invested in him as a teacher, in addition to his independent financial success, Jimmy Sullivan vicariously defended and justified their self-image.

Teachers need not have a black belt in karate, place a premium on machismo, swear in class, or have working-class roots like Jimmy Sullivan; however, they must be prepared to validate the identities that their students have taken on as part of growing up. Admittedly, this is not an easy task, especially as awareness of class, race, and gender stereotyping should be inculcated by teachers. If part of one's education should involve the confrontation of ingrained sexism and its consequences, Sullivan's class would not receive high marks. There were no girls in his class, and the uncritical affirmation of machismo confronted the observer in every aspect of the room, from the punching bags, posters of Bruce Lee, and *Soldier of Fortune* magazines to the frankly sexist attitudes of the teacher. But easy educational answers do not exist, and we must resist the tendency, all too prevalent among school reformers, to cling to single-solution, essentialist positions. On balance, I consider the Adjustment Class a failure because, for the most part, the students emerged with very few academic skills. Students must still learn the basics.

In my experience, academic rigor itself demands that the curriculum meet the needs and concerns of working-class and minority students. If the curriculum is made responsive to student needs, the gap between academic skill and maturity can be bridged. No one is going to get Shorty to read about the Hardy Boys; on the other hand, his reading ability may not be much above a fourth-grade level. Novels and poignant nonfiction works dealing with the concerns of working-class and minority youth could be incorporated into the curriculum. It is ludicrous, for instance, to expect students in the Adjustment Class to learn about social studies from a sixth-grade U.S. history textbook. Meanwhile, the thirteen-year-old younger brothers of the Hallway Hangers have managed to research prison life through books, movies, slides, seminars, and field trips and to produce a thirty-page anthology of interviews with former inmates, many of whom live in Clarendon Heights. Their achievement, *Behind Bars,* demonstrates what can be gained in educational terms when local history and culture are taken seriously and when students are actively involved in thinking and doing rather than being passively exposed to textbook material. These would-be Hallway Hangers did not memorize rules of punctuation, spelling, capitalization, subject-verb agreement, and other mechanics of grammar. Rather, they used them time and again in the process of putting together their magazine. Connecting the curriculum with the interests of pupils like the Hallway Hangers can be done; it only requires a commitment— both attitudinal and material—to meeting the needs of working-class students.

Material commitment is crucial. Many schools in poor neighborhoods lack the most basic resources: classrooms, desks, books, science labs, photocopy machines, cafeteria furnishings, functioning toilets, and properly trained teachers. Among the member-countries of the Organization for Economic Cooperation and Development (OECD), the United States has the lowest per capita expenditure on primary education. Inner-city schools, segregated by color and class, have been allowed to deteriorate to the point where they are downright dangerous. In this context it is worth remembering that the Hallway Hangers and Brothers actually attended a highly regarded public high school. Even a curriculum reformed along the lines I have outlined would neither dissolve a school's social reproductive function nor directly address the fundamental problem of the transmission of class inequality. Thus, educational reform should be pursued not as an end in itself but as a component of more fundamental change in the social fabric of American society.

The transformation of American class society is currently a political impossibility, and progressive social change is bound to be slow and piecemeal. One way forward is through education that fosters a critical understanding of social problems and their structural causes. As students develop tools of social analysis and begin to understand how class-based inequalities in wealth, power, and privilege affect them, this awareness of self in relation to society becomes a motivating force much more powerful than the achievement ideology. Reflection on their personal and social reality frees learners from the debilitating effects of the dominant "blame the victim" way of seeing the world. Consonant with the praxis of the Brazilian educator Paulo Freire,[25] when learners perceive the structural roots of their own plight, they develop a new sense of personal dignity and are energized by a new hope. Time and again I have seen poor students face up to long odds and vow to overcome them instead of resigning themselves to the marginalized fate of the Hallway Hangers. When their passions and intellects are stimulated by indignation, youths are often moved to challenge the heretofore hidden social, political, and economic forces that weigh so heavily upon their lives. For some, this means an intensely personal drive and ambition. Others begin struggling to create a better world. In still others, these impulses coexist; such youths work for social, political, and economic reconstruction as well as personal transformation. For all of them, in contrast to the boys in this study, education has recovered its mission: It has become emancipatory.

Class Dismissed

The experiences of the Hallway Hangers and Brothers, properly mined, highlight failures in economic, social, and educational policy, and the preceding pages offer a rough sketch of the book's broad policy implications. But this study points an accusing finger at one dominant dogma, itself a major obstacle to political change: the persistent belief that poverty is caused by the personal vices and cultural pathologies of the poor. Distinctively American, this old notion was rejuvenated in the 1960s by Oscar Lewis and Daniel Patrick Moynihan, who argued that a "culture of poverty" characterized by fatalism, family instability, and social irresponsibility promoted persistent urban poverty. Yet both Lewis and Moynihan contended that this "tangle of pathology" was rooted in sustained social immobility and chronic unemployment.[26]

Today, the link between economic opportunity and lower-class behavior has been completely cut in the popular press and the popular mind. Liberals such as Nicholas Lemann, keen to blame the poor for their plight, long to give ghettos an injection of bourgeois mores to cure the cultural malaise that black migrants allegedly brought up from the South, a theory he borrows from Edward Banfield.[27] Meanwhile, Banfield's archconservative heirs such as Charles Murray have set about convincing the public that welfare programs cause rather than contain poverty and that the social safety net should be scrapped altogether.[28] Egged on by Republican and even Democratic rhetoric, more and more Americans bewail the waste of their tax money on "the mythical black welfare mother, complete with a prodigious reproductive capacity and a galling laziness, accompanied by the uncaring and equally lazy black man in her life who will not work, will not marry her and will not support his family."[29] The war on poverty has become the war on the poor.

This book confirms that structural inequality causes poverty. The presumed behavioral and cultural deficiencies of the lower class are the consequence rather than the cause of poverty. Culture of poverty theorists consistently cite lack of ambition as a barrier to lower-class advancement. But the leveled aspirations of the Hallway Hangers can be directly traced to the impermeability of the class structure. Moreover, the ample ambition of the Brothers has been drained away by the tilted playing field under their feet. Over and over we discover beneath behavior cited as evidence of cultural pathology a social rationality that makes sense given the economic constraints these young men face. Born into the lowest reaches of the class structure, the Brothers and Hallway Hangers variously help and hinder the inertia of social reproduction. Their individual choices matter and make a difference, but the stage is largely set. Even the Hallway Hangers, far from authors of their own problems, are victims of a limited opportunity structure that strangles their initiative and channels them into lifestyles of marginality, and then allows the privileged to turn around and condemn them for doing so.[30]

But it is not merely the man driving by in the BMW who blames the victim. The Hallway Hangers and Brothers largely blame themselves for their plight. Schooled in the rhetoric of equal opportunity, the young men themselves confuse the consequences with the causes of poverty. Their self-blame is not total; many of the men in this study feel the constraining forces of social reproduction. But structural insight usually collapses into a feeling of personal responsibility for their failure to get ahead. Both the Brothers and Hallway Hangers see themselves as basically undeserving.

Class is not in the vocabulary of the Hallway Hangers and Brothers any more than it is in the vocabulary of other Americans. And yet class determines the grammar and idiom of their existence, if not the precise syntax. Yes, Frankie and company chose to follow the example of their older brothers and to hang out in doorway #13; chose to smoke and sell marijuana and angel dust at age thirteen; chose to deny rather than defer to teacher authority; chose to apply themselves to stealing rather than studying; and chose to drink and fight and assert their masculinity in displays of street aggression. Just like, as Benjamin DeMott imagines, a boy on the other side of town chooses to follow the example of his father (an engineer) and develop a science hobby in junior high (taking over the basement lounge for a lab); chooses to develop a research focus on robotics under the guidance of his brilliant young physics teacher (who already has two Young Scientist finalists); chooses at MIT to specialize in space robotics; chooses to take the NASA fellowship offer; and so on and on. In the American mind, life is about individual choices; social class matters not.[31]

The Brothers and Hallway Hangers live in a class society committed to the denial of class. Their lived experience attests to the power and pervasiveness of social class, but in the absence of any organizing and overarching ideology, their awareness of class is politically limp and inchoate. Where is such an ideology to be found? Democrats and Republicans fall over each other to please the mythically all-inclusive "middle class." Apart from conspicuously failing to address poverty as an issue, politicians pepper their public speeches with references to the "decent," "responsible," "hard-working" families they are so keen to court. "Symbolically cast out of the civic community," the poor, far from being a viable constituency, have become a political football to be kicked around in the debate about crime.[32] Politicians of all stripes want simply to lock up the likes of the Hallway Hangers, as if criminality and economic opportunity were not inextricably linked. Once again, social problems are reduced to problems of individual morality and pathology. In contemporary American politics, there is no critique of the class structure; instead, the poor find themselves pushed beyond the political pale.

If the tide and toll of advanced marginality in the United States is to be checked, new organizational forms of popular mobilization need to be nurtured: grassroots organizations, women's groups, community organizing outfits, and coalitions campaigning on issues of health, housing, schooling, child care, crime, and local neighborhood concerns. Political parties and trade unions alone are ill-suited to stop the steady advance of new forms of social inequality.

In many countries, trade unions still carry the cause of workers and promote class consciousness. But the American labor movement has been crippled by red-baiting, right-to-work laws, racism, corporate power, and its own conservatism. In today's postindustrial economy, unions are consumed by the fight for survival, and a comprehensive critique of the class system is far from their agenda. Still, some unions serve their members and instill class solidarity. If it weren't for his progressive hotel and restaurant workers' union, Frankie might still be strung out on coke. Mike, the other union member, makes far more money than the other men in this study. And as much as he rants about welfare cheats and raves about oceans of opportunity, Mike quotes with approval the literature distributed by his postal union about how "the Republicans are fucking us over, selling the working class down the river." Alone among the subjects of this study, Mike speaks of the "working class." And yet he is also the most reactionary, variously characterizing the Hallway Hangers as "fuckin' rejects," "fuckin' trash," and "a bunch of lazy, loser, fuck-up bums." Mike has forged his working-class identity by distancing himself from the "lazy" subproletariat. The class solidarity he articulates is defined as much against those below as against those above. Unfortunately, Mike's attitude is symptomatic of a working class that is severely fragmented.

The top tenth of the population owns 86 percent of the nation's wealth. But the rest of the wealth is distributed in such a way as to turn those in the bottom nine-tenths against each other. The working class is divided. White-collar workers vaunt themselves over manual laborers; skilled workers look down on the unskilled; those in low-status occupations belittle the unemployed. For the bulk of the workforce, there are always groups like the Hallway Hangers to whom they can feel superior. And the Hallway Hangers themselves, their peer group dissolved, seek solace and superiority in sexism and racism. They sense that the odds are stacked against them, but under the sway of New Right rhetoric and in the absence of any alternative political philosophy, the Hallway Hangers believe that they are victimized as white men. Victimized they are, but by a class system so clothed in the rhetoric of classlessness that the Hallway Hangers can be persuaded to pitch their tents with the powerful in a circle that excludes the Brothers. That is their tragedy, and ours.

Notes

1. J. Castro, "How's Your Pay?" *Time,* 15 April 1991, pp. 40–41.

2. "Corporate Executives Go to the Trough," *Dollars and Sense* 138 (1988):10–11. Cited in Thomas R. Shannon, Nancy Kleniewski, and William M Cross, *Urban Problems in Sociological Perspective* (Prospect Heights, Ill.: Waveland Press, 1991), p. 104.

3. David R. Francis, "Executive Pay in the U.S. Just Goes Up and Up," *Christian Science Monitor,* May 20, 1994, p. 9.

4. Cornel West, *Race Matters* (Boston: Beacon Press, 1993), p. 6.

5. Manning Marable, *Race, Reform, and Rebellion* (Jackson: University Press of Mississippi, 1991), p. 207.

6. Leonard Beeghley, "Individual and Structural Explanations of Poverty," *Population Research and Policy Review* 7 (1988):207.

7. Loïc J. D. Wacquant, "Morning in America, Dusk in the Dark Ghetto: The New 'Civil War' in the American City," *Revue française d'études américaines* 60 (May 1994):97–102.

8. See Roger Waldinger and Thomas Bailey, "The Continuing Significance of Race: Racial Conflict and Racial Discrimination in Construction," *Politics and Society* 19:3 (1991):291–323.

9. Loïc J. D. Wacquant, "Urban Outcasts: Stigma and Division in the Black American Ghetto and the French Periphery," *International Journal of Urban and Regional Research* 17:3 (1993):366–383. Wacquant refers to the historic all-black ghetto, but his insight also applies to the Brothers in their different context.

10. William Julius Wilson, *The Declining Significance of Race: Blacks and Changing American Institutions* (Chicago: University of Chicago Press, 1978), p. 12.

11. Loïc J. D. Wacquant, "The Puzzle of Race and Class in American Society and Social Science," *Benjamin E. Mays Monograph Series* 2 (Fall 1989):7–20.

12. Wacquant, "The Puzzle of Race and Class in American Society and Social Science," p. 15. See also Pierre Bourdieu, "Social Space and the Genesis of Groups," *Theory and Society* 14 (October 1985):723–744.

13. I am grateful to John Dickie for this point.

14. Paul E. Willis, *Learning to Labor* (Aldershot: Gower, 1977).

15. This objective dimension of race has nothing to do with the scientific category of race, which is biologically useless. Race is a sociohistorical concept rather than a biological one.

16. Loïc J. D. Wacquant, "The Ghetto, the State, and the New Capitalist Economy," *Dissent* (Fall 1989):508–520.

17. Diego Gambetta, *Were They Pushed or Did They Jump?* (Cambridge: Cambridge University Press, 1987). These schemes—of being pushed from behind and pulled from the front—are borrowed from Gambetta but take on a somewhat different meaning in the present context.

18. Loïc J. D. Wacquant, "On the Tracks of Symbolic Power," *Theory, Culture, and Society* 10 (August 1993):3–4.

19. To be fair, Bourdieu reckons that the structure-agency dilemma is improperly framed and leads to a theoretical cul-de-sac. It would be harsh to fault him for failing to resolve this dilemma, if it were not claimed by others that he succeeds in dissolving and transcending the structure-agency dualism.

20. Wacquant, "On the Tracks of Symbolic Power," p. 3.

21. Loïc J. D. Wacquant, " 'The Zone': Le métier de 'hustler' dans le ghetto noir américain," *Actes de la recherche en science sociales* 93 (June 1992):58.

22. Loïc J. D. Wacquant, "The State and Fate of the Ghetto: Redrawing the Urban Color Line in Postfordist America," in *Social Theory and the Politics of Identity*, ed. Craig Calhoun (New York: Basil Blackwell, 1994).

23. Wacquant, "Morning in America, Dusk in the Dark Ghetto," pp. 97–102.

24. Willis, *Learning to Labor*, p. 123.

25. Paulo Freire, *Pedagogy of the Oppressed* (New York: Continuum, 1981).

26. Douglas S. Massey and Nancy A. Denton, *American Apartheid* (Cambridge, Mass.: Harvard University Press, 1993), p. 5. See also Daniel Patrick Moynihan, *On Understanding Poverty* (New York: Basic Books, 1968).

27. Nicholas Lemann, *The Promised Land* (New York: Alfred A. Knopf, 1991). See also Lemann's "The Origins of the Underclass," *Atlantic Monthly* (June 1986):31–55, continued in (July 1986):54–68; and Edward C. Banfield's *The Unheavenly City* (Boston: Little, Brown, 1970).

28. Charles Murray, *Losing Ground* (New York: Basic Books, 1984).

29. Rosemary L. Bray, "Growing Up on Welfare," *The Observer Magazine*, 2 January 1994, p. 37.

30. Brian Powers, "Two Tracks to Nowhere," *Socialist Review* 19:2 (April–June 1989):157.

31. Benjamin DeMott, *The Imperial Middle* (New York: William Morrow, 1990), p. 186.

32. Wacquant, "Morning in America, Dusk in the Dark Ghetto," p. 5.

Appendix:
On the Making of
Ain't No Makin' It

Fieldwork: Doubts, Dilemmas, and Discoveries

Few sociologists who employ qualitative research methods discuss the mechanics of fieldwork in their published writings. A frank account of the actual process by which research was carried out might disabuse people of the notion that sociological insight comes from logical analysis of a systematically gathered, static body of evidence. If my own experience is at all typical, insight comes from an immersion in the data, a sifting and resifting of the evidence until a pattern makes itself known. My research methods were not applied objectively in a manner devoid of human limitations and values. Of course, I had access to books that describe the various methods used in sociological field research. But many of these statements on research methods, as Whyte argues in the appendix of *Street Corner Society,* "fail to note that the researcher, like his informants, is a social animal. He has a role to play, and he has his own personality needs that must be met in some degree if he is to function successfully."[1] If, as I would argue, the best fieldwork emerges when the sociologist is completely immersed in the community under study, it means that his or her personal life will be inseparably bound up with the research. What follows, then, is a personal account of my relationship with the Clarendon Heights community and the way I came to understand the aspirations of its teenager members.

Walking through Clarendon Heights for the first time in the spring of 1981, I felt uneasy and vulnerable. Entering another world where the rules would all be different, I was naturally apprehensive. I might have been closer in class background to the people of Clarendon Heights than the great bulk of my university classmates were, but neither my lower-middle-class origins nor my attendance at a regional high school in rural New Hampshire made me particularly "at home" in the project. Most important, I was a university student, a status that could breed resentment, for it implied an upward social trajectory to which these people do not have ready access. To undertake research under such conditions would have been inconceivable. But that spring sociological research was far from my mind. I was at the project with two other university students to begin the Clarendon Heights Youth Enrichment Program, with which I would be involved for the next four years. The youth program led to my interest in the aspirations of Clarendon Heights young people and also provided me with a role and an acceptance in the community without which the fieldwork would have been close to impossible.

Contrary to the expectations of the city's professional social workers, the youth program turned out to be a great success. We lived in the neighborhood during the summer months and established close relationships with the children in the program, their parents, and other project residents. Initial distance or coldness gradually gave way to trust and personal regard as the program's reputation and the rapport between counselors and community grew. Engaging nine boys aged eleven to thirteen in a varied mix of educational, cultural, and recreational activities, I gained more than acceptance by the project's residents—I also learned a great deal about their day-to-day problems and concerns. As my understanding of the community and sensitivity to the pulse of the neighborhood developed, so did my self-confidence and sense of belonging. Although class and racial differences could never be completely transcended, by September 1982 I counted among my closest friends many Clarendon Heights tenants.

It was during that second summer working in Clarendon Heights that my interest in the kids' aspirations really began to take shape. I was amazed that many of the twelve- and thirteen-year-old boys in my group did not even aspire to middle-class jobs (with the exception of professional athletics), but rather, when they verbalized aspirations at all, indicated a desire to work with sheet metal, in a machine tool factory, or in construction. The world of middle-class work was completely foreign to them, and as the significance of this fact impressed itself on me, I concerned myself more and more with their occupational aspirations. But at such a young age, these boys could not speak with much consistency or sophistication about their occupational hopes. To understand why aspirations were so low among Clarendon Heights youth, I would have to look to these boys' older brothers and sisters, to those in high school.

I say brothers and sisters because my study of aspirations should have included equal consideration of girls. That this study concentrates solely on boys puts it in the company of many other works in the male-dominated field of sociology that exclude half the population from research. But with class and racial barriers to overcome, I felt hard-pressed to understand the situation of the boys and would have been totally incapable of doing justice to the experience of girls because yet another barrier—gender—would have to be confronted. Already thus handicapped, I felt totally incapable of considering adolescent girls in Clarendon Heights, whose situation was so far beyond my own experience.

The boys presented enough problems. I'd had the least contact with Heights teenagers. I knew a few of the Hallway Hangers on a casual basis because Stoney, Steve, Slick, and Boo-Boo had younger siblings enrolled in the youth program. Still, no relationship extended much beyond the "Hey, how's it going?" stage, and although I was never hassled coming or going from doorway #13, I was still very much of an outsider as far as the Hallway Hangers were concerned. My previous involvement in the community, however, had gained me a small degree of acceptance. They knew that I had been around for more than a year, that I worked hard, and that I got along well with many of the tenants, all of which ensured that I would be considered different from the typical university student. Had I been seen in such a light, I'm not sure I ever would have been accepted by the group, for college students were not welcome in doorway #13. My work with the Clarendon Heights Youth Program, however, allowed me to get my foot in the door and paved the way for future acceptance by the Hallway Hangers.

The Brothers were not so difficult. I played a lot of basketball with the kids in my youth group; we had a team of sorts and used to practice a few hours each week during the day. In the evenings, I invariably could be found at the park a block from Clarendon Heights playing a game of pick-up basketball with the younger kids from the project. Many of the Brothers played, too, and I soon got to know them quite well. Some of them also had younger brothers and sisters in the youth program, so they were acquainted with me from the start. In addition, I had remained close to Mike, and my association with him helped me to befriend the others. For the Brothers my status as a college student was grounds for a measure of respect rather than suspicion. Nor did they seem to distance themselves from me because I was white. How they could endure the racist taunts of the Hallway Hangers and not come to resent whites in general is difficult to comprehend. It may be that I was insensitive to any covert racial strain between the Brothers and me, but I never felt its effects.

By November 1982 I had decided to write my undergraduate thesis on the aspirations of teenage boys in Clarendon Heights. I generally spent a few hours each week down at the project seeing the ten boys in my group anyway, but I began to increase my trips to Clarendon Heights in both duration and frequency. I also made more of an effort to speak to the older guys, particularly members of the Hallway Hangers. But I had an exceptionally heavy academic workload that semester; my real fieldwork did not begin until February 1983 when I enrolled in a course in sociological field methods.

The course introduced me to the mechanics of ethnographic fieldwork. From readings, discussion, and an experienced professor, I learned about the techniques of participant observation, oral history analysis, unstructured interviews, and unobtrusive measures. I realized that the real learning would take place through firsthand experience in the field, but discussion of methods and the examination of representative sociological work using qualitative methods served as a valuable introduction.

My initial research forays into Clarendon Heights were awkward and tentative. I wanted to determine the nature of the teenagers' aspirations and the factors that contribute to their formation. Sensing that there was a conflict between the achievement ideology promulgated in school and the experiences of the boys' families, I particularly was interested in how this tension was resolved. But although it was obvious that the Brothers and the Hallway Hangers experienced school in different ways, I had no idea of the extensive disparity in their outlooks. Most of my trips down to Clarendon Heights in February and March were spent as they always had been: in the company of the younger kids in the youth program helping with homework, talking with parents, and generally maintaining contact with the families to which I had grown close. I also was spending some time with the Brothers, casually asking them about their aspirations, their high school programs, and their family backgrounds. This was possible because I had struck up friendships with Mike's closest friends: Super, Derek, and Craig. But with the Hallway Hangers my acceptance was progressing much more slowly. Those I knew would return my greeting on the street, but I still was subject to the intimidating glares with which those outside the group are greeted when walking past doorway #13. There was also an element of fear involved. I knew of the fights that took place in and around doorway #13, the heavy drinking, the drugs, and the crime. I also knew of the abuse the Brothers suffered at the hands of the Hallway Hangers and realized that, in their eyes, I was to some extent associated with the Brothers. I was fascinated by the activity in doorway #13, but I needed an "in" with the Hallway Hangers if they were to be included in the study.

Basketball provided the opportunity I was looking for. The city's Social Services Department opened up the gym in the grammar school located just across the street from the Heights for a couple of hours on two weekday evenings. The Brothers were the first to take advantage of this opportunity for pick-up basketball, along with Hank White. Hank is a big muscular fellow, slightly older than most of the Hallway Hangers, who commands the respect or fear of everybody in the neighborhood. After his sophomore year in high school, Hank spent eighteen months in a maximum security prison for allegedly taking part in a rape behind the school building. With scars dotting his face, Hank conforms to the image of the stereotypical street "hood," and the manner with which he carries himself hardly dispels that impression. Nevertheless, he was the least racist of the Hallway Hangers, for in prison he had gotten to know and like a few blacks. He enjoyed playing basketball with the Brothers and was on good terms with all of them. We had seen each other around, but it wasn't until we were matched against one another on the basketball court one evening in early March that Hank took any real notice of me. Both of us are six feet tall, but Hank has the edge in strength and basketball ability. It was a good, hard game, and when it was over we walked back to the project together. It turned out he knew I was the student who ran the youth program. In parting, he grinned at me and told me to come back next week, "so I can kick your ass again."

Thus began my friendship with Hank. Only later would I discover that my new acquaintance was a convicted rapist, and by then I was prepared to believe the disavowals of his guilt. His apparent regard for me clearly influenced the light in which the other Hallway Hangers saw me and helped facilitate my acceptance by the group. If my team had won that evening, his friendliness may well have been enmity, and my status among his friends could have been of an entirely negative type. Still, basketball was turning out to be an important vehicle for gaining acceptance into the community.

The next week a number of the other Hallway Hangers turned up at the gym to play ball. Pick-up basketball, around Clarendon Heights at least, only vaguely resembles the game played at the college and professional level. Defense is almost nonexistent, passing is kept to a minimum, and flashy moves are at a premium. We had access to only half the gym, so we played cross-wise on a reduced court, a fortunate setup because none of us was in good shape. In fact, many of the Hallway Hangers would come in to play high or drunk or both. The games were nearly as verbal as they were physical. A constant chatter of good-natured kidding and self-congratulations could be heard from most players: "Gimme that fuckin' ball! I feel hot tonight. Bang! Get out of my face, Slick. I'll put those fucking fifteen footers in all day." Matched up against Hank again, I responded to his joking insults with abuse of my own, being ever so careful not to go too far. The Hallway Hangers present noticed my familiarity with Hank and treated me accordingly. I was making progress, but it was slow and not without its problems. Every step I gained was accompanied by apprehension and doubt. That night on the basketball court a vicious fight broke out between two people on the fringes of the Hallway Hangers. Everybody else seemed to take it in stride, but I was shaken by the bloody spectacle. I was entering a new world, and I wasn't certain I could handle the situations in which I might find myself. It was an exciting time, but it also provided moments of anxiety and consternation.

The next week, while waiting outside the gym with the Brothers, I was asked to play on a team they were putting together. I readily assented. I sensed that they were confused by my developing association with the Hallway Hangers and in a sense felt betrayed. That I could enjoy their company as well as those who openly and maliciously antagonized them was incomprehensible in their eyes. So I was anxious to reestablish my allegiance to the Brothers and saw participation on their team as a good way of doing so. That same evening, however, after the usual pick-up game, I was approached by Mark, one of Frankie's older brothers recently released from prison, who wanted me to play later that night for a Clarendon Heights team against another housing project across the city. I thought that there might be a league of some kind and, as I already was committed to a team, that I should forego the opportunity. But this was simply a one-time game he had arranged, and after checking with the Brothers, I consented.

About nine of us piled into two cars and sped, screeching around corners, three miles to a grammar school gym adjacent to Lipton Park Housing Development. We lost the game, and I played horrendously, but in terms of my project significant advances were made. There is nothing like a common adversary to solidify tenuous associations and dissolve differences. That night I felt in some sense part of the Hallway Hangers and was treated, in turn, simply as a member of the group. Of course, there were still barriers, and I obviously was different from the rest, a fact that was lost on nobody when they dropped me off at the university on the way home. Nevertheless, even while they jokingly derided me for my poor performance as I climbed out of the noisy, run-down Impala, I felt a sense of belonging that hitherto had eluded me.

Only a week later, however, the status I had managed to achieve in both groups was threatened. The Brothers challenged the Hallway Hangers and their older friends to a game of basketball. Although considerably younger and smaller than the white youths, the Brothers were generally more skilled on the court and, with Craig playing, promised to give the Hallway Hangers a good game. Knowing nothing of the situation, I walked into the gym to find the younger kids cleared off their half of the court. Instead of playing floor hockey or kickball, they were seated in the bleachers, which had been pulled out of the wall for the occasion. At one end of the full-length court the Brothers were shooting at a basket; at the other end the Hallway Hangers were warming up. I heard Super blurt out, "Oh yeah, here's Jay," but I also heard a voice from the other end bellow, "It's about fucking time, Jay; we thought we'd be playing without you." Both teams expected me to play for their side, and I had no idea what to do. To choose one team meant to alienate the other. My own inclination was to go with the Brothers. I remembered the contempt with which Juan had spoken of a white friend's neutrality when a fight had broken out at school between the Brothers and a gang of white kids. I had developed close friendships with Juan, Craig, Super, and Derek, and I didn't want to let them down. On the other hand, in terms of the dynamics of the fieldwork, I needed to move closer to the Hallway Hangers. Tying up my shoe laces, I frantically tried to think of a way out of the situation but came up short.

I walked out to the center of the court where a social service worker was waiting to referee the game. He seemed concerned about the possibility of the contest turning into a violent melee and looked none too happy about his own role. Trying to assume a noncommittal air, I sauntered over to the Brothers' side and took a few shots, then walked to the other end and did the same with the Hallway Hangers. The Hallway Hangers had Hank's older brother Robbie playing, a six-foot-four-inch hardened veteran of the army's special forces. I suggested that the Brothers could use me more, that with Robbie's playing for the Hallway Hangers the game might be a blowout anyway. The curt response was something to the effect that if I wanted to play with "the niggers," that was my prerogative. Before I could reply, the referee shouted for me to play with the Brothers to even up the sides, and, hoping this intervention would mitigate the damage done, I trotted over to play with the Brothers.

The game was close and very rough, with several near-fights and nasty verbal exchanges sparked off by elbows flying under the backboards. We were much smaller than the Hallway Hangers and somewhat intimidated, but with Craig playing we undoubtedly had the most skillful player on the court. I made one lucky play early on that probably did more to establish my credibility among teenagers in the neighborhood than any other single event. With Hank coasting in for an easy lay-up, I caught him from behind and somehow managed to block his shot, flinging the ball clear across the gym. The crowd, about fifty or sixty kids from the neighborhood, roared with surprise, for such ignominy seldom befell Hank. The Brothers whooped with glee, slapping me on the back, and Hank's own teammates bombarded him with wisecracks. I couldn't suppress a grin, and Hank, taking it well, just sheepishly grinned back. Fortunately, the referee had whistled for a foul, which enabled Hank to maintain some "face." We ended up losing the game by one point, not least because I missed a foul shot in the last minute, but although bitterly disappointed, the Brothers had shown a much bigger and older team that they would not back down to them. The significance of events in the gym extended well beyond its walls, which is why such games between the two groups were contested with intensity and vigor.

At game's end, I made a point of walking back to the Heights with the Hallway Hangers, despite the questions it must have raised in the Brothers' minds as to where my loyalties really lay. As far as both groups were concerned, there was no middle ground between them. Each wondered which side I was on; my attempt to sit on the fence, I began to realize, was going to be a difficult balancing job. There would be other instances, like the basketball game, where a choice would have to be made. It was an uncomfortable position, one that plagued me throughout the research, but I derived some comfort from the fact that at least it indicated I was getting on with the fieldwork.

The research, in fact, made some significant advances that night. I hung around with the Hallway Hangers outside doorway #13 while they smoked cigarettes and talked about the game. Frankie began to insult the Brothers in no uncertain terms, glancing at me to gauge my reaction. Sensing he was trying to find out where I stood, I let it all slide, neither agreeing with him nor defending the Brothers. Finally, apparently satisfied, he said that it was a good thing I had played for the Brothers, for it had evened up the teams. In fact, it hadn't made that much of a difference, but Frankie wanted to believe that it was the sole white player on the opposition who had made the game a close one. In any case, it became clear that although my playing for the Brothers had jeopardized my standing with the Hallway Hangers, I was to emerge relatively unscathed. Soon Frankie and the others were laughing about the confusion a white player on the other team had caused, about how they had nearly passed the ball to me several times, and about the look on Hank's face when I had blocked his shot.

When I boarded the bus heading for the university, I was surprised to find Frankie right by me. Heading to see a girlfriend, he took the seat next to me and struck up a conversation. When we passed Lincoln High School, he pointed to a window in the school and noted that inside was his classroom. "What subject?" I asked, in response to which Frankie launched into a fascinating description of the Adjustment Class and his teacher Jimmy Sullivan. He told me he hoped to graduate in June, that he'd be the first of his mother's six sons to do so. After describing his brothers' experiences in prison, Frankie related in a candid and poignant tone the vulnerability he felt in his role at the Heights. "I gotta get away. I gotta do somethin'. If I don't, I'm gonna be fucked; I know it. I ain't ready for fucking prison, man." I only had seen Frankie's hard exterior, and this quite unexpected glimpse of his feelings took me by surprise. In time, I became used to some of the toughest individuals confiding in me things they rarely could reveal to their peers. This particular episode with Frankie created a small bond between the two of us that had crucial implications for my fieldwork. My friendship with Hank was important, but he spent relatively little time actually hanging in the neighborhood with the Hallway Hangers. Frankie, on the other hand, was a fixture in doorway #13 and the undisputed leader of the group. I knew from other ethnographies that good rapport with one key member is often sufficient to gain entree to even the most closed group. William Foote Whyte's sponsorship by Doc allowed him access to the Norton Street gang,[2] and Elijah Anderson's relationship with Herman opened crucial doors to the social world of streetcorner men.[3] With Frankie's friendship, my entree into the Hallway Hangers' peer group was ensured.

I remember quite distinctly the first time I actually hung in doorway #13. Of course, I'd gone into that particular stairwell countless times, for one of the boys in my youth group lived in the entryway. Even then I felt uncomfortable making my way up the dark, littered stairway through the teenagers sitting sprawled on the steps and leaning against the walls laughing, drinking beer, and smoking marijuana. Walking in with Frankie, however, was entirely different. Everybody looked up when we came in, but when Frankie initiated a conversation with me, they all, as if on cue, continued on as if I weren't there. No one questioned my presence, and I found it not at all difficult to participate in the discussions. Frankie was collecting money to buy a half pound of marijuana, Chris was peddling cocaine, and at one point someone I'd never seen before came in wanting to buy some heroin but was turned away empty-handed. My presence seemed to have no effect; it was business as usual in doorway #13.

I knew then that I had crossed an important boundary. In the weeks that followed I was amazed at how quickly I came to feel accepted by the Hallway Hangers and comfortable hanging with them in Clarendon Heights. Despite the fact that my home was in rural New Hampshire and that I was a college student, neither of which I concealed from the Hallway Hangers, I was young (looking even less than my twenty-one years), and I was white. Those two characteristics and Frankie's friendship apparently were enough to satisfy the Hallway Hangers.

Without consciously intending to do so, I began to fit in in other ways. My speech became rough and punctuated more often with obscenities; I began to carry myself with an air of cocky nonchalance and, I fear, machismo; and I found myself walking in a slow, shuffling gait that admitted a slight swagger. These were not, on the conscious level at least, mere affectations but were rather the unstudied products of my increasing involvement with the Hallway Hangers. To a large degree I was unaware of these changes; they were pointed out to me by fellow students involved in the youth program.

The world of Clarendon Heights and the world of the university were at odds with each other in almost every conceivable way. To stand with one foot in each often proved a difficult posture. It was only a ten-minute bus ride from the dark squalid confines of doorway #13 to the richly decorated college dining hall with its high ceiling and ostentatious gold chandeliers. I remember turning up for dinner directly from the Heights and unthinkingly greeting one of my upper-class friends with, "Hey Howard, what the fuck you been up to?" His startled look reminded me of where I was, and I hurriedly added, "I mean, how's your work going?" The dichotomy between the university and Clarendon Heights and the different standards of behavior expected of me in each were not sources of constant angst, but I found it somewhat difficult to adjust to the constant role changes. That I talked, walked, and acted differently on campus than I did in Clarendon Heights did not seem inconsistent, affected, or artificial to me at the time. I behaved in the way that seemed natural to me, but as Whyte points out in describing his fieldwork, what was natural at the project was bound to be different from what was natural on the college campus.[4]

In Clarendon Heights I found myself playing a number of roles, and the conflicts among these caused me the greatest consternation. In the first place, I was Jay MacLeod, human being with personal needs, including that of maintaining a certain level of self-respect. The Hallway Hangers' racism angered me a great deal, and the feeling was especially pronounced because of my proximity to the Brothers. The deep emotional scars left on the victims of racial prejudice were only too apparent. So naturally I often had the inclination to confront the racism of the Hallway Hangers, to tell them, in their terms, to "fuck off." But as a researcher I was striving to understand the boys, not change them. Challenging their racism also would be of no great help in facilitating my acceptance by the Hallway Hangers. Thus, I generally kept my mouth shut, neither questioning their racist views or defending the Brothers against bigoted remarks, an exception being the conversation that is used to introduce the Brothers in Chapter 3.

If my roles as a person and as an ethnographer sometimes conflicted, then my role as director of the youth program complicated the picture further. What did the mothers of kids in the program think of me hanging in doorway #13 with Frankie and Hank and company? This was especially serious because by that time I was associated very closely with the youth program. I was seen not just as a counselor but as the major force behind its inception and continued existence. To invite disapproval was to invite condemnation of the program. I was particularly sensitive to this issue because the youth program was still my main priority in Clarendon Heights. I tried to minimize my visibility when associating with the Hallway Hangers, a feat not particularly difficult because they preferred to stay out of view of the police. Still, when lingering outside with the Hallway Hangers, especially if they were "partying," I stepped away from the group or otherwise tried to distance myself when a mother approached. Not surprisingly, this was not a very effective maneuver, and the problem was never resolved completely.

Late one Friday night, after a great deal of alcohol and drugs had been consumed and the noise level in the hallway reflected the decreased inhibitions of the group, a mother whom I knew quite well threw open her door and yelled at everyone "to shut the hell up." Noticing me, she shook her head uncomprehendingly and went back to bed more than a little bewildered. To ease the conflict between these two roles as much as possible, I simply kept up contact with the children's parents so they could see for themselves that I was undergoing no drastic character change. Although never confronted by any of the mothers about my association with the Hallway Hangers, I sensed that it was an issue for them and that it was discussed behind my back.

However, I was able to use this role conflict to my advantage in one respect. One of the stickiest issues with which I was confronted was whether or not to join in with the drinking and use of drugs in doorway #13. As the activity in the hallway revolved to a large degree around the consumption of beer, marijuana, and other intoxicants, I could fit in most easily by doing the same. Still, I was inclined to abstain for a number of reasons. First, both are illegal in the hallway because it is public property, and I had no desire to be arrested. I already had seen Stoney arrested in doorway #13 for possession of mescaline, and a number of older youths also had been apprehended for various drug offenses. Second, I needed to be alert and perceptive in order to observe, understand, and unobtrusively participate in the dynamics of the social relations. I had enough trouble participating in the discussions and writing up accurate field notes when I was completely sober. Third, drug and alcohol use would have hurt my credibility with the children in the youth program and with their parents. This last reservation was the only one I could express to the Hallway Hangers, but they understood and accepted it completely. Although I sometimes had a shot of Peppermint Schnapps or whiskey and smoked an occasional joint, I generally abstained from using intoxicants.

Other facets of the Hallway Hangers' subculture raised few problems. I learned to take and deal out playful verbal abuse; although my wit was never as sharp as Slick's or Frankie's, my capping ability certainly improved in time. I also became comfortable with the physical jostling and sparring sessions that took place in doorway #13, although I was more careful than the others to make sure they didn't erupt into serious bouts. My strongest asset was my athletic ability, but it probably was exaggerated by my sobriety, whereas the Hallway Hangers often were impaired in one way or another. In addition to basketball, we used to play football on the hardtop area between the project's buildings. The favorite sport of white youths in the Heights, however, was street hockey, and even individuals well into their twenties got involved in the neighborhood games. Once I rediscovered a long-abandoned affinity for goalie, I strapped on Jinks's old pads and attempted to turn away the shots Shorty, Chris, Stoney, and the others would blast at the homemade goal we set up against doorway #13.

Another element of the Hallway Hangers' subculture with which I had difficulty, however, was the blatant sexism. Involved tales of sexual conquest were relatively rare; the Hallway Hangers generally didn't discuss the intricacies of their sexual lives. Still, it was quite obvious that they saw the woman's role in their relationships as purely instrumental. Women were stripped of all identity except for that bound up with their sexuality, and even that was severely restricted; the Hallway Hangers always spoke about their own experience, never about their partners' experiences. Women were reduced to the level of commodities, and the discussions in doorway #13 sometimes consisted of consumers exchanging information. "Yeah, fuckin' right, Tracy'll go down on you, man. She's got that nice long tongue, too." Because of the discomfort these conversations caused me, I avoided or ignored them whenever possible. This was a serious mistake. An analysis of the gender relations of the Hallway Hangers could have been a valuable addition to the study, but with very few field notes on the subject, I was in no position to put forth any sort of argument. I managed to stomach the racial prejudice of the Hallway Hangers and in striving to understand their racism came to see its cultural, political, and theoretical significance. Put off by their sexism, I missed an opportunity to understand it.

My fieldwork with the Brothers did not pose nearly as many complications. Neither my status as a student nor my white skin seemed to be grounds for their distrust, and with the help of my long-standing relationship with Mike, I had little difficulty gaining acceptance by the group. But with his involvement in school athletics, Mike began to spend less and less time with the Brothers during the week, and I was often the sole white person in a group of eight or nine blacks, an anomalous position that was especially pronounced when we went into black neighborhoods to play basketball. I tried to fit in by subtly affecting some of the culturally distinctive language and behavior of black youths. It wasn't until I greeted a working-class black friend at the university with "Yo Steve, what up?" and received a sharp, searching glance that I finally realized how unauthentic and artificial these mannerisms were. I dropped the pretensions and found that the Brothers were happy to accept me as I was. Although I naturally picked up some of their lingo, I felt more comfortable with the honest posture of an outsider to black culture. My ignorance of soul and funk music became something of a joke in the group, and they found my absolute inability to pick up even the most basic breakdancing moves greatly amusing.

The Brothers were interested in university life, both the educational and social sides; after a discussion of their attitudes toward Lincoln High School I invariably was called upon to relate my own college experiences. On a couple of occasions I invited them to productions sponsored by the university black students' association—plays and movies—and they seemed to enjoy and appreciate these outings. Personal friendships with each of the Brothers were much more easily and naturally established than with the Hallway Hangers and were less subject to the vicissitudes of status delineations within the group. Whereas the respect I was accorded by many of the Hallway Hangers was based initially on my friendship with Frankie, with the Brothers I was able to establish a series of distinct one-to-one relationships. Spending time with the Brothers may have been less exciting than hanging in doorway #13, but it was certainly more relaxing and pleasurable. The only strain between me and the Brothers arose because of my continued association with the Hallway Hangers. Although I was never confronted directly on this issue by the Brothers (as I was by the Hallway Hangers), they began to recount with increased frequency stories of physical and verbal abuse at the hands of the Hallway Hangers. The implication of the stories and their searching glances was clear; although the Brothers never stated it directly, they wanted to know why I was spending so much time with the Hallway Hangers. Fortunately, it wasn't long before they were provided with an answer.

By April, having established a level of trust with both the Brothers and the Hallway Hangers, I felt ready to go beyond the unobtrusive research techniques I had thus far adopted. Hitherto I had been content to elicit as much information from the youths as I could under the guise of curiosity. I knew in which high school program each of the Brothers was enrolled and had an idea of the occupational aspirations of each boy. But for the Hallway Hangers, who were less tolerant of my questions, I had very sketchy data. I needed to explain to both groups the proposed study, my role as researcher, and their role as subjects. This I did in a casual way before initiating a conversation on their aspirations. I simply explained that to graduate from college, I must write a lengthy paper and that instead of doing a lot of research in a library, "I'm gonna write it on you guys down here and what kinds of jobs you want to go into after school and stuff like that." In general, they seemed happy to be the subjects of my research and patiently answered my questions, which became gradually more direct, pointed, and frequent.

Actually, I probably should have explained my project to them much earlier, but I wanted to be considered "okay" before springing on the youths my academic interest in them. I also was reluctant to be forthright about my research intentions because I was afraid some of the Brothers whom I'd befriended would see our relationship as based on academic necessity rather than personal affinity. This wasn't the case, although there was certainly an element of truth in it, which is doubtless why it bothered me. Neither the Brothers nor the Hallway Hangers, however, seemed as sensitive to this issue as I was. Although my researcher status added a new dimension to my relationship with each youth, all seemed willing to accept and distinguish between my academic agenda and my personal regard.

The revelation of my scholarly interest in the boys had one very important positive ramification. It gave me a special position in both groups, a niche that justified my continued presence but set me apart from the others. Whereas previously neither the Brothers nor the Hallway Hangers could understand my association with the other group, my involvement with both became much more explicable once I revealed in full my intentions. As Frankie explained to a fringe member of the Hallway Hangers who confronted me as I emerged from Super's apartment, "No man, see, to do his shit right for his studies he's got to check out the fuckin' niggers, too." Likewise, the Brothers had more tolerance for the time I spent with the Hallway Hangers. Although simultaneous affiliation with both peer groups still caused problems for which there was no solution and with which I found myself constantly burdened, the situation improved significantly.

This position of being at once of and yet apart from the group had other positive implications, especially for my standing with the Hallway Hangers. There are many things that go along with membership in that subculture of which I wanted no part: the violence, the excessive consumption of alcohol and drugs, and the strident racism and sexism. Had I completely integrated myself into the group, I would have been expected to partake of all of the above. Fortunately, the unwritten rules that govern the behavior of the Hallway Hangers did not always apply to me. Had I been vociferously insulted by another member, for instance, I would not be confronted necessarily with the only two options normally open to an individual in that situation: fight or lose a great deal of social standing in the group. For this special status within the group I was thankful.

I was not, however, totally free of the group's status delineations. The fact that I spent a good deal of time with the Hallway Hangers talking, joking, exchanging insults, and playing sports meant that I could not stay entirely outside the group's pecking order, even if my position in it was very fluid. My friendships with Hank and, especially, Frankie must have troubled those who received less attention from them when I was present. I wanted to excel in some of the things that matter to the Hallway Hangers in order to gain their respect, but attempting to do so necessarily threatened the status of others in the group. It was the same situation I faced on the basketball court that first evening with Hank: I wanted to play well, but I didn't want to imperil his status on the court. Hanging in doorway #13, I learned to be acutely aware of status demarcations and the threat I posed to the standing of other individuals. I would try to placate those whose positions suffered at my expense by self-disparagement and by consciously drawing attention to their superiority over me. I'm certain that I was not as sensitive to these situations as I could have been, but I did come to realize the importance of minimizing the degree to which I could be regarded as a threat by other members of the group. The success of my project depended on good relations not just with Frankie and Slick, but with Shorty, Chris, Boo-Boo, Stoney, Steve, and Jinks as well.

Once I told the youths of my sociological interest in them, I set about gathering information more aggressively. I was intent on amassing material on their attitudes toward school and subsequent employment, but I was still very much at the reconnaissance stage; these unstructured interviews were a preliminary ground survey. Still, my conversations with boys from both groups often were quite lengthy and covered a great many topics. Taping the discussions or taking notes, obviously, was out of the question, so I was forced to rely on my memory. After a conversation with one of the boys, I'd hop on the bus and return to my dorm room immediately, preferably without speaking to anyone, and promptly write up the interview. At first, I made summary notes of the interview, remembering as much of what was said as I could and putting it in paragraph format. I was able to recall more, however, when I tried to reconstruct the interview word for word and wrote it up in script form with each question and answer. The more interviews I conducted and recorded, the better my concentration and memory became, until I could recall most of what was said in a thirty-minute discussion. Writing up the interview as soon as possible with no distractions was crucial. I remember having an excellent discussion with Super, Mokey, and Craig on the way to play basketball at the Salvation Army gym. But after playing two hours of ball, conversing on the way back to the Heights, and finally returning to my room to write up the interview, I had forgotten a great deal of it. Writing up interviews was extraordinarily tedious, especially because after conducting a good interview one wants to relax, but the importance of good field notes was impressed upon me by my professor and was indeed borne out by my own experience.

The requirements for my field methods course spurred me to conduct as many unstructured interviews as I could, for by mid-May I had to produce a paper on my project. By that time I had managed to conduct interviews with fourteen boys, eleven of whom would end up in the final study. I had information on all seven of the Brothers, but only on Chris, Boo-Boo, Stoney, and Frankie of the Hallway Hangers. Except in the cases of Mike and Frankie, the material was very thin, often including not much more than their high school programs, their attitudes toward school, and their expressed aspirations or expectations.

To gain a measure of understanding of the high school curriculum I obtained a detailed course catalogue and conducted an interview with Karen Wallace, the school's career counselor. That I was compelled to examine and organize the data I had collected and search it for patterns and findings at that stage of the research was fortunate. Fieldwork is an organic process that should include a nearly continuous analysis and reorganization of the material into patterns and models that in turn guide the fieldwork in new directions. Writing the final paper for the class forced me to consolidate my research, and although a detailed picture of the social landscape did not emerge, I did gain a vantage point from which to formulate a strategy for exploring in greater depth the terrain staked out for study.

That strategy included fieldwork in the Lincoln School: observation in the classroom and semiformal interviews with teachers, guidance counselors, and ad-

ministrators. I also planned to interview as many of the Hallway Hangers' and
Brothers' parents to whom I could gain access as possible, a number I estimated at
about one-half the total. Most important, I decided to conduct semiformal, in-
depth interviews with all of the boys. My research demanded detailed data on
each boy's family background and their experiences in and approaches to school
and work, information I could elicit most effectively in private discussions relatively free of distraction. I was unable to construct with sufficient depth a portrait
of each individual by piecing together the bits and pieces of data I collected on the
street, no matter how much time I spent with each group; I needed to sit down
and talk with each boy for an hour or so to gather simple data, such as family
members' occupational histories, as well as to probe intricate issues like the degree to which each had internalized the achievement ideology. To this end, I drew
up an interview guide, a list of issues that I wanted addressed in each discussion. I
did not always stick to the guide, but having it before me in abbreviated form prevented me from missing crucial questions when the conversation got too intriguing. The guide also jogged my memory when I wrote up the discussion.

Unfortunately, the interview guide lay dormant for nearly two months, and
much of the ethnographic strategy never saw the light of day at all. I simply was
too busy with the youth program during the spring and summer to concentrate
on the research. I failed to do any substantive fieldwork in the high school aside
from conducting interviews with Bruce Davis and Jimmy Sullivan, and in
Clarendon Heights I only managed to undertake interviews with Derek and
Chris. But in September 1983 my work got a big boost.

Instead of returning to a university dormitory, I moved into a recently vacated,
rent-controlled apartment in a large tenement building directly across the street
from Clarendon Heights. It was a run-down, cockroach-infested dwelling, but it
was large, cheap, and gave me a much-needed base where people could find me
and I could conduct interviews. This move enhanced my research in vital ways.
Spending time with the Brothers and the Hallway Hangers was no longer a com-
muting hassle but rather a break from studying, a way to relax and enjoy myself.
Living so near Clarendon Heights, despite my continued status as a full-time student, also gave me a better feeling for the rhythm of the community and further
reduced the degree to which I was an outsider, both in their eyes and in mine. Although my residence in the neighborhood was not free of complications, it
marked a positive new development in my research and in my relationship with
the entire community.

I began interviewing individuals in the apartment in October. Each interview
would last approximately an hour, and I found that even if I made extensive notes
it was difficult to recall with precision all that had been said. Finally, I decided that
the formality of a tape recorder would be no worse than the formality of the interview guide. I tried it a few times, and although it certainly made people self-con-
scious at the beginning of the interview and probably deterred some of the Hallway Hangers from being as frank as they might have been about their criminal

exploits, the benefits seemed to outweigh the disadvantages. Transcribing the tapes, however, was just as tedious as writing up the discussions from memory, for it generally took at least four or five hours and sometimes up to seven.

Both the Brothers and the Hallway Hangers regarded these interviews as a favor to me. The Brothers generally were more accommodating; I had little difficulty cajoling them up to my apartment for the required session. The Hallway Hangers were more elusive. Theirs is a world in which something is very seldom had for nothing, and they saw quite clearly that there was nothing in this project for them. I was the one meeting an academic requirement for a college degree, a principal attainment in my own pursuit of "success." In a year's time I would be studying on a scholarship in Oxford, England; most of the Hallway Hangers would be back in doorway #13, in the armed forces, or in prison. To be fair, I had contributed to the community through the youth program, as the Hallway Hangers were well aware. They didn't see me as "using" them. However, they did sense an imbalance in the relationship, and when I requested an hour of their time to level a barrage of personal questions at them, many of the Hallway Hangers vaguely expected something in return.

It soon became clear, however, that I had very little to give. I couldn't help the Hallway Hangers with their academic work as I did with the Brothers because those who were still in school very seldom did any. I did assist Slick when he was struggling to finish the work required for his G.E.D., and some of the Hallway Hangers would approach me about legal or personal problems with the often mistaken hope that I could be of some help. More often, however, the requests were less innocent.

Like all the people aged twenty or so who spent any time in doorway #13, I was asked to buy beer for the Hallway Hangers. These requests put me in a difficult position. I wanted to be of some use to the Hallway Hangers, but, well aware of the debilitating role of alcohol in their lives, I didn't want to buy them beer. Moreover, although the risk of police detection was not particularly high, other Clarendon Heights tenants easily might discover what I was doing. Nevertheless, I did make a couple of trips to the local package store for the Hallway Hangers. Those two trips attest, I think, to the unease I felt about the one-way nature of my involvement with the Hallway Hangers, to my desire to maintain my standing in the group, and, of course, to their powers of persuasion and manipulation. One of the biggest mistakes one can make in the company of the Hallway Hangers is to appear hesitant or uncertain; after I decided that buying beer for them was ethically dubious and pragmatically stupid, I answered their subsequent requests with an adamant "no" and was frank and honest in dealing with their appeals and protests.

Despite the fact that there continued to be much take and little give in my relationship with the Hallway Hangers, I did manage to get them all up to my apartment for a taped interview that autumn. In the end, sensing how important it was to me, the Hallway Hangers did the interviews as a personal favor. Some of them consented immediately, and we did the interview as soon as we had some common time free. Getting some of the others up to my apartment in front of the tape recorder was a significant achievement. Stoney, for example, is a very private person. Rather than undergo the weekly ordeal of having to talk about his "drug problem" with a counselor at the city's drug clinic, Stoney opted for a three-month stint in the county jail. In trying to gauge the influence his mother has on him, I asked in the actual interview if they had ever discussed his performance in school. "I didn't talk to her that much. I'm not the type of person who opens up and talks to people. That's why it took you so long to get me up here. I go to the drug clinic, and the lady just asks me questions. I hate it. I just ask her back why she wants to ask me this for. I'm not into it. I'm just doing this for a favor to you."

Once up in the apartment, many of the Hallway Hangers actually seemed to enjoy the interview. Boo-Boo and Frankie both stated that it was good to discuss and examine their feelings and thoughts. I was impressed by the honesty and thoughtfulness with which the Hallway Hangers answered my often probing questions. The Brothers were no less candid, but I had expected the Hallway Hangers to be less forthright and honest. Only Shorty refused to take the interview seriously and maintained a level of distance and invulnerability throughout the session.

Chris and Jinks came up to the apartment together. As Chris already had been interviewed, Jinks and I left him in the kitchen and went into the small room I used as a study where we talked for nearly ninety minutes. We emerged to find Chris sitting at the kitchen table smoking a joint. On the table was a mound of marijuana, probably a half pound, which Chris was rolling mechanically into thin joints at an amazing pace. Chris must have seen the look of surprise on my face because he immediately offered up a couple of joints to placate me. Jinks and I had a good laugh but were interrupted by the doorbell. My mirth faded quickly as I figured that with my luck the police were onto Chris and had picked this opportune moment to make the arrest. Fortunately, it was only Craig and Super inviting me to play ball in the park. I declined and quickly shut the door before they could catch a glimpse of Chris and Jinks or a whiff of the joint. I sat in the study and began to transcribe the tape while in the kitchen Chris rolled his joints and Jinks smoked.

I conducted a number of discussions with more than one individual, but one really stands out in importance for the amount of information it produced. On a cold afternoon in December I managed to assemble Frankie, Slick, Shorty, Chris, and Jinks in my apartment. The discussion, which lasted more than an hour and a half, began this way.

FRANKIE: Okay, man, ask us a fucking question, that's the deal.

JM: I wanna know what each of you wants to do, now and ...

CHRIS: I wanna get laid right now (*laughter*).

JM: Everyone tell me what they wanna be doing in twenty years.

SHORTY: Hey, you can't get no education around here unless if you're fucking rich, y'know? You can't get no education. Twenty years from now Chris'll prob'ly be in some fucking gay joint, whatever (*laughter*). And we'll prob'ly be in prison or dead (*laughter*). You can't get no education around here.

JM: How's that though? Frankie, you were saying the other day that this city has one of the best school systems around (*all laugh except Frankie*).

FRANKIE: Lincoln is the best fucking school system going, but we're all just fucking burnouts. We don't give a fuck.

SHORTY: I ain't a fucking burnout, man.

JINKS: (*sarcastically*) You're all reformed and shit, right?

SHORTY: Shut up, potato head.

I had very little control of the interview and wasn't able to cover all of the ground that I'd hoped to, but the material that emerged as the conversation swept along from subject to subject was very rich and poignant. Disagreements and conflicts between individuals, some of which I actively probed, produced some fervid and well-argued viewpoints that never would have emerged from an individual interview. It took me an entire day to transcribe the discussion, and I never had time to conduct another one, but the yield from this group interview was very impressive. Although the ethnographer must weigh the impact of the dynamics of the discussion on its content, this added task should not deter researchers from cultivating this fertile area more thoroughly than I did.

By November, time constraints were cutting into more than my capacity to conduct group interviews. I had to scrap my plans to do any kind of extensive fieldwork in the school. Although I had interviewed only half the subjects in the study, I already had accumulated more than three hundred pages of field notes and interview transcriptions. I desperately wanted to interview as many of the youths' parents as I could, for I saw that as crucial to the study. In fact, I still see it as crucial to the study, but I simply did not have the time to conduct interviews with more than two mothers—Stoney's and Mokey's. Chapter 3 consequently is incomplete, and I think the study as a whole suffers from the limitations on my research into each boy's family. Another important item on my fieldwork agenda that I never was able to carry out and that would have been quite enjoyable was hanging at Pop's, the little store where the Hallway Hangers and their friends congregated during the school day. These casualties of my research strategy were the unfortunate results of my full-time student status and of the community work with which I continued to be involved in Clarendon Heights.

After I moved into the apartment, I found myself entwined in the lives of many families to a degree I hadn't experienced before. Youngsters in the youth program would stop by to say hello or to ask for help with their schoolwork, as did the Brothers. During this period I became very close friends with Billy, the former member of the Hallway Hangers who had won a scholarship to college as a high school junior the previous spring. Billy was struggling with the academic workload of the Fundamental School, having recently switched from Occupational Education, so I ended up spending about ten hours a week assisting him with homework, advising him about college admissions, and generally just hacking around. I also became a regular tutor to an eighth grader who had been in my youth group the previous three summers. He really was struggling in school, both academically and with respect to discipline, and at his mother's urging I met with his teachers, but to no particular avail. In none of these roles did I consider myself a social worker. I was simply a friend, and I probably got more out of these relationships in terms of personal satisfaction and fulfillment than they got from me. Sometimes the rewards were more tangible: A Haitian family to which I'd grown particularly close used to cook me a delicious West Indian meal about once a week, brought to my apartment wrapped in dish towels by nine-year-old Mark, fourteen-year-old Kerlain, or sixteen-year-old Rhodes.

Despite the fact that I never was viewed as a social worker, except perhaps as a very unorthodox and informal one, I was approached more and more often by people with serious problems. I stopped by to see Freddie Piniella, a tough little twelve-year-old kid whom I'd known for three years. He wasn't home, but his mother was. Mrs. Piniella always had maintained a cool distance from me, but suddenly she began to relate in a subdued, beaten tone her daughter Vicki's predicament. Vicki was a resilient fourteen-year-old girl whose violent temper, exceptionally loud voice, and strong frame made her at once an object of grudging admiration and resentment by her peers. Mrs. Piniella had found out that morning that Vicki was pregnant, well past her first trimester. She would need to have an abortion, but Mrs. Piniella had less than eighty dollars in the bank, and the cost of terminating such a late pregnancy was more than five hundred dollars. Mrs. Piniella, a part-time custodial worker at the university, was on welfare, but the state would under no circumstances, not even rape, fund abortions. I agreed to try finding a hospital or clinic that would carry out the operation at a reduced cost, but none of the places I contacted would do so for a pregnancy beyond the third month. Nor could Planned Parenthood or any other agency direct me to a hospital that would.

I returned the next day to report this news, only to hear from her very depressed mother that Vicki, it turned out, had gonorrhea as well. Eventually a social worker attached to the local health clinic located a hospital that would accept a reduced payment on a monthly basis, and Vicki had the abortion and was treated for venereal disease. I don't know how Vicki managed to cope with the strain of the whole experience, but I spoke with her the next week, and she seemed very composed. Her plight had quite an effect on me and pointed up the dichotomy between Clarendon Heights and the university more starkly than ever.

It was an ironic contrast to learn of her predicament and then to hear the consternation my student friends were expressing about their upcoming midterm exams.

One morning in mid-December I was awakened by the door buzzer at four o'clock. It was a very cold Super who had left home two days earlier after being beaten by his father. I found a blanket, and he slept on my couch. Later that morning we tried to decide what to do. Super was adamant in his refusal even to consider going home and trying to reach some sort of reconciliation with his parents. He had come that night from his uncle's apartment on the other side of the city, but reported that his uncle had a severe drinking problem and was prone to violent outbursts. With nowhere else to go, Super urged me to find a place for him in a home for runaways. So together we embarked on a very circuitous, time-consuming, and frustrating exploration of the social service bureaucracy. No shelter for teenagers would accept Super without a referral from a social worker, but the city's Social Services Department would not assign him one. Instead, they insisted on tracking down his family's social worker, a process that took four days. We finally got the woman's name and phoned her office repeatedly, but she must have been exceedingly busy because we never heard back from her. I called the high school, and Super finally managed to get one of the youth workers attached to the school to secure him a place in a teenage runaway home. By that time, however, all the beds were full, and he was put on a waiting list. Finally, after more than a week with me, Super moved into a youth home for ten days before returning to his family in Clarendon Heights. I always had assumed that the stories I'd heard from residents about the inefficiency and ineptitude of the social services bureaucracy were exaggerated. Now I was not so sure, although the problem clearly lay not with the social workers themselves; the problem was too little funding and too much work. It was, however, especially frustrating to be asked by those who could not deal effectively with Super's situation whether I was aware that it was against the law to harbor a runaway.

During the year I spent conducting research in Clarendon Heights I often was troubled by legal issues. By spending time with the Hallway Hangers in doorway #13 I quite clearly ran the risk of arrest, but this was not especially distressing. Had I been corralled in one of the periodic police raids of the hallway, the charges against me would have been minimal, if any were brought at all. Although being in the presence of those smoking marijuana was illegal, possession of narcotics, especially with intent to sell, is what the police were generally after. Still, I saw people arrested in Clarendon Heights for simply having a beer in their hand, so I had to contend with the possibility of arrest. Had that happened, I certainly would have had a lot of explaining to do: to kids in the youth program and their parents, to the Brothers, to university officials, and to my parents.

A greater cause for concern was my unprotected legal status as a researcher. Whereas lawyers, journalists, doctors, and clergy can withhold information to protect their clients, for academic researchers there is no clearcut right of confidentiality. If any law enforcement official came to know about my study, my field notes could be used as evidence, and I could be put on the witness stand and questioned. In such a situation I would have two options: incriminate my friends or perjure myself. To avoid such a dilemma, my field methods professor urged me to explain to the youths that I preferred not to hear about their criminal exploits or at least not to record their accounts in my notes. But I found the criminal activity of the Hallway Hangers very interesting and also quite relevant to the study. Besides, my legal position was no different from their own. The Hallway Hangers had all the information I did, undoubtedly more, and they had no legal coverage, nor were they particularly worried about it. I was a more likely source for the district attorney because as a university student I was presumably less concerned about indicting my friends than I would be about lying under oath. Not wanting to draw attention to this fact and risk losing the trust of the Hallway Hangers, I made no effort to remain ignorant of potentially incriminating information, although I destroyed or erased all the interview tapes and was exceptionally careful with my field notes.

In fact, one absolutely hallowed rule among the Hallway Hangers and a large proportion of the project's older residents was not to "rat" to the police. As an ethnographer I wasn't interested in passing an ethical judgment on this maxim. I was there to understand as much as I could, and selective noncooperation with the police seemed to make sense as a means of self-protection for a certain segment of the community. When I saw two young men who recently had been released from prison arrested while they sat quietly drinking bottles of beer on the steps of doorway #13 and realized that the "offense" would mean up to six months in prison for them as a violation of parole, I began to appreciate people's reluctance to cooperate with the police.

My own subscription to this maxim was put to a very serious test in mid-October. Paddy, a Green Berets veteran on the fringes of the Hallway Hangers, shot his girlfriend Doreen, and I was the sole witness. Doreen, whom I knew well, wasn't critically wounded; the bullet pierced her arm and lodged in her breast, and after undergoing surgery she recovered rapidly and was out of the hospital in a few days. The details of the incident and subsequent events are too involved to relate here, so I'll concentrate on the issues I had to face as a citizen, as a researcher, and as a member of the Clarendon Heights community.

I was questioned by the police at the scene of the crime first as a suspect and then as a witness. I hadn't actually seen the shooting itself, but I had overheard the preceding altercation from within my apartment and knew what had happened. My first inclination was to relate everything, but I checked myself and repeatedly told the officers only what I'd seen after hearing the shot and running out into the street, thereby leaving out the key incriminating material I had heard. Doreen, it turned out, also refused to incriminate Paddy, but the police were nevertheless quite confident that he had committed the crime. He was arrested, but when Doreen refused to bring criminal charges, it looked as though the case might be dropped. Instead, the state decided to press charges, and I soon received a letter from an assistant district attorney asking me to phone him.

I was faced with a serious problem. Do I tell the whole truth, incriminate Paddy, and see justice done the American way? I had a number of doubts about this course, not all of them pragmatic, such as my physical well-being, my standing in the community, and the future of the study. Practically speaking, to "finger" Paddy would have had disastrous consequences, and I think most people under the circumstances would have balked at full cooperation with the authorities. I also happen to think that withholding information was not only expedient but also morally justifiable. Such an opinion may be pure self-delusion, as most people to whom I've related the incident seem to think, but from my position I couldn't help feeling that way.

As a member of the Clarendon Heights community and more particularly as a trusted associate of the Hallway Hangers, I felt in some ways that it was incumbent upon me to subscribe to their behavioral codes. There were obviously limits to this adherence; other duties or commitments (e.g., to justice) could override this allegiance to the group's rules of conduct, but I definitely felt in some sense drawn to respect the code of silence.

There were, of course, competing impulses. Paddy had shot and could easily have killed Doreen, and no community wants to tolerate that sort of behavior. Yet they were both very high and very drunk, and a violent argument had precipitated the incident. In addition, the shooting was not completely intentional (she was shot through a closed door), and Paddy immediately had repented of his action, rushing her amid hysterical tears to the hospital. Moreover, Doreen herself had lied in order to protect Paddy, and the two of them were back living together within a matter of days. But although I was conscious of these circumstances, they failed to diminish my conviction that Paddy should be punished.

Still, having spent the bulk of the previous summer researching prison life as part of a project undertaken by the kids in my youth group, and having tutored inmates at a state prison, I knew only too well what kind of impact a stint behind bars was likely to have on Paddy. In the end, this proved decisive. I was unwilling to jeopardize all that I had gained in Clarendon Heights in order to put Paddy in prison when he was likely to come out a much more dangerous person.

I decided to say nothing about the argument that preceded the shooting. When the trial finally took place in midwinter after a number of postponements, Paddy was found guilty despite my incomplete testimony, so all my speculation turned out to be academic. Convicted of illegal possession of a firearm, illegal discharge of a firearm, and assault with a deadly weapon, Paddy was sentenced to serve two years in a state prison. I didn't feel good about my role in the proceedings, especially refraining from providing information under oath, but neither did I lose sleep over the incident. Bourgeois morality has diminished relevance in a place like Clarendon Heights where the dictates of practical necessity often leave very little "moral" ground on which to stand.

During the fall of 1983 I felt myself drawn into the community as I had never been before, into its political and social life and into the web of personal, economic, and social problems that plague its residents. At the university, I had a full academic schedule, a work-study job, and a large extracurricular load. It was a very busy time, and I also found it emotionally draining, especially in trying to reconcile the two lives I led: the one on the university campus and the other on the streets of Clarendon Heights.

It was, of course, this study that bridged the two worlds. One of the most challenging (and rewarding) aspects of an ethnographic study is the synthesis the sociologist must create between a perceived intellectual tradition and the data daily emerging from the fieldwork. Without a theoretical framework to make some sense of the overwhelming quantity and variety of empirical material, the researcher would be swimming in a sea of field notes, each new interview tossing him or her in a different direction. By the same token, there is all too much theoretical abstraction with no experiential grounding whatsoever coming from scholars who are locked in their academic offices. This book began with a review of reproduction theory and, after the ethnographic material was laid out, moved on to a reconsideration of the theoretical perspective. That is the way this intellectual enterprise was actually carried out, although the progression was not nearly so linear. Since the beginning of the fieldwork in spring 1983 I had been studying the theoretical literature. The thinking of Bowles and Gintis, Bourdieu, Bernstein, and especially Willis (I didn't read Giroux until long afterward) informed my own thinking at every stage of the research. My empirical data and the theoretical perspective were held in a kind of dialectical tension, and I found myself moving back and forth between the two until my own ideas coalesced.

The emergence of my ideas was a slow, circuitous process; I had expected to have problems analyzing the data, but the earlier stage of simply organizing the empirical material proved more difficult than I had foreseen. By January 1984 I had in excess of five hundred pages of field notes. By March I had to turn this mass of data into a senior honors thesis. I knew the analytical and theoretical sections would prove intellectually taxing, but I didn't realize how difficult it would be to organize my notes into the basically descriptive chapters on the peer group, family, work, and school.

I failed to make theoretical notes throughout the months of research. I had plenty of notes depicting events and conversations, but kept no record of my more abstract sense of the observed phenomena. By November, the ideas that make up the backbone of Chapter 7 were beginning to emerge, albeit in a rough and rudimentary form. I was especially cognizant of these ideas in carrying out the remaining interviews and strove to collect information that would help determine the validity of my fresh theoretical discernments. The entire research period, in fact, involved a nearly constant appraisal and reappraisal of abstract ideas I thought could help me make sense of the data. But, ludicrously, I kept no written record of the development of these ideas. I would mentally cultivate and modify my views in line with the empirical material, but I should have noted after every interview how the new data had forced revisions in or had affirmed my previous thinking. Had I kept such notes, the stage between the end of my fieldwork and the beginning of the actual writing would have been considerably less hectic and would have filled me with much less dread.

I remember spending days reading through my field notes again and again, sifting through the material trying to come up with an organizational framework. I began keeping a record of all new insights, some of which would come to me at the most bizarre times and places, often touched off by a chance incident or a stray comment. In order to get some sort of grasp on the data, I developed a one-page index for each youth, on which I recorded information that struck me as particularly relevant or important. Perhaps the most useful organizing tool I employed was a huge chart that contained for each individual information on the following specifications: race, peer group, high school grade level, school program, expressed aspiration, acceptance of achievement ideology, faith in the efficacy of schooling, father in the household, employment of father, employment of mother, educational attainments of parents, duration of tenancy in public housing, duration of tenancy in Clarendon Heights, and whether the subject smokes cigarettes, drinks alcohol, smokes marijuana, or has been arrested. Once the data had been systematically laid out, patterns began to emerge.

Such patterns gave form and further meaning to the lives of these boys and helped me measure the relative significance of the various structural and cultural factors that shape aspirations. Ultimately, however, it was on the basketball court with the Brothers or in doorway #13 with the Hallway Hangers that I gained whatever understanding I eventually achieved.

Second Harvest: Notes on the 1991 Field Experience

The fieldwork for the original study took place when I transformed a work site into a research venue in 1983. Having directed a youth program in Clarendon Heights, I was trusted by its teenage tenants, who agreed to help with my undergraduate thesis. When I returned eight years later to undertake research for the revised edition, Clarendon Heights had changed, and so had I. Moreover, the thesis had turned into a successful sociology textbook. I had maintained contact with some of the young men over the years, but many relationships had lapsed. Having taken up residence elsewhere, I no longer had a base in the community.

Thus I crossed the street to Clarendon Heights in July 1991 nearly as nervous as when I first arrived ten years earlier. I needn't have worried. "Hey Jay," Steve rang out, "what the fuck brings you back to the Ponderosa?" I was coming *back*. My history in Clarendon Heights meant that its residents were even more affable, accommodating, and forthcoming this time than they had been in the 1980s. The anecdotal account that follows gives a brief sketch of my field experience in 1991.

Although the Brothers and the Hallway Hangers had scattered, tracking them down proved less troublesome than I expected. Several lived nearby and seemed glad to see me. They were excited about being the subjects of a book and pledged to help me with an updated edition. Mostly, they wanted to know how many millions of dollars I'd made on the book, why I'd spent four years in a Mississippi backwater as a community organizer, and why I was shortly returning to a place even more obscure—England. Informed of my intention to become an Anglican priest, a disclosure that instantly kills conversations in sociology circles, these guys were apt to ask about discounts for christenings, weddings, and funerals. The Brothers and the Hallway Hangers also pressed me for details about my wife.

In turn, I pressed each of them for an interview to discover how they had fared in the eight years since I'd done the original research. Most of the interviews were undertaken in the back of a neighborhood bar and restaurant that a friend of mine owns about a mile from Clarendon Heights. I spoke with others in their homes, at their work sites, and in my car. With their permission I recorded most of the interviews on microcassettes. Only Super was understandably dubious. I started slowly in that interview, and as his wariness eased he forgot about the recorder and spoke with surprising candor about his drug dealing.

Boo-Boo also spoke frankly about his criminal activities. This interview was done in my car because Boo-Boo was living several miles from Clarendon Heights. We decided to drive around while we talked, a dumb idea. Doing an interview while wheeling around a city will result in a bad interview, an accident, or both. I pulled into a suburban shopping center and parked the car as we talked on. After describing his night-deposit robberies, Boo-Boo told of being confronted by a pistol-waving partner over a crack sale gone sour. Suddenly, there came a knock on my car window. In the same instant several police cruisers converged on our car. I looked up into the grim face of a policeman who motioned with one hand for me to roll down the window, the other hand on his holster. I looked helplessly at Boo-Boo as I eased down my window. The other cops stayed in their cruisers. Bidden to get my license and registration and to get out of the car, I surreptitiously turned off the tape recorder and did as I was told. Shoppers stopped and stared. I was stunned. I figured that with all Boo-Boo's violent drug troubles in Raymond, there was bound to be a warrant out for his arrest. So I vowed neither to divulge Boo-Boo's identity nor to let on about the book. I showed the police officer my license. He asked me what we were doing.

JM: Just talking.

PO: Just talking, huh?

JM: Yessir.

PO: You come all the way up from Mississippi to have a little chat? Who's your partner?

JM: Actually, I'm shortly off to England where I'll be training to be a priest.

PO: Uh-huh. Who's your partner?

JM: I'm not sure of his name.

This wasn't exactly convincing, so I explained that I studied at a nearby university years ago, ran a youth project in a poor neighborhood, and was close to Boo-Boo's sister Shelly. Because Boo-Boo is struggling with some traumatic personal problems, Shelly asked me to speak with him. As she is only his stepsister, I don't know his last name. It suddenly dawned on me that except for the last bit, this was quite true, and I stopped on a note of triumph. The officer showed rather less enthusiasm for the story. So I fumbled about in my wallet, hoping against all hope that I'd kept an old college ID, the only one with a decent photo. I found it, saved by my vanity. As the policeman turned the ID over in his hand, it seemed to dawn on him that my car trunk might not be full of heroin or assault weapons. Disappointed, he waved the other cruisers away but continued to question me closely. Pressed about Boo-Boo's identity and address, and about what we were doing, I ducked and drifted and parried weakly. I kept imagining the cop would reach into the front seat, pick up the tape recorder, and play back Boo-Boo's detailed disclosure of his criminal career.

Eventually the police officer called to his partner, who had been interrogating Boo-Boo, and they retired to their car. They seemed to spend ages on the radio, confirming our identities, checking my license and car registration, and comparing our stories. Then he returned to give me back my license and apologize for the half-hour inconvenience. He invited me to consider how suspicious we looked sitting outside a supermarket in a car with Mississippi plates. Instead of berating him for flouting police procedure and our civil liberties, I nodded meekly and he let us go. Evidently they didn't compare our stories too closely, for when I sank into the seat beside Boo-Boo and asked what he'd said, he replied, "Nuthin' really. Just our names, where I live, what we're doing, y'know, having an interview. He was real interested in your book."

As we drove away and resumed the interview (not such a dumb idea after all), Boo-Boo apologized for the incident as if it were his fault.

BOO-BOO: I'm sorry about that whole thing. You can't even sit in a car talking to me cuz I'm black. Shoot, these cops are so prejudiced around here.

Juan suggested I interview him as we drove to pick up his girlfriend. The drive took only fifteen minutes but he assured me she would be late. She was waiting at the curb when we drove up. Subsequently I struggled to set a time to speak with him. In the end, I went to Jim's Tow and caught him at work. I put in a tape, and Juan and I chatted as he painted a fender and then tinkered with an engine. When other employees began to pause as they passed by, I stuffed the small recorder into my pocket, thinking it would still pick up our conversation. That tape wasn't easy to transcribe. Juan's voice had been muffled even with the recorder perched on the car.

Slick's tape was also difficult to transcribe. I'd spent a few evenings hanging around his apartment, mostly playing with his baby son while he and Denise argued in an adjacent room. Without saying so, Slick seemed wary of doing an interview. The intervening seven years hadn't gone as he'd hoped. He was the proud father of two children. But he also had a difficult job, a girlfriend strung out on crack, and a rundown home. I stopped by one evening and the living room was full. Slick had just returned home from the construction site and was showering. Denise had three friends over, and there were three toddlers scrambling about on the floor. One child reached up and pulled a bottle of beer off a table. The women screamed, the babies shrieked, and Slick came in to suggest that we go out to do that interview. I knew that this was an escape from domestic duties and household chaos; I also knew that Denise was not pleased. But I jumped at the opportunity and lost little time in taking Slick to a cafeteria for dinner. "Turn the tape on," Slick commanded shortly after we sat down, "I don't give a fuck if people think I'm an FBI rat." We had an excellent talk over a good meal. Only later did I discover how easily voices are drowned out by background music and meal-time clatter.

The interviews done in prison were not tape-recorded. It shouldn't have been difficult to visit Stoney and Chris in prison, but it was. Stoney was in Carlisle State Prison twenty miles away. I called ahead to inquire about attire and was told not to wear jeans. I arrived fifteen minutes early, filled out the paperwork, placed the contents of my pockets along with my belt and wristwatch into a locker, and presented myself at the desk. "Sorry, you can't come in with that T-shirt on." I protested to no avail. Since it was a plain T-shirt, she explained, I could easily be confused with the prisoners. Shaking with anger, I extracted a promise that if I returned with a different shirt within half an hour, they would let me in. I ran back to the parking lot, jumped in my car, and raced into the surrounding countryside. Smack in the middle of a rural region, I sped along dusty lanes for fifteen frustrating minutes until I came upon a general store. They had one shirt, a massive T-shirt emblazoned with the cartoon character Roger Rabbit, protesting "I was framed." I bought it.

Back at the visitors' desk, I was told this time that no T-shirts whatsoever could be worn into the prison complex. Fairly bursting with rage, I demanded to see the supervisor and was eventually let in because he found my story and my shirt so funny. I took off my shoes, strode through the metal detector, stopped to be frisked, and stepped into the steel trap. Finally I was ushered into the visitors' room where I sat for thirty minutes. Eventually, a guard came up to tell me that Stoney had been moved that afternoon to Grassmoor Prison thirty miles away.

A few days later I turned up at Grassmoor and was told that Stoney was off the premises for a physical. I waited in the parking lot for an hour until a prison van drove up and Stoney and two other inmates climbed out, accompanied by two guards. Pleased to finally have Stoney in my sights, I waved like an idiot and received several searching stares. Then recognition broke over Stoney's face and he came to greet me. He had minimum-security status because of severe overcrowding in the state prison system, and so we went out in the yard and talked at a picnic table. He brought me up to date on his parents, brothers, girlfriend, ex-girlfriend, and children. He asked about Clarendon Heights, about each of the Hallway Hangers, and about me. I've always been close to Stoney's mother and brothers, but never had Stoney and I talked so easily. I felt less distance between us than ever before, and yet in an hour's time he would walk back to his cell and I would drive away in my car. And I wanted something first. I had come to interview Stoney, not just to visit him. Much as I hated to broach the issue directly, I knew better than to dance around it. I explained uneasily that the study had become a textbook and that I hoped to interview him for the revised edition. The subtext was plain: "Yes, Stoney, you're a friend, but first and foremost, you're an object of research. Otherwise, I wouldn't be here." Stoney was aware of the underlying message, I'm sure. But he graciously put me at ease and proceeded to pour his heart out for ninety minutes.

After the interview, Stoney led me around the prison and showed me a photo of his girlfriend. In the lounge area, we were surrounded by vending machines. He explained that prisoners had to pay for decent food, for clothes laundering, for most everything. Given only two dollars per day for his work in the prison kitchen, Stoney found this difficult. I offered him some money. He refused but then relented. Since it was against prison regulations and even a $5 bill would arouse suspicion, I tried to break up $20 as best I could. It wasn't easy making various vending machines spew out quarters by the handful and then sneaking the booty into Stoney's socks!

I failed to learn my lesson when I visited Chris at Broadbottom State Prison. Broadbottom is part of a large farm complex, a crumbling Victorian structure where prisoners still slop out their cells. I arrived late and hurriedly dumped all my belongings into a basket at the desk, filled out a form, stepped through the metal detector, submitted to a search, and was herded with the other visitors into a small cafeteria. Every time a prisoner was brought into the room, I examined him closely. I hadn't seen Chris for several years and wasn't certain I would recognize him, or vice versa. When they did bring him in, I knew him straightaway, but he needed reminding who I was. He was surprised to see me. No one else had driven the two hours from Clarendon Heights to see him. Without his saying so, it was obvious that the first thing he wanted was some food. Everyone around us was shuttling back and forth to various vending machines, munching on candy bars, and downing cold drinks. Chris looked at them hungrily and I apologized profusely. Thinking the rules were the same as at Grassmoor, I had turned in my money with the rest of my things at the front desk. I had made lots of money on *Ain't No Makin' It*, and here I was without a couple of quarters to buy Chris a coke.

In spite of this disastrous start, the interview went well from my point of view. Chris described in detached but vivid detail how his life had taken one disastrous turn after another. He'd alienated everyone, he told me. Having spent two hours with his mother the previous week, I knew this was no exaggeration. He had no money to buy deodorant or other essentials like socks and raised his foot above the table to prove the point. Before leaving, I promised to call his girlfriend, to visit his mother, to receive his collect call a week later, and to send him a $20 mail order the next day. As we got up, Chris flashed me his old grin and said, "I know you're gettin' rich off me, Jay, with this book."

The issue of my financial gain bubbled up in several interviews, sometimes at my instigation, sometimes at theirs, and it was always there, simmering beneath the surface. Sometimes I felt like a manipulative, exploitative bastard. It's not just the money. It's also the power, privilege, and prestige this book has brought me. To the Brothers and the Hallway Hangers it has brought nothing outside of the satisfaction that their lives have had passing significance for several thousand college students. Most of them took pleasure in their anonymous notoriety. Some didn't. Mike didn't want to be part of the second edition. He had kept in touch with me in Mississippi. He had also called several times and talked of flying down with Craig. Once, on a trip up north, I showed him the book and gave him a copy. A few months later, I asked him what he thought. "Man, I just flipped through and looked at the stuff about me. I couldn't make any sense of that shit." When I returned to Clarendon Heights to research the revised edition, he said to leave him out of it. "I don't want everyone knowing my business, my personal stuff. I know you change the names and everything, but still." In the end, he relented only as a personal favor to me and because I eventually pushed the right button. Whereas with most of the young men the money I made from the book embarrassed me, this is what Mike respected. He was always railing at me for squandering a university degree to work for a pittance as a community worker. When I said that I needed his input for the revised edition to be a success, Mike came 'round to being included.

Having just spent four years in rural Mississippi, I was sensitive to the issue of "using" the young men for my own ends. In impoverished Holmes County, articles and books were there to be written, but I just could not generate the requisite analytical and social distance to turn my friends there into research subjects. Instead, I helped teenagers do their own fieldwork. Kids much like the Brothers ended up publishing two volumes of oral history interviews. They spent countless hours doing research, honing their questioning techniques, conducting interviews, transcribing tapes, editing their texts, preparing the manuscripts for publication, and promoting their book. Basically, they democratized the research process by converting it from a scholar's lone enterprise into an empowering learning process. Having masterminded this little revolution, I rode north and charged back into Clarendon Heights—as the lone researcher.

In 1983 I had been a youth worker in Clarendon Heights for several years. In 1991, however, I was just breezing through to satisfy my own research agenda. And yet writing this book is a way of giving something back to Clarendon Heights for all it has given to me. By striving to understand the young male world of Clarendon Heights on its own terms and then trying to translate and interpret that world for the wider culture, I like to think I have rendered a service to both. The outlook reflected in *Ain't No Makin' It* grew out of my work in the youth enrichment program. I saw many things on the streets that I could not fathom during those first summers in Clarendon Heights. When I looked closely and tried to suspend the biases, values, and assumptions I had imported from my own rural, white middle-class social world, I was driven to the fairly radical conclusions of this book. And so my political commitment, whether it is played out in Clarendon Heights, Holmes County, or Chesterfield, England, becomes another way of repaying the community for the privileged access it gave me.

Not much of this would wash with the Hallway Hangers. They know I owe them personally, and I was repeatedly asked for loans during the months of fieldwork in 1991. I gave Shorty $10 late one night. The money went straight into Super's pocket. "Thanks, Jay," Shorty said, grinning as he walked away to smoke the crack crystals. In 1983 I wouldn't even buy the Hallway Hangers booze. Now I was subsidizing a far deadlier addiction. I stood there feeling angry, guilty, and confused. That's fieldwork: It generates personal and intellectual satisfaction but also worry, ambiguity, and uncertainty.

I lent money to nearly all of the Hallway Hangers. At the time I knew these were gifts, and evidently they did too. Slick made out well. On the eve of my departure to England, I sold him my beloved '69 Chevrolet Impala with its beautifully rebuilt engine. Slick bought it for $1,300 so basically it was a gift. He paid me $500 in cash and signed a contract to send me the rest in monthly installments. I'm still waiting for the first one.

Many of the young men seemed to appreciate the opportunity to talk about their lives. At the end of a long interview during which the Jack Daniel's flowed freely, I asked Jinks if he had anything else to add.

JINKS: I pretty much said what I gots to say. I hope it helps you out.

JM: I feel really privileged and lucky in a way that from way back people like yourself were willing to take me in, in a way. I mean, I'd worked down here for four years.

JINKS: Uh-huh.

JM: So you knew I wasn't a narc and that I cared about the place, cuz you'd seen me with the kids, but I felt privileged then and even more so now comin' back, cuz I haven't seen people for a long time. And yet people are willing to sit down and talk about fairly personal things. Umm, so I appreciate that.

JINKS: Hey, well, as I say, y'know, there are not too many people out there who you can sit down an' you can get stuff off your chest with. Y'know, a lot of times you don't want to talk to someone you're spendin' all the time in the world with. You'd rather talk to someone impartial, someone who you know it's gonna stay with. Y'know, cuz I keep a lot, I do, I keep a lot of shit in my system. An' then when the time comes, I let it out. Instead of letting it out when it comes, when it bothers me, I just absorb it all.

JM: When do you get a chance to talk about it?

JINKS: A lot of times I don't. A lot of times I don't.

Frankie, Shorty, Boo-Boo, and Stoney were also grateful to slip out of their street front and to speak candidly about their lives.

I was depressed to discover how poorly many of the young men had fared in the eight years since my original research. The Brothers especially had been shortchanged. Intellectually, this outcome confirmed the social reproduction thesis of the first edition. Emotionally, I was drained, disheartened, and disconcerted by their plight. As I listened to the men relate their experiences, my head was pulled in one direction and my heart in another. It was bizarre to feel simultaneously dispirited and vindicated by the poor employment prospects of the men, particularly the Brothers.

The interviews with the Brothers were more difficult for another reason. Whereas the Hallway Hangers had little stake in keeping up appearances, the Brothers' commitment to the American Dream meant that their relationship with me was more complex. The research relationship between a successful, white university graduate and a struggling, black high school graduate is inextricably bound up with the phenomena under analysis: class, race, education, opportunity, and marginality. In a sense, the subjects are inscribed in the object: The interview itself is a miniature realization of the broader topic under investigation. Friendship or not, there was a tendency for the Brothers to want to "look good" in my eyes and for the book. They may have been disposed, for example, to distance themselves from the twofold stigmata of race and poverty and to display their mastery of the dominant discourse of individual achievement. "No, we're not gonna use race and all the rest as an excuse." The crucial issue is whether their abiding belief in school and their dismissal of racism were trotted out for me as a white intruder, or whether the Brothers express these convictions among themselves.[5]

In 1983 I might have suspected that the Brothers' oft-stated belief in equality of opportunity was a symbolic gloss put on their experience for my benefit, had I not witnessed the practical outworkings of this belief in their everyday lives and conversations. Then I could corroborate their stories by firsthand observation; the new material relies on their word. Whereas an ethnography based on interviews *and* participant observation can compare a person's stated attitudes with his behavior, interviews alone have to be accepted at face value. Because every interview is partly an exercise in self-justification, then, my heavy reliance on interviews in Part Two is problematic. Lest this admission raise doubts about the data, let me say that I have complete faith in the candor and honesty of the interview material. When I suspected I was being fed less than the truth, I probed the issue and gently pushed the person to come clean. Invariably he did. If I was still unsure, I admitted as much in the text. In discussing Super's account of how the police planted drugs on him, for example, I allow that he "may be portraying his entry into the street economy in the best possible light." I am satisfied with the interview data, but the reader is required to trust my judgment.

To be sure, I was a participant observer as well as an interviewer in 1991. I spent countless hours hanging around with the Hallway Hangers and the Brothers, but often in their households and in neighborhood bars rather than on the streets. I stayed with Steve for a couple of weeks in Clarendon Heights. Given his hard exterior and often thoughtless behavior, I was surprised by his generosity as a host. It did me good to move back into Clarendon Heights, even for such a short time. It's so easy to forget the frustrations of project life: for example, the futility of keeping counters and cupboards clean when you're overrun by cockroaches anyway. One night I was awakened by a clamor in the living room. Steve was shouting, and I heard furniture shifting and things falling to the floor. I jumped out of bed and steeled myself for a fight as I peered through the doorway. There were Steve and his younger brother, hockey sticks in hand, chasing a rat around the room. Steve stunned the animal with a slapshot against the wall, picked it up by the tail, and flung it out the window to the street below. They collapsed in laughter. "Welcome to the Ritz," chortled Steve as I went back to bed. I moved out of Steve's place a few days later, the ever-present prerogative reserved for a researcher rather than a resident.

In late September 1991 I headed for Lincoln, England, to train for the Anglican priesthood. The contrast between Clarendon Heights and Lincoln Cathedral could not be sharper. In a moment of blind faith, I signed a contract with Westview Press to finish the revised edition by March 1992. I stole away from the library, lecture hall, and college chapel to transcribe the interviews and then to wrestle with 800 pages of transcripts and field notes that refused to be reduced to three new chapters. My wife, Sally Asher, and I devised all sorts of schemes to come to grips with the data. I highlighted the interviews using a complex color-

coded scheme. Sally created a one-page index on each youth with crucial information. I developed intricate outlines, made reams of notes, created subject indexes,
and distilled whole interviews down to a single sheet of paper. Reading the texts of
the chapters now, I find it all seems so simple and straightforward. It wasn't.

Still struggling as 1993 loomed, I asked the Bishop of Derby to postpone my or-
dination so that I could go home and finish the book that summer. I lived with my
parents and commuted to Dartmouth College's library. Suddenly surrounded by
more than theological tomes, I read far too widely and intensely. Important dis-
coveries were the works of Philippe Bourgois and Loïc Wacquant. In addition, I
gained access to census data for Clarendon Heights and the surrounding city. I
agonized over how to present the new material, made several false starts, and went
back to England to start my ministerial post in Chesterfield less than half finished
with the book.

This past year and a half has been crazy. Immersed in a poor parish in a declining mining and industrial town, I met plenty of indigenous hallway hangers. I began working with disaffected teenagers in addition to my full regimen of visiting,
counseling, praying, funerals, baptisms, and Sunday services. But still I had the
unfinished manuscript hanging over my head. I snatched bits of time in between
my ministerial duties to work on it. My sermons began to sound like sociology es-
says and the book began to preach. Meanwhile, the patience of Dean Birkenkamp,
my Westview editor, was wearing thin. I also wore out friends within and without
the ranks of academia with drafts of chapters for their comments. Now, finally,
with 1995 upon us, I print this file for what I trust is the last time.

I hope this book does justice to the young lives of the Brothers and the Hallway
Hangers. I hope it provokes further study and sparks a critical attitude toward the
American socioeconomic system. Most of all, I hope it spurs readers to struggle
for a society that doesn't trample on the aspirations of its people.

Notes

1. William Foote Whyte, *Street Corner Society* (Chicago: University of Chicago Press,
1943), p. 279.

2. Ibid.

3. Elijah Anderson, *A Place on the Corner* (Chicago: University of Chicago Press, 1978).

4. Whyte, *Street Corner Society,* p. 304.

5. I am indebted to Loïc Wacquant for making these points in correspondence with me.

Bibliography

Anderson, Elijah. *A Place on the Corner.* Chicago: University of Chicago Press, 1978.

Anderson, J., and F. Evans, "Family Socialization and Educational Achievement in Two Cultures: Mexican American and Anglo-American." *Sociometry* 39 (1976):209–222.

Apple, Michael W. *Education and Power.* Boston: Routledge and Kegan Paul, 1982.

———. *Ideology and Curriculum.* Boston: Routledge and Kegan Paul, 1979.

Atkinson, Paul. *Language, Structure and Reproduction.* London: Methuen, 1985.

Bailey, Thomas, and Roger Waldinger. "The Changing Ethnic/Racial Division of Labor." In *Dual City: Restructuring New York.* Ed. John H. Mollenkopf and Manuel Castells. New York: Russell Sage Foundation, 1991.

Banfield, Edward C. *The Unheavenly City.* Boston: Little, Brown, 1970.

Banks, Olive. *The Sociology of Education.* London: B. T. Batsfield, 1976.

Beeghley, Leonard. "Individual and Structural Explanations of Poverty." *Population Research and Policy Review* 7 (1988):207–219.

Beller, Andrea H. "Trends in Occupational Segregation by Sex and Race." In *Sex Segregation in the Workplace.* Ed. Barbara F. Reskin. Washington, D.C.: National Academy Press, 1984.

Bennett, T. *Popular Culture: History and Theory.* London: Open University Press, 1981.

Bernstein, Basil. "Social Class, Language, and Socialization." In *Power and Ideology in Education.* Ed. Jerome Karabel and A. H. Halsey. New York: Oxford University Press.

———. *Class, Codes and Control.* London: Routledge and Kegan Paul, 1975.

Bourdieu, Pierre. *The Logic of Practice.* Cambridge: Polity Press, 1990.

———. *Homo Academicus.* Cambridge: Polity Press, 1988.

———. *Distinction: A Social Critique of the Judgement of Taste.* London: Routledge and Kegan Paul, 1984.

———. "Cultural Reproduction and Social Reproduction." In *Power and Ideology in Education.* Ed. Jerome Karabel and A. H. Halsey. New York: Oxford University Press, 1977.

———. *Outline of a Theory of Practice.* Cambridge: Cambridge University Press, 1977.

Bourdieu, Pierre, and Jean-Claude Passeron. *Reproduction in Education, Society, and Culture.* London: Sage, 1977.

Bourdieu, Pierre, and Loïc J. D. Wacquant. *An Invitation to Reflexive Sociology.* Cambridge: Polity Press, 1992.

Bourgois, Philippe. *Selling Crack in El Barrio.* Cambridge: Cambridge University Press, forthcoming.

———. "From *Jibaro* to Crack Dealer: Confronting the Restructuring of Capitalism in Spanish Harlem." In *Articulating Hidden Histories: Festschrift for Eric Wolf.* Ed. Jane Schneider and Rayna Rapp. Berkeley: University of California Press, 1994.

———. "Growing Up." *The American Enterprise* 2:3 (May/June 1991):28–33.

_____. "In Search of Respect: The New Service Economy and the Crack Alternative in Spanish Harlem." Russell Sage Foundation Working Paper No. 21. May 1991.

_____. "Shooting Gallery Notes." Russell Sage Foundation Working Paper No. 22. May 1991.

_____. "Crack in Spanish Harlem." *Anthropology Today* 5:4 (August 1989):6–11.

_____. "In Search of Horatio Alger: Culture and Ideology in the Crack Economy." *Contemporary Drug Problems* (Winter 1989):619–649.

_____. "Just Another Night on Crack Street." *New York Times Magazine* (12 November 1989):52–94.

Bowles, Samuel, and Herbert Gintis. *Schooling in Capitalist America*. New York: Basic Books, 1976.

Bradbury, Katharine L., and Lynn E. Browne. "Black Men in the Labor Market." *New England Economic Review* (March/April 1986):32–42.

Bray, Rosemary L. "Growing Up on Welfare." *The Observer Magazine* (2 January 1994):35–38.

Burris, Val. Rev. of *Learning to Labor*, by Paul Willis. *Harvard Educational Review* 50 (November 1980):523–526.

Campbell, Anne. *The Girls in the Gang*. Oxford: Basil Blackwell, 1984.

Castro, J. "How's Your Pay?" *Time* (15 April 1991):40–41.

Centre for Contemporary Cultural Studies. *The Empire Strikes Back*. London: Hutchinson, 1982.

Chinoy, Ely. *Automobile Workers and the American Dream*. Boston: Beacon Press, 1955.

Clark, Burton. "The 'Cooling-Out' Function in Higher Education." *American Journal of Sociology* 65 (1960):576–596.

Corcoran, M., L. Datcher, and G. J. Duncan. "Most Workers Find Jobs Through Word of Mouth." *Monthly Labor Review* 103 (August 1980):33–36.

"Corporate Executives Go to the Trough." *Dollars and Sense* 138 (1988):10–11.

Corrigan, Paul. *Schooling for the Smash Street Kids*. London: Macmillan, 1979.

DeMott, Benjamin. *The Imperial Middle*. New York: William Morrow, 1990.

Dillon, David. "Does the School Have a Right to Its Own Language?" *The English Journal* 69 (April 1980):13–17.

Dimaggio, Paul. "Cultural Capital and Social Success." *American Sociological Review* 47 (April 1982):189–201.

Durkheim, Emile. *The Division of Labor in Society*. New York: Free Press, 1953.

Edwards, Richard. *Contested Terrain*. New York: Basic Books, 1979.

Erikson, Erik H. *Gandhi's Truth*. New York: Norton, 1969.

Erikson, Kai T. *Everything in Its Path*. New York: Simon and Schuster, 1976.

Farley, Reynolds. "The Common Destiny of Blacks and Whites." In *Race in America*. Ed. Herbert Hill and James E. Jones, Jr. Madison: University of Wisconsin Press, 1993.

Farrell, S., and J. Lorber, eds. *The Social Construction of Gender*. New York: Sage, 1991.

Featherman, David L., and Robert M. Hauser. *Opportunity and Change*. New York: Academic Press, 1978.

Findley, Warren G., and Mirian M. Bryan. *Ability Grouping: A Review of the Literature*, part 3. Washington, D.C.: Office of Education, 1970.

Foley, Douglas E. *Learning Capitalist Culture*. Philadelphia: University of Pennsylvania Press, 1990.

Fordham, Signithia. "Racelessness as a Factor in Black Students' School Success: Pragmatic Strategy or Pyrrhic Victory?" *Harvard Educational Review* 53 (1988):257–293.

Francis, David R. "Executive Pay in the U.S. Just Goes Up and Up." *Christian Science Monitor* (May 20, 1994):9.

Freeman, Richard. *Black Elite: The New Market for Highly Educated Black Americans.* New York: McGraw Hill, 1976.

————. "Employment and Earnings of Disadvantaged Young Men in a Labor Shortage Economy." National Bureau of Economic Research Working Paper No. 3444. September 1990.

Freire, Paulo. *Pedagogy of the Oppressed.* New York: Continuum, 1981.

Gambetta, Diego. *Were They Pushed or Did They Jump?* Cambridge: Cambridge University Press, 1987.

Gecas, Viktor. "Contexts of Socialization." In *Social Psychology: Sociological Perspectives.* Ed. Morris Rosenberg and Ralph H. Turner. New York: Basic Books, 1981.

Giroux, Henry A. "Theories of Reproduction and Resistance in the New Sociology of Education." *Harvard Educational Review* 53 (August 1983):257–293.

————. *Theory & Resistance in Education.* London: Heinemann Educational Books, 1983.

Goldthorpe, John H. *Social Mobility and Class Structure in Modern Britain.* Oxford: Clarendon Press, 1980.

Gordon, Liz. "Paul Willis—Education, Cultural Production and Social Reproduction." *British Journal of Sociology of Education* 5 (1984):105–115.

Gramsci, Antonio. *Selections from Prison Notebooks.* London: Lawrence and Wishart, 1971.

Granovetter, Mark S. *Getting a Job.* Cambridge, Mass.: Harvard University Press, 1974.

————. "The Strength of Weak Ties." *American Journal of Sociology* 78:6 (1973):1360–1380.

Grubb, Norton. "The Economic Returns to Post-Secondary Education." Mimeo, School of Education, University of California at Berkeley, 1990.

Hagan, John. "Destiny and Drift." *American Sociological Review* 56 (October 1991):567–582.

Haller, Archibald O., and Irwin Millers. *The Occupational Aspirations Scale.* Cambridge, Mass.: Schenkman, 1972.

Halsey, A. H., A. F. Heath, and J. M. Ridge. *Origins and Destinations.* Oxford: Clarendon Press, 1980.

Haraven, Tamara K., and Randolph Langenbach. *Amoskeag.* New York: Pantheon, 1978.

Hearn, J., and D. Morgan, eds. *Men, Masculinities and Social Theory.* London: Unwin Hyman, 1990.

Heath, Shirley Brice. *Ways with Words.* Cambridge: Cambridge University Press, 1983.

Hill, Herbert, and James E. Jones, Jr., eds. *Race in America.* Madison: University of Wisconsin Press, 1993.

Hout, Michael. "Occupational Mobility of Black Men." *American Sociological Review* 49 (1984):308–322.

Howell, Joseph T. *Hard Living on Clay Street.* New York: Anchor Books, 1973.

Jencks, Christopher. *Rethinking Social Policy: Race, Poverty and the Underclass.* Cambridge, Mass.: Harvard University Press, 1992.

Jencks, Christopher, and Paul E. Peterson, eds. *The Urban Underclass.* Washington, D.C.: Brookings Institution, 1991.

Jenkins, Richard. *Pierre Bourdieu.* London: Routledge, 1992.

Jones, Jacqueline. *The Dispossessed.* New York: Basic Books, 1992.

Jones, James E., Jr. "The Rise and Fall of Affirmative Action." In *Race in America.* Ed. Herbert Hill and James E. Jones, Jr. Madison: University of Wisconsin Press, 1993.

Karabel, Jerome, and A. H. Halsey, eds. *Power and Ideology in Education.* New York: Oxford University Press, 1977.

Kasarda, John D. "Urban Industrial Transition and the Underclass." *Annals of the American Academy of the Political and Social Sciences* 501 (January 1989):26–47.

Katz, Michael. *The Undeserving Poor.* New York: Pantheon, 1989.

Keddie, Nell. "Classroom Knowledge." In *Knowledge and Control.* Ed. Michael F. D. Young. London: Macmillan, 1972.

Kerkchoff, A. C. *Ambition and Attainment.* Washington, D.C.: American Sociological Association, 1974.

Kerkchoff, A. C., and R. T. Campbell. "Black-White Differences in the Educational Attainment Process." *Sociology of Education* 50 (January 1977):15–27.

Kirschenmann, Joleen, and Kathryn M. Neckerman. "'We'd Love to Hire Them, But ...': The Meaning of Race for Employers." In *The Urban Underclass.* Ed. Christopher Jencks and Paul E. Peterson. Washington, D.C.: Brookings Institution, 1991.

Kohn, Melvin L. *Class and Conformity: A Study in Values.* Chicago: University of Chicago Press, 1977.

Kornblum, William. *Blue Collar Community.* Chicago: University of Chicago Press, 1974.

Kornblum, William, and Terry Williams. *Growing Up Poor.* Lexington, Mass.: Lexington Books, 1985.

Lemann, Nicholas. *The Promised Land: The Great Black Migration and How It Changed America.* New York: Alfred A. Knopf, 1991.

_____. "The Origins of the Underclass." *Atlantic Monthly* (June 1986):31–55 continued in *Atlantic Monthly* (July 1986):54–68.

Liebow, Elliot. *Tally's Corner.* Boston: Little, Brown, 1967.

London, Howard B. *The Culture of a Community College.* New York: Praeger, 1978.

Mann, Michael. "The Social Cohesion of Liberal Democracy." *American Sociological Review* 35 (June 1970):423–439.

Mantsios, George. "Rewards and Opportunities: The Politics of Economics of Class in the U.S." In *Race, Class, and Gender in the United States: An Integrated Study.* Ed. Paula S. Rothenberg. New York: St. Martin's Press, 1992.

Marable, Manning. *Race, Reform, and Rebellion.* Jackson: University Press of Mississippi, 1991.

Marx, Karl. *Capital.* Harmondsworth: Penguin, 1976.

_____. *The Eighteenth Brumaire of Louis Napoleon.* In *Selected Works.* New York: International Publishers, 1968.

Marx, Karl, and Friedrich Engels. *The German Ideology.* New York: International Publishers, 1947.

Massey, Douglas S., and Nancy A. Denton. *American Apartheid: Segregation and the Making of the Underclass.* Cambridge, Mass.: Harvard University Press, 1993.

McNall, Scott G., Rhonda F. Levine, and Rick Fantasia. *Bringing Class Back In.* Boulder, Colo.: Westview Press, 1991.

Mehan, Hugh. "Understanding Inequality in Schools: The Contribution of Interpretive Studies." *Sociology of Education* 65 (January 1992):1–20.

Merton, Robert K. *Social Theory and Social Structure.* New York: Free Press, 1968.

Michels, Robert. *First Lectures in Political Sociology.* New York: Harper and Row, 1965.

Miller, Charles, John A. McLaughlin, John Madden, and Norman M. Chansky. "Socioeconomic Class and Teacher Bias." *Psychological Reports* 23 (1968):806–810.

Mollenkopf, John H., and Manuel Castells, eds. *Dual City: Restructuring New York.* New York: Russell Sage Foundation, 1991.

Moynihan, Daniel Patrick, ed. *On Understanding Poverty.* New York: Basic Books, 1968.

Murray, Charles. *Losing Ground.* New York: Basic Books, 1984.

Neal, Donald. "A Theory of the Origin of Ethnic Stratification." *Social Problems* 16 (Fall 1968):157–172.

Omi, Michael, and Harold Winant. "Racial Formations." In *Race, Class, and Gender in the United States: An Integrated Study.* Ed. Paula S. Rothenberg. New York: St. Martin's Press, 1992.

Osterman, Paul. "Is There a Problem with the Youth Labor Market and If So How Should We Fix It?" Mimeo, Sloan School, MIT, February 1992.

_____. *Getting Started.* Cambridge, Mass.: MIT Press, 1980.

Persell, Caroline Hodges. *Education and Inequality.* New York: Free Press, 1977.

Pomer, Marshall I. "Labor Market Structure, Intragenerational Mobility, and Discrimination: Black Male Advancement Out of Low-Paying Occupations." *American Sociological Review* 51 (1986):650–659.

Powers, Brian. "Two Tracks to Nowhere." *Socialist Review* 19:2 (April–June 1989):155–165.

Reich, Robert B. "As the World Turns." *New Republic* (1 May 1989):23–28.

Rist, Ray C. "Student Social Class and Teacher Expectations: The Self-Fulfilling Prophecy in Ghetto Education." *Harvard Educational Review* 40 (August 1970):411–451.

Rosegrant, Jane K. "Choosing Children." Thesis, Harvard College, 1985.

Rosenbaum, James E. *Making Inequality.* New York: Wylie and Sons, 1976.

Rosenberg, Morris. "The Self-Concept: Social Product and Social Force." In *Social Psychology: Sociological Perspectives.* Ed. Morris Rosenberg and Ralph H. Turner. New York: Basic Books, 1981.

_____. *Conceiving the Self.* New York: Basic Books, 1979.

Rosenberg, Morris, and Roberta G. Simmons. *Black and White Self-Esteem: The Urban School Child.* Washington, D.C.: American Sociological Association, 1971.

Rothenberg, Paula S., ed. *Race, Class, and Gender in the United States: An Integrated Study.* New York: St. Martin's Press, 1992.

Roy, David F. "The Role of the Researcher in the Study of Social Conflict." *Human Organization* 24 (Fall 1965):262–271.

Rubin, Lillian. *Worlds of Pain.* New York: Basic Books, 1976.

Sassen, Saskia. "The Informal Economy." In *Dual City: Restructuring New York.* Ed. John H. Mollenkopf and Manuel Castells. New York: Russell Sage Foundation, 1991.

Schatzman, Leonard, and Anselm L. Strauss. *Field Research.* Englewood Cliffs, N.J.: Prentice-Hall, 1973.

Schultz, Charles B., and Roger H. Sherman. "Social Class, Development and Differences in Reinforcer Effectiveness." *Review of Education Research* 46 (1976):25–59.

Scully, Maureen Anne. "Coping with Meritocracy." Thesis, Harvard College, 1982.

Sennett, Richard, and Jonathan Cobb. *The Hidden Injuries of Class.* New York: Vintage Books, 1972.

Shannon, Thomas R., Nancy Kleniewski, and William M. Cross, eds. *Urban Problems in Sociological Perspective.* Prospect Heights, Ill.: Waveland Press, 1991.

Sharff, Jagna Wojcicka. "The Underground Economy of a Poor Neighborhood." In *Cities of the United States: Studies in Urban Anthropology.* Ed. Leith Mullings. New York: Columbia University Press, 1987.

Shavelson, Richard J., Judith J. Hubner, and George C. Stanton. "Self-Concept: Validation of Construct Interpretations." *Review of Educational Research* 46 (Summer 1976):407–411.

Son, Soo, Suzanne W. Model, and Gene A. Fisher. "Polarization and Progress in the Black Community." *Sociological Forum* 4:3 (1989):309–327.

Spenner, Kenneth I., and David L. Featherman. "Achievement Ambitions." *Annual Review of Sociology* 4 (1978):373–420.

Stinchcombe, Arthur L. *Rebellion in a High School.* Chicago: Quadrangle Books, 1964.

Sullivan, Mercer. "Absent Fathers in the Inner City." *Annals of the American Academy of the Political and Social Sciences* 501 (January 1989):48–58.

———. *Getting Paid.* Ithaca, N.Y.: Cornell University Press, 1989.

Sum, Andrew M. Personal interview, August 1991.

Sum, Andrew M., and Neal Fogg. "The Changing Economic Fortunes of Young Black Men in America." *The Black Scholar* 21:1 (January–March 1990):47–55.

Sum, Andrew M., and Joseph Franz. "The Geographic Locations of Jobs Held by Employed High School Graduates." Unpublished paper, Center for Labor Market Studies, Northeastern University, May 1990.

Sum, Andrew M., and Joanna Heliotis. "Declining Real Wages of Youth." *Workforce* (Spring 1993):22–31.

Suttles, Gerald. *The Social Order of the Slum.* Chicago: University of Chicago Press, 1968.

Swartz, David. "Pierre Bourdieu: The Cultural Transmission of Social Inequality." *Harvard Educational Review* 47 (1977):545–555.

Tawney, R. H. *Equality.* London: Allen and Unwin, 1938.

United States Bureau of the Census. Public Use Microdata Sample File, 1980 and 1990.

Wacquant, Loïc J. D. "Morning in America, Dusk in the Dark Ghetto: The New 'Civil War' in the American City." *Revue française d'études américaines* 60 (May 1994):97–102.

———. "The State and Fate of the Ghetto: Redrawing the Urban Color Line in Postfordist America." In *Social Theory and the Politics of Identity.* Ed. Craig Calhoun. New York: Basil Blackwell, 1994.

———. "Bourdieu in America: Notes on the Transatlantic Importation of Social Theory." In *Bourdieu: Critical Perspectives.* Ed. Craig Calhoun, Edward LiPuma, and Moishe Postone. Cambridge: Polity Press, 1993.

———. "On the Tracks of Symbolic Power: Prefatory Notes to Bourdieu's 'State Nobility.'" *Theory, Culture, and Society* 10 (August 1993):1–17.

———. "Urban Outcasts: Stigma and Division in the Black American Ghetto and the French Periphery." *International Journal of Urban and Regional Research* 17:3 (1993):366–383.

———. "'The Zone': Le métier de 'hustler' dans le ghetto noir américain." *Actes de la recherche en science sociales* 93 (June 1992):39–58.

_____. "Making Class: The Middle Class(es) in Social Theory and Social Structure." In *Bringing Class Back In*. Ed. Scott G. McNall, Rhonda F. Levine, and Rick Fantasia. Boulder, Colo.: Westview Press, 1991.

_____. "Sociology as Socioanalysis: Tales of *Homo Academicus*." *Sociological Forum* 5 (1990):677–689.

_____. "The Ghetto, the State, and the New Capitalist Economy." *Dissent* (Fall 1989):508–520.

_____. "The Puzzle of Race and Class in American Society and Social Sciences." *Benjamin E. Mays Monograph Series* 2 (Fall 1989):7–20.

Wacquant, Loïc J. D., and William Julius Wilson. "The Cost of Racial and Class Exclusion in the Inner City." *Annals of the American Academy of the Political and Social Sciences* 501 (January 1989):8–25.

Waldinger, Roger. "Changing Ladders and Musical Chairs: Ethnicity and Opportunity in Post-Industrial New York." *Politics & Society* 15:4 (1986–1987):369–401.

Waldinger, Roger, and Thomas Bailey. "The Continuing Significance of Race." *Politics & Society* 19:3 (1991):291–323.

Weber, Max. *Economy and Society*. Berkeley: University of California Press, 1970.

Weis, Lois. *Working Class Without Work*. New York: Routledge, 1990.

Wellman, David T. *Portraits of White Racism*. Cambridge: Cambridge University Press, 1977.

West, Cornel. *Race Matters*. Boston: Beacon Press, 1993.

Whyte, William Foote. *Street Corner Society*. Chicago: University of Chicago Press, 1943.

William, Terry. *The Cocaine Kids*. Reading, Mass.: Addison-Wesley, 1989.

Willis, Paul. "Youth Unemployment and the New Poverty: A Summary of a Local Authority Review and Framework for Policy Development on Youth and Youth Unemployment." Wolverhampton Information Centre, June 1985.

_____. "Youth Unemployment: Thinking the Unthinkable." Mimeo.

_____. "Cultural Production and Theories of Reproduction." In *Race, Class, and Education*. Ed. Len Barton and Stephen Walker. London: Croom Helm, 1983.

_____. "Cultural Production Is Different from Cultural Reproduction Is Different from Social Reproduction Is Different from Reproduction." *Interchange* 12 (1981):48–67.

_____. *Learning to Labor*. Aldershot: Gower, 1977.

Wilson, William Julius. *The Truly Disadvantaged*. Chicago: University of Chicago Press, 1987.

_____. *The Declining Significance of Race*. Chicago: University of Chicago Press, 1978.

Yeakey, Carol Camp, and Clifford T. Bennett. "Race, Schooling, and Class in American Society." *Journal of Negro Education* 59 (Winter 1990):3–18.

About the Book and Author

"I AIN'T GOIN' TO COLLEGE. Who wants to go to college? I'd just end up gettin' a shitty job anyway." So said Freddie Piniella, an eleven-year-old boy from Clarendon Heights low-income housing project, to Jay MacLeod, his counselor in a youth program. MacLeod was struck by the seeming self-defeatism of Freddie and his friends. How is it that in America, a nation of dreams and opportunities, a boy of eleven can feel trapped in a position of inherited poverty?

The author immerses himself in the teenage underworld of Clarendon Heights. The Hallway Hangers, one of the neighborhood cliques, appear as cynical self-destructive hoodlums. The other group, the Brothers, take the American Dream to heart and aspire to middle-class respectability. The twist is that the Hallway Hangers are mostly white; the Brothers are almost all black. Comparing the two groups, MacLeod provides a provocative account of how poverty is perpetuated from one generation to the next.

Part One tells the story of the boys' teenage aspirations. Part Two follows the Hallway Hangers and the Brothers into adulthood. Eight years later the author returns to Clarendon Heights to find the members of both gangs struggling in the labor market or on the streets. Caught in the web of urban industrial decline, the Hallway Hangers—undereducated, unemployed, or imprisoned—have turned to the underground economy. But "cocaine capitalism" only fuels their desperation, and the Hallway Hangers seek solace in sexism and racism. The ambitious Brothers have fared little better. Their teenage dreams in tatters, the Brothers demonstrate that racism takes its toll on optimistic aspirations.

This edition retains the vivid accounts of friendships, families, school, and work that made the first edition so popular. The ethnography resonates with feeling and vivid dialogue. But the book also addresses one of the most important issues in modern social theory and policy: how social inequality is reproduced from one generation to the next. MacLeod links individual lives with social theory to forge a powerful argument about how inequality is created, sustained, and accepted in the United States.

A Rhodes Scholar, Jay MacLeod holds degrees in social studies and theology. He and his wife, Sally Asher, spent four years in Mississippi, where their work with local teenagers led to the publication of *Minds Stayed on Freedom: The Civil Rights Struggle in the Rural South, an Oral History* (Westview, 1991). Jay is now an Anglican Priest in Chesterfield, a declining mining and market town in Sally's native England.

Index